WOMEN IN
ENGLAND

1760–1914

A Social History

SUSIE STEINBACH

PHOENIX

For Benjamin, Sophie and Samantha

A PHOENIX PAPERBACK

First published in Great Britain in 2004
by Weidenfeld & Nicolson
This paperback edition published in 2005
by Phoenix,
an imprint of Orion Books Ltd,
Orion House, 5 Upper St Martin's Lane,
London WC2H 9EA

1 3 5 7 9 10 8 6 4 2

A CIP catalogue record for this book
is available from the British Library.

ISBN 0 75381 989 9

Typeset by Butler and Tanner Ltd, Frome and London

Printed and bound in Great Britain by
Clays Ltd, St Ives plc

www.orionbooks.co.uk

Susie Steinbach is Associate Professor of History at Hamline University, Minnesota. Previously she taught at Yale University, where she was a prize student. This is her first book. She lives in St Paul, Minnesota.

CONTENTS

List of Illustrations   vii
Acknowledgements   ix
Introduction   1

**PART ONE – Women's Lives:
The Influence of Class**
1 WORKING-CLASS WOMEN   9
Home
Agricultural work
Domestic service
Factory work
Outwork
White-collar work

2 MIDDLE-CLASS WOMEN   43
Home
Family income
Philanthropic work
New professions

3 ELITE WOMEN   83
Aristocratic women
Home
Politics
Royal Women
Queen Charlotte
Princess Charlotte
Queen Victoria

**PART TWO: Bodies, Souls and
Minds**
4 SEXUALITY   111
Understanding Sex

Advice and sexology
Reputation
Loving women
Courtship
Marriage
Pregnancy and childbirth
Controlling fertility
Prostitution and venereal disease

5 RELIGION   141
Religions in England
Anglicans
Non-Anglican Protestants
Catholics, Jews, and Atheists
Women's roles
*Clerical relations and
    missionaries*
Sisters
Messiahs
Preachers
The Salvation Army
Spiritualists and theosophists

6 EDUCATION   172
Before 1850
Elite girls
Middle-class girls
Working-class girls
    Dame schools
    Sunday schools
    Ragged, workhouse, and
        factory schools

National and British schools
Adult education
After 1850
Elementary schools
Grammar schools
Universities

PART THREE: Politics in the Imperial Nation

7 IMPERIALISM 199
Imperialism in popular culture
Race
Effeminacy
Sexual danger
Motherhood and sisterhood
English blacks, colonial whites
White domesticity
Consuming the Empire's goods
Travel narratives
Missionary work
Reformers and feminists
Emigration

8 DOMESTIC POLITICS 238
Women and politics
Conservatives, Liberals, and radicals
Electoral politics
Patriotism and protest
Patriarchal working-class radicalism
The Queen Caroline Affair
Owenism
Chartism and anti-Poor Law agitation
Middle-class radicalism
The Anti-Corn Law League
Local politics

Parties and auxiliaries
Feminist politics
Mid-Victorian feminism
Single women and work
Marriage and divorce
Repealing the Contagious Diseases Acts
Late nineteenth- and early twentieth-century feminism
The 'new woman'
Socialism and working-class women

9 SUFFRAGE 285
Early campaigns
The meanings of the vote
The case for suffrage
The case against suffrage
Working for the vote
Militancy and the founding of the WSPU
Non-violent militancy
The movement reinvigorated
Violence and imprisonment
The Conciliation Bill

CONCLUSION 317

APPENDIX: ENGLISH MONEY DURING THE LONG NINETEENTH CENTURY 320

NOTES 322

SUGGESTIONS FOR FURTHER READING 349

INDEX 359

ILLUSTRATIONS

Section One
A pen-grinding room (Weidenfeld & Nicolson Archives)
'The Needlewoman at Home and Abroad' (Mary Evans Picture Library)
A Spitalfields weaver at home (Mary Evans Picture Library)
An early 'typing pool' (Mary Evans Picture Library)
Interviewing for a governess (Mary Evans Picture Library)
Servants waiting to be called (Mary Evans/Bruce Castle)
A housemaid and a cook relaxing (Mary Evans Picture Library)
Upper-middle-class women at home (Mary Evans Picture Library)
Female emigration to Australia (The National Archives CO384/35)
Advertisement for 'female pills' (Wellcome Library, London)
A woman using a breast-exhauster (Mary Evans Picture Library)
'Poor Law Divorce' (Mary Evans Picture Library)
Cheltenham Ladies' College staff (Weidenfeld & Nicolson Archives)
Girls in a School Board classroom (Hulton Archive/Getty Images)

Section Two
Queen Charlotte by Benjamin West (The Royal Collection © Her Majesty
    Queen Elizabeth II)
The Dinner Hour, Wigan by Eyre Crowe (© Manchester Art Gallery/
    Bridgeman Art Library)
A female Salvationist in a Swiss Tavern (Mary Evans Picture Library)
Political cartoon of the Duchess of Devonshire (Mary Evans Picture
    Library)
A Christian missionary school in Shanghai (Felice A Beato/Getty Images)
Missionaries murdered in Africa (Mary Evans Picture Library)
A Women's Rights meeting (Mary Evans Picture Library)
The Empty Purse by James Collinson (© Tate, London 2004)
Abolitionist glass seals (Bridgeman Art Library)
The arrest of Mrs Pankhurst (Mary Evans Picture Library)
'The Appeal of Womanhood' (Mary Evans/The Women's Library)

Poster for a play, *The New Woman* (Mary Evans Picture Library)
An Anti-Suffrage League meeting (Mary Evans/The Women's Library)
Police photographs of suffragettes (The National Archives ARI/528)
WSPU bazaar (Mary Evans/The Women's Library)

ACKNOWLEDGEMENTS

Scholarly work, though a solitary endeavour, takes place in the context of a larger community. Many people made this book possible, and I have long looked forward to thanking them. My editor, Benjamin Buchan, has been unfailingly helpful. When I was an undergraduate, John Brewer, John Montano and Kathleen Wilson encouraged me, and Sam Sifton was my first historical colleague. Simon and Rebecca Pride gave a new researcher her first home in London and have remained valued friends. Later, in my postgraduate studies, Linda Colley was an exemplary adviser; I was also fortunate to work with Nancy Cott, John Demos, and Mark Micale.

Many scholars read sections of the manuscript, shared their expertise and their work, answered questions, suggested sources, and pointed out opportunities. Geraldine Forbes, Durba Ghosh and Marjorie Levine-Clark shared work with me before it was published. Peter Mandler, Cecilia Morgan, and Kathleen Wilson gave me crucial references. Carol Morgan, Jacqueline de Vries, Rohan McWilliam, Susan Mumm and Tim Hitchcock were generous with their knowledge. Deborah Cohen, Cynthia Curran, Jacqueline de Vries, Kristina Deffenbacher, Marjorie Levine-Clark, Jesse Matz, Carol Morgan and Anna Clark all read and commented on portions or versions of the manuscript. I would especially like to thank Kelly Boyd and Rohan McWilliam, who commented on early drafts of chapters and on the entire manuscript, and who supported the project in a variety of ways. Their intellectual generosity and rigour not only make them the heart and soul of the academy, but make that community one still worth belonging to. All of these friends and colleagues have saved me from many errors of fact, omission, interpretation and emphasis. Remaining shortcomings are my responsibility.

Every new publication is made possible by previous ones. Many historians who read this book will recognize my debts to their work, which I trust I have adequately acknowledged in notes and suggestions for further reading. Among those whose published work has influenced me most I must mention in particular Maxine Berg, Antoinette Burton, Barbara Caine, Elaine Chalus, Anna Clark, Elizabeth Crawford, Leonore Davidoff, Kathryn Gleadle, Catherine Hall, Lesley Hall, Ellen Jordan, Laura E. Nym Mayhall, F. K. Prochaska, June Purvis, Sarah Richardson, Deborah Valenze, Martha Vicinus, Amanda Vickery and Judith Walkowitz.

Many other kinds of help were also necessary. I am grateful to all of my childcare providers. Ginger Ammon, Stephen Lindberg, and Lila Savage were exemplary student research assistants. Holly Bell and Katina Krull gave crucial administrative support. The staff of the Hamline University Bush Library, especially Kimberly Feilmeyer and Gail Peloquin, were exceptionally helpful. Hamline University supported the project with six separate Hanna Grants for Faculty Research. The Institute for Historical Research (School of Advanced Study, University of London), the Feminist Faculty Seminar (Hamline University), and the Comparative Women's History Workshop (University of Minnesota) were supportive intellectual communities, as was the H-Albion Listserv group on British and Irish history. The Center for Advanced Feminist Studies (University of Minnesota), headed by Anna Clark and Jennifer Pierce, provided a home during the last year of writing.

Finally, family and friends outside the academy have been invaluable. My father, Samuel Steinbach, supported me and this project in a variety of ways until his dying day; my mother, Carole Steinbach, continues to do so. Most important to me are Benjamin, Sophie, and Samantha Elwood. This book is for them.

Saint Paul, Minnesota, August 2003

INTRODUCTION

ONE SPRING MORNING in 1872, V.R., a fifty-something widow residing in London, lies in bed thinking about her beloved husband, lost more than ten years earlier to typhoid fever, their nine children, and her current obligations at her workplace. In many respects, V.R.'s home and work experiences appear unexceptional, even typical, alongside those of other Englishwomen in 'the long nineteenth century' – the period between 1760 and 1914. She had chosen her husband from her own social circle, as was expected of her, and had been quite eager during their courtship; husband and wife had loved each other, and she had been devastated by his death. Due to quick-spreading infectious diseases, it was not uncommon for women to become widows in their fifties. Although she had delivered a higher-than-average number of children, more remarkable was the fact that all nine lived to adulthood. This past winter her oldest son had almost died of typhoid fever, and she was thankful he had survived, in part because he was expected to carry on the family's enterprise. Her own work in it was important to her; she had not done quite as much since being widowed, but as she emerged from her grieving she was gradually resuming her duties. She had kept up her philanthropic efforts since her husband died, giving money to schools and hospitals, and of late had renewed her interest in politics. As a woman she was not supposed to be too political, but she had always taken an interest in the affairs of England and its Empire, finding herself especially drawn to matters involving women and children less fortunate than herself.

This woman – Queen Victoria – was both entirely exceptional and quite typical of women in England during the long nineteenth century. She was the head of a nation, its Church and Empire, true; but like most English women, she married, had children, was active in a number of charities, was involved in her church, took an interest in politics, and helped pass the family's work and values on to the next generation. Nineteenth-century women were remarkable both for the restrictions within which they operated and for all they achieved in spite of them. Victoria was no exception.

This book intends to explore the tension between these restrictions and the impressive range of activities which women nevertheless engaged in. Nineteenth-century English women played many roles in society: daughter, sister, spinster, mother, wife, widow, neighbour, employer, worker, professional, philanthropist, recipient of charity, churchgoer, consumer, reader, imperialist, political activist, public servant, and monarch, among others. But women did not enjoy infinite possibilities; the political, legal, economic, and cultural limitations they experienced were severe. And while most of these were eased over time, few of them were wholly erased during the long nineteenth century; some are still in place today.

We know much about women of this era because the sources used by historians range in character from the depersonalized objectivity of institutional records to the intimate subjectivity of first-person narratives. Parish and later civil records list births, marriages and deaths; censuses give us information, albeit flawed, about household structures and occupations. While such sources tend to give priority to men's lives, they can help historians to make demographic calculations or understand regional occupational variations. At the other end of the spectrum are first-person narratives such as letters, diaries, and memoirs. These offer eyewitness accounts and perhaps even intimate glimpses into people's emotions and motivations. However, it is not safe to assume that these sources are always entirely trustworthy. Most memoirs are written many years after the fact and can be shaped by regret or discretion. Letters can be selectively edited for their intended readers. Even in diaries, writers explore different ways of understanding or presenting themselves. Another problem is that very few personal writings by women (or non-elite men) survive. This is partly because fewer were produced, as female literacy always lagged behind male literacy, but also because the personal papers of male heads of households were more likely to be preserved than women's papers.

In between the parish birth record and the diary there are many other sources of information that historians can mine. Women feature quite frequently in legal records: we know of many who would have left no traces had they not appeared in court – in small claims courts, as criminals or victims of crimes, as parties in a breach of promise of marriage or divorce suit. These records are extremely valuable because they often include the participants' own words. However, once in court women were speaking in a highly structured situation that must be taken into account: plaintiffs, defendants, and witnesses were presenting their cases in ways aimed at specific legal outcomes. Another important group of sources is newspapers and magazines, which tell us what kind of events the average person was aware of, and interested in. The advice manuals of the day can tell us quite a bit as well; they describe life, not as it was, but in an idealized form, as it was supposed to be. The images projected of the perfect young lady, housekeeper, wife, and mother give us important insights even though it was probably rare that their standards were met. Fictional sources such as plays, novels, short stories and poems can also be very valuable. While fiction should not be mistaken for reality, it can help us to understand the culture in which it was produced and of which it was a part. Finally, historians can draw on visual material, including 'high' art, political cartoons, and advertisements, which can often offer important new dimensions.

Using these and other sources, scholars have been able to explore women's lives in some detail. In the last twenty years the field has developed at an astonishing rate, and now includes many historical approaches, including those of social, economic, political, cultural, and imperial history. The history of women has also involved the exploration of theoretical issues, such as the function of gender in the creation of knowledge and in society as a whole.

Historians addressing nineteenth-century English women have tended to adopt one of two theoretical approaches. The first, commonly called 'women's history', emerged from the field of social history and 'second wave' or 1960s and 1970s feminism. This aims to rediscover and celebrate the lives of women from the past, though at its inception many scholars argued that women's history was neither rigorous, serious, nor, practically speaking, possible. It tends to focus on various forms of discrimination against women, and is often written by feminists. It emphasizes how the material aspects of women's lives shaped their experiences. Though based on solid evidence, it sometimes veers towards documentation rather than analysis, or concerns itself with merely celebrating 'women worthies'. Finally, women's history tends to assume that women were united by their shared status as women more than they were divided by class, race, nationality, ethnicity, religion, or sexual orientation.

The second approach, 'gender history', which emerged in the 1980s, draws on various academic trends which emphasize the importance of linguistic and textual analysis and argue that language does not just represent, reflect or report human experience; it helps to create our reality. Building on these approaches, gender history seeks to understand the relationships between men and women, and between the categories of 'male' and 'female'. Additionally, it studies the way ideas about masculinity and femininity are produced, and how these notions change over time. That women have vaginas and do not have penises is usually considered a biological fact; that women are emotional while men are rational, or dextrous and frail while men are strong and clumsy, are assumptions about what biology implies in the social realm. Assumptions like these are the subject of gender history.

Gender history emphasizes that gender is a relational and dynamic category. Ideas about men and women are created alongside one another, and are constantly developing. Gender history lends equal weight to the power of language as to the importance of experience; it relies on close readings of documents to tease out their varied and often conflicting meanings. Finally, gender history emphasizes how fractured the category of 'woman' itself is, since women of different nationalities, social backgrounds and sexual orientation differed significantly from each other and were often working at cross-purposes. Gender history often focuses on women, for instance, by noting their exclusion from formal politics on the grounds that politics were public and women were domestic. It can also focus on gender even where women are not present, as, for example, when aristocratic politicians were accused of being 'effeminate' and therefore incompetent rulers by middle-class men. (There are now many excellent works available on the topics of masculinity and male gender issues.') These insights and approaches have enriched the study of nineteenth-century English women. However, gender history can place too much emphasis on theory and ideology and not enough on lived experience, or it can confuse ideals for reality. In addition, its focus on texts and language can be misleading – women's behaviour was often quite different from that described as desirable or typical in advice manuals, sermons, novels, or magazines – and it can misinterpret texts by removing them from their larger context.

Here we will strive for the best of both worlds. In recent years, much of the finest historical work has attempted to combine women's history and gender history by looking carefully at the multifaceted relationships between lived experience and ideological concerns. Here we will do the same, concerning ourselves with the ideas about gender with which nine-teenth-century women lived, with the variety of social, economic, political, legal, cultural, religious, and other pressures brought to bear on women, and with women's responses to these challenges.

Two other brief explanations remain. The focus on England, rather than on all of Britain – England, Scotland and Wales – may seem overly narrow. Yet during the period 1760–1914, important national distinctions of religion, law, language and culture obtained, especially for the non-aristocratic majority of the population. Generalizations about an entire country are difficult enough to make; grand statements about three countries – four, if one considers the importance of Ireland in British history – would be impossible. (Happily, there are now growing literatures on the histories of women in Scotland, Wales and Ireland, which readers may wish to pursue.[2]) We will, however, occasionally look to the rest of the United Kingdom, as well as to Continental Europe and to the United States, for contexts, connections, and contrasts.

Finally, the notion of the years between 1760 and 1914 as a 'long nineteenth century' bears explaining. Many of the nineteenth century's most important features – industrialization, urbanization, the growth and dominance of the middle class, and the popularization of the monarchy – were evident from 1760. Similarly, the end of the 1800s did not mark the end of an era with anything like the decisiveness of the start of the First World War.

Throughout the long nineteenth century women were seen as more moral, more emotional, less sexual than men, and less capable of genius or even of rational thought; effeminacy was despised; 'mannish' women were regarded as suspect. Yet the period was a not wholly static one. While in 1760 many women worked in agriculture and almost none did secretarial work, the reverse was true by 1914. While in 1760 few women could read, England had achieved near-universal female literacy by 1914. In addition, dramatic changes in religious practices, legal institutions and the economy all affected women (though not all of them benefited women).

Most of these dramatic changes and developments are the explicit subject of this book, but two must be mentioned as necessary background. The first is the growth and urbanization of the English population. In 1760 the population of England and Wales together was slightly over 7 million; by 1911 it had more than quintupled, to 36 million people. In 1801 only 11 per cent of the English population lived in cities of over 100,000 people; a century later 44 per cent did so, and the vast majority lived in towns of over 10,000.[3] Northern textile towns grew fastest – Manchester jumped from a population of 75,000 in 1801 to 351,000 in 1871 – but almost all the English cities were growing. To take the capital as one example, when the British Museum opened in 1753, London – with a population of 700,000 people – had just become the largest city in the Western world.[4] In 1911 it was home to 7 million people, as many as comprised the total population of England and Wales in 1760.

Women were, of course, central players in population growth. Before 1860, population growth occurred because the birth rate was even higher than the mortality rate. Most women spent their adult lives raising children, and often died before their youngest children had left home. Death in, or as a result of, childbirth remained common until the early 1860s. For example Emily Lennox (1731–1814), an aristocratic English woman, raised not only her own twenty-two children but three of her sisters as well. Louisa, Sarah, and Cecilia Lennox were young children when their mother died in her late forties; they knew Emily as both older sister and second mother.[5] In the middle of the long nineteenth century, in 1851, the average woman did not marry until she was twenty-five but she still gave birth to six children.[6] High infant mortality rates meant that mothers did not get to raise all of their children; ten of Emily Lennox's offspring died young. In 1760 between 20 and 30 per cent of babies died before their first birthday, and a significant decline in infant mortality did not begin until the early twentieth century.[7]

After about 1860 a dramatic fall in the birth rate slowed the rate of population growth. Female life expectancy increased because women were risking their lives in childbirth fewer times. Many women bore their last child in their early thirties, saw their youngest child to early adulthood while still in their early fifties, and lived for a decade or more afterwards. While between 1837 and 1851, women who married in their twenties had between 5.9 and 7.4 children, during the early 1890s women who married at the same age had only 3.3 to 5.1 children. By 1940 the average married woman would give birth to only two children. These shifts in family patterns had profound effects on England and English women.[8]

Yet much remained the same. The ways in which things changed – and the ways they did not – are the subject of this book. It is organized into three sections. Part One – the first three chapters – considers the paid and unpaid work done by working-, middle-, and upper-class women. Part Two looks at sexuality, religion, and education. Part Three considers women in relation to imperialism and politics.

PART ONE
Women's Lives:
The Influence of Class

1

Working-Class Women

As the working classes comprised about three-quarters of the population of England in 1760, the large majority of English women were working-class. They needed to work to survive, principally through manual labour. While we tend to think of the working classes as being made up of working men and their relatives, women and their work equally helped to define the working classes and industrialization. Almost all working-class women spent their lives working, and almost all earned money. Their tasks included raising their children, shopping, cooking, cleaning, working in the homes of others, bringing paid work into their own homes, and working for wages outside the home. After about 1860, working-class women were more likely than men to rise into the lower middle classes, and by 1914 their social mobility had made the working classes slightly smaller than they had been in 1760.[1]

During the long nineteenth century women's work changed dramatically. From the late nineteenth century much of the labour associated with child-rearing became less intensive because working-class women began having fewer children. Indoor plumbing meant a cleaner home with less effort. In the workforce, women were the key workers of the Industrial Revolution. Industrialization was a long and complex process, and scholars disagree about its impact on women's lives. Of late, many have emphasized the dynamic relationship between gender and industrialization. Industrialization did not just mean the introduction of new technologies and products but a cultural process to which gender was key. The low-level white-collar jobs that were available from the 1860s were also examples of cultural, technological, and economic changes coming together.

Yet in many ways women's work remained the same. Throughout our period, women tended to pursue traditionally female employment such as housework and laundering. This concentration of women into gendered fields was not unique to the long nineteenth century. Long before industrialization we find women concentrated in occupations that were

considered female, many associated with domestic labour. At the beginning of the eighteenth century the four most common jobs for women in
London were domestic service, making and mending clothes, charring
and laundering, and nursing, in that order. A century and a half later,
the 1851 census listed the same four occupations in the same order.[2]
Throughout the long nineteenth century, homes remained small and
crowded; women cleaned and did laundry constantly. Because there was
little money saved up and little space, they also had to buy and prepare
food very frequently.

Most studies of nineteenth-century occupations and productivity have
focused on men and on paid labour; as a result they tend to render
women's work, both paid and unpaid, invisible. Many questions about
women's work were never asked, so we know far less about it than men's
work. The problematic nature of sources gives us an important clue to
the ways that people thought about work. For instance, historians rely on
the censuses (taken every decade from 1801) to provide information about
livelihoods, but for most of the nineteenth century, census enumerators
only inquired about the waged occupations of male heads of households;
women were simply recorded as millers' wives and labourers' daughters,
obscuring much of the work they may have done. (In the 1871 census,
women who did only unpaid housework were considered to work; in the
1881 census, for the first time, such women were considered idle. The
result was that enumerated female 'work' dropped from 98 per cent in
the 1871 census to 42 per cent in the 1881 census.) Other forms of evidence,
such as wage books and oral histories, suggest that the censuses substantially under-reported married women's work in agriculture, manufacturing, and some service industries. Most sources also failed to record
paid work that took place in the home or that was casual, intermittent,
or seasonal, as so much women's work was. Married women especially –
which is to say, most women – found themselves doing all sorts of occasional work that record-keepers overlooked: laundry, perhaps, or child-
minding for the neighbours, or taking in lodgers. These urban- and
service-oriented tasks were aspects of industrialization. For example, in
the town of Keswick, the 1851 census recorded no landladies (women who
took lodgers), while the directory of local services listed sixty-nine.[3]

In addition to focusing on men, census-takers saw the family, not the
individual, as the defining unit. Most working-class women shared this
view to some degree, and saw themselves and their work in the larger
context of the family economy. They were part of the 'economy of make-

shift' – the term was coined by historian Olwen Hufton – and were more intent on helping the family survive than with pursuing a career or even a single occupation. Almost all women cared for their young children and their households; some women also worked for wages in manufacturing, agriculture, or service. Many would spend part of the day, week, or year performing a combination of tasks. Sometimes, as part of the family economy, women contributed to a money-earning endeavour without earning an individual wage. Joseph Sherwin was a weaver in Stockport in Cheshire, who described his own wages as 6s. 6d. per week for weaving, and his wife's as 3s. per week for winding bobbins for two weavers. Yet at the same time she was winding bobbins for a third weaver, her husband, who did not pay her for her work. If we subtract from Mr Sherwin's weekly income the amount he would have paid his winder had she not been his wife, and add the same amount to Mrs Sherwin's weekly wages, their respective weekly incomes would be 4s. 10½d. and 4s. 7½d. – almost equal. The reported income of a male head of household, then, might disguise quite a bit of women's work.[4]

Throughout our period, women's work came second in several senses. Women were seen as secondary labourers; excluded from the highest-paying and most-respected roles, they more often than not undertook work that was preparatory, auxiliary, or ancillary to that engaged in by men. In general, women's wages were between one-half and one-sixth of men's.[5] Many working-class women spent their lives performing tasks so unskilled that they were also done by children. Thus, as their work was categorized as the labour of 'women and children', their status declined. Women's work was also seen as 'unskilled' even when it took a great deal of training, knowledge, or dexterity, simply because it was work done by women. In the metalworking areas around Birmingham, for instance, working metal presses in factories was considered unskilled women's work even though it required training and was physically taxing. Conversely, men's work was often classified as 'skilled' primarily because men did it. (Or sometimes a task that had previously been considered skilled women's work became re-categorized as skilled men's work; cheese- and butter-making are good examples of this.)[6] Finally, women's paid work was secondary in the sense that women already had jobs waiting for them: home, children, and the maintenance of respectability.

Very few working families could survive, and almost none could prosper, on a single male wage. Yet during the long nineteenth century, rhetoric about women's waged work as illegitimate and immoral (especially when women were seen as unfair competitors for men's jobs) became ever louder and more insistent. This was in part because of the 'ideology of separate spheres', which we shall explore in more detail in the next chapter. It dictated that middle-class women refrain from paid work and confine themselves to their homes, and this had ramifications for working-class women as well. For many working-class men, respectability came to be associated with certain aspects of the middle-class lifestyle, especially the ability to earn a 'breadwinner's' wage and so maintain a non-wage-earning wife. Over time, married women found it more difficult than single women to work; in 1851, 75 per cent of married women performed paid work, but by 1911 only 10 per cent of married women were recorded as employed (compared to 70 per cent of single women).[7]

This chapter will begin with a consideration of the domestic responsibilities of working-class women – their unremunerated work – and will then turn to the many other forms of work they engaged in. Throughout the century the principal waged occupations for women were domestic service, mechanized industrial work, and cottage industries; the last included sweated labour – work that, even when done full-time, did not generate enough income to keep even an individual alive, much less his or her family. After about 1860, more educated working-class women could also work at some non-manual jobs. In some ways these 'white-collar' fields held out the promise of upward social mobility; but they were also simply new ways of exploiting women's labour.

Home

The working-class home was a part of the world, not a refuge from it. Women of the working classes often worked as servants before they married but rarely had their own full-time servants. They did all of their housekeeping themselves or with the help of their older daughters. Before indoor plumbing and electricity, this involved quite a lot of heavy lifting, slopping out, and dirt. Women shopped, cooked, cleaned, laundered, and sewed, apparently ceaselessly. They might also grow vegetables or raise livestock. Food was, of course, a major preoccupation: in the early nineteenth century, about 70 per cent of a family's income went on food. Bread was a major staple of the working-class diet, though it was complemented by potatoes in parts of southern England. Tea was considered a necessity, but sugar and beer consumption fluctuated with wages.[8] All three were important ways of making a sparse and monotonous diet more pleasurable. Food preparation could be challenging in small, poorly-equipped kitchens. Women in late-nineteenth-century London found it especially difficult and often relied in part on prepared or semi-prepared foods such as fish and chips, meat pies, and pickles.[9]

Most women also spent a significant portion of their lives bearing and raising their children, tasks that were unpaid and labour-intensive even though emotionally rewarding. This was especially true since working-class women knew little about fertility control before the First World War and so tended to have large families. Most women were pregnant, nursing their babies, or both, for about twenty years of their lives; with very little household help or money to buy nourishing food, this took a tremendous toll. Many working-class women lost at least one if not more of their children as infants or youngsters. Decisions about breast-feeding choices depended in large part on employment options. Women who worked outside the home had to wean their children quite early; servants had to put their babies in the care of others to keep their positions; only those who worked in their own homes could nurse babies for longer. Most women, even if they were not verbally demonstrative, were devoted mothers who passed on to their children cultural and political values (such as respectability). Girls especially were watched closely so that they did not become 'fast' or otherwise sexually unrespectable during their courting years. That many children cared for younger siblings, received minimal schooling, or worked for wages from a young age should be interpreted in context: these choices were appropriate to a working-class culture and did not necessarily indicate an uncaring or demanding mother.

Women, whether or not they earned any part of the family's money, were usually in charge of making it last from one end of the week to the other. Because there were many degrees of affluence even within the working classes, household budgeting could be relatively easy or almost impossible. It depended on whether a woman was the wife of a skilled worker with a high and steady income, or of an unskilled worker with seasonal or otherwise unsteady work. Working-class affluence also varied by occupation, geography, and decade. Families in rural, mining, or industrial areas could have fairly high incomes between about 1810 and 1870; Londoners in such trades as saddle-making or hand-shoemaking, which had been industrialized, had low and insecure incomes between 1865 and 1915.[10]

Women also had to keep the family 'respectable' rather than 'rough'. Working-class respectability (which was quite separate from middle- and upper-class standards) emphasized community, political and economic independence for men, and good housekeeping and mothering skills for women. It was often measured at the local level by neighbours, who were far better able than middle-class observers to appreciate the finer points of respectability or lapses from it. The divide was central to working-class culture, but not rigid: many families slid from respectable to rough and back again, many people socialized across the divide, and few thought of themselves as rough, even when others did. Servants might find a factory girl's boldness rough whereas, compared with other factory workers, she would not have judged herself so.

Respectability was difficult to maintain and many of its most important aspects were controlled by women. It could be judged in many ways: how conscientious a woman was about returning borrowed items; whether a family needed its female head to earn wages year-round, seasonally, or not at all; whether a couple was legally married; whether a family had a parlour in which to entertain company; whether husband or wife drank and how often; whether a family could afford Sunday clothes, sent the children to Sunday school, attended church services, or enjoyed a proper Sunday dinner; whether the children ran around the neighbourhood unsupervised or used coarse language; whether a family could afford a proper funeral (which middle-class observers saw as irrationally extravagant).[11] Some saw the pawning of possessions as rough, others as an acceptable budgeting tool in lean times.

Presiding over home, family, and status were such time-consuming and difficult tasks that some women found it more sensible to confine themselves to unpaid family labour; housewifery was a hard job but, given the alternative occupations, sometimes a preferred one. Refraining from work was often more cost-effective than working outside the home, which would require paying for neighbourhood childcare when the children were young, paying more for food because of less time to devote to its preparation, and exhaustion from cleaning the house at night. Of course, as many women recognized, there were dangers inherent in depending on husbands for income too; men's work could be seasonal, they could decide that wage-earning gave them the right to domestic violence, or they could desert the family. When women worked, they had to crowd domestic responsibilities into their days as men did not. Women not only made less than men largely because they were paid less per hour or per piece, but also because they worked several hours each day caring for their families rather than earning money. Poor women from Lincolnshire, Berkshire, Northamptonshire, Devon, Surrey and Wiltshire who talked to parliamentary investigators all said the same thing: '[B]etween the woman who works and the woman that doesn't there is only 6d. to choose at the year's end, and she that stays at home has it.' A Surrey housewife, Mrs Hook, added: 'I used to go to work, and then had to sit up at nights to wash.'[12] Working-class women often saw full-time housework as the best way to improve their family's respectability and standard of living. With more time to shop and to prepare food, they could manage money more carefully and spend more time raising their children; these in turn increased their status in the family and the community. Less family stress could lead to a drop in marital violence as well. While women who did not earn money enjoyed less leisure time than others in their families, they enjoyed more than women who worked for money by day and for the family by night.

There were also ideological reasons for women to value their domestic labour and abilities. As the century wore on, a growing rhetoric of domesticity promulgated by more affluent working-class men and middle-class commentators helped to keep women in the home and out of formal employment. Despite being limited by it, working-class women used this rhetoric for their own purposes and took pride in doing their own housework and caring for their own children. Concomitantly, as domestic subjects occupied a larger part of the school curriculum of working-class girls from the 1880s, housewifery became distinguished from domestic service and seen as a profession from which men were excluded. This enhanced non-wage-earning women's prestige in their families.

Finally, charity – towards other struggling families and from middle-class women – was an important part of community life. Working-class benevolence took the form of visits to the sick and dying; of a purse passed around for a neighbour in need, into which everyone would drop a penny; or the gift of a Sunday dinner, which was a culinary and social high point of the working-class week. Tight as their budgets were, working and even very poor families made contributions to their church or one of its causes, frequently its foreign missions. Working-class homes were often the objects of much middle-class philanthropy as well; because lady visitors generally made their calls during the day, women were the immediate objects of their attention. It was up to working-class women to convince these visitors who were judging the family – usually by religious standards earlier in the century, and by social scientific ones later on – that their families were respectable and deserving of aid.

Agricultural work

Almost all working-class women spent at least part of their lives earning money, principally in farm work, domestic service, factory work, or cottage industries. In rural areas there was sometimes agricultural work available for women. While there was significant regional variation, in general, women worked in dairying, vegetable cultivation, and auxiliary tasks but rarely in grain production. They were considered especially suited to cleaning and planting jobs: they weeded, hoed, made hay, tended flax, and planted and harvested root crops like potatoes and turnips. The east and Midlands, where there were larger farms, offered less agricultural work for women than the smaller family farms in the west and north. Much of it was seasonal, casual, or performed alongside a father or husband who was paid for his family's work; such contributions went unrecorded and can only be inferred. While women's work was a small and shrinking part of agricultural labour overall, it could represent an important contribution to a family's budget; in Norfolk in 1851 a woman employed for the whole year could make £10, a large sum for a working-class family.[13]

Forms of agricultural employment varied by region, age group, and other work alternatives. In the south and east married women and their children were hired as day-labourers. In Norfolk, younger women worked as gang-labourers. During the 1850s and 1860s, many commentators disapproved of women's participation in casual gang-labour, which was thought unfeminine. However, female 'ganging', while it attracted much attention, was restricted to children and unmarried teenagers and limited to west Norfolk, and it was fairly rare even there. In the East Riding of Yorkshire young unmarried women were hired as farm servants on year-long contracts until the 1870s. Their work included outdoor tasks such as milking the cows and assisting in harvesting, and indoor jobs such as house-cleaning and meal preparation. In Norfolk and Yorkshire, women represented about one-third of the day-labourer force; in Bedfordshire, where there was other work for women in lace-making and straw-plaiting, women made up only 3 per cent of the agricultural labour force.[14]

In most places agricultural work for women became less plentiful over time. In the south and east, little work was available for women after the early nineteenth century. In the north, women's agricultural wages remained fairly stable until 1850, and then declined. The number of women working as farm servants dropped gradually during the first half of the nineteenth century, and sharply between 1851 and 1871 when less than one per cent of rural women were farm labourers. There were exceptions to this rule. In parts of the south-west, many women and children worked as agricultural day-labourers well into the nineteenth century. In Northumberland, women were an important part of the farm workforce into the twentieth century, and in Essex women and children still did traditional rural work such as weeding, and stone and potato picking, until the Second World War.[15]

After 1850 not only was there little agricultural work for women, but what work there was became more sex-segregated. In some areas wives and daughters of male agricultural labourers continued to perform agricultural tasks, but only at certain times of year. In the south and east women did only dairying, spring weeding, and early summer haymaking, tasks with short seasons. In the East Riding of Yorkshire female farm servants were increasingly pushed out of dairy and outdoor work and confined to work indoors. As women's role in agriculture became more limited, so their wages fell.[16]

Not surprisingly, women came to prefer employment in the town to working on farms. In the 1880s, many newspapers noted that local women would not take on farm work if they could get work as a domestic servant in town.[17] Many rural areas found themselves with noticeable gender imbalances. Flora Thompson (1876–1947) grew up in rural Oxfordshire. In her autobiographical trilogy *Lark Rise to Candleford*, she remembered that if one saw:

a girl well on in her teens, she would be dressed in town clothes, complete with gloves and veil, for she would be home from service for her fortnight's holiday ... There was no girl over twelve or thirteen living permanently at home ... The parents did not want the boys to leave home ... The girls, while at home, could earn nothing.[18]

More and more, rural women either left home for domestic service or factory work elsewhere, or stayed at home and did piece-work of some kind, such as straw-plaiting.

Domestic service

Domestic service was a form of work that certainly preceded industrialization. As the eighteenth century drew to a close, however, service
began changing and growing. The first important development was that
domestic service became dominated by female labour. While in the early
modern period there were at least as many men as women in service, by
the early nineteenth century women outnumbered men by eight to one,
and by the end of the century by twenty-two to one. There was an
expansion in the number of households which employed servants, though
most of these hired only one general servant rather than a large and
specialized staff. The 1891 census estimated that there were 1,649,000
people working as servants in England – almost all of them women.[19]

Most servants were required to live in the households they served and
to remain unmarried and childless (being married and not living in
became more common only a few years before the end of our period).
The typical servant was young and remained in service after she left her
parents' home and before she married and established her own household. Contrary to stereotypes about loyal family employees, most worked
on one-year contracts for a series of families. In Mrs Beeton's *Book of
Household Management*, a popular instruction manual for middle-class
women first published in 1861, the author gives a table of wages for
servants in or near London: an upper housemaid was to be paid between
£12 and £18 per year, while a lowly general servant or maid-of-all-work
made only £9 to £14 per year, which by the 1906 edition had risen to
between £12 and £28.[20] Wages were lower elsewhere in the country and
earlier in the period.

Domestic service existed all over England, but grew fastest in urban
areas (themselves growing quickly at this time). By 1801, one-third of the
population of England and Wales lived in urban areas with populations
greater than ten thousand. The demand for servants was met largely by
young women who left the country for the nearest city. Rural girls were
thought to make better servants than urban ones and were even preferred
to the workhouse girls who (after the introduction of the New Poor Law
in 1834) could be had very cheaply, for the cost of room and board, but
were considered uncouth and undesirable employees by those who could
afford better. (Workhouses were state-run institutions that provided food
and shelter for the poorest; working-class people saw them as a place of
last resort.) As a result girls who came from the countryside, though often

perceived as naïve and vulnerable, were sometimes better able to get posts in the homes of the middle classes, gentry, and even the aristocracy.

Domestic service was for most of the nineteenth century the nation's fastest-growing occupational category. By 1851, it had become the largest single occupation for women; by the 1880s, one-third of all women between the ages of fifteen and twenty-one were in service. These figures varied dramatically by region. In York, 60 per cent of employed women were in service in 1851. In Stockport and Preston, which had large textile factories that employed young women, only 3 per cent of working-class women were servants. Intriguingly, not every woman described as a domestic servant was a hired stranger; many servants were related to the head of the household in which they worked (although this does not mean they were treated as part of the family). Conversely, many women performed 'domestic service' for their own families, without being labelled 'servants'. Additionally, servants employed by farmers and retailers probably spent a significant part of their workdays farming and selling.

One reason that service was on the rise as an occupational category was the growth of the servant-employing middle classes, as a proportion of the population. To take only one lower-middle-class occupation, in 1851, office workers comprised less than one per cent of the working population; in 1951, this had risen to over 10 per cent. Because many considered keeping a servant to be a mark of middle-class status, they tried to hire at least one woman if they could afford it. As a result of this demographic shift, most servants in industrializing England worked for employers who were not wealthy aristocrats, but rather were middle-class professionals, shopkeepers, tradespeople, clerks, or even artisans.

Mrs Beeton's *Book of Household Management* counselled readers on how to manage a household staff, including butler, footman, coachman, groom, stableboy, housekeeper, lady's maid, laundry maid, nursemaid, and upper and under housemaids, the last of whose duties would include cleaning marble floors and crystal decanters and brightening gilt frames. But this description was more prescriptive (or fantastic) than real; only a tiny proportion of families enjoyed the £300 per annum income that was necessary to hire a second servant, let alone run the household described by Isabella Beeton.

The reality of service was often very different. Because the ability and desire to hire domestic help extended down to families with annual incomes of less than £100 (£100 to £150 was the boundary between the middle and working classes), households frequently employed not a vast retinue but one young woman. These solitary servants did not enjoy the relative luxury of differentiated duties; they were not ladies' maids or upstairs-maids but maids-of-all-work. The general servant was expected to perform a variety of services including shopping, cooking, cleaning, and laundry; she might also help out in the family's shop or mind the children. A typical general maid's day began at six in the morning and ended at eleven o'clock at night. Her work included blacking grates, cleaning boots, putting coal on the fire, emptying slops, making beds, sweeping, dusting, scrubbing walls and floors, washing windows and dishes, and cooking and serving meals. Hannah Cullwick was born in 1833, went into service when she was eight years old, and – unusually – remained a general servant for her entire working life. While working-class women rarely kept diaries, Cullwick (luckily for historians) did. Here she records a typical day:

> *Friday, 2 January [1863]* I open'd the shutters, lighted the fires & clean'd the hearths. Clean'd 1 pair o' boots. Swept and dusted the parlour & got the Master's breakfast up by a ¼ past eight & he told me to get a cab, so I fetch'd one and rode it in to the door. Of course I let myself out & am always on the pavement before the horse has well stopp'd – then I ring the visitors' bell & the Master waves his hand through the window to say it's all right. Had my breakfast & then clean'd the parlour things & wash'd up what was dirty & left the cloth on for Miss Very. Went to the Missis for orders and brought her breakfast things down. Clean'd the knives. Fill'd the scuttles & made the kitchen fire up. Got dinner ready. Clean'd away the dirty things & laid our cloth. Had dinner. Wash'd up after & clean'd up the kitchen ... I did some writing and got the supper ready. Laid our cloth. Clean'd away and wiped the knives. Lock'd up the doors – put a plate of beer to catch the beetles. Wound the clock up & put wood to dry & to bed at 11.[21]

Cullwick's day was long, unrelenting and physically demanding. One of the most difficult aspects of her job in this particular household was that the Foster family demanded that Hannah frequently change into clean dry clothes and perform some upper-servant work, such as answering the door or leaving the house to hail a cab. Like many middle-class families, the Fosters could not afford more than one servant, but they tried to make her do the work of two or more; they probably hoped that having Cullwick act as upper servant on occasion made them seem more affluent.

This particular form of service, maid-of-all-work to a less affluent family, probably accounted for much of the growing demand for domestic servants. We can, therefore, think of domestic service as an occupation that reveals both connections and discontinuities with the past. When we consider the tasks necessary to the maintenance of the home, little seems to have changed. But when we think of rural girls leaving home to become maids-of-all-work in modest urban homes, domestic service seems to be a new field indicative of dislocations and changes. Geographical disruption was a major consequence of industrialization, and many young women uprooted themselves to find work that was lonely and difficult.

Contemporaries had strong ideas about servants. Middle-class commentators criticized them for spending their cash wages on luxury goods. One 1846 article, 'Friendly Hints for Female Servants', reminded its readers that 'every day female servants are convicted of dishonesty; few weeks pass without cases of gross indecorum; thousands in the course of a year, lose their character and enter on vicious and destructive courses ...'[22] Critics also worried that servants adopted their masters' living standards as their own, and strove to replicate them in their own households when they left service.

It is hard to know how appealing domestic service was to women who needed to earn a living. Women who testified to parliamentary investigators about the conditions of their work sometimes talked about the differences between domestic service and work in factories or mines. Elizabeth Curnow commented that 'the work is harder at the mine for the time, but when one leaves work, there is nothing more to do.' Seventeen-year-old Elizabeth Davey, a pit worker in Cornwall, testified that 'she was in service before she came to the mine. Finds this employment agrees with her better than service', but lace-mill worker Anne Burgess, also fourteen, 'fancies she had rather be at service', and fourteen-year-old pit worker Ann Fern said she would 'rather go to service, but I never tried.'[23]

As servants were usually hired for full-year contracts, they did not need to worry about being seasonally unemployed. They were assured of year-round food and shelter plus a small cash wage, and if one includes the value of room and board, salaries for servants were competitive with other, more seasonal types of women's work. While most women worked as servants from the time they left their parents' household until they married and established their own, some women chose a career in service in preference to marrying and having children. Most female servants were not permitted to marry, and some women might have enjoyed being freed from the pressure to find a husband. Because of the demand for servants, especially experienced ones, few were dependent on or particularly loyal to a single employer. Many mistresses had difficulty maintaining their staff and despaired at the liberties taken by them. Many women in service, especially lower servants and maids-of-all-work, frequently left one household for another or for other types of work.

Domestic service also had its drawbacks. Because most servants were the only full-time household employee, the work could be very isolating. A servant might sleep alone in a room at the top of the house, or even in the kitchen, after a lifetime of sharing a bed with siblings. In addition, the constant scrutiny from their employers could be irritating. Servants had little time to spend away from the house and off duty, and little cash to spend on themselves. And they seem to have been a vulnerable part of the population: a disproportionately high number of prostitutes had been maids-of-all-work. While it is not entirely clear why this was so, one problem was that some employers would not give girls good 'characters' when they left their posts. Young women who were denied these crucial references had trouble finding new employment and could find themselves without homes or incomes. One doctor explained to a parliamentary committee that 'they get out of place and they have nowhere to go and they adopt this as a last resort, as a means of livelihood; some go back to service and again return to the streets.'[24] One of Jack the Ripper's victims, Polly Nichols, was a servant who had been dismissed for stealing and had turned to prostitution.[25] In contrast, factory work provided a support network of fellow workers and a higher cash wage but no room or board, and no guarantee of year-round work. The fact that domestic service had strengths and weaknesses, and that some women chose to enter it while others eschewed it, tells us that working-class women could exercise some choice regarding their working lives. To some women, the security of room and board, and the type of self-sufficiency that went with it, including freedom from cold, hunger, and economic or emotional dependence on a husband, made the restrictions of life in service acceptable. For others, the inability to choose their own food and lodgings, the lack of community, the impossibility of marrying or having children while continuing to work, and the danger of falling into a life of prostitution or ending up in the local workhouse, made service either a temporary occupation or one to be avoided altogether.

Factory work

Industrialized manufacture was another important source of jobs for women: by 1899 over half a million women worked in factories.[26] Most available factory work was in the great industrial centres of northern England, the Midlands, and Scotland; some was in the eastern parts of England and in South Wales. For those who lived elsewhere, it was usually not an option. The female population was a crucial source of workers. The female textile worker – the 'mill girl' – was the archetypal worker during industrialization, which could not have happened without women.

Factory work was quite different from service: the factory girl was not operating in a domestic space, her job was wholly new, and her wage symbolized independence. Factory work appealed to many because of the community provided by the workspace, in contrast to the lonely life led by many servants. While domestic service seemed to be an occupation in which women (when not developing dangerous aspirations) were closely watched and kept respectable, factory work appeared to observers to encourage a lifestyle in which employees often lived far from their families, were at liberty to fraternize with strange men, made enough money to buy baubles and bangles, and generally posed a danger to themselves and to the smooth functioning of society. Factory girls were also accused of lacking domestic skills and making poor wives and mothers, a charge many hotly denied. One factory worker from Stockport said in the 1830s: 'I have taken notice, in my own neighbourhood, that young women brought up in factories, against those that are brought up as servants, seem to take more care of their houses and children, and to be more industrious, than the other class.'[27]

Women were a prominent part of factory work from its beginnings, even as some worried that the working environment or the work itself was inappropriate. One observer in the 1790s described young women's work in a woollen factory:

> ... a girl of about fourteen years old ... placed [prepared wool flakes] on the Spinning Jenny, which has a number of horizontal beams of wood, on each of which may be fifty bobbins. One girl sets those bobbins all in motion by turning a wheel at the end of the beam, a wire then catches up a flake of Wool, spins it, and gathers it upon each bobbin. The girl again turns the wheel, and another fifty flakes are

taken up and spun. This is done every minute without intermission, so that probably *one* girl turning that wheel, may do the work of One Hundred Hand Wheels at the least. About twenty sets of these bobbins, were I judge at work in one room. Most of the Manufactories are many stories high, and the rooms much larger than this I was in. Struck with the impropriety of even so many as the twenty girls I saw, without any woman presiding over them, I enquired of the Master if he was married, why his Wife was not present? He said he was not a married man, and that many parents *did* object to send their girls, but that the poverty of others, and not having any work to set them to, left him not at any loss for hands. I must do all the parties the justice to say, that these girls appeared neat and orderly: yet at best, I cannot but fear the taking such young persons from the eyes of their parents, and thus herding them together with only men and boys, must bring up a dissolute race of poor.[28]

In fact, although the commentator Peter Gaskell claimed that factory work created 'an habitual indifference' to marital fidelity and the 'destruction of domestic habits',[29] women who worked in factories were no more sexually promiscuous than others and were less likely than domestic servants or sweated workers to become prostitutes.

Employment in textiles (including cotton, wool and worsted, linen and fustian) tripled between 1750 and 1800. By the end of the eighteenth century, the woollen and worsted industries were concentrated in Yorkshire, Norfolk and the West Country; knitting was centred in the East Midlands and especially in Leicestershire and Nottinghamshire, with hand-knitting localized in the north and in Scotland. Silk, a luxury industry, was found in Spitalfields in London, and silk ribbon weaving was done in Coventry. The English demand for linen was met by workers in Ireland and Scotland.

Cotton, the largest and fastest-growing of the thriving textile industries, was concentrated in Lancashire, Cheshire, and Scotland. In 1818, women comprised over half of the labour force in the cotton industry in England – in Scotland, the figure was 61 per cent – and they were important in other forms of textile production as well, including silk and largely domestic industries such as lace-making. In 1831, cotton represented over one-fifth of British industry, while continuing to maintain a largely female labour force. By 1871, 57 per cent of adult workers in the Lancashire and Cheshire cotton industry were women. As the industry grew, it mechanized: the first factories in England were cotton factories, and again the labour force was made up predominantly of women and children. But while textiles increasingly depended on steam power, the clothing trades, which expanded rapidly in the 1840s and 1850s, still relied on the hand tech-nology of needlewomen (those in the dressmaking and needlework trades). Not all cotton factories were huge: as time went on small factories became rarer, but as late as 1835, the average cotton mill employed fewer than two hundred people.

As with domestic service, wages varied by process, employer, and loca-tion. In the 1760s, women in silk mills in Sheffield earned 4s. to 6s. weekly. In the 1790s, women in cotton mills in Yorkshire made at most 5s. per week. In Manchester between 1809 and 1819, weekly wages for cotton pickers were 7s. to 11s., carders about the same. Between 1803 and 1833 spinners in Manchester made between 8s. 5d. and 10s. 5d. By 1842, throstle spinners in Manchester made an average weekly wage of 9s. to 11s., though women in Wigan made only 7s. 6d. for the same work. Later in the period, cotton weavers in Lancashire made 21s. to 27s. weekly, while carpet weavers in Kidderminster made only 16s. weekly.[30]

Women's work in textile factories was often unpleasant and unhealthy even where it was not arduous. Before the Factory Acts of the 1830s and 1840s limited the number of hours per day which women and children could work, most women worked alongside children in cotton and other textile factories for twelve or more hours per day. Flax had to be damp while it was spun, and so spinners in flax mills were constantly being sprayed by water coming off the frames.[31] When, in 1831 and 1832, the Member of Parliament Michael Sadler headed a parliamentary committee investigating the conditions of work in factories, the committee was appalled by its findings. In one interview, Elizabeth Bentley, a worker in Busk's flax mill in Leeds, who had started work at the age of six and was now twenty-three, described life for herself and her mother:

> I was a little doffer. [I worked f]rom 5 in the morning till 9 at night, when they were thronged, [and f]rom 6 in the morning till 7 at night [at other times] ... When the frames are full, [doffers] have to stop the frames, and take the flyers off, and take the full bobbins off, and carry them to the roller; and then put empty ones on, and set the frame going again ... there are so many frames, and they run so quick ... [M]y mother had been up at 4 o'clock in the morning, and at 2 o'clock in the morning; the colliers used to go to their work about 3 or 4 o'clock,

and when she heard them stirring she has got up out of her warm bed, and gone out and asked them the time; and I have sometimes been at Hunslet Car at 2 o'clock in the morning, when it was streaming down with rain, and we have had to stay until the mill was opened.[32]

Bentley was by this time a young woman, still doing tedious, relentless, difficult tasks at the mill; her mother (who may or may not have worked in the mill herself) also had a hard life simply getting her children to their jobs.

Much of the work done by women in cotton factories was unskilled or auxiliary labour and was also performed by children. When, as part of the Children's Employment Commission Inquiring into the Factories in 1833, Commissioner John Spencer asked workers in Newcastle-under-Lyme and the Staffordshire Potteries about conditions at their place of work, he used two separate questionnaires. One was for 'adults'. The other was for 'women and children'.[33] However, women were often thought superior to men at designated female tasks; for instance, of women in the Leicester hosiery industry it was said that on 'many machines, owing to their intricacy and delicacy the women are superior'.[34]

The number and proportion of married women working in factories varied by region, family income, and their husband's trade. In Lancashire's cities, by 1851 most women workers were between sixteen and twenty-one, and 75 per cent were single. This means, of course, that one in four factory workers was married, a significant number that is probably an under-estimate. Eleven per cent of the young children in Preston at mid-century had mothers who worked in factories. In the 1830s and 1840s evangelical and other middle-class commentators criticized mothers of babies and young children for working, especially in factories, and throughout the nineteenth century various critics blamed the ignorance and paid employment of working mothers, rather than poverty and poor sanitation, for the high infant mortality. Some factory workers were local girls and women; others had migrated from the surrounding countryside in search of work. Women who married weavers were more likely to continue their factory work than were those who married spinners. While commentators worried that girls receiving high cash wages and who had no family living nearby would behave wildly, young silk workers in Essex who lived in boarding houses that operated as surrogate families sent the better part of their wages home.

Spinning was the first task to be mechanized and brought into the factory. Until the late eighteenth century, it had been the quintessential female task, with women and children making up as much as 90 per cent of the workforce. Spinning was done at home, by hand, by women, between other chores. Even the invention of the spinning jenny by James Hargreaves in the 1760s, which allowed a single spinner simultaneously to work eight spindles, then sixteen, and by 1800 one hundred spindles, did not immediately transform spinning; many of the early jennies were used at home by women, and even when spinning first moved into cotton factories, the large industrial jennies were worked by women.

It was the introduction of Samuel Crompton's 'mule' which transformed spinning into a task done by men. From around 1820 to 1833, women worked in factories on short-handled mules, but in the next ten years these were replaced by long-handled and double mules, which required so much physical strength that it was difficult for women to operate them. But whereas cotton manufacture was revolutionized by the new machinery, mule-spinners could not make strong enough woollen or worsted yarn, so women continued to dominate spinning in those industries. In due course, spinning, which had been performed by women in domestic settings all over England, became entirely mechanized and concentrated in certain regions of the country, notably south Lancashire. Mule-spinning became a skilled male task, now called 'minding', and women were able to perform only preparatory and unskilled work relating to it. Some women remained at work on short mules, but they were few and far between. Even when the self-acting mule, which took less strength to operate, came into wide use in the late 1840s, women remained unskilled piecers rather than skilled minders, because by then there were not enough women to hand their knowledge down to the next generation and because male workers now insisted that mule-operating was men's work. With factory spinning now established as men's domain, and weaving as yet done outside the factories, the women who worked there were confined to auxiliary tasks such as tenting and carding, for which they were paid at most half of what male spinners made.

Weaving was mechanized soon after spinning, with power looms first appearing in cotton factories in the 1820s. In contrast to spinning, weaving had traditionally been a skilled male task. The male handloom weavers, whose artisanal craft was being rendered obsolete by the new power looms, resisted them fiercely for several decades, refusing to allow their skilled independent work to be replaced by the new, less skilled power-loom weaving now being done in the factories. By the 1840s, the handloom weavers had been forced by circumstances, including dire necessity, to give up this stance and work in the factories as power-loom weavers. But their initial resistance meant that women were an integral part of the weaving workforce as it mechanized and entered the factories. The first power-loom weavers were agricultural workers, both male and female, and many of the first power looms were worked by women and children. Some female factory hands, then, became skilled weavers, working alongside and receiving the same piece-rate as male weavers. The contrast between the effects of the transition into factories of spinning and weaving on male and female workers is striking. Where men embraced new technology, as in spinning, women were excluded; and where men resisted new forms of work, as in weaving, women had more opportunities. As power-loom weaving expanded and women were no longer confined to auxiliary tasks, their role in mechanized cotton production changed. The result was that in the weaving-only factories of north-east Lancashire, women became conscious of themselves as workers with rights, and weavers saw themselves as a group of workers whose interests cut across gender lines.

Gender was not the sole determinant of women and men's experiences or identities as workers.[35] Frequently, though, it was a decisive factor. Women weavers in weaving-only factories were exceptional in doing the same work as men for the same wages; even female weavers in factories that employed both weavers and spinners did not fare as well as their colleagues. And as the century wore on, women's work came to be defined as work that was light, clean, semi-skilled, requiring dexterity – women were praised for their 'nimble fingers' – and close attention, but not much expertise.[36] This definition restricted women to a small number of processes, including the operation of sewing machines (in the factory or at home).

Trade-union activism, an important part of the history of men's work, is less relevant to women's work. Before the late nineteenth century trade unions were usually aimed at skilled workers, and as we saw above, skill was defined in ways that excluded women. Also, women who did domestic service, home work, or any form of sweated labour usually worked alone and changed jobs frequently, which made them difficult to organize. More importantly, the union movement conceptualized the worker as a male head of household, and so usually overlooked the needs of female workers. Some trade unionists were willing to address the needs of women as members of the working classes, but not as workers themselves, insisting on men's rights to work and act politically and on women's rights to remain at home and pursue respectability via domesticity.[37]

In some industries, organized male workers resented female labourers (and immigrants) and excluded them from their unions. Middle-class women therefore formed unions for working-class women, starting in 1874 with the Women's Trade Union League (WTUL), from which they lobbied the government for legislation on hours and conditions. In other industries, women and men agitated together, as for example in the chainmakers' strikes between 1910 and 1913. Overall, though, trade unions protected the rights of skilled male artisans and labourers and did little for women.

Outwork

It is impossible to know how many women worked at home in manufacturing. While farm work became more rare, domestic service and factory work loomed large on the cultural landscape: the servant and the factory girl were the focus of much attention and anxiety, as both seemed simultaneously to pose a threat to, and be victimized by, various segments of society. While advice manuals for middle-class women were full of cautions about the help, radical commentators worried about the assault on working-class women's virtue waged by vicious aristocratic employers (in spite of the fact that most illegitimate pregnancies were the result of seductions by working-class, not elite, men). Victorian stage melodramas and industrial novels such as Charles Dickens's *Hard Times* (1854) depicted female factory hands as virtuous women who struggled to earn a living without resorting to prostitution and were therefore deserving of attention and pity. Others portrayed mill girls as dangerously independent of family and community controls.

The stark contrast between these two extremes gives us an inaccurate picture of women's options. Between the employer's home and the factory floor lay the thriving, sprawling, and complex world of cottage industry, also called home work, domestic industry, domestic manufacture, the domestic system, domestic work, outwork, or the putting-out system; the multiplicity of terms suggests the importance of these endeavours to English culture and the economy. In cottage industries, workers laboured at home, turning raw goods into finished products for very little money. For women, such work was an essential part of their 'economy of makeshift', in which a variety of never-ending tasks helped to make ends meet.

Such putting-out systems might seem pre-industrial, but many industries, even as they expanded during our period, maintained some or all of their production as domestic work. This was especially true of the wool industry, where power looms could not handle finer threads or delicate weaving processes. Home work also remained very important in lace-making, gloving, leather, and straw-plaiting. Almost all of this home work was done by women. In the following description, women prepare cotton for weaving:

> The raw material was first separated from the bale, laid out on a wire riddle or tightly stretched cords, and beaten well with willow switches to free it from dirt ... Cotton intended for fine spinning was then carefully washed, while in other cases it was simply drenched in order to make the fibres cling in spinning. The younger Crompton has described how his mother prepared the cotton for the inventor of the mule. 'I recollect that soon after I was able to walk I was employed in the cotton manufacture. My mother used to bat the cotton wool on a wire riddle. It was then put into a deep brown mug with a strong ley of soap suds. My mother then tucked up my petticoats about my waist, and put me into the tub to tread upon the cotton at the bottom. When a second riddleful was batted I was lifted out, it was placed in the mug, and I again trod it down ... When the mug was quite full, the soap suds were poured off, and each separate dollop of wool well squeezed to free it from moisture. They were then placed on the bread rack under the beams of the kitchen-loft to dry. My mother and my grand-mother carded the cotton wool by hand, taking one of the dollops at a time, on the single hand cards. When carded they were put aside in separate parcels ready for spinning.'
>
> Drying the cotton for spinning was not always an easy matter in the cottages and was sometimes attended with risk [of fire] ... When dry, the cotton was ready for carding ... [then] converted into rovings by twisting on the spinning wheel ... into yarn fine enough for the weaver.[38]

Domestic industry could turn a home into a workplace, as the image of wool drying by the bread in the kitchen makes vivid.

Once thought to have been quickly replaced by factory production, cottage industries are now recognized to have thrived alongside newer technologies and systems of organization throughout the nineteenth century. The two coexisted, often as different facets of a single production effort. Many processes were performed in homes and in factories sim- ultaneously, and even for the same employer. Sometimes employers would invest in new technologies, or decide to open large factories, but they were just as likely to decide that it would be easier and cheaper to expand their existing domestic system. This was especially true in the textile industry, which as we have seen was a main provider of factory jobs for women. Because the labour of women and children was cheap, it was often more cost-effective for employers simply to continue using them in a putting-out system. Indeed, much outwork was so poorly paid that its workers could not support their families or even themselves on their income; this was even more true as the century progressed. One needlewoman told the journalist and social investigator Henry Mayhew (1812–87) at mid-century that:

> at all kinds of work . . . I cannot earn more than 4s. 6d. to 5s. per week – let me sit from eight in the morning till ten every night . . . and my clear earnings [after paying for coal and other supplies] are a little but more than 2s. . . . I consider trowsers [sic] the best work . . . Shirt work is the worst, the very worst, that can be got . . . A mother has got two or three daughters, and she don't wish them to go to service, and she puts them to this poor needlework; and that, in my opinion, is the cause of the destitution and the prostitution about the streets in these parts . . . Most of the workers are young girls who have nothing else to depend upon, and there is scarcely one of them virtuous . . . As [my daughter and I] sit to work together, one candle does for the two of us, so that she earns about 3s. per week clear, which is not sufficient to keep her even in food . . . My husband is a seafaring man, or I don't know what I should do. He is a particularly steady man, a teetotaller, and so indeed are the whole family, or else we could not live. Recently my daughter has resigned the work and gone to service, as the prices are not sufficient for food and clothing.[39]

This woman's family could not survive without her husband's regular (if inadequate) income. Others were not so lucky. As we shall see below, needlewomen turned to prostitution out of desperation. Yet while some commentators deplored the low wages of cottage industry, others approved of it because it took place in the home.

Some women may have been drawn to cottage industry because it allowed them more flexibility and independence than either domestic service or factory work, and because it enabled them to supplement their husbands' income even if it could not feed a family. Historians have long thought that home work may have appealed to women with children, who could spin or make lace at home while breast-feeding or caring for babies. This may have been true. However, the assertion that the two roles were complementary is only speculation, and it would surely have been difficult, even impossible, for a woman who was breast-feeding, caring for older children, cooking, and cleaning, to add yet another task to her day – especially as those who did piece-work usually did it fourteen to eighteen hours per day.

Outworking women performed a variety of tasks, many of them in clothing and textiles or related fields. One was spinning, the very process that was revolutionized by technology perhaps more than any other in this period. As noted above, Hargreaves's spinning jenny allowed a single spinner to work many spindles. But jennies with fewer than twenty spindles were used widely in domestic or small-workshop settings, even after the introduction of the many-spindled jennies which were designed for use in the factory. Crompton's mule was also used at first on a putting-out basis. The domestic system remained just as vital in the woollen and worsted industries until at least 1860. And although the steam-powered rotary frame was becoming widely used in the hosiery industry, it could not produce the intricate patterns required for 'fancy' work, which remained the province of hand-loom knitters.

Female home-workers were important in the silk industry as well: in Coventry, where silk ribbons were made, in Spitalfields, and in Essex. Their tasks included throwing (similar to spinning in the wool and cotton industries) and winding silk yarn on to bobbins and quills in preparation for weavers. Women also did some weaving, although they tended to be restricted to work on plainer fabrics, while men wove brocades and satins. A nineteenth-century observer noted that in one household in Spitalfields, '[t]he mother was engaged in warping silk with a [warping] machine ... One of the daughters was similarly employed at another machine, and three other girls were on separate looms',[40] giving us a sense of how industrious a home could be.

Women outworkers would also make, mend, and finish lace, seam and embroider hosiery, sew gloves, cover and sew buttons, and plait straw. Since domestic industries tended to be geographically specific, women in different parts of the country had different outworking options. The silk industry was centred in Essex; most shirt buttons were made in Dorset. Women in Birmingham and the Black Country worked in the small metal industries, making nails and chains, and this was often criticized because it seemed too dirty and difficult to be done by women. Home-workers all over the country were engaged in one or another of the needle trades, making shirts, trousers, and waistcoats, or repairing frayed collars and buttonholes. Still others were laundresses, collecting dirty clothes from employers' homes and returning with clean bundles.

Later in the nineteenth century many outworkers were engaged to finish items such as matches that had been partially manufactured elsewhere. In London Arthur J. Munby, a middle-class man who made a habit of observing working-class women, wrote in 1861 that on London Bridge:

> One meets them at every step: young women carrying large bundles of umbrella frames home to be covered; young women carrying cages full of hats, which yet want the silk and the binding, coster-girls often dirty and sordid, going to fill their empty baskets, and above all female sackmakers.[41]

Outwork allowed women to take on work sporadically and to work at home while caring for – or with the assistance of – their children; neither domestic service nor factory work offered such flexibility (though families could sometimes do farm work together). But women chose outwork from a narrow range of options because they needed to earn money, and much of it was back-breaking, tedious, exploitative, and poorly paid. Indeed, needlewomen were by the 1840s icons of distressed poverty. Henry Mayhew revealed the tragedy of needlewomen forced into prostitution by their low wages. One 'good-looking girl' who had been doing 'slop-work' or low-paying piece-work for three years told him that:

> I struggled very hard to keep myself chaste, but I found that I couldn't get food and clothing for myself and mother, so I took to live with a young man ... He did promise to marry me, but ... I have not seen him now for about six months ... He told me if I came to live with him he'd take care I shouldn't want, and both mother and me had been

very bad off before. He said, too, he'd make me his lawful wife, but I hardly cared so long as I could get food for myself and mother. Many young girls at the shop advised me to go wrong ... There isn't one young girl as can get her living by slop work.[42]

Another young woman sobbed as she explained that:

I used to work at slop-work – at the shirt work – ... working from five o'clock in the morning till midnight each night ... still it was impossible for me to live. I was forced to go out of a night to make out my living. I had a child, and it used to cry for food ... On my soul I went to the streets solely to get a living for myself and child. If I had been able to get it otherwise I would have done so ... for the sake of other young girls I can and will solemnly state that it was the smallness of the price I got for my labour that drove me to prostitution as a means of living...[43]

While these poor women knew the melodramatic conventions of the day well, and may have used them to shape their stories, their desperate economic circumstances were quite real, as was, one suspects, their grief. An industrialized England, full of cheap and available mass-produced goods, was built, to a large degree, on the backs of poor girls.

White-collar work

From mid-century, changes in England's economy and culture led to important developments in working-class women's employment. The growth of state and commercial bureaucracies, of retail shopping, and of state-sponsored education led to the creation of new jobs for women in clerical work, elementary-school teaching, nursing, hospital dispensing, and retail sales work. The related growth of the service sector meant that positions in office-cleaning, or waitressing in inexpensive restaurants and tea shops, were also available, especially in London and other large cities. All of these jobs represented a dramatic departure from previous options. They were especially appealing to lower-middle-class and upper-working-class women because they required education and provided respectability, and were therefore set apart from more menial work. They became available to women not only because employers needed new sources of cheap labour but in part because of the campaigns of middle-class feminists to raise public awareness of women's abilities.

Most of these jobs required years of schooling that not all working-class women could afford. Women who went into white-collar work had to stay at school until they reached sixteen (the law required schooling only to the age of ten in 1880), which represented a cultural and financial commitment on the part of their families. In 1891 Amelia Fidoe, a widow who was receiving Poor Law assistance in Stafford, applied to be allowed to take her twelve-year-old daughter out of school. When the Poor Law Board of Guardians refused, Fidoe apparently chose to forgo assistance so that she could remove her daughter from school and have her start earning a wage.[44]

Most employers required female employees to remain unmarried and childless. But for those who could afford the preparation and accept the restrictions, white-collar jobs offered work that was clean and light and felt like a career. They also offered the possibility of an exciting urban lifestyle in which women walked the city streets alone, dressed up to go to the theatre or a music hall with friends, read the latest popular literature and mass circulation periodicals, and generally lived an independent and cultured life as 'latchkey girls'.[45] However, these jobs quickly became overcrowded, and large numbers of women were restricted to the few tasks considered feminine. And in some forms of white-collar work, educated working-class women had to compete with middle-class women looking for ladylike employment as well. During the second half of the nineteenth century teachers, nurses, shop assistants, clerks and civil servants found their working conditions improving; as regards status, though, teaching and nursing became professionalized and more respected, while by the turn of the century shop assistants, clerks and civil servants lost some of the sheen of middle-class respectability they had enjoyed earlier.[46]

In 1861 fewer than 200,000 women worked as teachers, nurses, shop assistants, clerks, or civil servants. But by the turn of the century that number would rise to almost 562,000. This means that working-class women were flooding into white-collar work faster than into any other fields. Between 1881 and 1911, the number of women in manufacturing and domestic service increased by a quarter, while the number engaged in teaching, retailing, office work and nursing almost tripled. In 1911 teachers, nurses, shop assistants, and privately- or state-employed clerks, most of them women, made up over 14 per cent of the employed population.[47]

These new jobs had many disadvantages. Work as a salesgirl in a small shop or in one of the new department stores in London or other cities was low-paid and highly regimented. There were strict requirements: only girls with genteel accents, proper grammar, and excellent manners could hope to obtain posts, so poor and workhouse girls had no chance. Shopgirls did not get paid much more than factory workers: room and board and £10 to £12 per annum to start with, plus commissions for some.[48] Most employers required salesgirls to live in, where conditions, especially in the dormitories provided by large stores, were cramped and uncomfortable. Shopgirls were also vulnerable to predatory advances from customers and employers. In spite of all this, sales work was appealing to many women because it was higher in status than factory work or domestic service. Shop assistants wore neat, middle-class clothes and did not do heavy labour. Many women felt the cultural distinction between their work and manual labour to be crucial.

Nursing, on the other hand, had been little more than domestic service and the province of uneducated older women until the middle of the nineteenth century. Nurses cared for the sick, and, in this period, were expected to provide as much tea and sympathy as medical expertise. Because nursing involved both caring for others and domestic labour it was deemed feminine even though it involved back-breaking work and long hours. Its feminine appeal, along with its roots in women's religious and philanthropic work, meant that it attracted middle-class as well as working-class women, especially in the years after the Crimean War due to Florence Nightingale's efforts to raise the status of nursing. Only late in the century did it become a medical profession that required education beyond the elementary level. By 1890, hospital nurses in London earned £20 to £30 per annum; by 1914, they earned £24 to £40 per annum, and matrons (head nurses) earned from £100 to £350 annually.[49] However, working-class nurses were often made subordinate to middle-class colleagues, and could rarely advance to the higher levels of the profession. Like servants and shopgirls (and teachers in rural areas), nurses were offered room and board, but were closely supervised and enjoyed little personal freedom.

The largest and fastest-growing field for women was clerking or office work, or what is now referred to as secretarial work: women comprised 2 per cent of English clerks in 1851 and 20 per cent in 1911. Although clerking was previously a male profession, it was so ideally suited to social expectations about women that one historian suggests that 'had it not existed, it would have been necessary to invent it'.[50] Office work was clean, light and respectable, performed in single-sex settings (male and female clerks were segregated) that appealed to middle-class and aspiring women, and it allowed women to use their education. Hours were shorter than for factory work, home work, or domestic service: usually from ten to five on Monday to Friday with a half-hour break for lunch, and nine to one on Saturday.[51] As with factory work, though, women were restricted to auxiliary tasks deemed female and unskilled, were paid less than men, and had little hope of career advancement. But it provided a new world of work and cultural opportunities for women, who could combine safe and comfortable employment with exciting and respectable lives.

The first female clerks were hired in the 1870s. They were from families who had educated their daughters before the passage of William Forster's Education Act in 1870; by 1890, that Act had transformed the nation into a literate one, so that more women were potential clerks. The civil service and local government were the largest employers of women, 4,657 in 1881 and 27,129 in 1911. The General Post Office was one of the first institutions to hire women in large numbers: by 1880 a quarter of its clerks were female, and this had increased to 40 per cent by the start of the First World War. Commercial offices also welcomed women, as did some insurance firms like the Prudential. But banking, railways, and law firms remained decidedly male-dominated; in 1906 the Great Western Railway became one of the last employers to start hiring women.[52]

At the same time as women were being recruited into a previously male-only field, that field was changing. Clerking had been a sphere in which young men advanced from apprenticeships doing routine work to more challenging work and increased responsibility and pay. As women entered it, new technologies for word- and number-processing, including typewriters and adding machines, new means of data storage such as card indexes and vertical files, along with new methods of communication such as telegraphs and telephones, all meant that clerical work was increasing in volume and complexity, but it was also becoming more monotonous. The volume of routine work resulted in a field in which a small number of men could pursue fulfilling careers while a much larger number of women remained mired in rote work and low pay.

As was the case in all of the new white-collar fields, this division was maintained in a number of ways. One method was the segregation of work tasks. Even as women flooded into offices, they did different work from men and were mostly restricted to two tasks, shorthand and typing.

These tasks obviously had no necessary gender affiliation, and when they first became part of office work, male clerks sought to acquire the necessary skills. However, shorthand and typing soon came to be seen as dead-end tasks, men eschewed them, while female clerks were hired exclusively to fulfil them. Indeed, for a period at the end of the nineteenth century the term 'typewriter' referred not only to the machine but to its female operator. In the Post Office, telegraph and later telephone work was also female, auxiliary, low-paid work, without the opportunity for promotion.

Lower wages for women were a feature of clerical work from the beginning; indeed, one reason that women were first hired by the Post Office and the Prudential Assurance Company was that employers were looking for cheap labour. At the Prudential, lady clerks started at an annual salary of £20. Men began at £15 as junior clerks but could expect to move up in time to salaries of £180 to £350 per annum. In contrast, the highest salary lady clerks could hope to attain was £95, and in 1891 only seventeen of the Prudential's two hundred lady clerks made more than £60. The average female clerk earned £1 per week in 1910; very few female clerks ever earned more than £2 per week, and many earned as little as 10s. weekly. Clerks in London in 1914, who were probably the highest paid of all in our period, earned an annual average of £83. In the same year the average wage for women was 12s. to 14s. per week, servants in London earned around £18 per year plus room and board, and female cotton workers earned 19s. per week. The only women who earned more than clerks were teachers.[53]

On these low wages, female clerks were expected to look respectable at work, which could be expensive. Some lived nearby and walked to work; others commuted on the cheap trains that ran before 8 a.m. and then lingered over tea and buns at one of the new ABC or Lyons cafés until work began. Those who did not live with their parents needed to pay for lodgings, usually at the local semi-charitable Home for Business Ladies, in a furnished room without board or service, or in a third-rate boarding house, which left no money for health care or emergencies and little to spend on leisure. In spite of all this, clerical work was an overcrowded field. The Post Office received seven hundred applications for five positions in 1874 and 300 applications for 25 posts in 1901.[54]

In addition to doing gender-segregated work, female office clerks were physically separated from their male colleagues into Ladies' Departments that occupied separate floors, rooms, or sections. Some employers argued that this protected women from sexual advances, but a Bank of England report from March 1921 admitted that the hope was that women who could not see the more interesting work being done by men would remain satisfied employees. Women who worked for insurance firms entered and exited the buildings through separate entrances, and worked different hours from men so that they would not run into male colleagues outside the buildings. Many employers did not permit women to leave the premises for lunch – female clerks at the Post Office only secured this right in 1911, after a concerted campaign and direct appeals to the Postmaster General. In most banks and insurance companies, women who were waiting for a new task could read, write, or do needlework at their desks, while their male colleagues were permitted to retire to the local pub.

Although office workers led lives that were far more independent, respectable, and middle-class than domestics, clerks, like servants, laboured under a marriage bar. Employers required all clerks to be single and to retire upon marriage. Marriage bars meant that women could work in these fields when young, but had few prospects of independent, self-supporting adult lives. The bars also reinforced the social expectation that women worked between school and marriage, then stopped working to raise children. Since most women did marry, the marriage bar gave the false impression that women chose to leave work for marriage before they could advance, disguising the fact that there were no opportunities for promotion. To many women, marriage must have seemed the most viable career opportunity available. While the majority of employers dropped their marriage bars during the war, not all did; the Post Office maintained one until 1963. These so effectively buttressed the idea that clerking and similar jobs were appropriate only for young single women that barriers to female advancement lingered long after the official marriage bars were gone.

Upper-working-class and lower-middle-class women were especially attracted to teaching because it was so respected, and unlike clerking could be made a long career; at least 80 per cent of teachers in London were in this social category.[55] They usually taught at elementary level, grammar-school and university teaching being reserved for upper-middle-class, university-trained women. Elementary-school teachers were noted by contemporaries for their uncertain class status. From the 1870s they usually came from families of skilled workers or lower-middle-class professionals (clerks, sales people, or small shopkeepers) – families proud of their skill and status but only tenuously differentiated from the respectable working class. Becoming an elementary-school teacher reinforced this ambiguity.

Teachers were educated, usually at state schools, and stayed at school until they were sixteen (unlike less affluent working-class girls, they were not kept at home to do domestic work, and unlike wealthier middle-class girls, they were not sent to finishing schools). From 1846 most learned to teach by working as pupil-teachers, serving as junior or apprentice instructors while still attending school themselves or soon after leaving; the Education Act of 1902 phased out apprenticeships in favour of scholarships for attendance at state secondary schools. Following either, young women attended a teacher training college for two or three years, and then took examinations to receive teaching certificates before going on to teach in state elementary schools. Training colleges were in the nineteenth century religiously denominational boarding colleges; the Education Act of 1902 established non-denominational day colleges, creating more places and allowing students to commute. The high demand for teachers, however, forced the state to allow untrained or uncertificated teachers to teach as well.[56]

Teachers' days were long. They taught from nine to twelve and from two to half-past four, with duties before and after school and paperwork at the break for most. They had to satisfy many groups including students, parents, administrators, and School Board inspectors. They faced many challenges, including teaching students whose poverty and family responsibilities made their attendance and their attention erratic. And then there was needlework, which occupied an increasingly prominent place in the girls' curriculum.[57]

As with clerking, women teachers were paid less than men, and this was one incentive for hiring them. However, they made more money than clerks or nurses, let alone women in lower-paid fields. In 1870 teachers earned from £30 to £60 annually, depending on their qualifications, and by 1914 between £54 and £122, depending on whether they were heads or assistants and whether they were certificated. They were also more likely than women in other lines of work to make their job their profession. For example, between 1870 and 1914 two-thirds of London's elementary-school teachers worked for ten years, and almost half stayed for twenty years. Many who started working after 1890 were confident enough to fight for professional issues like better pay and pensions and political ones like suffrage.[58]

Like clerks, some teachers lived at home with their parents and contributed to the family economy; others lived in the most respectable lodgings they could afford. In some places teachers faced marriage bars, but in others (such as London) many teachers continued working after marriage, although maintaining such work alongside a family caused the health of many teachers to break down. Educated and educators, betwixt and between class positions, teachers enjoyed more community respect than affluence. But in spite of the challenges, most seemed to experience job satisfaction and even a sense of identity from their work.[59]

Most working-class women earned money, whether in agricultural work, factories, service, domestic industry, or the new white-collar and service jobs, and their work was an important contribution to their families' well-being or even survival. In late Victorian London, for a family with young children, a wife's earnings could mean being able to afford to rent two rooms instead of crowding into one. For some, working in cotton factories or at elementary-school teaching, industrialization and the expansion of the educational, commercial and bureaucratic spheres profoundly touched their lives. For others, in prostitution, laundering, or charring, little changed. Women dominated the textile industry, from spinning to mending and laundering clothes, whether they worked at home or in factories. Women did the vast majority of the housework performed in England, whether for the immediate family, distant relatives, or strangers. They also raised the children. In the last part of our period they came to provide most of the country's skilled nursing and to do the bulk of its secretarial work. Once women married, they preferred not to work for wages when their children were young. They were far more likely to earn money as young women without children, and again when their children were older and somewhat less dependent on them for care.

In some important respects, women's relationship to work remained the same before, during, and after the revolutions in industry, commerce and education. Most women spent long hours doing important unremunerated work at home, caring for children and keeping house. When doing paid work, female employees were almost always segregated into sex-specific jobs which were considered less skilled forms of labour and were less secure. Women made between one-third and one-half of what men earned, and the fact that women were so low-paid helped to make possible the mass production of a wide array of affordable goods.

Economic and cultural developments changed women's lives even as they were shaped by women's participation. The availability of factory work altered the rhythm and quality of life, as did the newly common position of maid-of-all-work; even cottage and sweated industries sometimes took on new meanings as the economy changed. The notion of skilled women's industrial or farm work virtually disappeared over time. Women who performed paid labour were largely restricted to unskilled work that was done alongside children, or to dead-end jobs without any hope of advancement, and this 'deskilling' or excluding of women from more desirable jobs indicated the low social status of their work.

By 1914, however, the average working-class woman enjoyed a higher standard of living than was typical in 1760. She was better fed, better educated, her housework was less labour-intensive, she had fewer children, and she had a somewhat wider choice of jobs. But industrialization was a rocky process that affected various generations differently. For some, the process was one of radical and disruptive change, which they endured for their entire working lives; its cultural legacy as regards women and work was apparent into the twentieth century. Education also transformed the lives of those who could take advantage of it. Some women were a crucial part of the growing lower middle class, though this rise was often a matter of status rather than income. For others, the empowering potential of education remained chimerical in the face of manual labour and child-minding.

2

Middle-class Women

MIDDLE-CLASS WOMEN, and the rules by which they lived, have
been the subject of a great deal of historical inquiry, so much so
that it is sometimes surprising to learn what a relatively small proportion
of the population was middle class. (It may be that many scholars, themselves from middle-class backgrounds, choose to study women like
themselves.) While less numerous than working-class women, middle-
class women were more literate and more leisured, and so left written
records of their own lives that make them rich fields of study.

The middle classes – those families whose members did not perform
manual labour and did not rely solely on income-generating land, who
were generally in commerce, manufacturing, the civil service, and the
professions – were growing during the long nineteenth century. In urban
areas, there were approximately 475,000 middle-class people in 1801,
almost three times as many as there had been in 1700, and their numbers
continued to grow over the next century.[1] The middle classes made up
almost one quarter of the population by 1850, and between 1851 and 1871
the number of solidly middle-class families doubled. In the late nineteenth
century the number of men and women who became lower middle class
by virtue of their white-collar employment increased dramatically; in the
last fifty years of our period the number of men doing office work
increased by a factor of five, and the number of women by a factor of five
hundred.[2]

Although affluent by national standards, income and status among
the middle classes varied widely: the head of the family might be a
local shopkeeper or the owner of a large factory, a bank clerk or the
town banker, a village schoolteacher or a prominent London barrister.
During the eighteenth century, families from the middle ranks had
annual incomes between £50 and £2,000, with most hovering between
£80 and £150.[3] When Victoria took the throne in 1837, the upper-
middle-class family income was somewhere around £300, and until the
First World War most middle-class families had an annual income of

£100 to £300. Only the very tiny upper middle class was better off.

If we read advice manuals aimed at middle-class women, or some of the many essays written on correct behaviour, deportment, and decorum, a picture emerges of what historians have called the 'ideology of separate spheres' (or 'domestic ideology'). This ideology dictated that respectable middle-class women were domestic creatures. They were concerned with home, children, and religion; they avoided politics, commerce, and anything else which was part of the 'public sphere'. This ideology was most clearly articulated in middle-class evangelical Christianity, which encouraged women to cultivate their godliness in domestic ways.

A division of the world into women's and men's spheres was not new to the nineteenth century; we would be hard-pressed to find any period of English history – indeed of human history – in which gender did not shape identity and men and women performed the same tasks in the same spaces. But some argue that the notion of separate spheres, with its specific understanding of women as the morally superior but socially and politically subordinate sex, and its emphasis on connecting women with domestic spaces, was enforced with particular vigour after 1760.

Yet it remains unclear how middle-class women experienced this separate-spheres ideology. If we look at the actual lives of women, rather than the advice aimed at them, a more nuanced picture emerges, one in which engagement with the world beyond the domestic hearth was typical and women deployed the rhetoric of separate spheres to their own ends as well as being limited by it. Even women who claimed to adhere to domestic ideology often interpreted domesticity in extraordinarily broad terms. On the other hand, we should not simply dismiss the separate spheres as empty rhetoric. Rhetoric they may have been, but they were not empty. There were real restrictions on what middle-class women could do without compromising their reputations and respectability. Respectable middle-class women did not engage in pre- or extra-marital sex or romance, did not earn money, and did not do anything considered by their contemporaries to be work. They did, however, work. The nineteenth-century definition of work (to which we still adhere) as a paid, extra-domestic activity rendered invisible much of women's valuable endeavour.

The separate-spheres dictum that respectable middle-class women should not be gainfully employed, coupled with the fact that most middle-class women had one servant, might make it seem as if middle-class women had little to do, and indeed the stereotype of the bored and frustrated Victorian housewife lingers even now. The reality was quite different. Most middle-class women spent their lives in purposeful action, maintaining their homes, raising their children, acting as hidden partners in their husbands' work, and engaging in their own charitable work. Whether married or not, the skills exercised by women outside the home mirrored those they used inside it – planning, managing money and staff, and caring for, educating, and working with children, women, and the working classes.

Women made varied and crucial contributions to family businesses and incomes. Historians Leonore Davidoff and Catherine Hall have dubbed these the 'hidden investment' in middle-class economic life. In addition, middle-class women worked, some occasionally or sporadically, others extensively and tirelessly, in and through religious or philanthropic organizations at a wide range of valued activities. Later in the century their work for these causes became professionalized, but remained focused on women, children, and the poor, and on the benefits of domesticity.

True, their work was unpaid and was construed as 'domestic' and 'feminine'. But these two terms were exceptionally flexible and many middle-class women used the ideology of feminine domesticity to justify such activities outside the home. The prominent writer and phil-anthropist Hannah More's insistence in the early nineteenth century that 'the care of the poor is her profession'[4] helped to establish philanthropic work as a natural part of middle- and upper-class women's domestic role. Women maintained that in their purposeful engagement outside the home they were not leaving the domestic sphere for the public one; rather they were widening the domestic sphere – through bringing its softening influence to others in need – or feminizing the public one. Their work was seen as an extension of domesticity rather than as a transgression of its boundaries. For many, their cloak of domesticity granted them the right to superintend those they helped, so that philanthropy was a key sphere of authority for middle-class women. At the same time as helping the less fortunate, they maintained the distance and differences between themselves and the needy, building bridges rather than tearing down walls. Acting as guardians of poor and working women and children secured their class status even as it provided assistance.

The range of benevolent activities undertaken by middle-class women is astonishing. Because they favoured institutional forms of giving, middle-class women's organizations left records which give us a fairly full picture of the work they did. Donating money, visiting the poor in their homes, in prisons, in orphanages, hospitals and workhouses, and organizing charity bazaars, were all part of their role in establishing and maintaining the class status of their families. For many, these activities were also personally fulfilling. So were later efforts in professions that grew from, and resembled, the philanthropic work which women already did, such as nursing, teaching and social work. By the turn of the twentieth century, the continuum between domestic affairs, philanthropy, and female professions was so well-established that when Mrs Arthur Lyttelton published a book entitled *Women and their Work* (in 1901), her chapters were on 'The Family', 'The Household', 'Philanthropic and Social Work' and 'The Professions', one after the other.[5]

Before exploring their contributions to the family income, philanthropy, and the professionalization of their work in the second half of the nineteenth century, we will look at the home lives of middle-class women. By the end of our period, they had far more options than they had had at the beginning. This was in part because, as we will see in Chapters 7 and 8, anxieties had arisen about an apparent 'surplus' of middle-class women compared to the men available to marry them. The writer Harriet Martineau (1802–76) claimed that fully half a million middle-class women were going to have to earn their own keep. Feminists responded to this and similar claims by pressing employers to consider women as potential workers in a variety of fields. Nevertheless, in many ways middle-class women's lives were as circumscribed by appropriate gender roles in 1914 as they had been in 1760.

Home

In the middle classes, marriage signified a woman's entry into adulthood and so was a key status marker. As we will see in Chapter 5, many middle-class people practised evangelical Christianity, which stressed the importance of marriage and family. While husbands and wives were both expected to play an active role in their married and family life, and to take them seriously, their contributions were not the same. Women were expected to be the subordinate partners and dependent on their husbands. As symptoms of this expectation, women were supposed to remain passive in courtship, allowing themselves to be wooed but not wooing, and marital love was seen as something tender rather than erotic. Wives were often significantly younger than their husbands, especially among professional and upper-middle-class couples. Once married, middle-class women were expected to act as their husbands' helpmates, and to centre their identities and energies on home, husband, and children.

Many in the middle classes spoke of the home as a refuge from the outside world. For adult women, at least, this was not really the case. The home was a public as well as a private space. Most families entertained relatives and friends; in their homes, women might also hold meetings of associations or charities in which they were active. Once married, a middle-class woman was expected to run her household, directing the servant or servants, and managing the budget through detailed planning and account keeping.[6]

Upper-middle-class women had more servants and did less physical work themselves, but few were so lucky (in a very modest home, mistress and servant might work side by side). Most families, with an annual income of £100 to £300 per year, had one servant, plus an occasional 'girl' to help out on big tasks or at busy times of year. Middle-class women were therefore the primary caretakers of their homes and children; they scorned the aristocratic tendency to have children cared for by servants. Mistresses were intimately involved in the smooth functioning of the household, shopping, planning meals, overseeing the help, and performing domestic duties themselves, including cleaning the house (which probably had six to ten rooms on three or four floors), cooking, shopping, washing, and sewing much of the family's clothing.[7]

There was a wide range of middle-class lifestyles. The difficulties faced by lower-middle-class housekeepers increased over the century as middle-class standards of living rose faster than incomes; during the second half of the century it was even more difficult than before, on the modest income enjoyed by a shopkeeper's or clerk's family, to present a middle-class façade. Rents doubled between 1831 and 1881, while meat prices rose almost every year from 1852 to 1882. Piped-in hot and cold water became necessities, as did a bathtub, in its own room rather than the kitchen. Kitchen ranges, washing and sewing machines, all made the middle-class woman's life easier, but were expensive.[8] It is no wonder that Mrs Eliza Warren's book explaining *How I Managed My House on Two Hundred Pounds a Year* sold 36,000 copies in its first year of publication, 1864. Remaining middle-class was a full-time job for most, and must have seemed an impossible task to many. Women had to work hard to maintain a proper middle-class home without seeming to expend any effort. A family's middle-class status depended in part on the fact that the wife did no paid work (as her husband did) or heavy domestic work (as her servants did). But this presentation of women as leisured was not realistic. Middle-class women did much domestic labour behind the scenes while trying to appear as if they did none. Housework was hard work, and making it invisible was a task in itself.

The tension created by the gap between expectations and incomes is evident in such works as Mrs Beeton's *Book of Household Management* (1861), the most popular handbook and recipe book of the period. The work seemed to be addressed to a wide range of middle-class homes, offering both precise instructions on a frugal life with a single servant and more expansive descriptions of well-appointed households. It was filled with tips on running a household economically, from the general comment: '[i]n marketing, that the best articles are the cheapest, may be laid down as a rule; and it is desirable, unless an experienced and confidential housekeeper be kept, that the mistress should herself purchase all provisions and stores needed for the house', to specifics such as the reminder that '[t]he shank-bones of mutton, so little esteemed in general, give richness to soups or gravies.' It also included directions for giving large balls and directing fleets of servants, implying that these were far more typical than they actually were or perhaps that they were the proper goal of every middle-class household. Surely the majority of middle-class women, who had one servant and many children, did not 'change the dress, jewellery and ornaments' as part of their 'full dress for dinner' every evening.[9]

Most adult middle-class women had children and viewed the task of raising them as central to their lives. By the late eighteenth century, women bore more children and saw more of them live to adulthood than had been the case previously; this meant that mothering was more time-consuming than it had been and helped to promote the new social convention that women's lives were focused on the home. However, like women in the working classes, middle-class women usually suffered the pain of seeing some of their babies through serious illnesses and of burying others. Mary Jesup of Essex was distraught after her infant son died. Struggling to maintain both her daily routine and her religious faith, she recorded that:

I have often found it difficult on awakening in the morning to fix my whole heart in meditation on my God and my duty, as I had been much favoured to do in time past. But thou, Oh Lord! knowest when the feelings of nature were awakened in viewing the dear child's sufferings, and anticipating of the separation which would probably soon take place – how often I was able to say in sincerity, 'Not my will, but thine be done.'[10]

Gaps between births suggest that most women in this class breast-fed their babies. Although the majority of middle-class people did not marry until their late twenties, before the middle of the nineteenth century they went on to have over seven children. Large families meant that mothers were frequently exhausted, and older daughters and unmarried aunts often helped to look after younger children. From mid-century, middle-class couples began controlling their fertility and had smaller families, arguing that good parents provided a higher standard of living and more individual attention to fewer children.

Women were viewed as naturally maternal and were expected to see mothering as the better part of their adult identities; during the first half of the nineteenth century a middle-class woman's full-time commitment to mothering became a sign of her family's gentility. Mothers were expected to care for their children emotionally and physically. They performed many of the intimate tasks of childcare, educated their young children (some instructed older daughters as well), and took responsibility for their children's religious development. For example, Catherine Gurney, mother of the philanthropist Elizabeth Fry (1780–1845), presided over a comfortable home, focusing especially on the education of her daughters and on religion until her death in 1792. In *The Memoir of the Life of Elizabeth Fry* (1847), written shortly after her death by two of her daughters, Catherine Gurney is quoted as believing that

> As piety is undoubtedly the shortest and securest way to all moral rectitude, young women should be virtuous and good, on the broad firm basis of Christianity ... a great portion of a woman's life ought to be passed, in at least regulating the subordinate affairs of the family ... she should not be ignorant of the common proprieties of a table, or deficient in the economy of any of the most minute affairs of the family ... gentleness of manner is indispensibly necessary [so that] children may be led without vanity or affectation, by amiable and judicious instruction.[11]

(By 'family', Gurney included her domestic help as well as her husband

and children.) And her notes on a typical day reflect these priorities: upon awakening she prayed, went to see her children, attended to her husband's needs, took a walk with her younger children, gave instructions to the servants, and then began her work on 'the claims of the poor'.[12]

Family income

Many women contributed to their families' incomes without being recognized as workers. Like working-class women, middle-class women saw their adult lives in the context of a family strategy and tied their identities more closely to family than to any one occupation. Their economic role was part of their commitment to family. A principal contribution was hidden labour; while manual work was seen as unfeminine, women could do almost anything else in the guise of helpmate. Some women worked in the family business. Others might assist their husbands by giving dinner parties for business associates, copying documents, or fending off insistent creditors. Sometimes wives stepped in to run things when their husbands were ill, or even ran their businesses as widows. Many middle-class men took positions that required an unpaid female assistant. For instance, a schoolmaster would often be employed on the understanding that his wife would work in this capacity, feeding the boarding students and teaching the girls needlework. These wives – and the wives of shopkeepers, who often fed apprentices and sales assistants – were therefore required to be surrogate mothers, responsible for the moral and emotional development of their young charges. Women also contributed to family businesses by donating small sums, often from inheritances; for lower-middle-class families these modest amounts could be crucial. And they created useful networks of contacts through socializing and marriage; sisters' and daughters' spouses often became business partners. Middle-class women tended to see these varied tasks as part of their duty rather than as work.[13]

Some middle-class women never married, either from choice or circumstance. They might run a household for a male relative, live in some kind of female community (as so many female professions demanded), with friends, or alone. Some devoted themselves to religion; during the second half of the nineteenth century many became Catholic or Anglican sisters. One prominent single woman was Louisa Twining (1820–1912), a member of the London family of tea merchants, a leader in workhouse visiting and reform, and a supporter of suffrage, whose philanthropic and political commitments we will explore below. She and her sister Elizabeth cared for their elderly mother in the family's London residence; after her mother's death, Twining opened her house as a home for impoverished elderly women. When she got older she preferred not to live with married relatives, probably because she feared a loss of independence, and instead kept her own household in Kent (with a live-in servant) near a niece who provided companionship and support.

Unlike Twining, many single women and widows had to earn their own keep. Some did so all their lives; others were forced to do so by a turn in family fortunes. The need to earn money was a serious problem, given how few suitable positions were available to middle-class women before the 1860s. Single women found work as governesses, teachers, or dressmakers. Probably the most common position was that of governess, which was considered respectable but poorly paid and meant living somewhat like a servant. The fact that there were fewer governess positions than there were young middle-class girls in need of work, and the terrible employment prospects facing respectable middle-class girls generally, became a topic of frequent discussion in the middle of the nineteenth century. Governesses became iconic of impoverished middle-class spinsterhood.

There were other ways in which women, single or married, kept themselves. Some women owned their own businesses; between 1775 and 1787 over 11 per cent of shopkeepers were women. During the nineteenth century 20 per cent of all British firms were owned and operated by women. G. J. Holyoake recalled that in his mother's button workshop, which she ran in the early nineteenth century before and after she married:

> She received the orders; made the purchases of materials; superintended the making of the goods; made out the accounts; and received money besides taking care of her growing family. There were no 'Rights of Women' thought of in her day, but she was an entirely self-acting, managing mistress.[14]

Many women-owned firms catered to elite women and were run as conspicuously genteel and feminine establishments. Others worked as innkeepers or in various manufacturing trades, though these became less respectable for single women as the century progressed.

Women novelists were an interesting exception to the rule that middle-class women could neither earn money nor enter the public sphere. Some are well-known today: they include Jane Austen (1775–1817), author of *Pride and Prejudice* (1813) and *Emma* (1816); Mary Shelley (1797–1851), daughter of Mary Wollstonecraft and William Godwin, wife of the Romantic poet Percy Bysshe Shelley, and author of *Frankenstein* (1818); Charlotte Brontë (1816–55), author of *Jane Eyre* (1847), *Shirley* (1849), and *Villette* (1853); her sister Emily Brontë (1818–48), author of *Wuthering Heights* (1847); Elizabeth Gaskell (1810–65), author of the 'industrial novels' *Mary Barton* (1848) and *North and South* (1855); and George Eliot (1819–80), author of *Adam Bede* (1859) and *Middlemarch* (1872). All of these women wrote novels that have entered the canon of English literature and have been studied by generations of students and scholars, as well as being read, discussed, and reviewed by contemporaries. But these few were not alone. Indeed, they were not even the most popular female authors of their respective generations; while Jane Austen's four major novels published during her lifetime earned her less than £700, her more popular contemporary Maria Edgeworth (1768–1849), author of *Castle Rackrent* (1800), earned £1,500 to £2,000 per novel.[15]

From the novel's appearance in the mid-eighteenth century, many women were prominent producers as well as readers; by the Victorian period, women dominated the novel market and were the almost exclusive writers in certain genres, notably 'sensation' fiction. Like their male colleagues, they also wrote essays and reviews for various periodicals, and were important contributors to print culture. Popular women writers included 'sensation' novelists such as Mrs Henry Wood (1814–87), whose *East Lynne* (1861) became an often-produced melodramatic play; Dinah Mulock Craik (1826–87), author of *John Halifax, Gentleman* (1858); Mrs Margaret Oliphant (1828–97) who wrote *Miss Marjoribanks* (1866) and nearly a hundred other novels, and Charlotte Yonge (1823–1901) whose popular novel *The Daisy Chain* (1856) was one of the two hundred works she published; 'new woman' novelists of the 1890s, such as Mona Caird, Emma Brooke, Sarah Grand, and Olive Schreiner, whose work is discussed in Chapter 8; and Marie Corelli (1855–1924), spiritualist author of the bestselling *Sorrows of Satan* (1895) and *The Treasures of Heaven* (1906).

One of the most popular and prolific novelists of the period was Mary Elizabeth Braddon (1837–1915), who worked in several genres but was best-known for her sensation novels. This genre, so named because of its ability to cause physical reactions such as shivering in readers, emerged in the 1860s; it was considered feminine – authors and readers alike were overwhelmingly female – and of low artistic quality, dependent on flashy plot mechanics and shock value. Its passionate and unrestrained heroines were condemned as 'unnatural' and dangerous by critics, who saw the characters as 'depraved' and the genre as 'diseased'. Braddon's two most popular novels, both of which featured bigamy in their plots, were *Lady Audley's Secret* (1862) and *Aurora Floyd* (1863); they brought her lifelong fame and success. *Lady Audley's Secret* went through eight editions in its first three months alone; its total sales outnumbered all other novels of the period, and a dramatic version became a staple of Victorian theatre.[16]

Female authors fell into two distinct groups – eminently respectable women who circulated private copies of their writings for the amusement of their families and friends, and distinctly less respectable ones who published their work for profit. The place of female authors in the public sphere was always an ambiguous one. The fact that they earned money by competing in the publishing market was at odds with models of middle-class female virtue that forbade wage-earning, the adoption of professional status, or any other engagement with the market-place. While cultural standards certainly changed over the course of the long nineteenth century, the respectability of women writers was always suspect, as evidenced by the fact that many wrote secretly, like Jane Austen, or pseudonymously, like the Brontë sisters and George Eliot. Women who published under their own names always insisted that they had some good reason for doing so, usually impending poverty. Most women asked a male relative to negotiate terms with publishers.[17] Elizabeth Gaskell felt that being a professional writer made her a scandalously 'public' woman. She wrote to her daughter Marianne that she 'hate[d] publishing because of all the talk people make, which I always feel as a great impertinence, if they address their remarks to me in any way;' after the publication of her controversial novel *Ruth* in 1853, she worried that she must have made herself 'improper' because she had 'manage[d] to shock people'.[18]

Some female writers supported themselves and their families through their writing. Jane Austen's gentry family did not need the income from her novels, but the Brontë family was not so well-off and Charlotte worked as a governess and a schoolteacher before turning to writing. When Dinah Mulock Craik's mother died, Mulock – who had taught at her mother's school – chose writing over other available options, including working as a governess or living with relatives who could have supported her. Interestingly, most contemporary accounts of her early life insist that poverty forced her to publish her work: that she assumed responsibility for supporting her mother and two brothers when her father had treated her invalid mother badly, and that after her mother's death her father deserted his three children entirely, leaving Mulock to care for her brothers (who in reality were probably already working).[19] Such stories helped to preserve Mulock's public reputation by providing her with a good reason for choosing to become a public and money-earning woman. Mary Elizabeth Braddon came from modest middle-class circumstances as well; her mother had been deserted by her father and made a living taking in lodgers. Before she was thirty Braddon was writing so prolifically for the market that she could support her lover (later her husband) John Maxwell, his five children by his first wife, and their six children.

The experiences and choices of Brontë, Craik and Braddon suggest that many female novelists were members of the struggling or lower portions of the middle class. Some needed to earn money although their families, who had perhaps suffered an economic fall, were uncomfortable with the idea. The conflict between status and the need to earn a living helps to emphasize the cultural and economic difficulties that middle-class women so often faced. Others were from lower-middle-class families in which female wage-earning was seen as perfectly respectable, reminding us that many of the standards now remembered as 'middle-class' were in fact the privilege only of its wealthiest sections.

Philanthropic work

In addition to their contributions to family income, the majority of middle-class women devoted time to philanthropy. In our period, charitable activity was more widespread than it had been previously, and charity was to a great extent associated with and administered by women. In 1857 the medical journal *The Lancet* commented that 'there was not a town in the kingdom which did not have its lying-in society, female school, visiting association, nursing institute and many other charitable organizations exclusively managed' by women.[20]

As women came to dominate charitable institutions over the course of the century, their efforts permeated the lives of most English people, especially women and children of the working classes. Female philanthropy was called 'women's mission to women'; Sarah Lewis wrote a book called *Women's Mission* in 1842, as did William Lovett in 1856.[21] In the nineteenth century few publicly-funded safety nets existed (with the exception of the Poor Law, whose grim workhouses were avoided at all costs by many in need); at the same time life was far less predictable and more hazardous than it is today. Financial ruin, illness, and death were common; one in seven children died in infancy in the late nineteenth century, and the figures were worse earlier in our period and for poorer people. Many families experienced the illness or death of a child or parent; widows with children were common. The upheavals of industrialization also caused suffering.

Female philanthropy was organized around helping the poor by bring-ing middle-class values to the less fortunate. These values included Chris-tianity, especially the evangelical emphasis on women as naturally virtuous (and many took the evangelical Christian description of women's intrinsic morality to heart and spoke of their charitable works as 'missions'); middle-class feminine respectability, which dictated that women did not engage in pre- or extra-marital sex; and the softening influence of female domesticity. The last of these was especially important: many charities operated on the assumption that the home was an inher-ently moral and stable venue, and that charity was a matter of bringing domesticity – in which the moral and the material were inextricably intertwined – to those in spiritual and physical need.

Until late in the century middle-class women did not try to transform English society or the economy; only a few politically radical middle-class women agitated for higher wages for working women, or challenged cultural norms by promoting birth control. In this sense many middle-class women could be said to be politically conservative. They tended to concentrate on helping individuals, not on changing the world; on the other hand many, inspired by their religious beliefs, believed themselves to be saving souls and therefore the world. Additionally many were reformers in practice, if not in theory; often female philanthropy exposed misery that was then addressed legislatively or otherwise. Most, even those who advocated parliamentary solutions, believed that poverty was the result of ignorance, misfortune, or some defect of character, such as laziness, and sought to address it through face-to-face contact, education, and religion. They also tended to see poorer women as passive victims of Fate. These beliefs and approaches were not peculiar to women: they were typical of the Victorian period and were shared by most middle-class men and many working-class people. Much of the help women provided came with an explicit moral judgement, as for instance in the aid offered to 'fallen' women. They also expected the poor to live austerely. Yet these realities should not prevent us from appreciating the work that middle-class women did, work that gave them satisfaction and a sense of identity while easing hardship for many people.

As evangelically-influenced domestic ideology came to hold sway over the lives of respectable middle-class women, philanthropy offered opportunities for agency and action that could be found in few other fields. Philanthropy implicitly valued women's experiences and abilities, since through it women's domestic skills – broadly qualified, and including the ability to manage a budget and keep careful accounts – qualified them for important service outside the home. By the end of the century it was estimated that half a million women were professional or semi-professional philanthropists, with many more working as part-time volunteers. While all of their opportunities and methods were limited, they led purposeful lives, asserted themselves in the social hierarchy, and made a difference in the lives of the poor.

One philanthropic activity was donating money. In the nineteenth century England was an astonishingly charitable nation; in 1885, money donated in London alone was larger than the national budget of Sweden. The middle class believed in giving and did so generously. More affluent families spent as much on charity as on rent or food; less well-off families gave what they could. Crucial too were women of all classes who, over the course of the century, donated as much to charitable causes as men. Poor and working-class women gave small sums to institutional charities, usually to their churches' missionary funds, and practised much informal philanthropy. At the other end of the spectrum, the wealthy philanthropist Angela Burdett-Coutts (1814–1906) gave away over a million pounds during the course of her life, and Queen Victoria subscribed to many charities, as well as being a patroness of hospitals and other philanthropic endeavours all over Britain.

In between lay those at the heart of organized philanthropy, middle-class women. They usually gave money by a system of subscription, in which individual donors would subscribe a fixed sum. Subscriptions were a popular way of raising money for a variety of causes. In the late 1790s, many women supported the wars against France in this way, either by joining men's lists or by starting their own female lists. For most of the nineteenth century, subscriptions – largely to small and highly specialized causes – were a major source of activity for women and income for the institutions in question. Women often subscribed to a ladies' auxiliary, a local women's organization that was affiliated with an existing cause. Most of the largest and fastest-growing charities received much of their income from female subscribers. Women could also donate money in other ways: many single women and widows left legacies to charities, which married middle-class women could not do because they rarely owned their own property.[22]

Women gave discriminately, focusing on women and children who were vulnerable or in need. They favoured charities which aided those who were poor, pregnant, ageing, or 'fallen', and raised money for the anti-slavery movement, which we shall explore in more detail in Chapter 7. Many middle-class women must have been quite aware that they were only one generation or one catastrophe away from being working-class or poor themselves; this knowledge may have inspired them to help those less fortunate, perhaps in part to solidify their own class status. And in an age when middle-class men entered the formal political sphere by winning the vote (in the Reform Act of 1832) and middle-class women did not, supporting a charity financially was a key way for them to assert their values in public.

In addition to giving their own money, women raised money, largely by organizing bazaars, balls, and other social events. Bazaars were one of the most important sources of revenue for charities. These festive events, at which baubles and ornaments were sold to benefit a cause, were organized mostly by middle-class women. Also called fancy fairs, or fancy sales, they were used to raise funds by hospitals, orphanages, asylums and churches. A small local fair might raise £20 or even less; the British Orphan Asylum fair held in London in October 1832 made £1,460. Nationwide fancy fairs raised tens of millions of pounds. Missionary and anti-slavery societies even tried to hold fancy fairs abroad, in India, Africa, Australia, and North America; although shipping British-made items was cumbersome, the latest London fashions in lace and embroidery were desirable in mid-century Boston and Philadelphia. These popular, ubiquitous, and remunerative sales were a quintessentially female form of charity, and their economic and cultural impact demonstrates how important middle-class women and their work were to English society.

The rise of bazaars as a fund-raising tool is an intrinsic part of philanthropy and the expanding role of women within it. As charity increased in scale and scope, a wide variety of causes needed new ways to raise money. The solution, bazaars, was probably suggested by women and these were certainly run by them: no records survive of a bazaar run by men, and one of the synonyms for 'bazaar' was 'ladies' sale'. Ladies' sales allowed women to participate in civic culture in prominent, public, but feminine ways.

Bazaars utilized women's domestic abilities – preparing and serving food, decorating stalls and so forth – outside the home. Women used many other management skills gained at home as well. They set dates, procured and prepared venues, arranged advertising, printed and sold tickets, planned opening celebrations and entertainment (such as kaleidoscopes, palm readers, magicians and musical recitals), and recruited patrons and stallholders. A prominent female patron could greatly enhance the prestige and profitability of a fancy fair, so the task of enticing one was an important one. Depending on the fair, the patron might be a titled lady, an actress (Sarah Bernhardt and Ellen Terry both served as stallholders), the wife of an MP or of the local cleric. When the Anti-Corn Law League (a largely middle-class organization which opposed tariffs that benefited aristocratic landowners and kept grain prices high) held its bazaar for three weeks at Covent Garden Theatre in the spring of 1845, the ladies' committee shipped goods from all over England and even arranged special trains to London for customers. Eight thousand people attended each day, and the event made a profit of £25,000.[23]

Contemporary criticism of the fancy fair was perhaps predictable. Some complained that bazaars turned respectable young women into pushy shopgirls. Many objected to the flirting that went on (some evangelical mothers forbade their daughters from attending). Charles Dickens satirically praised the bazaars as the only places that young ladies could 'exhibit themselves for three days, from twelve to four, for the small charge of one shilling per head!' and mocked lower-middle-class women who, entranced by 'visions of admiration and matrimony', tried to imitate the better fairs by putting on their own in a 'dingy' hall somewhere. Fairs and bazaars were certainly held in modest as well as smart neighbourhoods. One writer warned that the Anglican Church was in danger of becoming 'womanized' by them. These criticisms express only very thinly-veiled anxiety about a new field of female expertise.[24]

Nineteenth-century philanthropy was founded on the notion that close, individual contact between poor women and their more fortunate sisters was a crucial part of every charitable endeavour. The most common way for women to become involved in the lives of the poor was through visiting them, either in their homes or in the institutions, public and private, that cared for them. Middle-class women brought 'domesticity' to the people and spaces they visited.

Visitors hoped to alleviate the sufferings of the poor without wishing to acknowledge them as their social equals; one manifestation of this was the habit of knocking and entering private homes before being invited in. This sort of overbearing behaviour was reproduced in surprising conditions. In 1849 Mary Barnier kept up with her visiting duties even on a ship bound for Australia by attending the birth of a baby in steerage. She noted in her on-board journal that she and her friend Mrs Ashworth had been 'gracious' enough to name the baby Edith Woodstock, and claimed that 'its mother thinks [it] is a most beautiful name'.[25] We have little information about how the objects of all this attention felt about it. Surely many of the poor and working-class women who were at the receiving end of this philanthropic aid often felt more judged than helped by their well-meaning visitors.

Individual visiting to the homes of the poor had a long history with both upper- and middle-class women. Elite women were more likely to visit their own tenants in rural areas, while middle-class women gravitated towards urban visiting. In the late eighteenth century the activity became more organized with the founding of visiting societies, supported by subscriptions and run by committees. Localities were divided up into visiting 'districts', and each visitor was responsible for several households, which they would supply with Bibles, blankets, and food. By the early nineteenth century women had formed visiting societies in towns and cities all over England; even in male-run societies the proportion of female to male visitors was three to one or more.

Visiting societies focused on specific groups: they might help the sick, post-partum women (those 'lying-in'), distressed needlewomen, or poor widows. These societies were sponsored by, or affiliated with, Anglican parishes, other religions, and large and small charities. A single poor or working-class household might receive visitors from large national or regional societies, small local ones, and the parish, not to mention casual visits from other well-meaning women.

Visitors were required to follow their organization's guidelines; most arrived once a week during the day, and so usually saw the woman and younger children of the household. Some societies afforded visitors much discretion in their giving, others required formal applications for relief and an interview with the committee. Some organizations handed out cash, others saw this as encouraging idleness and poverty. Some asked the poor for money each week to be put into savings accounts. Most requested that visitors take notes in specially made little black books, another aspect of the careful accounting which middle-class women practised at home. Almost all societies' guidelines, as well as books such as *The Ladies' Companion for Visiting the Poor* (1813) or *The Female Visitor to the Poor* (1846), recommended that women visit regularly, be sympathetic without encouraging dependence, give advice on household management and child-raising, quote the Scriptures, and distinguish real distress from laziness and deception (considerable energy was devoted to the problem of feigned distress).

Institutional visiting was also popular and also dominated by women. From 1810 female visitors were being admitted to prisons, asylums, orphanages, workhouses, and homes for destitute women of various sorts, mostly widows, prostitutes, and servants. Some were casual visitors, women working under their own aegis; many were representatives of large charities. Some institutions welcomed lady visitors; in others there was friction between officials and visitors as to policy and goals. Institutional visiting's recognition as analogous to domestic female endeavour seems tenuous in the extreme, since women worked in large public institutions and with their bureaucracies (upper-middle-class women's connections were often invaluable in gaining access). But contemporaries perceived institutional visiting as feminine, and so it was.

Women founded and managed many homes for women and children in need; the 'rescue' of prostitutes by placing them in strictly-run, domestic-style 'magdalene homes' was an especially popular cause. Some, like the Manchester and Salford Asylum for Female Penitents, were under church supervision, run by men and managed by women who visited and talked with inmates. Others were founded by individual women; a Miss Stride managed several homes in Tottenham, London.[26]

Prisons were some of the earliest institutions to admit visitors, and female prisoners were abundantly visited from the 1810s. One well-known prison visitor, Sarah Martins (1791–1843), was working-class, an evangelical dressmaker who even led services in Yarmouth prison on Sundays and gave her own sermons. Most visitors, though, were middle-class. The most famous was Elizabeth Fry, who began visiting Newgate Prison in 1813 and founded the nationwide British Society of Ladies for Promoting the Reformation of Female Prisoners in 1821. Later, in 1840, she also founded the Institution of Nursing Sisters to visit and nurse the poor. Fry knew of Martins' work and supported her financially, but her own status as a well-connected and affluent middle-class woman meant that she had more extensive philanthropic opportunities. When she wanted to start a visiting association to Millbank Prison, prominent friends wrote to the Prime Minister supporting her and she was invited to give evidence to parliamentary committees on conditions in prisons.

The work of the British Ladies' Society is a good example of how visitors interacted with public officials and institutionalized women, how they sought to promote specific values while they provided personal contact and material assistance, and how the way of life they offered their charges was very like their own. As she wrote in her *Observations on the Visiting, Superintendence, and Government of Female Visitors* (1827), Fry believed in emphasizing prisoners' and visitors' common humanity and sought to treat each prisoner as an individual. Believing in the softening influence of women and the dignity of prisoners, members of the British Ladies' Society campaigned for female prisoners to be housed in all-female prisons or wards, attended by female officers, wardens, and visitors. An emphasis on the personal touch in institutions for the poor and needy was common; many women opposed larger institutions as impersonal. Mary Carpenter (1807–77), a Unitarian educational reformer from Bristol, argued that smaller institutions replicated family life and domesticity and therefore valued the individual in a way that larger institutions could not.

Mrs Fry and her colleagues recommended a combination of religion and diligent domesticity for female prisoners. British Ladies' Society volunteers read the Bible to prisoners and gave them religious books and tracts. They created a small business within Newgate in which female prisoners sewed baby linens that were sold in the prison shop by a Society volunteer; profits went to the prisoners, but recidivists got smaller shares. Prisoners whose needlework was not fine enough for baby clothes were put to work on coarser fabrics, calico and flannel; women who were no good at needlework were given knitting to do. On Saturdays no ladies visited, and prisoners did laundry and ironing. The British Ladies' Society was quite influential – it shaped policy at Newgate, published guidelines for other local prison visiting societies, and its model was flexible enough to be applied to other institutions. The Society's work decreased over the century as the government regulated prisons more tightly, but its style pervaded institutional visiting.[27]

Also popular was workhouse visiting. After the passage of the 1834 Poor Law, lady visitors began paying close attention to the poor staying in the workhouses created by the new law. Over time many visiting societies replaced evangelical rhetoric with more punitive arguments that were in keeping with Poor Law policy, although whether they were using these for strategic purposes is not always clear. The most prominent workhouse visitor was the Anglican Louisa Twining, who founded the Workhouse Visiting Society in 1858. Like Fry, Twining was very well-connected – her friends included Mary Carpenter, Florence Nightingale (1820–1910), and a leading Christian Socialist F. D. Maurice (1805–72) – and as a result her society's managing board was filled with prominent male and female philanthropists. The society was quite successful and in the 1860s and 1870s mobilized huge numbers of female visitors. It was centred in London but sought national influence. Twining's status should not distract us from thinking that workhouse visiting was the exclusive province of the upper middle classes; many visitors were lower-middle-class women.[28]

Visitors often discovered and exposed appalling conditions in which the inmates were living and working. Twining herself did so in many essays, including her 'Workhouse Cruelties', in which she described a mentally disabled 75-year-old man who died after being beaten with a strap and a man with epilepsy who died of burns because he was left unsupervised near a fire; she also remarked that 'improvement' had begun in the workhouses due in part to 'the fact that women have come forward ... and done good service to the cause of the poor and helpless, of whom women and children form so large a proportion.'[29] In 1858 Twining published her book *Workhouses and Women's Work*, whose title indicates her special interest in the female poor.

The Workhouse Visiting Society provided libraries, put up pictures, offered lectures and teas, and gave toys to children. Visitors also gave Christmas parties – at the Leeds Workhouse in 1863 lady visitors provided decorated trees, presents, and a musical performance. With all of these small touches, workhouse visitors were typical middle-class phil- anthropists. They did their work by bringing middle-class female expert- ise – entertainment, decoration, religious influence – to the world outside their own homes. They did not address the root causes of poverty, but they ameliorated misery (by imposing, it must be said, their own cultural standards). They wished to add dignity and respectable amusement to the lives of the poor even though they did not consider them equals.

The Workhouse Visiting Society, like many nineteenth-century visiting societies and other philanthropic agencies (rescue homes in particular), sought to train (or retrain) poor young women for work in domestic service. This strategy is subject to a number of interpretations. On the one hand, service was one of the most respectable forms of employment a working-class woman could find; it was steady work that provided food and shelter as well as a small salary. It also involved close supervision by a middle- or upper-class woman, which most female philanthropists believed was beneficial. On the other hand, the focus on service seems a bit self-seeking, given the middle and upper classes' unquenchable need for servants; it was sometimes said that female philanthropists seemed to be driven in equal parts by the desire to do good and the need to maintain a steady supply of help.

The Workhouse Visiting Society was disbanded in 1878 because its success had rendered it obsolete: workhouse visiting had become so widely accepted that most institutions were now open to visitors, and so popular that other more general charities had embraced it as part of their missions. But its history, in which one affluent woman turned an interest into an organized society, many of whose members were lower middle class, its emphasis on small domestic touches and on religion, and its philosophy of embracing proximity while maintaining a gap between rich and poor, typified middle-class visiting societies.

New professions

All the female philanthropic work available during the late eighteenth and early nineteenth centuries – supporting causes financially, planning and executing bazaars, visiting the poor – was unpaid and perceived as feminine. Before about 1860 there were few paying professions open to respectable middle-class women. As we have seen, women could make a living writing novels; they were also notable writers in other genres, including botany books and children's literature.[30] But many middle-class women in reduced circumstances who had to earn their own keep found that their only options were to become a governess or a dressmaker, poorly paid positions that were structured like domestic service and indicated genteel poverty and a descent in class status.

From mid-century, however, there was a profound shift in opportunities and attitudes. While 'hidden investments' in family income and unpaid philanthropy continued vigorously until the First World War and beyond, middle-class women's work became professionalized. Better education made some posts attainable. Some tasks of a philanthropic nature became paid work; others were unpaid but required training, appointment, or election. For some posts – clerk, shop assistant, teacher, nurse, hospital dispenser, and hairdresser – middle-class women competed with the aspiring working-class or lower-middle-class women. Other positions – like librarian, doctor, social worker and researcher, Poor Law Guardian, and School Board official – were either unpaid or required so much education or social status that they were only open to middle- and upper-middle-class women. In the words of one historian, 'Many of the sort of girls who, in 1850, believed that to leave their homes to work for money would destroy their status as ladies and unsex them as women were [from the 1870s] happily training for occupations and earning a living at them.'[31] Given contemporary fears that marriageable middle-class men were hopelessly outnumbered, and that 'superfluous' women were doomed to a life of spinsterhood, the possibility of ongoing meaningful paid occupation was critical.

Middle-class women's professions at once challenged and confirmed middle-class gender roles. Among the middle classes, getting paid or elected to a post was previously a privilege accorded only to men. Lower-middle-class women expected to earn money, at least until they married, and felt no need to justify their work. But for women from the more comfortable middle classes, and especially the evangelical middle class, the shift to the belief that earning was compatible with respectability was a dramatic change. Yet, throughout this transition, middle-class women's work retained several key features. The radical political potential of professionalization was modified by the fact that most of the jobs women were paid to do closely resembled earlier philanthropic work: it was feminine, moral, domestically oriented, and often religiously inspired; it involved caring for and superintending women, children, and the sick, and overseeing the lives of the poor. It used what were seen as women's natural abilities to nurture others and maintain domestic spaces and it often involved reaching out to other women without erasing class and racial boundaries. For many, including the philanthropist Louisa Twining, the responsibility for caring for others was inseparable from the very notion of women's work.[32]

In addition, the paid work open to middle-class women in the second half of the nineteenth century did not threaten men who needed employment or the virtue of the employed women. Women took jobs in fields dominated by women, such as nursing and teaching; even in medicine, most of the first lady doctors justified their work in terms of the special needs of female patients, and so laid little claim to men's work. (Strangely, this was also a period that saw the masculinization of obstetric medicine.)

Women trained and worked in all-female or otherwise protected environments. Grammar-school teachers trained at women's colleges and worked in schools for girls, while those in retail work lived on the premises; both groups seemed safely under surveillance at all times. Some fields also still had official or unofficial marriage bars that helped to guarantee turnover. Post-1860 professionalization was an important development in the liberation of women, but it did not change everything.

Not only did middle-class women become comfortable with working; employers came to accept the notion of employing women. This was not simply a logical decision based on economics – if it had been, women would have been employed as clerks, teachers, doctors and nurses decades earlier than they were. Women were hired because female employment began to be perceived as acceptable and respectable. Feminists were the key agents of change here: while their efforts to find jobs for specific women were of limited success, their campaigns to raise public awareness of women's abilities in many fields resulted in the opening of those fields to middle-class women. Starting in 1859, feminists of the Langham Place circle, founded by Barbara Leigh Smith (1827–91) and Bessie Rayner Parkes (1829–1925), successfully argued that women could be trained in the professions and work for as long as they remained unmarried; the Society for the Promotion of the Employment of Women (SPEW), a creation of the Langham Place group, also helped to open some employers to the idea of hiring young ladies.[33]

All of these factors together helped to change the nature of middle-class women's work after 1860. 'Hidden investments' of money, time and expertise into family businesses or husbands' careers remained important alongside emerging new options. Though the number of professional middle-class women was always small before the First World War – women doctors, secondary-school teachers, School Board officials, and others taken together never numbered more than a few thousand – they were none the less significant. Education and social work accounted for most middle-class employment (though a few women became doctors) and give a broad but nuanced picture of women's working lives.

Clerking, hospital dispensing, and nursing, while having some appealing characteristics for women, had others which rendered their class status less than perfectly secure. One tension was that these fields were, as we have already seen, crowded with lower- and lower-middle-class women, from whom many more affluent middle-class women wanted to be distinguished. Yet the same criteria that enticed upper-working-class and lower-middle-class women made them relatively safe choices for more affluent middle-class women, some of whom also went into clerking. One of the first large firms to hire women, the Prudential Assurance Company, explicitly restricted its hiring to 'ladies'. The workplace was organized so that the lady clerks rarely interacted with anyone of inferior class status, the low pay made the work seem ladylike because the salary could not have supported a family, and the firm offered amenities including a library, concerts, and a piano.[34] Lower-middle-class women tended to work in firms that hired a wider range of female clerks. Clerking allowed young women – mostly from the lower middle class or below – to go out to work after leaving school and before getting married without casting doubts on their respectability.

Like clerking, hospital dispensing was a field in which the demand for low-level employees was growing just as women started to enter it. Until the First World War, it was a popular career choice for middle-class young women, who saw it as a suitable form of work before getting married.[35] Female dispensers accepted lower pay in voluntary hospitals and work-house infirmaries, and left the field after five or ten years rather than seeking promotion. In contrast to nurses, hospital dispensers, most of whom trained and worked after 1895, were not supervised during their leisure time, either as students or as workers; they were paid a salary and otherwise left to their own devices. (Male dispensers, who were more highly qualified, often opened their own chemist's shops.)

The appeal of nursing as a feminine, care-taking occupation drew a wide range of middle-class women to the profession, especially after Florence Nightingale's work in the Crimea in the 1850s became well known. Nursing was associated in the minds of many with religious women because it had traditionally been the province of sisters – indeed, one historian calls the history of nursing 'a sub-plot [in] the history of Victorian Christianity.'[36] However, it was also connected with untrained working-class women, which cast doubts on its respectability. Even though most middle-class women became hospital 'sisters' who managed working-class nurses rather than toiling alongside them, they found that associations with both selflessness and manual labour persisted. Lucy Rae, a middle-class nurse, felt strongly that:

> ... a well-born woman will more easily enter into the feelings of her patients than a woman who belongs to the lower orders ... The matter [of raising nursing standards] could be easily accomplished if hospital

officials would recognise the fact that the question of 'class' is at the root of the evils in the nursing profession; there might then be some chance of a remedy.[37]

At mid-century nursing was undergoing a series of radical changes. Nightingale's popularity had attracted funds and attention to nursing. A public subscription raised £44,000 to set up a Training School for Nurses in 1860.[38] Several London teaching hospitals began implementing a new training system to produce 'Nightingale nurses'. Women in reformed nursing hoped to transform it into a skilled profession and, at the same time, they considered that their moral superiority, as a function of their class status, formed the crux of their qualifications: middle-class values would infuse the wards through which they walked.

Yet the emergence of a reformed training system did not resolve the tensions that persisted as to whether a nurse was, in the words of Dr Lionel S. Beale, professor of medicine, 'a sort of medical maid-of-all-work ... [or] a member of a profession [with] rights as well as duties.'[39] Another disadvantage of nursing was that it was messy and required an intimacy with the bodies of strangers, including men, that also rendered it less than solidly respectable to middle-class women.

While lower-middle-class nurses trained alongside their working-class colleagues, more affluent middle-class nurses were keen to distinguish themselves from them. A separate system of training 'special' or 'lady' probationers was therefore instituted in the late 1860s; ladies lived in separate and more luxurious quarters, trained for only a year (rather than for two or three), and paid a guinea a week for their training. Nursing became fashionable for more affluent young women to pursue as a form of charity until they married. Before about 1880 most nursed for only a few months after their training. There were, of course, exceptions; after working in 'ragged schools' for poor children and as a district visitor, Agnes Jones (1832–68) became committed to a career in nursing. She trained as a Nightingale probationer and became the head nurse at the Liverpool workhouse, where she died of typhus after several years of work.[40]

By 1880, nursing had been reconfigured from being the province of poorly-educated, dirty and, according to stereotype, drunken old women (Dickens's Sarah Gamp was commonly invoked) into being the work of well-trained young women. As a result, when hospitals expanded and needed more nurses in the 1880s, they were willing to hire upper-middle-class women as managing sisters and lower-middle-class as working nurses. These women were in turn able to enter the profession without losing their respectability. As the field grew in popularity, nursing schools became crowded, and nurses in consequence far less well paid. Whereas reformed nursing started out by paying better than other professions available to upper- and lower-middle-class women, by the 1890s it was relatively poorly paid. Promotion, too, came more slowly as more women entered the field.

In 1888 the British Nursing Association emphasized that a nurse's most important quality was character, and two years later a probationer described herself as 'behaving exactly like a general servant', which suggests that she was not raised to be one.[41] By the turn of the century class hierarchies, always a feature of the profession, had been fixed: head nurses were from the upper parts of the middle classes, while other nurses were from the lower middle and working classes and were comfortable with their place in the hierarchies, with physical work, and with the idea of themselves as wage-earners.

Teaching was far more popular than either clerking or nursing. In contrast to the stereotype of the amateurish schoolmistress, even before the 1870s many middle-class governesses and other teachers were educated women who took their work seriously. By the last third of the nineteenth century, more and more middle-class women were educated at secondary schools and even universities. Education improved women's minds and, many argued, made them more able wives and mothers. As adults, some women also went on to work in state schools. Other middle-class women became teachers at private girls' schools and women's colleges. Teaching provided more middle-class women with paid employment than any other field. Its connotations of public service and domesticity made it attractive to many women. Secondary schools became producers of their own faculties and intimately linked to women's colleges. By the 1890s attendance at a university college for women was the standard qualification for a secondary-school teacher, and the majority of graduates who took paid employment did so as teachers.[42] For instance Sara Burstall (1859–1939), headmistress of the Manchester High School for Girls, attended North London Collegiate School for Girls and Girton College (at Cambridge University).

Teaching was a suitable profession because it allowed middle-class women to use their education but also fitted perfectly with expectations about middle-class femininity. Secondary-school teachers were generally accorded professional status and had a relatively high degree of control over their classrooms, rather than being at the mercy of a variety of officials and visitors as elementary-school teachers were. Sara Burstall claimed that 'the teacher is an expert professional and is entitled therefore to the deference shown to the skilled professional opinion of the doctor, lawyer, or architect'.[43] Although secondary-school teachers did not teach poor or working-class children, teaching was promoted as a form of public service in that it was a way of training young girls to be wives and mothers and for their adult lives of philanthropic work. And because many schools were boarding schools or residential female colleges, teachers operated, at least in part, within a domestic sphere. The communal life of the boarding school was not for everyone, but for some it was ideal. (In general, secondary-school teaching was seen as incompatible with marriage and family life, which made it more appealing to some than others; many women compromised by working as teachers until they married.)

When women first began working as secondary-school teachers in about 1860, salaries were high, opportunities for advancement abounded; the few women who had benefited from a university education could expect to make between £120 and £220 per annum and to rise to the post of headmistress. By 1890, the field had, like so many areas in which only women were employed, become crowded; starting salaries were now only £70–£80 (less if the position was residential) and few could expect to become headmistresses. Yet secondary-school teaching remained the career of choice for most educated middle-class women. It was still relatively well-paid and required professional yet genteel training while confirming middle-class status.

University teaching was an unusual field for women in the nineteenth century but became a recognized one by the start of the twentieth; by 1930, women constituted perhaps as much as 14 per cent of university and college faculties (though few reached the upper levels of the professoriate, and women were not even eligible for the most prestigious Oxbridge positions). As with other women's fields, the pay was poor (especially at non-residential colleges). Resident women tutors at Newnham College, Cambridge, made about £100 per annum, while men at Cambridge made more like £500 per annum and often much more. In 1892 Margaret Tuke could accept the position of French tutor at Newnham only because she had her own income to live on.[44]

University life was rewarding as an intellectual pursuit but socially kept women out of the mainstream because it was so rarified and often involved communal residential living. Those who did enter academe found it difficult to combine with marriage, and so most – 79 per cent in 1884 and even more in 1904 – never married (others left academia after a few years for marriage).[45] As a result, university teaching carried the stigma of spinsterhood, although women able or willing to accept the communal, female-only life of the residential women's colleges often found their work extremely rewarding. Colleges not only allowed women to teach, research, and generally lead the life of the mind; they also provided amenities such as private rooms, domestic servants, meals, and institutional support.

Women often worked as tutors. Louisa Lumsden (1840–1935), one of Girton College's first students, tutored girls in Greek and Latin there in the 1870s. By the 1880s all the women's colleges at Oxford and Cambridge had at least one woman tutor, and the older ones each had five. They engaged in scholarship as well as teaching. Jane Harrison (1850–1928) graduated from Newnham, lectured on and studied the classics in London for several years, then returned to Newnham as a faculty member in 1898. She knew sixteen languages (five of them dead) and in the early twentieth century revolutionized classical studies. She gloried in the female communal life of the college and had many close and passionate friendships with women and men, but was also self-conscious about her spinster status. She was greatly admired at Newnham, where her lectures were always crowded, and was a mentor to many students. While university women were rare, the fact that there were women who devoted their lives to scholarship and to the higher education of other women broadened the professional boundaries for middle-class women.

In addition to teaching, some of the most rewarding work that women did during the second half of the nineteenth century was in the social services. This included work as school managers, charity workers, Care Committee members, and School Board members in elementary schools; Poor Law Guardians in workhouses; rent collectors and settlement workers in housing; and inspectors, social investigators, and advocates of better conditions for working women. Some of these were volunteer positions; others were paid, elected or appointed and attitudes varied towards them: Octavia Hill (1832–1912) opposed women's suffrage and claimed to eschew formal politics, while Louisa Twining pushed for women's right to be elected as local officials. All were variations on the female philanthropic tradition and allowed women to continue offering aid and overseeing the lives of poor and working families. Unsurprisingly,

given what we know of the earlier part of the century, late nineteenth-
and early twentieth-century social theory saw domesticity, family, and
female influence as the key to solving a wide range of social problems,
and so offered many opportunities for women's involvement. Social work
gradually acquired professional status, so that by the end of our period
university courses of study in social work had been developed in London,
Liverpool, Birmingham, Bristol, Leeds, and Manchester, all emphasizing
a combination of theoretically-oriented coursework and practical field
experience.

In the first half of the century some women ran their own free schools
for the very poor, called 'ragged' schools. Mary Carpenter ran ragged
schools in Bristol in the 1840s, which she kept small so that they would
be more family oriented. She later became a well-known authority on
juvenile delinquents. Once state schools had been established in 1870,
elementary-school teaching was an important career for lower-middle-
class women, as we saw in the last chapter. A few more comfortably placed
middle-class women also went into elementary teaching, combating the
social stigma of taking a job that was usually regarded as beneath them.
Gertrude Tuckwell, for instance, a parson's daughter, reminded herself
that her work was 'honourable instead of ... undignified'.[46] The professional training of elementary-school teachers indicated that they were
from a lower social stratum: they generally went to state elementary
schools, worked at apprenticeships, then attended vocational colleges.
More affluent women, educated at private primary and secondary schools,
and at women's colleges at universities, felt uncomfortable at training
colleges. One attempted solution was Bishop Otter College in Chichester,
founded expressly for middle-class women so that they could train
without coming into contact with lower-middle-class women, but it
did little to change the field. Once on the job, the professional lives of
elementary-school teachers on the one hand seemed too independent to
be entirely respectable, yet on the other hand involved being too much at
the mercy of others – school managers, School Board members, local
inspectors, nurses and volunteers – to allow a proper sense of philanthropic mission.

Upper-middle-class women became involved in elementary schooling
in ways more in keeping with their class and gender positions. Though
their own children virtually never attended state elementary schools,
which were for lower-middle-class and working-class children, they
oversaw the lives of elementary-school children and their families in a

variety of ways. Some worked, in an unpaid capacity, as school managers, which meant taking charge of the daily administration of the school, hiring, evaluating, and firing teachers, handling parent and teacher complaints, and visiting the school periodically. In London in 1884, one-fifth of the managers appointed by the School Board were middle-class women.[47] Some managers wanted to learn about working-class life; others were there to promote middle-class values and behaviour among teachers and students. Still others hoped to be more accessible to women teachers than male managers; indeed, one teacher in London in 1888 admitted that her maternity leave had not been properly arranged because she had been too uncomfortable to discuss the issue with the male manager of her school.[48]

Food was another point of entry into elementary schools for middle-class women. From the 1880s, some schools attempted to provide meals for their hungriest students and from 1906 many did. Middle-class philanthropists used the opportunity to define themselves as domestic nurturers, and occasionally to criticize working-class mothers (for instance, by their tendency to refrain from allowing the children bread, which they felt poor mothers served too often instead of a hot meal). After 1908 middle-class women in London also worked on Care Committees alongside schoolteachers, managers, and others on issues of student welfare. They assessed which children needed, and were deserving of, free meals, medical care, clothes, spectacles and the like. In their quest for the information they needed for their assessments, middle-class women often invaded the realms of teachers and parents – lower-middle-class and working women – but these services were needed and valued by the poorer students.

Finally, state-provided education offered women their first foray into electoral politics in the form of local School Boards, for which rate-paying women could vote and on which women could serve. The School Board decided many key issues, including curriculum, attendance policies, and budgets. School Boards were directly elected from 1870 until 1902, during which time twenty-nine women served on the London School Board (LSB) (out of a total of 326) as well as many others in other areas.

Board work was full-time, unpaid, and involved overseeing the lives of women, children, and the working classes. Augusta Webster (1837–94) put her name forward in 1879 because she was unhappy that the education of working-class girls was being 'planned and ruled almost entirely by men'.[49] Female members of the LSB had close ties with various philanthropic societies or related causes such as settlement work, and most were politically liberal. For example, Jane Chessar (1835–80), elected to the LSB in 1873, also prepared girls at North London Collegiate School for their Cambridge examinations, belonged to the Royal Geographical Society, founded a ladies' debating society, and worked as a journalist. Elizabeth Garrett (1836–1917), the first woman doctor in England and a member of a prominent Liberal family, also served on the London School Board.

Less prestigious positions were available at the local workhouse. From 1875, women were able to serve as Poor Law Guardians, unpaid locally-elected officials who oversaw the workhouses. This was a continuation of the Workhouse Visiting Society's service to inmates; significantly, though, working as Guardians meant that rather than serving as watchdogs from without, philanthropic lower-middle-class women were now pursuing their mission from within the state-provided system.

While election to local office was an important political step for middle-class women, the positions they filled were – as they themselves pointed out in pursuit of them – extensions of widely accepted female philanthropy. Women articulated the importance of a female presence on local Boards of Guardians in much the same ways that they had spoken of earlier work as institutional visitors: they argued that women provided a necessary domestic and caring perspective without which local government was inexcusably unfeeling. Louisa Twining mocked the notion of male Guardians choosing the crockery and examining the laundry at workhouses, declaring that they were 'large households which are none the less such because they are public institutions and not private families' and that 'where domestic and household management is concerned, there women should have a place and a power of control'.[50] Twining acted on this conviction by serving as a Poor Law Guardian for Kensington in the 1880s and in Tunbridge Wells in the 1890s. The suffragette Emmeline Pankhurst (1858–1928), in her autobiography, criticized the men who ran the Manchester workhouse before her election as unfeeling 'guardians, not of the poor but of the rates'. In her description of the inmates' terrible living conditions and the steps she took to remedy their discomforts and indignities, she focused on those traditional objects of women's attention:

old folks … sitting on backless forms, or benches … little girls seven and eight years on their knees scrubbing the cold stones of the long corridors … pregnant women … many of them were unmarried women, very, very young, mere girls ... What became of those girls, and what became of their hapless infants?[51]

The position of Poor Law Guardian, whether man or woman, was of a lower social status than School Board official because the work was unpleasant. Women, however, who were especially interested in the workhouses and had few chances to work in local government, flocked to guardianship. So did suffragists, who wanted to demonstrate women's fitness for participation in national politics by working on a local level. Many of the earliest women Guardians were also School Board managers or were on local committees that enforced school attendance policies, demonstrating a broad range of philanthropic interests.

Until 1894 Poor Law Guardians were required to own property, which meant that few women were eligible. The first female Guardians in London included Martha Merrington, also a School Board manager, elected for Kensington in 1875. The first married female Guardian, Harriet McIlquham, was elected for Tewkesbury several years later, and her husband was publicly criticized for allowing her to stand.[52] Another Guardian was Amelia Charles (1830–1900), whose candidacy was supported by the Society for Promoting the Return of Women as Poor Law Guardians. A generous subscriber to a number of charities, she took a particular interest in workhouse children, who she felt should be boarded out in the country rather than living in urban workhouses. Charles served on the Paddington Board of Guardians from 1881 until her death in 1899. Pro-suffrage Guardians included Emmeline Pankhurst and Louisa Twining. In 1894 the property qualification was abolished and a much wider range of people, including lower-middle-class women, were able to serve as Guardians. By 1910 there were 1,655 female Guardians, though over two hundred local boards had no women on them.[53]

Other women superintended the poor as housing managers and rent collectors. Here middle-class women sought to provide them with decent accommodation while imparting their own moral standards through close contact. Housing management was first promoted by Octavia Hill, a devout woman who spoke of her work as a calling and strongly believed that the middle-class women who worked with her should not be paid. During years of philanthropic work among the poor she became especially concerned with sanitation and overcrowding, arguing that working-class people could not be expected to live decent lives unless they were decently housed. In the 1860s she began (aided by friends including John Ruskin) acquiring and renting out working-class housing that was managed by unpaid middle-class women. By 1874 she managed fifteen housing schemes that accommodated over two thousand tenants; at her death in 1912 she controlled over two thousand properties, in which perhaps ten thousand people lived, and women trained in the Olivia Hill system, as it was called, worked in the United States and Northern Europe as well as in England and Scotland.

Hill insisted that housing management was properly women's work. 'Ladies must do it,' she wrote, 'for it is detailed work; ladies must do it, for it is household work.'[54] She believed strongly in the value of face-to-face contact between middle-class and working-class women, and so trained a fleet of lady housing managers – who oversaw properties – and lady rent collectors – who appeared in person every week. Keenly aware that her workers had contact mainly with the women in tenant families, Hill insisted on warm relations between workers and their working-class tenants. The Octavia Hill system combined middle-class expectations of working-class behaviour with affordable rents. Managers and rent collectors were to provide tenants with examples of middle-class standards of order and cleanliness to which, it was hoped, they would aspire. In keeping with the philanthropic tradition of making the lives of the poor more pleasant, the ladies also provided their tenants with playgrounds, saving clubs, workshops, classes, gardens, and trips to the countryside. Housing managers and rent collectors were expected to observe and comment on the homes they entered, just as home visitors did. They made sure repairs were carried out and enforced a policy of prompt payment of rents so as to promote self-reliance on the part of tenants. Those who fell behind with their rents were evicted. (We would be foolish to think that all tenants were as grateful for these interventions as Hill and others hoped.) The work was demanding, but housing managers and rent collectors enjoyed a level of professionalism along with a sense of purpose and usefulness.

Many other middle-class women were involved in the settlement house movement. This was a scheme in which university-educated students lived in very poor neighbourhoods and, with the help of other volunteers, tried to create a safe and welcoming community. Living among the poor required a different type of commitment from visiting them, although the ideas, approaches, and beliefs of settlement women were not dissimilar from those of visitors and rent collectors. Women in the settlement house movement continued older traditions by visiting neighbours; they also worked as School Board managers. They sought to relieve the poverty of their new neighbours and to educate them to become more culturally middle class, which they believed would be beneficial. Most settlement women were unmarried and childless; many had already enjoyed communal life at their boarding school or women's college and found settlement houses appealing as female communities of like-minded workers.

Women worked in men's settlements as well and also founded their own, often under university auspices. University women's settlements included Lady Margaret Hall Settlement in Lambeth and, the first to be founded, Blackfriars Women's University Settlement in Southwark (WUS). The Southwark settlement sought '[t]o promote the welfare of the people of the poorer districts of London and especially of the women and children, by devising and promoting schemes which tend to elevate them physically, intellectually and morally, and by giving them additional opportunities for education and recreation'.[55] By 1888, WUS women were working on various projects with the Metropolitan Association for Befriending Young Servants, the Charity Organisation Society, the Children's Country Holiday Fund, and the Recreative Evening Classes Association. They also established a settlement library and installed a piano at the Blackfriars Settlement. From the 1890s, settlement women and others working in slums offered prenatal care, girls' clubs, and various classes and clinics for working-class mothers; they also placed settlement children with rural families for two weeks during the summer. Settlements were most effective at providing services which the state did not; their efforts to remake the poor as culturally middle-class were less successful. Settlement women insisted on rigorous training for those who wanted to do social work, insisting that good intentions were not enough. They were instrumental in establishing social work as a trained and paid profession, though this was not fully realized until after the First World War.

Other middle-class women worked as government-appointed inspectors. The first female workhouse inspector, Jane Nassau Senior, was appointed in 1872; her father-in-law had helped to draft the 1834 Poor Law that created the workhouses, and her friends included Octavia Hill and Louisa Twining. Women worked as factory inspectors from the 1890s and as inspectors of reformatories and prisons from the 1900s. Factory inspectors investigated workplaces to uncover unsafe or illegal working conditions for women. While some men opposed their entry into the profession – in 1870 the chief factory inspector argued that a woman's presence in a factory was 'opposite to the sphere of her good work in the hospital, the school, or the home'[56] – women argued that their sympathies for fellow women and their access to private female spaces (such as bedrooms in which piece-work was being done) made them useful and necessary. A separate women's branch of the Factory Department was established in 1893, with the help of the upper-middle-class socialist, suffragist, and women's trade union organizer Emilia Dilke (1840–1904), who pressed her friend, the Home Secretary Herbert Asquith, on the matter. Lady inspectors took a separate exam from male inspectors and earned £200 per annum, two-thirds of what male inspectors were paid but a good salary relative to other middle-class women's work. Tellingly, the women were from the start called 'lady inspectors'. Middle-class women were expected to use their social status, education, and philanthropic experience in pursuit of justice on behalf of working-class women, who were not considered able to help themselves. As a result there were tensions between lady inspectors and the women whose lives they investigated and with the local sub-inspectors who were working- or lower-middle-class men.

Factory inspectors travelled the country, living in hotels or in short-term flats while they investigated women's workplaces. The work was lonely but exciting. May Abraham, one of the first lady inspectors, visited textile mills in Lancashire and Cheshire, and ribbon and braid factories in Coventry and Derby, and reported on unsanitary and dangerous working conditions and on unfair wage practices (such as charging workers for cleaning the lavatories or fining them for talking while working). Lady inspectors helped combat the lead poisoning that plagued workers in the Staffordshire Potteries and helped to improve the pay and working conditions of home-workers in Ireland. They also addressed the domestic spaces in which so many women worked: Lucy Deane and Rose Squire, for instance, spent years investigating laundry work, which was done mostly at home by women with families. Deane first reported in 1893 that '[e]very little house in a network of mean streets ... was a hand-laundry ... the steam from the wet clothes drying overhead condensed and dripped on the shoulders of the ironers, sweating at their work.'[57] She spent several years systematically keeping records of accidents in laundries, campaigning for safer machinery, and prosecuting managers and owners for compensation to injured workers. By 1904, after more than a decade of this work, reported accidents in laundries had decreased significantly, and in 1907 laundresses' working hours were limited to sixty per week (and children's to thirty). By that time lady inspectors were established professionals who, while they might have seemed overly intrepid to some, raised few eyebrows. In 1908 there were fifteen ladies (and 172 men) working as inspectors. In 1926 – by which time there were more than three hundred women in the profession – the women's branch was absorbed into the Factory Department of the Home Office.

Some middle-class women sought to improve women's wages and working conditions by helping working women to form unions, joining consumers' pressure groups, and pressing for factory legislation and a minimum wage. The writer and social investigator Clementina Black (1854–1922) devoted years to the problems of women of the working classes. Black refused to condemn working-class women's work, writing in her *Married Women's Work* (1909) that '[w]hat is wrong is not the work for wages of married women, but the underpayment.' She and other middle-class women pressed their case with a variety of organizations such as the Women's Trade Union League (WTUL), the Consumers' League (which tried to get middle-class customers to exert pressure on employers for better wages for women), the Anti-Sweating League, and the Women's Industrial Council (WIC) (which investigated and published details of women's working conditions and, by 1914, had investigated 117 trades).

Clara Collet (1860–1948) worked with Charles Booth on his social survey, *Life and Labour of the People in London* (1889), investigating living and working conditions in London's East End and living there herself in 1888. In 1892 she was appointed to the Royal Commission on Labour, where as one of four Lady Assistant Commissioners she investigated and collected statistics on women's work all over England. The following year she entered the civil service as a senior investigator for the Board of Trade (a precursor to the Ministry of Labour), where she remained for thirty years. While her long career and high government position made Collet unusual, she was typical in that she was a middle-class woman who was using new channels to continue the traditional work of helping women and children in need. The social reformer Beatrice Webb (1858–1943) also worked with Booth. She began her career as an active philanthropist with the Charity Organisation Society (COS) but later departed from that group as she – unusually for a middle-class female philanthropist – came to see the causes of poverty as structural rather than the fault of the individual.

Women in all of these fields expanded gender roles and exploited career opportunities without necessarily challenging contemporary notions about middle-class femininity. That many had no chances of promotion, and that most were unpaid or not paid enough to live on, blunted the radical potential of their activities. However, their explicitly professional and vocational presence in the public sphere was a dramatic change from previous decades, especially for those from the upper middle class.

Medicine was the profession with the highest status which women entered during our period, but unlike the fields discussed above it was considered a definitively male field until the late nineteenth century. The fact that its male practitioners were uneasy and defensive of their territory meant that it was extremely difficult for English women to train to become doctors. At the start of the First World War, medical co-education was rarer in England than in the United States or any Western European country. Most of the women who went into medicine sought to carve out a separate space for women's medical work instead of arguing that they were like men or could do men's jobs.

All of the early women doctors came from wealthy middle-class families, and were able to spend a number of years – and pounds – in pursuit of their career goals. Most were also suffragists, which makes sense given that lady doctors, like the early suffragists, were challenging contemporary gender roles rather than working within them as most professional women did. There were not many lady doctors at first. Elizabeth Garrett Anderson, sister of the leading suffragist Millicent Garrett Fawcett (1847–1929), became the first English woman on the Medical Register in 1865. She was followed by Sophia Jex-Blake (1840–1912) in 1877. In 1900 there were only two hundred women on the Register and in 1914 one thousand, not all of whom managed to practise.[58]

Although nurturing was thought to be natural to women, they were generally considered unfit to be doctors. They were thought to be even less qualified for its rigorous training than for other courses of university study. (Medical faculties were on the whole more conservative and more opposed to female students than others). In particular the thought of women attending classes in anatomy and physiology was repugnant to many, especially if those classes were mixed. One hospital doctor told Elizabeth Garrett Anderson in 1863 that:

> I have a strong conviction that the entrance of ladies into dissecting rooms and anatomical theatres is undesirable in every respect, and highly unbecoming ... it is not necessary that fair ladies should be brought into contact with such foul scenes – nor would it be for their

good any more than for that of their patients if they could succeed in leaving the many spheres of usefulness which God has pointed out to them in order to force themselves into competition with the lower walks of the medical profession.[59]

Eventually, as was the case with nursing and other professions, feminists were able to shift public perceptions so that women were seen as potentially competent doctors, at least under some circumstances. Imperialism played a key role in this process. Advocates of female medical education not only emphasized that many British women would prefer being attended by a lady doctor (especially for gynaecological and obstetrical problems), but insisted that it was impossible for Indian women in zenanas (sex-segregated spaces) to be attended by male doctors.

The first two female doctors, Garrett Anderson and Jex-Blake, were quite different in their approaches and attitudes. To be legally qualified to practise medicine, a man typically had to obtain a university degree in medicine and have his name placed on the Medical Register (established in 1858). Garrett Anderson was able to register by qualifying for an apothecary's licence, which was not explicitly forbidden to women, and she finally attained a medical degree in Paris in 1869. The apothecary loophole was closed once she had used it, so that although Garrett Anderson was an inspiration to other women, they could not follow in her footsteps.

Sophia Jex-Blake, in contrast, wanted to blaze a trail for herself and others by receiving a medical degree from a British university, as men did. In 1869 she and seven other women began attending Edinburgh University, where they were the objects of much hostility – in 1870 male students physically barred them from the Anatomy Room – and were denied clinical training and their degrees. Jex-Blake completed her education on the Continent and in 1877 sat for her examinations at the Irish College of Physicians in Dublin. Soon afterwards the University of London and other universities allowed women to take their medical examinations but Oxbridge remained closed to aspiring lady doctors throughout our period.

Experiencing at first-hand the difficulties of being accepted into degree-granting institutions that admitted men, Garrett Anderson and Jex-Blake came together to found the London School of Medicine for Women (LSMW), which opened in 1874. (Elizabeth Blackwell (1821–1910), who trained in Geneva and was the first woman to qualify as a doctor in the United States, worked with them.) By emphasizing the need for qualified

British women who could treat zenana-imprisoned Indian women, the
LSMW defined medicine as part of middle-class women's mission to
serve less fortunate women. The school used images of Indian women as
silent, passive victims both to promote the professionalization of 'lady
doctoresses' and to establish a place for women in the Empire. Its work
was continued in the 1880s by the Dufferin Fund (established by Harriet
Countess of Dufferin, Vicereine of India), which helped send medically
qualified women to India. The image of British women helping Indian
women was sufficiently compelling to quieten the anxieties even of those
who saw medicine as an unsexing profession for women. One of the
LSMW's first students, aspiring missionary Fanny Butler (1850–99),
worried that medicine was unwomanly but embraced it none the less as
an essential part of her evangelizing mission in India; in her last year of
practice, in Srinagar, Kashmir, she claimed to have seen over 5,000
patients, and to have introduced over 2,000 of them to Christianity.[60]
While some of the LSMW's early students were, like Butler, missionaries,
others were not, and were eager to establish themselves as secular professionals distinct from unskilled medical missionaries. But both groups
saw themselves as civilized healers of uncivilized natives. Over time more
British universities accepted female medical students. In addition, the
First World War inspired many more women to pursue medicine as a
career, and many more parents to drop their objections, so that by 1921
over two thousand women had qualified as doctors.

The term 'middle class' covered a wide range of incomes and experiences.
While all women who considered themselves middle-class shared housekeeping standards to some degree, some found these easy to keep up,
while others struggled to maintain their class status. Women's labour and
resources were often a 'hidden' part of the family enterprise. For much of
the century middle-class women expressed themselves in the public
sphere through philanthropy. They had a wide range of attitudes towards
wage-earning. Less affluent middle-class women – the wives and daughters of shopkeepers, teachers, and clerks – grew up expecting to earn their
keep and saw nothing disreputable about doing so. But among the upper
middle classes – who along with the minor gentry were considered 'polite'
society – paid work and female gentility were incompatible before the
1850s. Employment as a governess or dressmaker was a sign of tragic
(though relative) impoverishment. After 1860, when more women found
it necessary or desirable to work for pay, definitions of gentility changed;

by 1906 a periodical had appeared called *The Working Gentlewoman's Journal*.[61] Some of these women worked alongside lower-middle-class women as clerks or nurses; others entered new professional fields such as factory inspection or medicine. Some professions resisted women into the twentieth century. Women were not permitted to become accountants or bankers until 1910, and in 1914 there was not a single woman diplomat, barrister or judge. All middle-class women remained restricted to a handful of employment opportunities that were considered feminine, and offered little in the way of advancement or pay. Yet the fact that middle-class women's ability to earn their own money as individuals had become quotidian was a dramatic change from the conditions that prevailed at the start of our period.

3

Elite Women

Royal and aristocratic women were a tiny but important elite during the period under discussion. While their wealth, social status, and political influence made them atypical, they were afforded by their positions unique opportunities for political, social, and economic action that render them worthy of attention. Yet until recently elite women were rarely topics of serious historical inquiry; histories of the aristocracy usually neglected women, while histories of women and gender focused almost exclusively on those from the middle and working classes.

While Britain's royal family is easy to identify, the country's aristocracy – probably the smallest and wealthiest in Europe – is not. (The aristocracy was by this time British rather than English, as the titled families of England, Wales, Scotland and Ireland had merged into a single elite.) The narrowest definition includes only the peerage, that is, those who bore the hereditary titles of baron, viscount, earl, marquess, or duke and therefore sat in the House of Lords. In Britain, unlike the Continent, only the male head of the household was a peer; wives and children bore courtesy titles, and women, who could not sit in the House of Lords until 1958, were technically commoners. What we think of as the female peerage was in reality royal women and the wives and daughters of peers. A broader definition of aristocracy could include those who could afford its lifestyle. During Victoria's reign, the heads of four to five hundred families sat in the House of Lords, but many more – nine hundred families in 1870 – had the minimum annual income of £10,000 per annum necessary to afford an elite standard of living. Of course annual incomes varied widely – the Earl of Clarendon had a landed income of only £3,000, while the Dukes of Devonshire and Northumberland amassed over £50,000 in the early nineteenth century.[1] The aristocracy could also include the gentry, or untitled large landowners (one historian defines the gentry as those landowners who could not afford to participate in the London Season and the aristocracy as those who could). Historian David Cannadine prefers the term 'the British landed establishment', to include the aristocracy and the landed gentry, because it emphasizes power and landownership over title and conveys the economic, political, and social importance of the country's elite. Others emphasize the notion of 'polite' society (which included the gentry and upper middle class), whose members shared a culture that was defined not by a family's source of wealth but by its relative affluence and lifestyle.

By any definition the English elite was a very small part of the population – less than one per cent by the strictest definitions, and never more than 5 per cent. In 1873 more than 80 per cent of the land in the United Kingdom was owned by 7,000 people, less than half of one per cent of the population. This chapter will focus on an elite that is broadly construed, exploring the lives of women of Cannadine's 'landed establishment', from landed gentlewomen dispensing charity on their country estates to London's great political hostesses. We will be concerned less with lineage for its own sake and more with the context of political and social power and prestige within which aristocratic women operated.[2]

The chapter begins by examining the lives of aristocratic women in relation to their own families and households, then turns to their philanthropic, social, and political activities. Almost all elite women engaged in some form of philanthropy, and many performed social and political work officially and unofficially, in public and behind the scenes, as individuals and as female relatives of powerful men. We can best understand the lives and work of elite women if we embrace an understanding of their socializing as what the historian Elaine Chalus calls 'social politics – the management of people and social situations for political ends'.[3] Turning to the royal family, the chapter also examines key aspects of the lives of the four royal women who figured largely in the politics, culture, and national imagination of England during the long nineteenth century.

Aristocratic women

The lives of aristocratic women were clearly quite different from the lives of other women. For most of our period, from 1760 until the Reform Acts of the late nineteenth century made England's politics more democratic, aristocratic power was great. Aristocratic women fared well: they were respected for their roles in family life and estate succession, and were often loved companions of and collaborators with their husbands.

The enviable position of aristocratic women stemmed in part from their financial independence from men: upper-class women, married or single, usually had their own wealth separate from their husbands. Women who did not marry simply inherited family wealth; they could be left money or valuables, and could even inherit family land, although law and tradition ensured that lands and titles usually went to male descendants. Married women could not legally own any property until 1870. However, when elite women married, property was given to them, and kept out of their husbands' control, through the use of complex legal fictions called 'trusts'. Trusts were technically controlled by male trustees (usually relatives), not by the women on whom they were settled, but in practice most women – though they might be badgered by their husbands for money – controlled their own property. Individual wealth gave aristocratic women a sense of independence, in contrast to middle-class women, who, while they were crucial to their families' enterprises, neither earned nor possessed wealth and were dependent on their husbands' incomes and investments. The combination of membership of a powerful class and of personal wealth has led some to argue that aristocratic women were aristocrats first and women second, sharing much privilege with noblemen and little subordination with other daughters, wives, sisters, and mothers of England.

Yet aristocratic women, like other women, spent much of their adult lives bearing and raising children; they embraced evangelical religion in droves, especially during the early nineteenth century; they devoted themselves to philanthropy, claiming it as a female sphere while using it to act publicly. Perhaps most importantly, they, like other women, were subordinate to men of their own class. Aristocratic women did not vote. They could not sit in either chamber of Parliament, and until the 1830s could not even watch those bodies in session. And with relatives who were so politically powerful, they could not have helped noticing that they themselves were not. A number of elite women were key players in the fight for women's education and women's suffrage. As aristocratic political power declined at the end of the nineteenth century, many women disdained democracy; but others were, perhaps, more willing than the men of their class to forgo class privilege in pursuit of gender equality and even democracy.

HOME

Like less privileged women, aristocratic women were expected to spend their adult lives as wives, mothers, and housekeepers. However, housekeeping was less isolating for elite than for middle-class women, since on large estates home and work were inextricably linked. Aristocratic men did not earn wages or salaries or leave the home every morning for the workplace (although they attended Parliament when the family was in London); indeed, the house was both home and the centre of the family estate, and therefore a simultaneously public and private sphere by middle-class standards. Aristocratic men and women both worked at managing the household and the estate, and both directed servants and hosted large parties of guests. Stereotypes of oppressive aristocratic marriages, uninvolved and uncaring aristocratic parents, and aristocratic households and estates being run entirely by servants are unfounded. However, many marriages were marked by a public reserve that disguised the spouses' private intimacy.

The aristocratic home was not a female space. Its drawing rooms, billiard- and smoking-rooms were male spaces, and the home was frequently a site of political activity. Moreover, the family's private life was often quite public. The commemoration of family birthdays and other celebrations, the notice of such events in the London newspapers during the Season, and the constant presence of many servants also detracted from the privacy of the home.

Most aristocratic women, like most other women, married and spent the greater part of their adult lives as wives (though we should note that aristocratic widows could wield a great deal of power). While the aristocratic household was certainly a patriarchal one, most marriages seem to have been affectionate and companionable unions in which husbands and wives respected each other and valued each other's company and opinions. Spouses usually had gender-specific responsibilities with regard to child-rearing, estate management and politics, but they often performed their intertwined tasks side by side. Adultery did occur in aristocratic marriages, but it was usually discreet and infrequently the cause of divorce. Whereas divorced men were able to acknowledge and retain custody of their illegitimate children, divorced women were socially stigmatized and were separated from their legitimate children.

All married landed women, and especially those whose families were titled or owned much property, were under pressure to produce a male heir. Elite wives were rewarded for giving birth to boys; in 1821 Lady Stewart (later the Marchioness of Londonderry) received a string of pearls worth £10,000 from her husband when she produced a son.[4] Women who

were unable to produce healthy live children were considered dis-
appointments to their families.

The emphasis on large families meant that the typical aristocratic
woman spent a large part of her adult life either pregnant or as a nursing
mother. To take three of the political hostesses discussed below as
examples, Elizabeth, Lady Holland (1771–1845) had fifteen pregnancies
and ten children during her two marriages; Sarah Sophia, Countess of
Jersey (1785–1867), had ten pregnancies and eight children; Frances Anne,
Marchioness of Londonderry (1800–65), had ten pregnancies and seven
children. As these numbers indicate, even elite women often suffered the
loss of a pregnancy, infant, or child. The landed classes adopted birth-
control strategies relatively late in our period and continued to have large
families until the end of the century. Elite marriages that began in the
1860s and lasted more than two decades produced an average of 6.16 live
births; for those that started in the 1890s the figure was still a relatively
high 4.13.[5] Most elite women, however, did not allow themselves to be
significantly inconvenienced or cloistered during their pregnancies. There
was no social taboo against aristocratic women appearing at social events
visibly pregnant, and women decided for themselves whether to socialize,
even when near delivery. While the short intervals between births in many
elite families suggest that most women did not nurse their own babies,
some certainly did. Breast-feeding may have been more common among
the lesser gentry than the greatest landed families, however, and seems to
have been most prevalent between 1840 and 1880.[6]

Like middle-class families, aristocratic ones became increasingly
domesticated and child-centred over the course of the early nineteenth
century; an eighteenth-century model which emphasized child-bearing
as an elite wife's principal duty was replaced by one in which child-rearing
was seen as both paramount and a lifelong responsibility. Domesticity
(aided by evangelicalism) had become the rule by the 1810s or 1820s, and
most memoirs, diaries and letters reveal loving and attentive parents who
wished to provide their offspring with happy childhoods even while
instilling religious, moral, and class values and social skills. Louisa Yorke,
gentry mother of two in Erddig, often played with her sons and, when
their nanny was sick, took over in the nursery.[7] In 1825, when the Countess
of Gower went abroad with her husband and was separated from her first
child, she wrote to her sister:

My dearest Caroline, the parting with one's child is most dreadful . . .

You have no idea of the treasure her little likeness is to us; we have it out and look at it constantly when by ourselves. I tell you all these things because I know you will not think them affected and would feel them very much the same *à ma place*.[8]

While upper-class mothers were more involved with their babies and young children than were upper-class fathers, parents on the whole were relieved of the messy and tedious aspects of child-rearing. Separate nurseries and staff should not, however, deceive us into confusing a lack of physical labour for the absence of physical or emotional intimacy. Elite mothers spent much time with their children, breast-feeding, overseeing the nursery, and teaching reading and religion while their children were young. Later on, both parents took a serious view of their children's marriages; mothers would manage their daughters' comings-out into London Society, and many adult women participated in the Season only when it would benefit their children.

Aristocratic and gentlewomen were to varying degrees involved in housekeeping and estate management, overseeing and even participating in housework. Women in the wealthiest and most powerful families would generally delegate day-to-day responsibilities to their staff; the more modest the household, the more likely that its mistress would be directly involved in its smooth running (many smaller estates employed no housekeeper, and one in ten had only a few female servants). No aristocratic household was left entirely to the staff; the mistress might meet daily with the housekeeper, keep the household accounts, pay bills, order food and other supplies, and plan menus. When her family moved from one property to another, as happened seasonally for many, she managed the smooth transfer of goods and servants. When the family entertained, the mistress oversaw the extensive planning necessary as well as the event itself.

Women were very important to the running of the estate; while they received little formal recognition, they were usually substantially involved in the family's economic enterprises, and found this a meaningful occupation and a valuable source of self-identification. In addition, women were responsible for providing social events for the staff in their households, tenants on their estates, and voters in their areas, ranging from celebrations on the coming-of-age of the heir to Christmas and rent-day festivities. In all these ways aristocratic women were responsible for the family's role as employer, landlord, and political representative.

In her role as mistress of the house, the aristocratic woman was also an employer. She hired, paid, supervised, and fired most of the family's staff, which might be quite large. When the Sutherlands came to their London home in 1841 they were attended by forty or so servants.[9] This meant that aristocratic women had power over the working lives of others. They had a tendency to intrude into the lives of those in their employ (preferring, for example, unmarried servants), and their references were crucial to any hope of future employment; the refusal to provide a 'character' would make it nearly impossible for a departing employee to obtain a new position. Conversely, ladies could be of much help to their servants or other young women on the estate in finding employment elsewhere (almost always in service). Some ladies even provided suitable outfits for job-seekers; Lucy Arkwright helped young girls to find their first places as servants. Lady Jersey and the second Duchess of Sutherland both founded servants' training schools on their estates. The Marchioness of Buckingham started the straw-hat industry in Essex as a way of creating work for women, and the field later became a profitable one.[10] The influence of aristocratic women over those below them on the social scale was of course not confined to their power over their servants. On the estate and in the surrounding local community, aristocratic families were expected to provide for 'their' poor, regardless of personal inclination. Philanthropy was for them an unavoidable duty. This had its roots in older traditions of paternalism as well as newer sources of inspiration such as evangelicalism and separate-spheres ideology. Ladies took their social duties seriously, and were often quite deeply involved in charity, education, and the church on their country estates and in London, although their activities contrasted markedly with the work of middle-class women in similar realms.

Most aristocratic philanthropy was proffered in a fairly haphazard and intensely personal way. While middle-class women tended to create and maintain highly organized systems of charity, aristocratic women usually dispensed money, food, clothing and advice to their own poor without any structured programme. While they might be assisted by their daughters (who were also being trained for their own adult duties) or other relations, they reported to no board, formed no committees, and kept no records. They also tended to focus their charitable activities on their own estates and villages rather than on London or provincial urban areas.

Like middle-class women, aristocratic women believed that face-to-face interactions between charitable donor and recipient were a crucial way of having a positive influence over the poor. Visits to the sick and the poor were a central part of their efforts, and they usually knew the needy on their estates better than middle-class visitors to the urban poor. While some view the highly personal style of the nineteenth-century 'Lady Bountiful' as an attempt at benevolent social control and as crucial to the maintenance of patriarchal dominance and plebeian deference, others are less suspicious of elite women's good intentions.

The discharging of duty took several forms. Unlike middle-class women, aristocratic women were mistresses of large estates and possessors of individual wealth. They could use their kitchens and gardens to provide for the needy by having surplus food saved and soup made for the poor. When the American heiress Consuelo Vanderbilt married into the British aristocracy in 1895 and became Duchess of Marlborough, she discovered that she was responsible for putting the remains of each day's lunch into large tins for the poor (she was the first duchess to take the time to put separate courses into separate tins). Young girls might be expected to carry soup to cottagers in their homes. The mistress of the estate would also give away old clothing, have shawls, petticoats, and Sunday-school frocks made for the deserving, and even make items herself on occasion, especially layettes for new-born babies. Aristocratic women would also provide bedding and medicine for sick cottagers if necessary. While in London, they organized balls and parties to support various charities. They also joined middle-class women in visiting the poor in workhouses, prisons, hospitals, and homes for fallen women, as well as in their homes, and were in demand on charity boards and as patronesses and stallholders of charity bazaars. Such work had its appeal, especially for sheltered young women, and by the end of the nineteenth century 'slumming' was a typical part of the seasonal London whirl.[11]

Religion was a key field in which the relationships of aristocratic women to the wider world were played out. While maintaining their state church affiliations – most belonged to the Churches of England, Scotland, and Ireland – many elite women embraced active evangelicalism during the late eighteenth and early nineteenth centuries. For example, Sarah Trimmer was a devotee of Hannah More's writings on elite women as moral examplars. Countess Spencer helped to make religious and philanthropic training fashionable for elite girls. Lady Westminster transformed her son, Lord Robert Grosvenor, from a roué into a leading evangelical politician.[12] As part of their evangelicalism, aristocratic women came to celebrate domesticity and to focus on the religious education of children, both their own and those of the poor for whom they felt responsible. They also supported local and village schools and the poor children who attended them. Some founded and financed their own and even taught at Sunday school; in the 1870s, Ishbel Marjoribanks taught at a London Sunday school (until her marriage made her the Countess of Aberdeen).[13]

The emphasis of evangelicalism on good works and proselytizing may have appealed to some women from the aristocracy because it provided an alternative model of public action to the narrow political one in which their husbands participated. The publication of Hannah More's 1809 novel *Coelebs in Search of a Wife* inspired much charitable work by gentry and aristocratic women, who took to heart its message that they were the natural moral leaders of England. Even those who did not admire More conceded her great influence; Lucy Aiken wrote to a friend in the United States that:

> It has always been the practice of the better kind of country ladies to distribute benefactions among the cottagers ... but Hannah More in her *Coelebs*, by representing her *pattern* young lady as regularly devoting two evenings a week to making her rounds among the village poor, unfortunately made it a fashionable and a rage.[14]

More's work encouraged elite women to take their personal moral values seriously and to extend their public influence, and was therefore attractive to many.[15] After her conversion to evangelical religion Marianne Francis (1790–1832, a niece of the well-known novelist Fanny Burney) read *Coelebs* 'with great delight'. The daughter of fellow-evangelical Arthur Young wrote that Francis and Young would often take 'a two hours' walk on the turnpike road to some cottage or other, and they take milk at some farmhouse; and [Miss Francis] distributes tracts (religious ones), and questions people about their principles, and reads to them and catechises them.'[16]

Many elite women's understanding of their traditional duties was coloured by evangelical notions of women's special fitness for charitable work and of the large sphere of public activism envisioned by evangelicalism. The relationships of aristocratic women to the churches they attended was distinctly marked by their class; they were the principal patrons or prominent attenders of their rural parish churches, or of fashionable churches in London. They were often the socio-economic superiors of their clergy and were frequently involved in deciding who to appoint to the family's church livings. In 1871 Lady Constance Stanley invited her clergyman for dinner and took the opportunity to instruct him on what she would like to hear on future Sundays: 'I had an opportunity of saying I liked short sermons & quick service & I advised the leaving out of the Litany.'[17] Aristocratic women might be deeply religious, even evangelical, faithful churchgoers, and religiously-inspired philanthropists, but in their endeavours they were far less likely than other women to be subordinate to the non-elite men with whom they worked. At the same time, evangelical elite women often tried to convert family and friends, with mixed success – Caroline, Georgiana, and Blanche Howard influenced their husbands and children, but their mother Lady Carlisle and their uncle the sixth Duke of Devonshire were never persuaded.[18]

POLITICS

Aristocratic women were perhaps most unlike other women in their ability to act politically. Middle- and working-class women were involved in a variety of extra-parliamentary political activities, but were denied direct input into parliamentary politics even as the men of their classes obtained the vote in the Reform Acts of 1832, 1867 and 1884. At the elite level, however, politics were eminently susceptible to female input. Even as some protested 'petticoat politics', women canvassed, visited, and influenced patronage. Before 1832 it was custom, not law, that prevented property-owning women from voting, and there is scattered evidence that some single women and widows may have voted, and that other women who owned property appointed male relatives as proxies to cast their votes. In some places women seem to have had at least the potential for direct involvement in politics and until the 1830s they had some rights in the local electoral process.[19]

Even after that date many elite women took an active role in elections. Before the election of 1868, Mrs E. H. Bruton wrote a note to each of her tenants that simply stated: 'SIR – I request you will vote for my father, J. W. S. Erle-Drax, Esq., on receipt of this.' Such a direct request indicates that Mrs Bruton saw such a demand as entirely within her prerogative. More rarely, requests might be less direct (though no less obvious) and accompanied by greater ceremony. Also in 1868, Mrs Gwynne Holford paid visits to electors in the borough which her son was contesting.

Arriving at modest country cottages in an elaborate carriage drawn by four horses and attended by several servants, she explained to 'each poor man and his wife [that] no one who served a Gwynne *ever* had cause to repent it'. Her visit was followed by the delivery of a food basket. The message could not have been lost on voters or their wives that Mrs Gwynne Holford expected her electoral request to be honoured.[20]

The most brazen female aristocratic canvasser was Georgiana, Duchess of Devonshire (1757–1806), who in 1784 helped her friend Charles James Fox to campaign for a Westminster seat. The Duchess was a glamorous woman and an extremely visible canvasser, who was at one point accused of kissing butchers in exchange for their votes. She was attacked quite viciously in the press for this, especially in cartoons which depicted her as sexually voracious. While her behaviour in the public sphere made her notorious to contemporaries and historians alike, her presence there was not controversial, and many Whig men encouraged her to continue her canvassing in the face of a hostile press. Female electioneering was not only condoned but was seen as part of a woman's responsibility to her family.

In addition to public canvassing, women could write letters on behalf of candidates. They could also socialize, usually by visiting or giving dinners. During election years, the female relatives of candidates for office, or female patrons who controlled seats, visited the female relatives of voters and dined with aldermen. Where a parliamentary seat or clerical post was controlled by their families, women could influence patronage decisions. Perhaps 10 per cent were landowners in their own right and made their own choice of candidates. And most of the fashionable elite were always interested in gossip or 'news'.[21]

Another way in which aristocratic women interacted with others of their class was in their participation in Society and their use of the London Season, which served as an annual period of entertainment, culture, and conspicuous consumption, for political purposes. During the Season (which coincided with the parliamentary session and, by the end of the eighteenth century, kept families in town from January to July), politicking took place in social settings. Corresponding with large networks of friends, relations, and acquaintances, and hosting literary and political salons, were both important aspects of this. In general socializing was, for the elite, another venue in which the political could be debated, and resolved, and it was a part of life largely controlled by women.

Lady Charlotte Guest's journal records a week in June of 1852:

Monday – dinner and dance at the Londonderry's
Tuesday – ball at Lady Cavendish's
Wednesday – concert Landsdowne House
Thursday – French play
Friday – Maria's fête for 8th birthday. Duchess of Bedford presided
    at tea table for adults. Dined Lady Kinnoull's
Saturday – dinner Duke of Somerset's[22]

Such busy social schedules must have been typical for many elite women.

The Season was also a marriage market for the younger members of Society. While it was considered important that young men and women should choose their own partners, this was effected by the maintenance of controlled social events – many during the Season – at which young people only met others of acceptable backgrounds. Within this limited field, they were expected to make an appropriate choice of partner based in part on love.

One of the most important ways in which aristocratic women could engage in social politics during the Season was by acting as political hostesses. Until the start of the First World War, virtually all politicians were aristocrats, and upper-class socializing – from daytime visits to dinners to grand balls – was inevitably political. In Anthony Trollope's novel *Phineas Finn* (1869), Lady Laura Standish is described as having 'semi-social and semi-political' evening gatherings. Home and politics overlapped gracefully and perhaps inevitably at this social level. Parties and other social activities were a key part of the milieu in which politicians operated and much of the socializing that took place at home was more from political duty than personal preference. Some of the most important political hostesses of the late eighteenth century were Ladies Hervey, Salisbury, Liverpool, and Mansfield, the Marchioness of Stafford, and the Duchesses of Rutland and Gordon. In the nineteenth century the Whig Ladies Holland, Palmerston, Molesworth, and Waldegrave, and the Tory Ladies Jersey, Londonderry, and Dorothy Nevill were hostesses not simply in the service of their husbands' careers but of their political parties. Emily Palmerston once received the news that votes were needed to support her husband's ministry with the spirited declaration, 'Stay! We will have a party!'[23] Lady Nevill reminded various political men that 'You know how discreet I am,' and many confided in her.[24] Her Sunday luncheons were political salons well-attended by artists, journalists, Liberals and even Radicals, as well as Tories. While it is difficult to measure

precisely these women's influence on high traditional politics, it is clear
that their contemporaries respected the political power such women
wielded.

In a tightly-knit community that was at once social and political,
society hostesses were well placed to exert their influence; but as the
growing franchise broadened the political nation, after 1880 this form
of socializing became a less effective political tool. Even so, hostessing
opportunities remained: after the split over Home Rule of 1886, the
Unionist faction of the Liberal Party gathered at Devonshire House in
Piccadilly, while Tory ministers assembled at Lansdowne House in Berkeley Square. Grosvenor House was the base of operations for opponents
of the 1909 Budget and House of Lords reform.[25] However, as the end of
the century approached, with the democratization of society and politics,
there were signs of the decline of the aristocracy as a closed social elite. A
young woman's presentation to the Queen was a good indication that her
family participated in Society, or intended to do so. During the last third
of the nineteenth century, the number of women presented at court
increased dramatically, while the proportion whose families were aristocratic (rather than gentry, professional, industrial, or otherwise previously unsuitable) dropped from 72 per cent in 1841 to 24 per cent in
1891. Apparently, those contemporaries who complained, as did Hamilton
Aide in 1890, that '[t]he "upper ten thousand" ... ought to be called the
"upper million", were perceiving a real decline in the insularity of the
British landed establishment.[26]

The deterioration of this previously small and well-defined social group
was part of a larger transformation of England's political culture. As
Society became more socially and economically diverse, various political
changes (including the Second and Third Reform Acts in 1867 and 1884
and the rise of middle-class men in national politics) weakened the
hegemony of aristocratic political culture in which elite women enjoyed
informal but crucial access to politics. They retained social and cultural
influence, but not political power.

By 1884 Britain had achieved almost universal male suffrage. However,
the Corrupt Practices Act (1883) made the payment of canvassers illegal,
and so women came into their own as volunteer canvassers. The new laws
about electioneering heralded a new organization of party politics that
made it possible for some upper-class women to use their skills as organizers and as charitable visitors in the service of politics. In the 1880s, the
parties formed women's auxiliaries. The Tory Primrose League had a

separate Ladies' Grand Council, whose members were elite women; women also worked alongside men in local groups called 'habitations'. The Primrose League was the most successful of the party auxiliaries at harnessing elite women's skills to party interests. This was partly because the League tried to avoid controversial issues and direct ties to the Conservative Party, preferring to wield indirect influence and to use social events to political ends. These methods fitted squarely into traditions of female aristocratic power. The League especially welcomed upper-class women, and titled members came to include Jenny and Clementine Churchill – the future Prime Minister's mother and wife – the Duchess of Newcastle, the Countesses of Jersey, Malmesbury, and Shrewsbury, and Lady Gwendolen Cecil. The League also had many rank-and-file female members from the middle and working classes.

While the Ladies' Grand Council was clearly subsidiary to the (male) Grand Council, aristocratic women were often financial officers, public speakers, and leaders of their local habitations. Just as women's charitable work had been represented not as a public activity but as an extension of womanly influence in the private sphere, this female political activity was promoted as an extension of appropriate female duties. The Primrose League consistently dissociated itself from turn-of-the-century militant feminism (although some local habitations held debates on women's suffrage) and emphasized the womanly qualities of its 'Dames'.

The Primrose League was far more successful than its liberal equivalent, the Women's Liberal Federation (WLF), perhaps because its activities capitalized upon the traditional skills of elite women. One of their main duties as Primrose League members was to volunteer as unpaid door-to-door canvassers for the Tory Party; as many contemporaries noted, aristocratic ladies were well-suited to the job by charitable visiting, which gave them the skills to charm listeners and the traditional right to enter working-class homes. The Primrose League also held many local social events, a duty to which aristocratic and gentry women were accustomed and at which they excelled.[27]

While the nineteenth-century cult of domesticity made aristocratic women more centred on their homes and families, they were not constrained by strict middle-class evangelical domesticity; rather, they were empowered by the message of evangelicalism to engage with the public sphere even as they broadened it. Although definitively subordinate to the men of their class, many of whom mocked women's claims to political influence, aristocratic women wielded power over women and men of other classes, as mistresses, employers, philanthropists, hostesses and patrons. They also worked effectively, if indirectly, before and during democratization, in local and parliamentary politics.

Royal women

Curiously, male-dominated English society has a long history of prominent royal women, including rulers. This tradition stretches back to Queen Elizabeth in the sixteenth century and Queen Anne in the early eighteenth century. In the long nineteenth century, the women of the royal family came to figure centrally in the national imagination. That the feminization of the monarchy was contemporaneous with the development of a popular press and of industrialized mass production meant that images of female royalty reached a wide public. The prominence and idealization of female royalty in Britain helped to make a distinctively female form of patriotism possible while providing women of all backgrounds with a way to celebrate their domestic roles as daughters, wives, and mothers.

As the first women in the land, royal women served as political and domestic symbols of conflicting hopes and fears about women and about the nation. Politicians, writers, producers of souvenirs and memorabilia, and the public projected their political needs and cultural fantasies on to them. The modern cult of royal women began with George III's consort Charlotte and continued with her namesake, George IV's daughter Princess Charlotte, whose death at a young age was nationally grieved. George's wife, Queen Caroline, enjoyed notoriety and extensive support from radicals and women of all classes and political persuasions before fading from public view and dying in ignominy. Caroline's niece and Charlotte's first cousin, Victoria, inherited the throne and ruled the country for sixty-five years. Recently scholars have sought to make an understanding of Victoria central to an understanding of gender and power during the period that bears her name.

QUEEN CHARLOTTE

George III's queen, born Princess Sophia Charlotte of Mecklenburg-Strelitz (1744–1818), has received less scholarly attention than her daughter-in-law Caroline or her granddaughters Charlotte and Victoria. Those who do not dismiss her as a hard German princess believe that she was a quiet and domestic woman whose chief accomplishment was her large family. While she was the mother of thirteen, her presentation of herself as virtuous and maternal was also key to the politics of the monarchy.

George III's marriage was different from those of the previous two Georges, in that it was happy and faithful (and lasted for the whole of his effective reign (1761–1810)). But this truth was especially important in a broader political context: together with her husband, Charlotte was the first Queen to embark on the project of portraying the royal family as domestic, familial, and familiar. Cartoons mocking the Queen as a frugal housewife seemed to attack her, but in another sense prove that her presentation was convincing.

Charlotte's main emphasis was on the royal family as first and foremost a family and on herself as a virtuous woman, the King's partner, and an idealized mother. From the 1780s the family attended church in Windsor every Sunday and greeted the assembled townspeople after the service; lining the route from St George's Chapel to the Royal Lodge became a local tradition. Whenever a new clergyman was installed Charlotte was present next to the King on a throne in the sanctuary, rather than looking on from a balcony as her predecessor had done.[28]

Charlotte had many portraits painted of herself as a mother. One excellent example is that from Benjamin West's pair of portraits of the King and Queen, from the late 1770s. While the King appears against a background of soldiers and cannon, the Queen is depicted – just as regally – with her many children. Simultaneously grand and maternal, deemed 'a pattern of domestic virtue'[29] by The Times in 1789, she must have been a role model for more typical English women who were exhausted by frequent childbirth and large families.

That she was popular was made clear in 1789, when the King recovered from his first bout of mentally-incapacitating illness. Fully one-fourth of the addresses sent on this occasion were to the Queen herself.[30] She was the wife of the King and the mother of the nation.

PRINCESS CHARLOTTE

Queen Charlotte's granddaughter, Princess Charlotte Augusta of Wales, was born in 1796, the only child of the Prince of Wales (later George IV) and his wife Caroline of Brunswick. Because she was heir presumptive to the British throne, the young Princess was always politically significant. This is evident in the press coverage that attended her first engagement to William of Orange and her subsequent marriage to Leopold of Saxe-Coburg (later the King of Belgium and a favourite uncle and adviser to Queen Victoria). Charlotte's rejection of William in 1814, which she claimed was based on the fact that the marriage would have forced her to spend time away from England, was used by the radical press to embarrass her father, an unpopular ruler who had favoured and arranged the match. Whig and radical opponents of the government wrote about the Regent's oppression of his daughter as a way of drawing attention to other forms of government oppression.[31]

Charlotte's decision was used to position her as a national and nation-alist heroine to Britons of all classes. She was depicted in popular prints with, or as, Britannia. Similarly, her 1816 marriage to Leopold, a suitor of her own choosing, was interpreted as a triumph of British liberty and of national pride. Charlotte had stood up to her father and her advisers and had made a happy marriage, unlike that of her parents, and was to pave the way for her own stable and domestic reign. In both alliances, the stakes were simultaneously domestic and political, and newspaper and print coverage reflected this conflation.

But a long and happy life as a British wife and mother and a queen of England was not to be Charlotte's fate. In the autumn of 1817, at the age of twenty-one, she died in childbirth. Harriet Granville noted in a letter to her sister Lady Georgiana Morpeth:

> I feel quite unable to write upon any subject but one. We are all heart sick at this terrible event. Poor Princess Charlotte ... She bore her whole labour with a patience and courage that were quite heroic. It is true that she never shrunk or complained but only held out her hand to him [Prince Leopold] and pressed it when the suffering was great. It is said that ... [her] constitution was in so bad a state that she could not possibly have lived long.[32]

Charlotte's death introduced significant problems of royal succession and sent the Prince's brothers (none of them young men) scrambling to trade their mistresses for wives in a sudden race to provide a new heir (the Duke of Kent won when his wife gave birth to Princess Victoria in 1819). It also changed the nature of obstetric practice in Britain; after all, the Princess had died while receiving the best care possible. After her death, obstetricians (who mainly served elite women; most births were attended by midwives) were far more likely to intervene in births and hasten them where they could.[33]

The entire nation mourned Charlotte's death. Churches all over England, including local parish churches, conducted funeral services; the day's sermons, in which the Princess was described as a moral exemplar, were published soon after. Many commemorative poems were written and published in the months after the Princess's death and continued to appear even years later (for instance, Letitia Elizabeth Landon's poem of 1833, 'Princess Charlotte'). In addition, a tremendous amount of mass-produced memorabilia, including memorial cards, imprinted mourning ribbons, handkerchiefs, tea services, and jewellery was manufactured, indicating the creation and existence of a large group of consumers who commemorated Charlotte's death through the purchase of such items. Mourning rings containing locks of hair were popular in the first part of the nineteenth century; here they were used to commemorate a princess rather than a family member. Such jewellery recalls the Christian reliquary tradition, and indeed Charlotte was, in material culture and printed works, often portrayed as the Madonna herself. James Wyatt's monumental sculpture of the dead princess installed in St George's Chapel at Windsor also recalls earlier images of the Virgin Mary's assumption into Heaven.

The historian Linda Colley argues that part of the importance of the female royals from the early nineteenth century to the present has been their ability to serve as Protestant or secular substitutes for older cults of the Virgin, and that in her early death Charlotte was the first to do so.[34] The Charlotte memorabilia reveal not so much a national memory of Charlotte herself as a national cult of the death of Charlotte. This cult created a national community of sympathy, and as such was politically important (as well as being quite profitable for purveyors of mass-produced memorial ephemera). The British government may also have used the nation's grief over Charlotte's death to distract the populace from an unpopular ruler, a tenuous government, widespread calls for political reform, and the popular oppositional politics of the mass radical platforms. The political and cultural uses to which Princess Charlotte's life and death were put were tremendous and far-reaching.[35]

In 1820 (three years after Charlotte died) Caroline of Brunswick returned to England upon the death of her father-in-law, George III, to be crowned Queen alongside her husband. The Regent, who had for some time wished to be rid of the wife he had never loved, was outraged. The Queen Caroline Affair, including the Queen's trial for divorce before the House of Lords, her acquittal, and the popular support she received, will be discussed more extensively in Chapter 8. Here it is worth noting that many of the politicians and writers who had supported Charlotte as a way of attacking the Regent and his government now rallied to Caroline with the same end. And indeed, the forms of support daughter and mother received, from both radical politicians and women of all classes, are comparable. Caroline was also held up as the paragon of British motherhood and a virtuous spouse (however tenuous such arguments in her case), and was the subject of addresses, ballads, chapbooks, and political cartoons. Caroline's funeral, like that of her daughter, was a national cultural event. Both were part of a new fascination with royal women, both had their lives pressed into the service of larger cultural narratives of political freedom and domestic virtue, and both died young.

QUEEN VICTORIA

As the person who ruled Britain and its Empire for sixty-five years, Queen Victoria (1819–1901) was in some ways the most important woman of the nineteenth century. And yet one could also argue that she was a mere figurehead. She reigned over Britain, it is true, but by the end of her life this meant much less politically than it once had. As the monarch of an increasingly democratic nation, and as the female ruler of a male political system, Victoria is easy to dismiss. And yet she kept her throne while many other European rulers lost theirs. Celebrations of her reign were astonishingly popular. Her image was ubiquitous. What, then, are we to make of Victoria Regina et (after 1877) Imperatrix? We can begin by investigating her seriously, rather than taking her for granted; as the literary critic Margaret Homans points out, 'We use the word "Victorian" without thinking about Queen Victoria; her name designates a diffuse global culture before it designates a person who once lived, wrote, and made aesthetic judgements.'[36]

The Princess Alexandrina Victoria was born in 1819 and ascended to the British throne in 1837 upon the death of her uncle, William IV. She was awakened before dawn on 20 June 1837 and received the Archbishop of Canterbury and the Lord Chamberlain still in her nightgown; as she recorded in her journal, they informed her 'that my poor Uncle, the King, was no more ... and consequently that I am *Queen*.'[37] She married her German cousin, Prince Albert of Saxe-Coburg-Gotha, in 1840. Because of Victoria's rank, the marriage proposal had to come from her, prompting a broadsheet poem that reveals contemporary anxieties about what it meant for a woman to stand higher than any man:

> Since the Queen did herself for a husband 'propose',
> The ladies will all do the same, I suppose;
> Their days of subserviency now will be past,
> For all will 'speak first' as they always did last!
> Since the Queen has no equal, 'obey' none she need,
> So of course at the altar from such vow she's freed;
> And the women will all follow suit, so they say –
> 'Love, honour', they'll promise, but never – 'obey'.
> Our cups to the dregs in a health let us drain
> And wish them a long and a prosperous reign;
> Like good loyal subjects, in loud chorus sing
> Victoria's wedding, with Albert her king![38]

Albert was by all accounts a loving spouse. He believed in the responsibilities of the throne and encouraged Victoria's desire to act as patron and to subscribe to many philanthropic endeavours. By 1851 she was contributing to over two hundred charities, including schools, hospitals, and asylums; in 1882 she gave away almost £11,000.[39]

Like other elite women, Victoria spent a large portion of her adult life pregnant: she had nine children in the first eighteen years of her marriage. (The Queen was in favour of wet-nurses and was upset when two of her daughters chose to breast-feed their babies.[40]) Her insistence on obstetric anaesthesia in 1853 during the birth of her eighth child, Prince Leopold, made the use of chloroform respectable among the aristocracy. Her husband's death in 1861 devastated her; she secluded herself at Osborne House on the Isle of Wight, was unwilling to perform most of her ceremonial duties, and was rarely seen in public for over a decade thereafter (although the London papers printed daily reports of her activities and she made many prison and hospital visits). She definitively returned to public life in 1872 when she attended the thanksgiving service for the recovery of the Prince of Wales from serious illness, was crowned Empress of India in 1877, was fêted at the jubilees of 1887 and 1897 (celebrating the fiftieth and sixtieth years of her reign), and died in 1901 at the age of eighty-one.

The problem of a female monarch – who answered to no man – in an age when women had no formal political rights, were socially subordinate to men, and were legally subordinate to their husbands – was a perplexing one to contemporaries (as the above poem indicates). But while on the face of it this seems an unresolvable conflict or irony, in some ways a married woman was the ideal person to have on the throne during this period of change. Historians agree that the British monarchy survived the nation's transition to parliamentary democracy because it was represented as middle-class, domestic, and patriotic, and because it became a public spectacle.[41] Victoria was the key to this success: she was an excellent performer when she chose to be, and as a women she was easily made to seem both ordinary and an object of display.

The successful depiction of the royal family as middle class was made easier by the fact that the monarch was a wife and mother and therefore tended to be projected as unthreatening, typical, and domestic, however inaccurate such portrayals may have been. Representation of the Queen and her family as ordinary were important to the survival of the monarchy into the twentieth century. The emphasis in the press and elsewhere on the glamorous and yet typical episodes in the Queen's life, such as her wedding and the births of her children, imbued the same events in lives of other British women with larger meaning.

Scholars have recently noted the resemblances between nineteenth-century conceptions of the monarch's role and that of a middle-class wife. Both were to refrain from ruling or leading but were expected to offer advice; Walter Bagehot's influential treatise, on *The English Constitution* (1867), argued that the monarchy was one of the 'dignified' parts of government, that its political rights were 'the right to be consulted, the right to encourage, the right to warn',[42] and that the monarch had a duty to be theatrical and ornamental, and so to uphold British stability. The Queen's role, then, was to entertain her people, to advise her ministers, and to refrain from direct action: in some ways Bagehot's description of the monarch's proper role was simply an application of separate-spheres language about women and men's roles to Crown and Parliament. Where a male ruler might have seemed to conflict with Parliament, Victoria always seemed merely to influence it.

Rather than being a problematic figure or figurehead, then, Victoria, as mother, wife and widow, was the ideal sovereign to lead her country into an age of stable parliamentary democracy while maintaining the strength of her throne. We can explore Victoria's role as queen during this complex period of transition by examining the Bedchamber crisis early in her reign, her decade of seclusion following Albert's death, including her opening of Parliament in 1866 and her obsessive memorializing of the Prince Consort, and the Thanksgiving and Jubilee celebrations of the second half of her reign.

Only two years after Victoria came to the throne, her favourite adviser and the leader of the Whig government, Lord Melbourne, lost his majority in the House of Commons and was forced to resign. The Queen reluctantly summoned Tory leaders, first the Duke of Wellington and then Robert Peel. Peel had every right to expect that, as leader of a new government, he would be entitled to ask her to replace the Whig ladies who were members of her royal household with women from Tory families: positions in the royal household were understood as political appointments that changed with the administration. The Queen, however, asserted that her ladies of the Bedchamber were personal friends; that she never discussed politics with them; and that even though she was the sovereign, when at home she was not political. Victoria's refusal to yield on this point forced the Whigs and Lord Melbourne back into office for two more years.

By standing up to Peel as a girl of nineteen, Victoria asserted herself as sovereign and made her wishes politically felt. However, her victory was based on an affirmation of royal prerogative that was also an assertion of herself and her house as female and apolitical. Peel argued that a monarch had no private life separate from affairs of state, but Victoria rejected that claim. She insisted that even as queen her household was a separate, domestic sphere that was immune to, and a respite from, political intrigue.

The strategy used by the Queen during the Bedchamber crisis affected perceptions of her household throughout her reign; appointments to the royal household subsequently were seen as apolitical and dependent on family connections.[43] Victoria used these offices as opportunities to distribute patronage to aristocratic ladies in need, who could thereby be assured of an income as well as a residence for much of the year. She insisted that the women who served in her household be unmarried (just as aristocratic women themselves preferred unmarried servants in their households). Some single and widowed women served in the court for many years, and it became a substitute family and female community for them. The *London Gazette* reported their activities daily for public consumption and emphasized their decorative role (although the fact that their comings and goings were on the front page of the newspaper demonstrates how public their allegedly private household activities were). The domesticity of the court was used to disguise how active the Queen was in governing the country (and to mask her political disagreements with Prime Minister Gladstone in the 1880s). Court domesticity also disguised the degree to which members of the female royal household could in fact reinforce the Queen's political preferences.[44]

The ladies of the Queen's household became a political issue again during her self-imposed seclusion following her husband's death. During this period, Victoria used her ladies as go-betweens, and some, most notably Lady Ely, Horatia Stopford, and Harriet Phipps, came to be recognized as her political agents. But by the time the Queen returned to public life in the 1870s, the monarchy had been transformed from a political institution into a ceremonial one, and so the question of who had political access to her became less highly charged.

One reason that the royal household was an issue during the Queen's seclusion was because of her refusal to conduct public business. This created great political difficulties and anxieties in Britain, partly because of the Queen's gender. As a woman, Victoria was expected to grieve and to be incapacitated following her husband's death. As a monarch, however, she was expected to continue carrying out her political and ceremonial duties. That she refused to do so caused considerable consternation; Victoria was derisively referred to as 'the widow at Windsor' and was called upon to abdicate in favour of her son. The republican movement to abolish the monarchy, which was strongest in the 1860s and early 1870s, was motivated in part by the Queen's abdication, not of her crown but of what was seen as her duty to be visible and visibly public-spirited.[45]

Interestingly, Victoria did not simply disappear from public life between 1861 and 1872; instead, she provided continuous evidence of her widowhood by her constant dedication of various national and local shrines to Albert's memory. These included a cairn; an English national memorial on the site of the Crystal Palace; Welsh, Scots, and Irish national memorials; the Hyde Park memorial; and commemorative sculptures, windows and paintings in various towns and cities all over Britain. Royal memorials included busts and full-size sculptures for the various royal residences, the mausoleum in the grounds of Frogmore in Windsor Home Park, an indoor statue for Balmoral, and the Albert Memorial Chapel in Windsor Castle. Typical of the royal memorials, the Memorial Chapel in Windsor portrays Albert in effigy and the Queen mourning him. In her obsession, Victoria portrayed not Albert's life (he had requested 'not a single marble image in my name'[46]) but his death and her own grief.

Just as she performed her mourning, Victoria also dramatized her reluctance to appear in public. Newspaper notices of her activities continued to appear daily and to emphasize how infrequently the Queen left home. They did not, however, report the political work she did, reading and signing documents out of the public view. When she grudgingly agreed to open Parliament in 1866 (as she was expected to do every year), she refused to wear her crown or robes of state or to read her speech; the Lord Chancellor read it for her, while she sat with her royal robes draped behind her on her throne. Rather than simply becoming invisible, Victoria acted out her own refusal to perform. The gap that opened in the 1860s between Victoria as queen and Victoria as grieving widow helped to complete the process by which the monarchy was rendered emblematic.[47] Victoria the widow Queen was wholly symbolic; when she returned to her public duties in 1872, it was as the ceremonial ruler of her people.

When Edward Albert, the Prince of Wales, recovered from a serious illness in February of that year, Prime Minister Gladstone (of whom the Queen was not fond) convinced Victoria that her attendance at a service of thanksgiving was necessary and important. Indeed, her appearance at St Paul's Cathedral was a turning point. The thanksgiving service (and the Queen's gracious willingness to perform in it) was an opportunity for public celebration that brought Victoria back into favour and silenced the republicanism of the 1860s. This new emphasis on a spectacular monarchy was reinforced throughout the rest of Victoria's life, with her coronation as Empress of India in 1877, her Golden and Diamond Jubilees of 1887 and 1897, and even with her funeral. The Crown was seen to personify the British nation and its Empire, rather than ruling over them.

Like the thanksgiving service, the Jubilees were gorgeous pageants, celebrations of Victoria's reign, of nation, and of empire. For her Golden Jubilee the Queen rode in an open carriage from Buckingham Palace to Westminster Abbey, escorted by Indian cavalry whose presence emphasized Britain's imperial power. She then appeared on the balcony of Buckingham Palace to be cheered by an enormous crowd and watch a fireworks display. The Golden Jubilee was marked by the use of advertising, souvenirs, memorabilia, and quotidian objects of all sorts featuring the Queen's face or coat of arms, including portraits, embroidered samplers, rugs, plates, cups, toys, dolls, bracelets, and scent bottles.[48] At the Diamond Jubilee, too, the Queen travelled through London, waving to ecstatic crowds over a six-mile route that took her over London Bridge and through south London, back over Westminster Bridge, and past the Houses of Parliament to the Palace. The Queen was a willing participant in both events, if mainly as a spectacle whom her subjects were eager to see. People stood for hours to get a glimpse of Victoria as she passed by. The monarchy came to be defined by these gigantic festive ceremonial occasions, which celebrated Britain's prosperity and stability and the Queen as the embodiment of the nation's success. As the monarchy became more ceremonial and less political, and as it came to be seen as proof of the nation's prosperity rather than an integral part of that prosperity, so it became ever more commodified (as had the death of Princess Charlotte).

Victoria's uncles had undoubtedly wielded more direct political power than she, and this was probably connected to their gender as well as to the period of their rule. The late nineteenth century's great statesman, William E. Gladstone, also wielded more power than the Queen he served. But, tellingly, Victoria's funeral was more spectacular and offered more cause for public mourning than his.[49] Victoria presided over a surprisingly successful transformation of both the monarchy and the country. Like the women of the aristocracy, she adapted to changes in England's political culture. Under Victoria, the British monarchy evolved into something less powerful but in some ways no less potent: the embodiment of Britain.

Victoria's role as queen also spoke to the lives of more typical English women. As we shall see in Chapter 8, all English women had a complex relationship with politics. They too were often more important as symbols than as actors, yet were never wholly barred from the political sphere. Furthermore, the representations of Victoria as domestic that were so crucial to the survival of the monarchy relied on the associations they suggested between the Queen and her female subjects. The Queen was, it was implied, virtuous insofar as she obeyed the same standards of respectability as other women. While she was not subject to the same economic, political, and social limitations faced by most women, her life was shaped by the fact that she was a 'Victorian' woman, just as nineteenth-century English women's lives were shaped by her reign.

PART TWO

Bodies, Souls and Minds

4

Sexuality

DISCUSSING WOMEN AS sexual beings is more difficult than it might appear. You might expect that the topic of sexuality would unite all women: women are defined as a group by the fact of their genital resemblances to each other and differences from men. Women have vaginas, ovaries, uteruses, and the ability to bear and nurse children, and these facts seem more firmly fixed and determinative than notions about domesticity or paid work outside the home. Yet these realities are no more 'real' than any others. Sexuality has a history. It is not fixed and it does not exist in isolation from language, culture, or politics; instead it is created by and helps to form all of these. Human beings' understanding of sexuality – their own and that of others – has always been influenced by ideas that vary dramatically in time and place.

The long nineteenth century has been depicted as, well, 'Victorian' – prudish, repressive and repressed, with a horror of the body so great that even the legs of pianos were covered. This version of history has been discredited for some time. In truth, the long nineteenth century was characterized less by a refusal to talk about sex than by an obsessive debate over sex that was distinguished by dire warnings of its dangers, detailed discussions of its effects, and a powerful insistence on the necessity for discretion.

Sexual behaviour and feelings are intimate and therefore largely undocumented. The records that do survive are usually of those speaking for some official audience, so we must interpret their words cautiously. A prostitute who applied for admission to a home for 'fallen' women was anxious to receive food and shelter, and her promises of penitence and reform should be seen in that light. A young mother hoping to place her newborn baby at the London Foundling Hospital was more intent on presenting her sexual history so that her child would be accepted by the hospital (which had strict standards) than on leaving accurate records for historians. Prosecutions for rape or seduction, and actions for breach of promise of marriage, divorce, or the custody of children, all produced records that give us a window into private lives, and these too must be used with caution because of the emotive issues involved. All of these sources can, however, be read alongside one another to compensate for the shortcomings of individual sources. In addition, statistical evidence about patterns of marriage, divorce and birth can help us to understand the history of sexuality.

Ideas about anatomy, desire, and appropriate sex acts all changed during the late eighteenth century, and so this chapter will begin with an examination of the ways in which people understood sexuality during the long nineteenth century. The topics it goes on to explore include the roles of advice manuals and sexology, the importance of women's reputations, sex and love between women, courtship, marriage, pregnancy, and childbirth; various ways in which women could control their fertility; prostitution and venereal disease, which were almost always discussed together during this period; and the new ways of thinking about sex that emerged in the early twentieth century.

Understanding Sex

'Some time during the second half of the eighteenth century,' the historian Thomas Laqueur argues, 'human sexual nature changed.'[1] This change – which was of perspective rather than biological – was characterized by three things. The first was a reconceptualization of male and female genitals and anatomy, and by extension of men and women. Before the late eighteenth century, a 'one-body' model, in which female genitals were thought to be male genitals turned inside out, prevailed. The uterus and ovaries were analogous (though inferior) to the penis and testicles; indeed, there was no separate term for ovaries. In the 1770s the physiologist Pierre Roussel remarked that the organs on either side of the uterus were 'alternatively called ovaries or testicles, depending on the system which one adopts',[2] and popular verse supported him even into the nineteenth century:

> ... though they of different sexes be,
> Yet on the whole they are the same as we,
> For those that have the strictest searchers been,
> Find women are but men turned outside in.[3]

Women were therefore inferior to, but made from the same material as, men.

This model was replaced by one in which female genitals were wholly unlike male genitals. Women were not lesser men; they were quite different from men. This reconceptualization could work for and against women. On the one hand, it suggested that women were simply other beings, perfect in their own way rather than an inferior version of men. This 'two-bodies' model was used to support the idea that women were happiest and most powerful following their biological destiny to be mothers, and many women derived satisfaction and empowerment from this idea. On the other hand, since assertions of difference almost never exist without implicit hierarchies, in practice this new understanding meant that women's bodies were seen as different from, and lesser than, men's. This shift in outlook was not prompted by new scientific knowledge; rather it was part of a set of social, political, and economic changes – many of which we have already seen – that limited women's opportunities. Science was not separate from society. Anatomical thinking changed not because of new scientific discoveries, but because of a cultural need to redefine women as unlike men.

The second key shift was a re-evaluation of the relationship between women and desire. During the early modern period, women were thought to be the more sexually voracious of the sexes; during the nineteenth century, though, women, or at least respectable ones, were thought to be less sexual than men. The most important symptom of this shift was in popular and scientific thinking about female orgasm. Previously the occurrence of female orgasm was accepted without any debate. Moreover it was considered as necessary to conception as male orgasm; sexual pleasure was thought to release the female 'seed' from the ovary and was therefore essential to reproduction. But while ovulation was not observed in women until the twentieth century, experiments on dogs and pigs prompted doctors to argue from the mid-nineteenth century that women's ovaries did in fact produce seeds independently of intercourse or sexual excitement, that ovaries were the key to reproduction, and that orgasm was not. By 1841, the fourth edition of *A Manual of Midwifery* could explain that:

the character of a woman's mind is chiefly determined by the part she bears in relation to generation ... we must never forget that indescribable, or perhaps mysterious influence on the female system, which predominates ... and is subservient to reproduction.[4]

In 1869, the anthropologist J. M. Allen argued similarly that with regard to women's intellectual capacities there were: 'radical, natural, permanent distinctions in the mental and moral conformation, corresponding with those in the physical organisation of the sexes'.[5]

The fundamental distinction was the difference in sexual desire. 'Respectable' women were reconceptualized as 'passionless'; they had sex in the interests of procreation, marital harmony, or motherhood, but rarely if ever in response to their own desire.[6] Men, in contrast, were if anything governed by their sexual desires. The 'fact' that they needed to ejaculate to remain healthy – but that male masturbation was widely held to be unhealthy – was often invoked to justify prostitution. (Military officials worried that soldiers who were denied sexual release with prostitutes were at risk of engaging in homosexual sex with each other, and of thereby compromising the virility of colonial rule.[7]) As with the two-bodies anatomical model, the doctrine of passionlessness could be useful to women, who used it to demonstrate that they were moral and intellectual beings who were above carnal desire. Yet it also restricted men's and women's ideas about female pleasure. Furthermore, as the notion of passionlessness was medicalized over the nineteenth century, it became less empowering for women.

Motherhood and desire came to be seen as incompatible. Women – especially respectable middle-class women – were politically and rhetorically reduced to, and defined by, their bodies as reproductive, not desiring. The effect was to render women passive vessels who satisfied men's desire and bore children because it was their destiny. Connected to this was a new emphasis on women's virginity and on the loss of virginity as the key sexual moment in a woman's life.

Finally, the second half of the eighteenth century saw a narrowing of the scope of normal sexual behaviour so that any activities outside of penetrative heterosexuality were seen as unnatural. As sex came to mean heterosexual intercourse, non-penetrative sexual play was replaced by penetration as typical premarital sex. This shift seems to have started in London and spread to the provinces and is reflected in eighteenth-century pornography, which came to emphasize vaginal penetration. For instance, in his autobiography, the radical Francis Place (1771–1854) notes the prevalence of premarital penetration among the London poor at the end of the eighteenth century:

[E]ach of my companions, had a sweetheart who was the daughter of some tradesman . . . [the girls were] in their general conduct respectable. With these girls I and my companions were as familiar as we could be, each with his own sweetheart. These girls however turned out much better than the boys . . . I could name several of them now living long since married to young men who were as well acquainted with them before marriage as afterwards . . . These cases must be very numerous.[8]

At least in artisanal circles like Place's, couples clearly began having intercourse before they married. More intercourse did not necessarily lead to more happiness or pleasure all round. Heterosexual couples were more likely than in previous generations to have premarital intercourse, leading to earlier marriages, pregnant brides, and deserted women who bore illegitimate children. The shift to vaginal penetration as the main expression of heterosexuality made women more vulnerable and left many solely responsible for their children.

Quantitative evidence concerning the sexual behaviour of the non-elite confirms these changes. Compared to the early eighteenth century, by the early nineteenth century the age at marriage had dropped, the bastardy rate had soared from less than 2 per cent to 5 per cent of births, and the percentage of pregnant brides had risen from 15 to 33 per cent. England had gone from being a society in which many remained single and celibate, much sexual expression was non-penetrative, and those who married did so in their late twenties, to one in which most people had sexual intercourse, got pregnant, and then married at a young age. These changes were one cause of the rise in population from five million in 1701 to almost eight and a half million in 1801.

Another important influence on sexuality was religion. Until the 1750s the Anglican Church had legal jurisdiction over marital and sexual issues, so much so that the Church courts were known familiarly as the 'bawdy courts'. Even after that date the Church continued to influence people's marital and sexual practices: many couples who never set foot in a church otherwise were married and had their children baptized in one. Evangelicalism was another major influence, and has often been seen as the sole source of sexual repression and oppression during our period. It is more accurate to say that it was a factor in prudery, and a complex one at that. Evangelicals preached narrow sexual standards and expected women to be faithful wives, but also preached a doctrine of forgiveness and sought to rescue, not reject, those they considered fallen. Overall, religious influence on sexual behaviour varied markedly by class and faith. Upper-class evangelical Anglicans felt that women were subordinate to their husbands, while middle-class radical Unitarians pursued equal rights for women. Working-class members of the Salvation Army believed that temperance kept men sober and women safe. Each of these Church's doctrines would have a different influence on a female congregant's understanding of herself and her sexuality. After the Church lost its legal jurisdiction over sexual matters, in the middle of the eighteenth century, it was in part replaced by the medical establishment and later by sexology as well, both of which played a part in defining women's anatomies, desires, and potential.

Advice and sexology

One place we can see evidence of all these dramatic shifts in thinking about women and sex is in sexual advice books. *Aristotle's Masterpiece*, first published in English in 1684, was the most important sexual advice manual in early modern and modern England and was the most widely read of its kind throughout the eighteenth century. It seems to have been aimed at upper-working-class and lower-middle-class readers, but sales were great enough to suggest a socially mixed audience. In it, sex was not held to be frightening or dangerous but rather pleasurable, fun, and purposeful. Ignoring homosexuality and male masturbation, and rejecting the notion that women are passionless or that sex is sinful, it presumed that couples wished to conceive and that men and women both desired sex unproblematically. The book aimed to instruct them in how to have intercourse for the purposes of enjoyment and reproduction. Much of the text detailed specific positions and practices that encourage conception. Readers were encouraged to marry early, to 'copulate not too often, nor yet too seldom', and to enjoy a glass of wine before sex, 'that their spirits may be raised to the highest pitch of ardour and joy'.[9] Many eighteenth-century advertisements for medicines for women similarly indicated that sex was to be enjoyed and reproduction was its aim.

During the first few decades of the nineteenth century, though, *Aristotle's Masterpiece* lost its dominance of the market. And while it remained popular, new versions began appearing that were far less explicit, providing no anatomy of the genitals, and far more dire in their treatment of sex. These editions offered no advice on creating an enticing atmosphere or tips on how to conceive a boy or a girl. Instead, they contained chapter titles such as 'Words of Warning' and reminders that, while sex was not inherently debasing, marriage should always be prudently delayed until the suitor was prepared to offer 'adequate means of support'.[10]

From the 1850s to the 1880s, the most popular book to offer sexual advice was William Acton's dour text *The Functions and Disorders of the Reproductive Organs in Youth, Adult Age and Advanced Life* (1857), which pronounced firmly that 'the majority of women ... are not very much troubled with sexual feeling of any kind'.[11] The medical journal *The Lancet* noted Acton's book with approval; it seems that by 1857 women had been firmly categorized as passionless. Yet at the same time another doctor, Isaac Baker Brown, was surgically removing women's clitorises to cure a wide range of ailments that he claimed were rooted in excessive sexuality and/or masturbation. The author of *On Some Diseases of Women, Admitting of Surgical Treatment*, Baker Brown operated on several hundred women. He was condemned by many and expelled from the London Obstetrical Society; he was certainly not typical of English medicine or society. But his work demonstrates that the Actonian position on female sexuality was not unchallenged; even as many insisted that women were 'naturally' passionless (and those who were not were aberrant and needed to be surgically cured), fear of women's sexuality persisted.

In the last part of the nineteenth century, following the publication of Darwin's *Descent of Man* (1871) – in which he considered the role of sexual reproduction in evolution – the field of sexual science or 'sexology' emerged. Sexologists sought to make sexuality, sexual behaviour, and gender differences the object of serious scientific and sociological study. They attempted to classify and catalogue a wide range of sexual behaviour, and were instrumental in changing perceptions of homosexuality from sin to perversion or to some intermediate sex, as the sexologist Edward Carpenter (1844–1929) argued. Their work has often been seen as biologically determinant and oppressive to women, and there is evidence to support this interpretation. In *Sex and Character* by the Austrian sexologist Otto Weininger (1903), which was misogynistic and anti-Semitic, but widely read by many feminists, sexologists, and radicals, Weininger wrote: 'To put it bluntly, man possesses sexual organs, but [woman's] sexual organs possess her.'[12] However, sexologists put forward varied and opposing arguments, some of which were positive for women. And the field's view of sexuality as a key part of human society was liberating for many of its readers. In attempting to approach sex rigorously and rationally, sexologists provided new ways of revising and creating sexual knowledge.

The most important British sexologist was Havelock Ellis (1859–1939), author of the seven-volume *Studies in the Psychology of Sex* (1898–1928), who combined biological determinism with cultural relativism to produce an alternately (and sometimes simultaneously) conservative and radical corpus. He saw female modesty as a natural phenomenon, and female sexuality as responsive to male sexuality, but he also advocated the 'erotic rights of woman'.[13] His rich and multifaceted work is a good example of the complexities of sexology and the many uses – feminist and misogynist, radical and conservative – to which the field could be put. Although Ellis is best remembered for his work on sexual deviancy, he wrote on a wide range of sexual topics. While many sexologists sought to classify deviant sexualities as distinct from normal ones, Ellis stressed the continuity between the normal and the perverse. He also helped to popularize works by other sexologists: *The Evolution of Sex* (1889) by Scottish biologists Patrick Geddes (1854–1932) and J. Arthur Thomson (1858–1935), was the first volume of Havelock Ellis's Contemporary Science Series and therefore widely affordable and available. Geddes and Thomson saw human sexuality as an important field of study and argued that the two sexes had evolved quite differently, into active males and passive females. They famously declared that this reality, 'decided among the prehistoric protozoa[,] cannot be annulled by Act of Parliament'.[14] Yet Geddes and Thomson also upheld the importance of women and female influence to society.

In the 1910s, British sexology turned away from human behaviour and society towards laboratory experiments on animals and became more conservative. The sexologist Blair Bell added a scientific veneer to contemporary notions of sexual difference as predictive; he saw women's minds as controlled by their 'internal secretions', which gave them an 'ardent desire to be loved'.[15] Clearly not all sexology was a departure from the nineteenth-century doctrine of passionlessness. While sexology provided important new bodies of evidence and ways of thinking, for most of the long nineteenth century sex seemed a world of limits.

Reputation

Sex was simultaneously private and a key part of women's public personas. The most important identifying characteristic a person had in the nineteenth century was his or her reputation. Men's and women's reputations were assessed quite differently. While men were judged on many factors, including wealth and work, women were judged by their sexuality (and to a lesser extent by their housekeeping skills). Women took their reputations very seriously and recognized that their sexual behaviour was not a private matter. For a young woman from the comfortable middle classes, nothing less than an entire lack of sexual experience before her engagement would do. Middle-class girls were constantly reminded of the importance and fragility of a good reputation – even flirtation or romance could taint one – and many must have not only been aware of, but internalized, these standards, along with the doctrine of passionlessness.

Working-class culture could be very forgiving of a once-'fallen' woman, though less so of one seen as habitually promiscuous. Too many partners could be problematic, but pre-marital sex, conception, and even delivery could be compatible with a good reputation if they took place within a family- and community-approved courtship. The woman might still marry her children's father, and many communities recognized that respectable women could be jilted by their lovers. To take one example, in the 1827 breach-of-promise case of *Hawkins* v. *Pring*, Jane Hawkins was furious that Pring had reneged on his promise to marry her after his father died, but she was not at all ashamed of their out-of-wedlock relationship. She indignantly explained in court that 'she had had two small children with him, and would have no more of it . . . she had seven years of it with him and that was enough . . . all I want is thee to make me thy wife.'[16] Other women won breach of promise of marriage damages from the men who had broken their hearts even though they had reputations for being 'gay' or 'fast';[17] for working-class and lower-middle-class women, sexual experience was not incompatible with respectability.

While most Victorians, and all Victorian statisticians, distinguished sharply between legitimate and illegitimate births, in many ways there was actually not much difference between them. As marriage rates rose and fell, so did illegitimate births; high bastardy rates were a by-product of cancelled marriage plans. Some children registered as illegitimate were actually the products of stable non-marital unions, and a baby's parents could marry months or even years after its birth. When a child was definitively a bastard – born out of wedlock to parents who never married or formed a household – its birth usually occurred not in the absence of marriage plans but in the wake of their collapse. Since the nineteenth century was a period of social and economic disruption, many occurrences could have thwarted even the best-intentioned courtships, but most women were aiming for respectability. And many achieved it: between 1821 and 1871 in rural Kent, many women who gave birth out of wedlock went on to marry, and 40 per cent of those who did so married men who were not the fathers of their children.[18]

On the other hand, many women – widowed as well as deserted – lived for years as single mothers, a position that was economically extremely difficult. This was especially true from 1834 to 1845, when the new Poor Law in its first and harshest incarnation made it almost impossible for unmarried mothers to get support from their children's fathers. Throughout the century, mothers of illegitimate children faced harsh criticism from middle-class commentators and had difficulty finding work; many, especially those in service, gave up their children because childlessness was a condition of employment. Servants were especially vulnerable to having illegitimate offspring because the single-and-childless requirement for domestics led them to conceal their relationships for as long as possible; expecting to leave their employment and marry once pregnant, they were sometimes unpleasantly surprised. For example, in 1840 Jane Watson, in service in the West End, was engaged to Alexander Hay, a watchmaker. They met for seven months on Sundays after church; he bought her an engagement ring (a luxury few working men could offer) and even put his promise to marry her in writing:

> Dear Jane Watson
>   I solemnly promise to marry you
> my dear girl.
>   18 December 1840
>   Yours affec.
>   Alex Hay

Once engaged, Jane had intercourse with Alex twice. When she became pregnant, his affections cooled, and he eventually wrote her a letter admitting that he had 'basely seduced you under a solemn promise of marriage', that he was emigrating to America, and that he hoped she would find support 'in the trouble in which you are involved by my shameful rascallity'.[19] Jane took her baby to the London Foundling Hospital, whose records reveal that milliners, furriers, hat-binders, shoe-stitchers, embroiderers, and seamstresses, among others, also found themselves in trouble and sought to give up their babies. Extramarital as well as premarital sex could lead to trouble. Aristocratic wives who gave birth to babies not their husbands' could also be made to suffer: the Duchess of Devonshire was forced to live on the Continent for two years, from 1791 to 1793, after giving birth to her adulterously conceived daughter Eliza, during which time she missed her other children horribly.[20] Elite women who publicly acknowledged their illegitimate children risked divorce and a loss of social position and reputation.

Loving women

Sex meant danger as well as pleasure. Sex inside and outside marriage was often accompanied by oppression, physical violence, and sexual violence including rape. And of course the social and economic effects of pregnancies (including the stigma that could accompany extramarital ones) were disproportionately borne by women. One way to avoid pregnancy was to have sex with women. The social expression and meaning of sex and love between women (or lesbianism, although the term did not exist during our period) changed as the eighteenth century became the nineteenth. Frustratingly for historians, sex and relationships between women – even more than those between men and women – have left few records. Sex between women did not result in progeny, and unlike male homosexuality, it was not a crime in England. As 'sex' came more and more to mean heterosexual intercourse, and 'sodomy' came to refer to anal intercourse between men, sex between women remained unprosecuted and in some ways invisible, which perhaps gave those who engaged in it a certain freedom. While we do not know much about what Victorian women did in bed together, this should neither delude us into thinking that they did nothing (at least until sexologists labelled them in the early twentieth century) nor fool us into thinking that every time women shared a bed they made love. The truth is undoubtedly somewhere in between.

The eighteenth century was an age fascinated by cross-dressing women (many but not all of whom were lesbians), and many tales of adventurous cross-dressers survive. Most cross-dressers seem to have been working-class women seeking more freedom and better job opportunities, and cross-dressing, with the role-playing and gender boundary-crossing it implies, was the dominant form of lesbian presentation. By the early nineteenth century, however, tales of cross-dressing were almost nowhere to be found; if women were still doing it, they were no longer celebrated for it. At the same time, all women were given to understand that they were 'passionless' (though affectionate). The dominant cultural image of women who loved women as cross-dressers was replaced by the notion of the 'romantic friendship', in which female friends expressed their affection in ways that were clearly loving, romantic, and physical, and perhaps sexual. The 'romantic friendship' paradigm, though, is a fairly privileged, upper-middle-class one; we know far less about sex between plebeian women. In the late nineteenth and early twentieth centuries, while sexology for the most part defined normal sex – the only kind healthy women were to desire – as heterosexual penetration, it also made more open discussion of lesbian sex possible.

Where and when did sex between women happen? Although we cannot be sure, one likely place is in same-sex environments such as schools and workhouses. Half the population of English workhouses were adult women (only a fifth were men), and one historian remarks drily that 'it is difficult to accept that no "grubbling" took place late at night'.[21] Better-off women seeking same-sex relationships probably gravitated towards homosocial environments such as girls' schools and women's colleges. There was no English urban centre with a female subculture like those in New York, Berlin and Paris.

We have several good examples of love and sex between women during the long nineteenth century. Probably the most famous in England in their own day (though they were of the Irish gentry) were Lady Eleanor Butler and Sarah Ponsonby, who in the 1770s, ran off together to rural north Wales, in defiance of their families who objected to the intensity of their romantic friendship. They became internationally known as the 'Ladies of Llangollen'. While a gossipy newspaper unkindly described their situation as one of 'Extraordinary Female Affection', they seem not to have suffered any serious oppression or opposition, and lived together for forty years, until Butler's death. Some observers derided them and insisted on seeing them as inhabiting male and female roles (Butler 'tall and masculine', Ponsonby 'effeminate, fair and beautiful') though in fact they wore matching riding clothes and wigs; others assumed, at least publicly, that their love was platonic and praised them for what they saw as sexless selflessness. A leading scholar of English lesbianism, Martha Vicinus, points out that this second misinterpretation was encouraged by the pair, who tried to deflect unpleasant remarks by appearing intellectual and desexualized.[22]

Another well-known example is Anne Lister (1791–1840). She was born in Yorkshire to an old family of lower-gentry status; less affluent than the Ladies of Llangollen, she was comfortable but not independently wealthy enough to live openly with a lover until late in her life. Lister was an educated, well-travelled, sophisticated, and purposefully mannish woman who kept a long and sexually explicit diary. It allows us access to the intimate thoughts of a woman struggling to create a place for herself at a time when few models of female love existed. While there were very small, cosmopolitan intellectual and theatrical circles in London and Bath that welcomed women like her, she did not discover them until after she had had several lesbian affairs. Lacking a community or even a set of available role models or images – she was obsessed with the Ladies of Llangollen and was certain that their relationship was indeed a sexual one – Lister read widely in an attempt to create a social and sexual identity for herself. In particular she used her extensive knowledge of classical and romantic literature, including references to Sappho in Juvenal, and the romantic writers' notion of the individual's secret self that was bursting with forbidden passions. Lister spent most of the 1820s flirting with and seducing middle- and upper-class women in Yorkshire and abroad, had a long affair with a married woman named Marianna Lawton, who seems to have been her greatest love and whom she wanted to 'marry', and in the 1830s settled down with fellow Yorkshire heiress Anne Walker. While she was careful with whom she flirted and often used coded language and references to figure out if women were potential lovers, her targets either accepted or rejected her advances but never expressed horror at her perversion. In other words, what is noteworthy about her life was its normality.[23]

Of course, the Ladies of Llangollen and Anne Lister all had independent means. Among lesbian women who had to earn their own living we know of Mary East, who went by the name James How, owned a pub, and lived with a wife for thirty-five years, beginning in the 1730s. When Mrs How died in the 1760s, Mary East went to the local magistrates to complain about the blackmailer she had been paying for years; they declined to arrest her for fraudulently living as a man but imprisoned the blackmailer. Jane Pirie and Marianne Woods were Scottish schoolteachers who in 1811 were tried and acquitted for indecent and criminal behaviour; Sarah Geals lived as William Smith and was married to Caroline Smith for twelve years.[24] These few surviving examples imply the existence of many same-sex-oriented women of all classes in nineteenth-century England.

Courtship

Most girls and women, though, had sex with boys and men, usually in the context of courtships that led to or were supposed to lead to marriage. In the elite ranks of society, since the political and financial stakes were high, courtship was closely monitored. Within the controlled environment of gentry social circles or the London Season, though, young people chose their own mates and got to know them before becoming engaged. Among the upper middle class as well, parental supervision and economic safeguards such as trusts were common. Less affluent middle-class women were free to choose their mates from available suitors, but all middle-class women had to be careful not to appear too eager.

Among the working classes, courtship practices varied widely over the country and the century. Francis Place commented that in London:

> When I was an apprentice [in the late 1780s] ... [girls] wore no stays, their gowns were low round the neck and open in front, those who wore handkerchiefs had theirs always open in front to expose their breasts this was a fashion which the best dressed among them followed...[25]

Furthermore, young women might have several sweethearts or even fiancés before they married. Place remembered that in the 1790s his oldest sister was courted by a cook named Ben Ward. She left her position as a servant in preparation for their wedding, but then met a chair carver named James Pain and married him instead.[26] This indicates that working-class women had more choice and freedom than we might have expected.

Most working-class women became involved with men of their own social standing whom they met through family, friends, or work. While an upper servant in London might hide her relationship from employers and co-workers for fear of losing her position, most romances were known to others, and their public nature was in some measure meant to guarantee their stability. Couples would court, become more serious, and then marry and have children; if they could afford it, the woman would stop working. In the upper working and lower middle classes, where men sought respectability by delaying marriage to save money or advance in their careers, long engagements were not uncommon; as we saw above,

Jane Hawkins and her fiancé were engaged for seven years, and had two children during that time.

Premarital sex between affianced working people made a good deal of sense in the early modern period, when much premarital sex was non-penetrative and the plebeian understanding of marriage was of a multi-step process involving courtship, betrothal, banns or licence, church service, consummation, and the birth of the first child. If courtship resulted in pregnancy or even an infant at the altar this was not necessarily problematic so long as the marriage took place.[27] Over the course of the long nineteenth century, though, this courtship style became less effective for women. Urbanization and industrialization meant that young people moved away from the family in search of employment before they married, and community surveillance of courting couples declined. This led to greater freedoms for young people, but also to greater dangers for young women, who could more easily be jilted. The ability to court away from the prying eyes of family and friends was not necessarily to the advantage of women who, unlike their erstwhile fiancés, might be stig-matized (by middle-class people or even other members of the working classes) or face economic difficulties if they bore children out of wedlock.

As we saw in the case of *Hawkins* v. *Pring*, some upper-working-class and lower-middle-class women who were deserted by their fiancés took their jilting lovers to court and sued them for breach of promise of marriage. In court they had to prove that there had been a promise of marriage (written evidence was not necessary), that their hearts had been broken, and that their reputations were damaged. If they could do this, they usually won awards from sympathetic juries. This demonstrates that while many middle-class commentators were quick to blame young women for sexual experience or extramarital motherhood, some people, including judges and juries (made up of middle-class men at this time), saw the jilted fiancée or single mother as a victim.

Marriage

Whether or not it was their first suitor or even their first fiancé, most women in the nineteenth century married. Some historians emphasize the fact that the nineteenth, more than previous centuries, saw the rise of affectionate, companionable marriages in which spouses were friends and monogamous lovers as well as household partners. Others point out that many marriages, at all levels of society, were rife with physical and emotional cruelty as well as companionship. In and out of marriage, abuse, including rape, was extremely difficult to prosecute (marital rape was not even a recognized concept until the late twentieth century). Divorce was expensive and difficult to obtain, and divorced women usually lost custody of their children. Whether their marriages were marked by intimate companionship, cruelty, or both, most adult women's experiences of sex were with their husbands. While some undoubtedly enjoyed sex, many factors, including lack of confidence in a lover's intentions or competence, fear of (yet another) pregnancy, fear of sex, and fear of the possibility of violence must have conspired to make enjoying sex less than inevitable.

Sexual violence – often difficult to separate from other forms of violence and from alcohol – was an ever-present possibility in women's lives. Women could be forced, coerced, or seduced into sex by strangers, acquaintances, friends, or suitors, in their neighbourhood, walking home at night, or at their workplaces. Women might be attacked by fiancés for trying to end the relationship, or by husbands for announcing a pregnancy and therefore another mouth to feed, or in a confrontation about adultery or venereal disease. Much domestic violence that was not explicitly sexual took place in sexual spaces such as the couple's bed or bedroom. Drunken husbands beat their wives, but it is unclear whether they struck because they drank or drank so as to batter. Sex and violence were often intertwined.[28]

Pregnancy and childbirth

Just as most women married, most became pregnant and gave birth more than once during their lifetimes. In an age before reliable contraception – and virtually all of the long nineteenth century could be so characterized – pregnancy loomed large for sexually active women. Whether married or not, women bore the brunt of intercourse: they, not men, got pregnant, faced the dangers of childbirth, and experienced exhaustion and permanent physical damage from closely spaced and/or multiple pregnancies. For most of our period, doctors and scientists understood little, and the general public even less, about conception. Many lay people still believed that female orgasm was necessary to conception. Few understood that ovulation was independent of sex, and when doctors first established a connection between menses and ovulation it was thought they occurred simultaneously – the result being that any medical advice that relied on an understanding of women's fertile periods was wrong and best left unheeded.

The connection between breast-feeding and lowered fertility had been noted. Some women made use of this information; for instance, aristocratic women who wished to conceive frequently might send their babies to wet-nurses. Women who wanted to space births might choose to nurse their babies for long periods. Others might not be able to put their knowledge to good use: a woman who wanted to delay subsequent pregnancies, but needed to keep her factory job, had to wean her babies early. Nor was breast-feeding a foolproof method of contraception. For most sexually active women, pregnancy might be hoped for or dreaded but could rarely be planned or avoided. Overall, royal, aristocratic, and working-class women tended to have the largest families, while women in the middle classes and the aspiring working classes seem to have started controlling their fertility from the middle of the century because they had smaller families.

Then, as now, pregnancy could be tiring for women, especially for those who had to continue working. Many suffered from depression or malnutrition; poor pregnant women in London of the 1880s described themselves as 'often weak and low spirited', and 'half starved'.[29] Most had no medical care until they went into labour. Delivery could be dangerous and was approached with apprehension by many women. It could also result in long-term debilitating conditions such as perineal tears and uterine prolapse, especially in women who gave birth many times. Working women usually gave birth at home, attended by a midwife, nurse, or knowledgeable friend or neighbour (the distinctions were not always clear). In London, though, where most medical personnel were trained, poor women could receive excellent care from doctors, midwives, and nurses in training through the Poor Law medical services. In the decade before the First World War national insurance also gave the poor access to private doctors. Working women almost never relied on drugs to ease the pain of giving birth, or interventions meant to speed up the process, in spite of their concern to have a quiet labour so as not to frighten their young children.[30] More comfortably-off families were, especially as the century progressed, given to hiring doctors, who were far more likely than midwives to use interventions such as forceps for hastening birth and chloroform for mitigating pain. As these techniques were sophisticated but risky, the delivery practices of doctors were actually less reliable than those of midwives. Anaesthesia was difficult to administer safely; physical interventions increased the likelihood of infection, which was the leading cause of women's death in or after childbirth. After giving birth, most women rested and then gradually resumed their daily duties, although very poor women often returned to piece-work almost immediately.

Controlling fertility

Quite understandably, the physical, economic, and social implications of becoming pregnant led many women to wish to plan desired pregnancies and avoid unwanted ones. And to a significant extent they succeeded: birth patterns show that from about 1850 many English women were controlling their fertility to some extent. This is all the more extraordinary because no new technologies were developed during our period. In other words, women began controlling their fertility because they wanted to, not because they suddenly could.

Nineteenth-century contraceptive goals were quite different from twenty-first-century expectations of perfect control and choice. Some portions of the population were resolutely against controlling births. These included royalty and the aristocracy, who for dynastic and property reasons continued to have large families (although some women may have wanted to use birth control for adulterous affairs). They also included some portions of the urban working classes. For instance, we know that in the later nineteenth and early twentieth centuries poor married mothers were extremely fatalistic about many aspects of their lives, including family planning. While they might have dreaded successive pregnancies and large families, they did not have a sense that they could control their fertility. One woman speaking of the early twentieth century said of conception and children, 'Well, I mean, we never thought of it. They just came and that was it.'[31] Even among those who did practise some form of birth control, goals might be quite limited: to delay the birth of the first child, to have children several years apart, or to avoid extramarital conception or venereal disease.

Certain chemical, hormonal, and mechanical devices – such as spermicide, birth control pills, or condoms – are the contraceptives of today, while abstinence from sex is considered a separate sort of choice and abortion another thing altogether. In the long nineteenth century, though, in the minds of most people, a wide spectrum of strategies and behaviour aimed at preventing the arrival of new children existed on a continuum. Abstinence from intercourse was considered a form of contraception, as it was during certain parts of a woman's menstrual cycle. Coitus interruptus was the most popular method of birth control, and the most widely used, until well into the twentieth century.[32] Taking herbs or medicines to re-establish a woman's 'interrupted' menstrual cycle was another solution.

Occasionally the most desperate of mothers – young, poor, and frightened – killed their infants immediately after giving birth, usually by smothering. This was a capital crime, but most people saw a difference between the typical person guilty of infanticide, a poor woman without resources who had just given birth alone, and other killers. Very few trials for infanticide resulted in a verdict of murder, as lawyers, judges and juries alike were hesitant to convict women they saw as innocent young victims of heartless seducers. While there were infanticide panics during the 1860s, most of these involved scandals about 'baby farms' to which infants were fostered out; these scandals tended to focus popular attention on the fact that mothers were not caring for their own older babies rather than on the infanticide of newborns.

Women's choices about less desperate forms of contraception were limited by the available options, which were few and unreliable, and by the fact that contraception was not considered respectable; condoms, in particular, were associated with prostitutes and disease prevention, and were almost never used to prevent births within marriage. (Condoms had been invented in the early modern period; there is a mention of a linen one in 1564, and by the early 1700s they were being made from animal bladders and skins.) In her divorce of 1872, middle-class Louisa Birch even charged her husband with 'insisting on using against the wish of your petitioner French letters [condoms] when he had connection with her', implying that she regarded condoms as unnatural, foreign, and dangerous.[33] Doctors would not discuss contraception with their patients: even those who cautioned patients about becoming pregnant for health reasons often refrained from advising them on how to accomplish this without practising abstinence. Many feminists opposed the use of contraception in marriage because they felt it turned wives into prostitutes by making them perpetually available to their husbands for pleasure.

In public discourse, contraception was associated with political and sexual radicalism. One of the few medical men to favour it, Henry Arthur Allbutt, was a political radical from Leeds. He published a cheap pamphlet, *The Wife's Handbook*, that explained to poor and working-class women how to use contraception. The Malthusian League, founded in 1877, was the first organization dedicated to the promulgation of birth control information. Its activities were declared illegal and its publications pornographic, in part because they were priced to be affordable by working-class people. The same year two of its members, Annie Besant (1847–1933) and Charles Bradlaugh (1853–91), were tried for republishing Charles Knowlton's *Fruits of Philosophy*, an obscure American tract on birth control which went on to sell hundreds of thousands of copies by the end of the century. Newspaper reports of the trial spread as much practical information as the pamphlet. Besant's own pamphlet, *The Law of Population*, sold 175,000 copies between 1877 and 1890. By the late nineteenth century, then, there was a much wider dissemination of information about birth control.

Where the respectable feared to tread, opportunists as well as principled radicals rushed to fill the gap. Quacks – unofficial medical practitioners – did a huge business in cures for various sexual ills. Most of their pills, salves, and devices claimed to solve the two great undiscussed problems of the day, unwanted pregnancy and venereal disease. They operated largely through advertisements in newspapers and other print media. By the end of the nineteenth century, advertisements for contraceptives and abortifacients appeared in newspapers and magazines, while the products themselves were sold in barber shops, rubber goods stores and chemists, and were brought to working-class urban neighbourhoods and rural villages by door-to-door pedlars. Most advertisements for abortifacients did not openly state the use to which the product would be put. Instead, they promised to 'remove obstructions' or 'restore vitality' to exhausted women. While some women may have sought help for just these problems, perhaps even to restore or increase their fertility, most were reading between the lines and understood that any mixture that would restore a woman's menstrual flow would also terminate a pregnancy. At least some quack providers seem to have done quite well for themselves; when an abortifacient provider, Madame Douglas (real name Louisa Fenn), was tried in 1897 in Exeter, it was revealed that in six months she had spent £600 – a comfortable annual income for an upper-middle-class family – on advertising alone.[34]

There were an increasing number of products that could help prevent unwanted pregnancies. Condoms were only used to protect against venereal disease but also prevented pregnancy; mass-produced rubber condoms, available from 1900 and a more acceptable alternative to the earlier types, were affordable (at ½d. each). Contraceptive sponges also existed but were associated with adulterous sex. The later nineteenth century saw the invention of the diaphragm, which when accompanied by douching after intercourse was an effective method of birth control, but a relatively expensive one that had to be fitted by a physician. In the 1880s quinine pessaries (which also required douching) and suppositories were developed. At the turn of the twentieth century commercially prepared spermicidal jellies and powders became available (but were not necessarily widely or successfully used); many women approximated these methods by making cocoa butter- or glycerine-based spermicidal barriers themselves at home. Birth control pills were not invented until the 1960s.

Advertisements for these products were opposed by social purity activists, those who wished to create a more sexually pure and continent nation by means that many considered coercive, such as inspecting music halls for indecent costumes and lyrics and shutting down prostitutes' places of work. They united with doctors to silence advertisers by lobbying for the passage of the 1889 Indecent Advertisements Act, which when passed made posters and handbills illegal. They also worked to strip doctors of their medical licences. Henry Allbutt became a target of the Leeds Vigilance Association (LVA), a social purity group, because the low cost of his birth control pamphlet, *The Wife's Handbook*, was subsidized by advertisements. The LVA brought the pamphlet to the attention of the General Medical Council, and in 1887 Allbutt was struck from the Medical Register. Disseminating contraceptive knowledge could be quite risky. Quacks and the public spoke to one another across the barrier of silence maintained by the medical profession and purity activists.

Finally, abortion was a widely used form of fertility control. During the second half of the nineteenth century doctors and birth control advocates sought to distinguish contraception from abortion, but with little success; most people saw abortion as another way of preventing childbirth. This understanding was aided by the popular belief that a woman was pregnant only when she could feel the foetus's movements; called 'quickening', this generally occurred at eighteen to twenty weeks after conception. Some women probably took medication to 'restore' their menstrual regularity prior to quickening without consciously believing they were aborting a pregnancy. Medicinal abortifacients – pills, herbs, or other substances taken by mouth – were more common than surgical methods. Taking hot baths and long walks and drinking gin were two folk prescriptions for 'restoring regularity'. Traditional medicine offered a variety of strategies including bleeding, purgatives, emetics, and suppositories. Women also tried ingesting Spanish fly, mercury, powdered savin, juniper essence, and a variety of herbal teas. By mid-century colocynth, quinine, and a concoction of gin and gunpowder were widely used, and at the turn of the twentieth century lead pills, although poisonous, were very popular.

A law passed in 1803 made it an act of felony to provide an abortion before quickening occurred and a capital crime afterwards. Ironically, the same act that produced this law made it more difficult to prosecute a woman for infanticide of her own newborn, and was a victory for activists who had sought to make such convictions more difficult to obtain. Doctors were displeased because the new law lent weight to the concept of quickening, which – since only a pregnant woman herself could say when she felt the foetus move – gave authority to pregnant women instead of medical men. Amendments to the law in 1828 and 1837 abolished the concept of quickening and made abortion in essence legal if performed by a doctor and illegal in all other cases.

Taken all together, these various contraceptive methods had a clear impact on the population. Statistics show that from the middle of the nineteenth century onwards, overall rates of marriage remained fairly stable while children per marriage dropped dramatically. English couples who married in the 1860s had an average of 6.16 children, but those who wed in the 1890s had only 4.13 children. Those who married in the early 1920s had a mere 2.31 children. The most common pattern was to have children early and frequently in the marriage, and then to cease having children while the woman was still fairly young.[35]

So in spite of imperfect options, diffident doctors, opportunistic quacks, legal repercussions, and a general culture of silence around the matter, people were practising birth control. Of course, they did not all start at once. Occupation, region, and subculture played a large part in determining who regulated fertility. For example, in Sheffield and York, birth control first became popular among the respectable lower middle classes, such as small shopkeepers, perhaps as early as the 1840s. Miners and agricultural workers continued to have many children, while textile workers and those working in urban industries had fewer.[36] While not all professional people controlled births, doctors nationwide were clearly limiting the size of their own families even as they declined to tell patients how to do so.

Women were more eager to control family size than men, and used many strategies without consulting or even informing their partners. This is unsurprising since men and women experienced the consequences of fertility quite differently. Some working-class people believed that as family matters were women's responsibility, so too was family planning. Women often learned about birth control techniques from other women, including family members, friends, and neighbours. Annie Besant promoted the contraceptive sponge over the condom partly because using the sponge gave women more control. Many advertisements for female-controlled birth control emphasized that the method in question could be used without a husband's knowledge, which suggests that this was an important or even necessary feature.

Why did English women and men start controlling their fertility when they did? There are many possible reasons, including rises and falls in national prosperity, and declines in infant mortality that led more children to survive to adulthood. Some emphasize rising or changing expectations, arguing that a greater number of people wanted to give their children a more affluent life, or that as middle-class women came to see mothering as a profession they found greater fulfilment in having fewer children. Others claim that as women became more emancipated they wished to leave mothering behind as their primary role. A number of scholars explain the falling birth rate by the fact that existing contraceptives became more easily available, or that advertising made more people aware of them; certainly from the 1890s contraceptives were better produced and advertised. In sum, there is no single convincing explanation for this revolution in sexual behaviour and family size; most likely a combination of factors were involved, which impacted differently on different areas and individuals.

Prostitution and venereal disease

Just as many were controlling fertility without talking about it, many had venereal disease without mentioning it. One of the most widespread health problems in England and its Empire during the long nineteenth century was sexually transmitted diseases. (Venereal disease was also a huge problem in the military and especially among soldiers in the Indian

Army. The rate of infection among enlisted men was rarely under 20 per cent and was as high as 50 per cent in some regiments.) In the eighteenth and nineteenth centuries, venereal disease was associated in the popular mind with prostitution, so much so that neither was discussed without reference to the other. Prostitutes were believed to be the main source of infection to 'decent' society.

Given the tendency to divide women into virtuous and fallen camps in the late eighteenth and nineteenth century, it is no surprise that one of the central figures in English culture was the prostitute. Alternately scorned and degraded, regulated and harassed by the legal and judicial systems, and pitied by charity workers intent on 'rescue', intimately linked in the public mind with venereal disease and immorality, prostitutes were the subject of exceptionally intense scrutiny. The result, strangely, is that we know more about society's preoccupations and beliefs than about the number of women working as prostitutes or the conditions of their work. Contemporary statistics are unreliable, fluctuating between 5,000 and 220,000, or 7 per cent of its population, for mid-nineteenth-century London alone. We know that while some women worked full-time as prostitutes, many others cycled in and out of the profession. English prostitutes usually worked for themselves, in contrast to women on the Continent who generally worked in brothels. Women who worked in seasonal or very poorly paid jobs were especially likely to work part-time as prostitutes. Rescue workers recognized that domestic servants, in particular, but also seamstresses, milliners, and shopgirls, among other poorly paid women, turned to prostitution.

From the start of the long nineteenth century the prostitute was sim-ultaneously considered a 'fallen' woman who had been seduced and thereby trapped in a life of prostitution, and a dangerous public health risk in the form of the moral contagion and venereal disease she passed on to 'innocent' middle-class men and their even more innocent wives. Indeed, many seemed to consider prostitutes as a separate race. Through-out the century rescue workers, mostly middle-class women inspired by their religious beliefs, their feminist principles, or both, sought to save prostitutes. This often involved confining them in rescue or 'magdalene' homes where strict discipline was key: women were not allowed to talk at meals or in bedrooms, rudeness and noisiness were frowned on, and swearing was forbidden, as was any discussion of their past lives. Women performed domestic labour most of the day – reform institutions were funded in part by inmates' laundry work – as they were transformed, it

A pen-grinding room, 1851. Industrialization meant that women worked in large, crowded rooms, performing monotonous tasks.

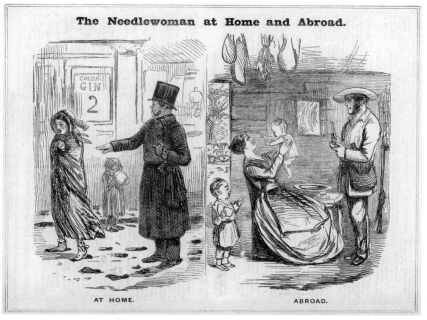

The Needlewoman at Home and Abroad.

AT HOME. ABROAD.

'The Needlewoman at Home and Abroad', 1850 engraving. The plight of impoverished English needlewomen – of whom there were many – was dire. Here their pathos reflects poorly on the entire nation.

Left. A Spitalfields weaver, 1885. For women in cottage industries, home and work were not separate; a bedroom was also the site of industry.

Middle. The typing office of the Society for the Promotion of the Employment of Women, 1889 illustration from *The Quiver* magazine. By the 1880s women did most of the routine clerical work in England. It was considered of higher status than factory work, but resembled it in some ways.

Left. Interviewing a prospective governess, 1853 engraving from *The Leisure Hour*. The applicant's demure posture contrasts with that of her interrogators and suggests the reduced class position that governesses found themselves in.

A photograph *c.* 1870. Elite leisure relied on the labour of others. Two servants wait discreetly to be called.

In this *Punch* cartoon of 1853, a housemaid and a cook sit by the range. Their sullen demeanour reflects middle- and upper-class anxieties about whether their servants were sufficiently respectful and hard-working.

Young women at home, 1858. Elite and upper-middle-class girls were expected to excel at polite and 'decorative' pursuits rather than academic accomplishment.

Female emigration to Australia, 1834 poster. Advertisements aimed at potential emigrants promised a choice of well-paid jobs, but demanded that applicants be of good character. This example was aimed at the working classes; it was not until 1851 and the 'redundancy crisis' that promoters of emigration turned their attention to middle-class women.

Dr Patterson's Famous Female Pills, advertisement, *c.* 1911. Abortifacients, sold by quacks, promised to 'restore' women's 'usual health', that is, their menstruation.

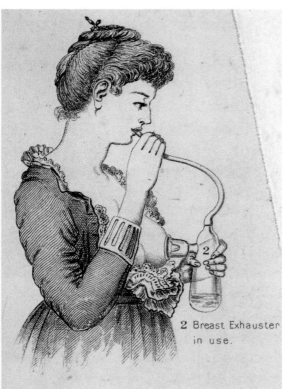

Illustration of a woman using a breast-exhauster, *c.* 1880. Some women hired wetnurses or fed their babies from bottles. Others nursed, and faced the occasional discomfort of engorged breasts.

2 Breast Exhauster in use.

'Poor Law Divorce', from the *Pictorial Times*, 1846. The image protests at the way the new Poor Law and its workhouses divided families.

Top. Dorothea Beale, principal of Cheltenham Ladies' College, and staff in the 1860s. Beale strived to make Cheltenham appear domestic so that the education of girls would seem unthreatening. This portrait could almost be that of a middle-class family.

Above. Girls in a School Board classroom, 1876 engraving from *The Graphic*. Only a few years after the passage of Forster's 1870 Education Act, girls were partaking in state-provided education in large classrooms like this one.

was hoped, from raucous prostitutes into quiet and respectable servants. By the 1880s it became clear that these efforts at reform were largely unsuccessful, and the attention of social purity activists shifted to an insistence on male chastity and on repressing the trade of prostitution itself, rather than on attempting to save individual prostitutes.

The non-poor reading public was most concerned about prostitution as a threat to its way of life. The second half of the century was marked by a series of 'white slavery' scandals, in which it was revealed that innocent young girls were dragged forcibly into child prostitution abroad. The most famous 'exposé', which turned out to have been at least partly fabricated, was W. T. Stead's article 'Maiden Tribute of Modern Babylon' which appeared in The Pall Mall Gazette in 1885. Stead claimed to have uncovered a ring that sold children into white slavery and even to have himself purchased a fourteen-year-old from her mother. Such things rarely happened – the mother in question vehemently disputed Stead's version of events – but received far more attention than the widespread problem of young working women who were forced into prostitution to survive. The Jack the Ripper murders in London in 1888 focused attention on the East End prostitutes who were Jack's victims, but for many they offered a titillating glimpse into another world rather than provoking sympathy.

While prostitutes were thought to be the main spreaders of disease, in reality venereal disease was also passed from clients to prostitutes, from husbands to wives, and between lovers. Children of infected mothers could be born with syphilis or gonorrhoea. They could also be infected by breast-feeding mothers or wet-nurses, or could infect their wet-nurses, who could then carry the disease to other children they nursed. The two most common forms of venereal disease were gonorrhoea and syphilis. Gonorrhoea was for most a localized and non-fatal infection. When first infected, male sufferers experienced uncomfortable discharges of semen and burning during urination. These symptoms would eventually subside, whether treated or not, but the infection could then worsen and produce pain and complications in the urethra, bladder, and prostate, and might cause sterility. Infected women were often unaware of the disease or suffered only slight genital inflammation, and could therefore be unknowing carriers.

Syphilis was much more prevalent and far more dangerous. Today easily treated with antibiotics, the disease was, until the advent of penicillin in the 1940s, contagious, painful, progressive, and incurable. The first symptom for both men and women was a chancre or ulcer that formed a few weeks after infection where the bacterium had entered the body, be it the mouth, genitals – women could get internal or external chancres – or buttocks. Some also had secretions of pus from the vagina or urethra or swollen lymph nodes near the chancres. Months after these primary-stage symptoms had subsided, secondary-stage syphilis would manifest itself in the form of reappearing chancres, other skin rashes and lesions, and sometimes the infection of an internal organ. Some victims suffered from swollen or hardened glands (called buboes), fevers, aching bones, or warts. Like primary symptoms, the manifestations of secondary-stage illness would disappear after several weeks (although they could reappear). In those who developed tertiary, or third-stage, syphilis, the disease spread to their brains or cardiovascular systems and produced dementia and eventually death. Death by tertiary syphilis was slow and very painful.

While venereal disease was associated in the popular mind with poverty, non-respectability, and especially with prostitution, the reality was that men and women of all social stations had syphilis and infected one another with it. Evidence of its prevalence is plentiful in a variety of sources. We see poor people being treated for the disease in charity hospitals: in the 1840s eighteen-year-old Elizabeth McCaw, a domestic servant, and Ann Price and Mary Austin, married women in their forties, were all treated for syphilis at University College Hospital in London. Well-off married women who brought divorce cases sometimes accused their husbands of infecting them. For example, in one 1859 divorce case, Bernard Brocas infected his wife, Jane, with syphilis while she was pregnant. When she experienced painful symptoms, he told her that they were features 'of being in the family way, and that all women in that state suffered in the same way'; even when her doctor advised against sexual intercourse, her husband continued to insist on it. She finally left him and went to stay with her father, Sir John Rose; when Bernard promised to be kinder she returned to him, only to be reinfected with syphilis.[37]

Venereal disease was never treated simply as an illness. Instead, it was seen as shameful and often called the 'secret malady'. This is evident in attitudes towards those infected, towards those providing cures, and in the cures themselves. One of the most obvious aspects of this is the ongoing association between prostitutes and venereal disease, despite the prevalence of syphilis throughout the general population. We can see how shameful venereal disease was by looking at the first charity hospital dedicated to its cure. The London Lock Hospital opened its doors in January 1747; by the end of the eighteenth century it had treated 26,800 men, women, and children, from the ranks of the London poor alone. Clearly, the need for medical help across the English population as a whole was far greater. The hospital had more trouble finding patrons than other charities, and had fewer annual and lifetime governors than other hospitals for the poor. The organization of the hospital's wards also demonstrates contemporary mores regarding venereal disease. In the 1760s the hospital was reorganized so that married women and infants – supposedly innocent victims – were placed in separate wards from single women, who were presumed to have collaborated in their own downfall.[38] The implication was that single women had sought sex, either for pay or because they enjoyed it and deserved what they got, while married women were presumed to have been infected by their husbands and were therefore deserving of pity, not censure.

As was the case with many other medical problems at the time, all available treatments for sexually transmitted diseases were ineffectual. Because the diseases were so shameful, cures were provided and sought out in secret; as the historians of sexuality Roy Porter and Lesley Hall have noted, 'Secret diseases bred secret remedies.'[39] The most widely used cure, mercury, was used in ointments, plasters, injections, and liquids and pills taken orally, in spite of the debilitating effects of mercury poisoning. Other cures included various drugs and poultices, courses of bleeding, emetics, surgery, fumigation, and baths. These remedies were over-whelmingly provided by quacks, and often euphemistically advertised in posters and handbills as well as cheap periodicals. As was the case with birth control, doctors – furious with quacks for impinging on their still-new professional territory – castigated non-professional hucksters for providing poor information while offering none at all themselves.

In general, those willing to overcome their shame and seek medical treatment for a venereal disease found themselves with few options beyond quackery. Nationwide, medical training did not address the diseases; voluntary hospitals were supposed to turn away patients suffering from them, though not all did; Poor Law medical policy ignored them; and friendly societies refused to pay benefits because they considered such diseases self-inflicted. It is no surprise that people of all classes resorted to quack remedies or that men tried the folk remedy of inter-course with a virgin. It was not until 1905 that *Treponema pallidum*, the bacterium that causes syphilis, was identified. During the First World War the development of the Wassermann test for the diagnosis, and the drug Salvarsan for the treatment, of syphilis marked the first effective steps towards containment. After the Second World War penicillin was made available to the civilian population and made a complete cure of both gonorrhoea and syphilis possible.

As we will see in Chapter 8, from the 1860s venereal disease became a feminist issue. Feminists were concerned with two specific aspects of venereal transmission: the role and rights of prostitutes, and the infection of wives by their husbands. The Contagious Diseases Acts, passed during this decade, allowed police in port and garrison towns to apprehend any women who were suspected of prostitution. The fight to repeal these laws was one of the major feminist campaigns of the nineteenth century; repealers were appalled by the double standard inherent in the Acts, by the trampling on women's civil rights, and by the degradation of the examinations, which they called 'instrumental rape'.

Feminists were also horrified by the high rate of disease transmission from husbands to wives, which is most obvious in divorce court petitions. The spousal abuse that divorce cases revealed was protested by feminists for decades. The 1912–13 Royal Commission on Divorce heard testimony to the effect that few wives from the upper working classes would admit to the main causes of marital unhappiness and divorce, namely the infliction of unwanted pregnancies and infection with venereal disease.[40]

From the 1890s professionals including doctors and lawyers were aware of the scale of the syphilis problem. At the turn of the century, new anxieties about racial and population decline combined with existing fears about nation, gender, and sexuality to produce a country-wide concern about venereal diseases. Feminists began to speak of venereal disease not just as an issue of immorality or a double standard but as a threat to both nation and race. In 1896 feminists and doctors came together to write a memo to the government requesting that a Royal Commission on the subject be formed. A commission was appointed in 1913 and became the National Council for Combating Venereal Diseases. During the First World War, the prevalence of syphilis and other diseases among troops made the issue ever more difficult to ignore. In 1916 the Royal Commission brought out a report that emphasized its seriousness – as much as 10 per cent of the urban population seemed to have syphilis, and more had gonorrhoea – and recommended that public health officials and the public at large stop stigmatizing sufferers and presenting the problem as one that pitted men against women or culpable women against innocent ones.[41] At last venereal disease was starting to be seen as a public health issue rather than an individual's moral failing.

The shift in attitudes towards venereal disease from the start of the twentieth century was indicative of the fact that the sexual climate of England was changing. One aspect of this was the emergence of the 'new woman', who will be discussed in Chapter 8. 'New women' were in part a creation of journalists and novelists, but articles and novels that depicted these young, middle-class, independent, and sexually adventurous women had some basis in reality. The 'new woman' rejected traditional marriage as stifling, rather than embracing it as women's best protection, as was more common during the nineteenth century. In its place she preferred 'free love', a term used to indicate freely giving oneself to a life partner outside of legal marriage; she might even pursue sexual pleasure for its own sake or have more than one sexual partner. The 'new woman' novelist Cicely Hamilton (1872–1952) not only wrote about such topics but personally approved of both free love and birth control.[42]

A small number of feminists began to explore the possibility that women might claim for themselves not only freedom from unwanted sexual advances but freedom to experience and act on their own sexual desires. Many read and wrote for the new journals *Shafts* (published 1892–6) and *Freewoman* (published 1911–12). These late-nineteenth- and early-twentieth-century feminists were a minority even among their own kind, most of whom continued to stress women's essentially pure nature and the dangers of sex. They were an even smaller minority of women overall. Pro- and anti-sex feminists agreed on many issues. Both argued for women's sexual autonomy from men. Both criticized the institution of marriage and were vociferously opposed to the double standard that demanded the chastity of women but winked at the sexual misbehaviour of men. Both believed that women should not have to become mothers unless they wished to, and that ideally sex was spiritual at least as much as it was physical.

But where most sought a haven from sex for women, pro-sex feminists claimed women's right to act as sexual agents. Social purity women, some feminist, some not, opposed the use of birth control because they felt that the threat of unwanted pregnancy was an important tool for women who wanted to refuse to have sex with their partners. Pro-sex feminists, on the other hand, favoured birth control as a way of evading unwanted pregnancies while being able to have sex. Many were in favour of limited monogamy and 'free love' rather than self-control.

New feminists were influenced by sexology; both heterosexuals and homosexuals seem to have used the field selectively, using some of its approaches and insights to clarify their own positions and construct their own identities. For instance, they agreed with sexologists that male masturbation was natural so as to emphasize that it was a far more benign solution to the alleged problem of men's relentless sexual needs than prostitution.[43]

By the start of the First World War, the combination of sexology and early-twentieth-century pro-sexuality feminism had helped to make female spinsterhood and celibacy seem unnatural and unhealthy. The old duality of the (good) virtuous and passionless married woman versus the (bad) sexualized and immoral prostitute had been replaced by one of the (good) sexualized married woman versus the (bad) sexless spinster. Whether this constituted progress for women is certainly a matter of debate. But it was a clear departure from the approaches to women's sexuality that had reigned for over a century.

5

Religion

IT IS IMPOSSIBLE to understand English society in the long nineteenth century without understanding religion in all its diversity and complexity. This reality has critical implications for our investigation of women's lives. Most theology and religious practice during the nineteenth century was unkind to women or even misogynistic; many religious leaders held that, spiritually and otherwise, women were properly subordinate to men; most faiths had explicit bans on women as leaders of any kind. In spite of all this, women were more religiously active than men. And even as people endlessly debated the source, essence, and purpose of morality, it was generally agreed upon, as it had not been earlier, that women were naturally more moral than men.

Religion provided many opportunities for women in the long nineteenth century. In their daily lives, women of all classes and faiths could pursue personal, familial, communal, national, and imperial engagement via religion. While the belief in women's superior moral nature rarely translated into the granting of congregational leadership to women, it did offer certain crucial opportunities for both typical and unusual women, many of whom worked tirelessly in and through religious organizations. In these realms they could perform in ways that would have been frowned upon or even prohibited anywhere else, particularly in commerce or politics.

Religion shaped life in ways that are difficult to imagine today. The Anglican Church was supported by taxes, and its parishes were the local unit of government. Many English people were not active in their churches or even particularly pious, and lived without any well-articulated theology. Nevertheless their religions dictated their forms and styles of worship and of celebration, with whom they socialized, where they shopped, and how they spent their leisure time. Furthermore, since most denominations attracted a narrow socio-economic range of adherents, to know someone's religion could be to know their class. Anglican evangelicals were well-off, for example, while most Methodists were from the working classes. Religion, along with class, gender, and race, played a key part in the formation of identities.

This chapter will survey the diverse faiths of England and explore the influence of evangelicalism on women's roles in religion. It will then consider endeavours such as preaching, mission work, and sisterhood. It will conclude by looking at spiritualism and theosophy, which emerged in the late nineteenth century.

Religions in England

The long nineteenth century was the evangelical century. Evangelicalism swept all churches and affected all aspects of life. Characterized by an emphasis on good works as an expression of faith, the use of lay leaders and preachers, the Bible (and especially the Christian Gospel), individual salvation, an opposition to ritual, and a proselytizing zeal, evangelicalism in many ways set the tone across denominations, inside and outside of Protestant churches and even beyond the religious sphere as it is narrowly defined. Evangelicalism also provided a new set of opportunities and challenges for women.

Membership of evangelical dissenting churches increased rapidly from the 1780s and peaked during the third quarter of the nineteenth century, and many more people were evangelically inclined although they were not formal members of any church. All of England was affected but not united by evangelicalism. Class, ethnic, racial, geographic, and national boundaries continued to exist in shifting and complex ways. A religious census taken in 1851 revealed that Methodist, other nonconformist, and Catholic church attendance was, taken together, slightly higher than Anglican church attendance. In spite of this growing pluralism, many Protestant Britons took religious belief and their style of worship to be intrinsic to national identity, and considered Jews and Catholics, whether immigrants or natives of England, to be definitively foreign.

Evangelicalism's message about gender and family varied by class: middle-class women were encouraged to cultivate their godliness in domestic ways, while working-class women were more likely to see the wider world as an appropriate audience for their religious enthusiasm. Yet in many ways the message was consistent: Anglican and Methodist evangelicals alike focused on the family as a religious unit, and almost all evangelicals gathered for family prayers once or twice each day.

ANGLICANS

Evangelical or not, most English people observed some form of Christianity. The Church of England, also known as the Anglican Church, was the state church. Indeed, Anglican doctrine held that church and nation were coeval, and that every citizen of England was technically a member of the Church. By the early nineteenth century, however, the growth of other religions made this notion largely theoretical. The Anglican Church and its members also enjoyed certain official governmental privileges. Before 1828, otherwise qualified men who were non-Anglican Protestants could not vote. Until the passage of the Marriage Act of 1836, which established the civil registration of marriages, the Anglican Church was virtually the only body that could record marriages (Quaker meetings and Jewish synagogues, which served but a small percentage of the population, were exceptions). The Church of England, like most nineteenth-century churches, stressed the primacy of the family and family life to religious endeavour, and thereby provided a range of spiritual opportunities for women. (One notable but relatively minor challenge to this was the enthusiasm of Anglo-Catholics – Anglicans who wanted the state church to employ Roman Catholic doctrines and styles of worship – for clerical celibacy.) Most Anglicans were fairly well-off, and their religious activities reflected this.

Aristocratic, gentry, and upper-middle-class (or 'polite') Anglicans assumed that women would refrain from working outside the home but expected them to infuse family and nation with their superior morality. While imposing strict limitations on women, this also provided areas for female action. In their own homes, Anglican women might read illustrated Bibles with their children, or help them to memorize the Anglican prayer book. Middle-class Anglicans reached out to their less fortunate neighbours in many ways. They were active and often aggressive parish visitors to the sick and poor. Maria Havergal (1821–87), a devout evangelical who was the daughter of a clergyman and the sister of hymn-writer Frances Havergal (1836–79), relied on divine guidance to help her uncover immorality in those she visited. Women also taught Sunday school to children and Bible school to uneducated adults, supported the Anglican Girls' Friendly Society for poor industrial workers, and were active in the Church of England Temperance Society. In the 1830s and 1840s, many took part in local efforts to open new churches or enlarge old ones (over 2,000 were built and many more expanded) so as to attract people to the faith and thereby instill morality. Women were especially concerned about illegitimacy.[1] Church women were active in various purity campaigns such as William Wilberforce's Society for the Suppression of Vice (founded 1802), Josephine Butler's National Ladies' Association, which sought to repeal the Contagious Diseases Act in the 1860s, 1870s, and 1880s, and Jane Ellice Hopkins's Church of England Purity Society (founded in 1883).

Conservative Anglican women celebrated their roles as mothers via the Mothers' Union (founded in 1876), which encouraged members to unite in prayer and to see their maternal responsibilities as religious. The Union had members of all classes but they met separately, in 'Drawing Room' meetings for the middle and upper classes and 'ordinary Mothers' Meetings' for the working classes.[2] The Mothers' Union was typical of late Victorian Anglicanism in that it was staunchly imperialist, nationalist, classist, and eugenicist; its members argued that the fittest societies gave religion and family pride of place. Evangelical Anglicans shunned novels, but many others believed that novel-writing could be a virtuous Christian endeavour if undertaken correctly. Charlotte Yonge's novels, featuring self-effacing Christian heroines, were popular, as were the poems of Christina Rossetti. Hymn-writing could also be a vehicle for female self-expression; Mrs Alexander's *Hymns for Little Children* (1848) ran to several editions.

During the nineteenth century the Church faced many challenges to its hegemony, including the rapid growth of Methodism and of the (largely Irish) Roman Catholic population. By the 1880s England was a religiously pluralistic country. The Anglican Church failed to keep pace with population growth, especially in urban areas in the north and the industrial Midlands. For industrial workers, the nearest parish church was often miles away, and Methodist chapels filled the gap. Non-Anglican forms of Protestantism were known collectively as 'dissent' or 'nonconformity'; in 1851 the religious census reported 3,153,490 nonconformists, including various Methodist denominations (who would by 1900 count over half a million members), Congregationalists, Presbyterians, over 125,000 Baptists, 37,000 Unitarians, and 18,000 Quakers. Members of these groups had fewer rights than Anglicans regarding both worship and participation in political life, although by contemporary European standards they enjoyed religious freedom. Many of these churches had more democratic or inclusive forms of worship and governance than the Anglican Church.

A sharp contrast between Anglican and non-Anglican Protestants

should not be assumed. Many non-elite families who considered themselves dissenters turned to the Church for certain functions, most notably
for baptism. Before the Civil Registration Act of 1837 an Anglican baptism
certificate functioned much like a secular birth certificate. While this was
a source of complaint among older nonconformists such as Quakers, in
many areas Methodists, especially Wesleyan Methodists, continued to use
their local parish church for baptism and other rites of passage such as
marriage and burial. For them, the Anglican and Methodist churches
served separate and complementary functions until at least mid-century.
One nonconformist family, while having their twins baptized in the parish
church in 1862, explained to the vicar that it was always best to 'begin and
end with the Church whatever you do between-whiles'.[3]

NON-ANGLICAN PROTESTANTS

Nonconformist churches were of two types: older denominations that
dated from the seventeenth century or before, such as Quakers and Unitarians, and newer evangelical ones that split off from the Anglican church
in the late eighteenth and early nineteenth centuries, notably various
forms of Methodism. Members of the Quaker faith, founded in the mid-
seventeenth century as the Society of Friends by George Fox (1624–91),
were by the nineteenth century a small but influential, mostly middle-
class group. Quakers regarded all people as equal before God and rejected
worldly finery; to this end they wore sober clothes and refused to acknowledge rank or title. Many were politically liberal or radical. In the nineteenth century, several Quaker families were prominent in manufacturing
and industry; Cadbury's chocolate, Barclay's Bank, and the Stockton and
Darlington Railway were all founded by Quakers.

The Quaker system of Women's Meetings gave women status within
the community and allowed them to gain administrative skills. Quaker
women's belief in the equality of men's and women's souls (although by
the nineteenth century women's preaching was banned), and their refusal
to see religion as isolated from politics, led them to be public activists in
various philanthropic and radical movements.[4] One was the anti-slavery
movement, in which Elizabeth Heyrick (1769–1831) led the Quakers' fight
to convince the national anti-slavery organization to pursue an immediate
rather than a gradual end to slavery. The English Quakers Anne Knight
(1786–1862) and Elizabeth Pease (1807–97) worked in the American campaign for abolition.

The term Unitarian entered European vocabularies at the beginning of the seventeenth century; the faith was well-established in England by the late eighteenth century. Unitarians' central belief was in the oneness of God. This rejection of the Holy Trinity, an illegal belief until 1813, was their only unifying doctrine; congregations did not need to belong to any larger organization or subscribe to any creed or doctrine to call themselves Unitarians. Like Quakers, Unitarians were a numerically small, mostly middle-class group. Most congregations were in large industrial cities such as Manchester, Birmingham and Leeds. Also like Quakers, Unitarians were disproportionately influential because many, including the Wedgewoods and the Courtaulds, were prominent in industry. Unitarians saw education and religion as crucial to politics and society, and they strove to improve themselves and the lot of others through anti-slavery activism and other reform efforts as well as educational endeavours.

Unitarianism's theological insistence on Jesus's humanity and the spiritual equality of all people informed the political and educational activism of its adherents. The relative gender equality of Unitarian communities helped ambitious and able women to flourish. Unitarian women were especially prominent in education reform. The Roman Catholic Church responded to the mass Irish immigration of the nineteenth century and to English, Welsh, and Scottish prejudice by establishing separate schools for Catholic children after 1847. Unitarians, in contrast, educated children and adults of all religious persuasions. They believed in the empowering and liberating effects of learning and were committed to meaningful, non-sectarian education for girls as well as boys. They emphasized small groups and personal interaction and founded 'ragged' and night schools for the working classes and day schools for middle-class children.

The career of Mary Carpenter exemplifies the opportunities available to Unitarian women. A devout believer of middle-class origins, Carpenter was deeply involved in education for all of her adult life and became famous for her work with child criminals. She was greatly influenced by evangelicalism and tried to model her own compassion after Jesus's. In Bristol in the 1840s she ran a night school for working-class children, a reformatory home for girls, and a middle-class girls' school. She was fiercely opposed to the impersonality of large institutions for the needy, arguing that smaller schools and dwellings offered orphaned children and others the chance to form the surrogate families that were as necessary to their success as more formal schooling. As a young woman she sought to appear retiring; later in life she read her own papers in public at meetings of the National Association for the Promotion of Social Science, and became so well-known that she was approached as an authority on young criminals by an 1852 Parliamentary Committee.

Middle-class evangelicals who were of the newer nonconformist faiths became a growing presence in English life during the last decades of the eighteenth century and the first decades of the nineteenth. Less politically engaged than Quakers and Unitarians, more prosperous and less radical than most Methodists, these evangelicals – some Anglican, some not – emphasized the centrality of domesticity and the home to their religion. Middle-class evangelical ideology held that women were morally superior but socially subordinate to men. This contradictory set of prescriptions celebrated the home but confined women to it, dictating that they care for house, husband and children and refrain from paid employment. Women were expected to bow to the wills of their husbands, but were also given responsibility for the religious and moral education of their children and the atmosphere of their homes. While men were spiritual leaders of their households and usually led the family's morning and evening prayers, other forms of day-to-day piety with regard to children and servants were often left to the womenfolk.[5]

The evangelical spirituality of women could also be expressed in personal journals, activities in church groups, and philanthropy. Many women who considered themselves serious Christians kept spiritual journals, some intended solely for private reflection and others for publication as a way of spreading the Gospel. They might also evangelize in person to household servants, friends, and the local poor. Most were active in various church activities, working in ladies' auxiliaries and visiting the sick and the poor on behalf of the congregation. They might give hand-made gifts to the minister, ask local merchants and professionals to help sponsor various events, or bake and pour tea for celebrations. Middle-class evangelicalism, then, separated women from men and confined them to a morally elevated but restricted domestic sphere where they practised the professions of wife and mother. And many middle-class women used the evangelical ideology of feminine domesticity to justify activities outside the home, especially religious and philanthropic work. If domesticity and morality were natural to women, they argued, then a true woman was domestic no matter where she was.

For working-class evangelical women, most of whom were Methodist, the situation was somewhat different. The rise of evangelical Methodism was one of the most notable developments of the century. Founded in

1738 by John Wesley (1703–91), who spent much of his adult life as an itinerant out-of-doors preacher, the movement grew quickly, especially among the lower middle and upper working classes: by 1800 there were 94,000 English Methodists and by 1830 Methodism claimed 286,000 adherents (the sect remained within the Church of England until Wesley's death in 1791 but broke away soon afterwards). Between 1790 and 1830 Wesleyan Methodism expanded from its eighteenth-century urban base into the smaller towns, villages and rural areas of the north and west (remaining weaker in London, the south, and the south-east) and appealed to the miners, artisans, small tradesmen and shopkeepers of early industrial England. It also divided into other sects, including Primitive Methodists and Bible Christians.

Methodism took religious control away from the pulpit and gave it to those in the pews, who often expressed themselves in raucous and uncontrolled ways. Methodists sang, prayed aloud, and testified to their spiritual experiences and to God's presence in their lives. Above all, they stressed individual salvation as their central religious experience. All of this could be quite threatening to traditional or 'high church' Anglicans. Many Anglicans found the Methodist style of worship disturbingly enthusiastic and disapproved of its emphasis on lay preachers and on personal relationships with God over learned theology. But to many working people it seemed a better way of expressing their spirituality than that of the Church of England. Methodist services put the emphasis on music and singing rather than theology and set liturgies. Adherents were encouraged to feel the spirit of God moving them rather than worrying about whether they were educated enough to understand fine doctrinal points or well enough off to sit in the front pews. (For much of the century pews were rented out in Anglican churches. Those in front were most expensive, while those further back were more affordable. In some churches people who did not rent pews could not attend; in others, benches were provided in the back at no charge.)

Working-class Methodist women were largely immune to the pressures of the middle-class evangelical celebration of home as a place apart; for them home was part of, rather than a haven from, the world around it. Working-class nonconformist women had many ways to express their spirituality in their daily lives. While some defied their husbands to express their faith, after conversion to a sect such as Primitive Methodism or Baptism, others were able to pursue their beliefs in a family context. Most could use their parental roles and domestic space to religious ends.

It was women's job to educate the next generation into religion, a task that was described as praiseworthy by preachers and denominational magazines. A well-kept house was often taken as a sign of godliness: Emma Robson's 1870 obituary in *Primitive Methodist Magazine* stated that she was 'near to our ideal of the model wife and mother', partly because her home was 'the picture of neatness'.[6] Hospitality could also be a spiritual endeavour, especially the accommodation of Methodist itinerant preachers in need of beds. Women might volunteer their houses for weekly female prayer meetings or girls' Bible classes, as Baptist Marianne Farningham (1834–1909) did. Working-class evangelical spirituality was also expressed in workplaces; in early-nineteenth-century Yorkshire, evangelical women who worked in the woollen industry were said to alternate hymn singing with conversation.[7]

Perhaps the best illustration of the far-reaching potential of evangelicalism is the temperance movement, which emphasized personal purity and salvation from the socially and morally destructive influences of drink. In the 1830s, 40s and 50s, many small, local, non-sectarian women's temperance societies were organized, especially in the north of England, Birmingham and London. Some opposed only hard liquor or excessive drinking, others wished to prohibit all spirits, wine, and beer. In all its guises, temperance was noticeably female in membership and evangelical in style. Working-class women, many of whose lives were rendered violent and impoverished by the alcohol consumption of the men in their families, spoke out in their communities and wrote prolifically, usually for audiences of women and children, in an effort to convert others to their cause. Within the Chartist movement there were several female Chartist Abstinence Unions, which held Chartist Temperance Tea Parties. Later more elite women also became involved, usually concentrating their efforts on the damaging effects of drinking on working families. In the 1860s the state Church began its own organization, the Church of England Temperance Society, whose Women's Union was at first dominated by upper- and middle-class women but later came to include working-class women. The Union was especially concerned with the problem of women's drinking, and targeted certain professions: laundrywomen were thought to be heavy drinkers. Others, such as Mrs Julia Wightman, a clergyman's wife and leading temperance advocate who wrote a widely read account of temperance work, *Haste to the Rescue* (1859), reached out to clergymen and Sunday school teachers in an effort to interest the middle and upper classes in the cause.

Temperance became national in scope with the founding of the British Women's Temperance Association (BWTA) in the late 1870s. Inspired in part by the Gospel Temperance movement that was so influential in the United States, women in it specifically spoke of their temperance activism as a form of mission, making explicit the connection between religious commitment, evangelical style and opposition to drink. Temperance was seen as a female morality crusade: the BWTA received many requests specifically for female speakers, and women who were willing to speak publicly were in demand. This was a tricky path to tread, as meetings could become rowdy, and because women often went to public houses to proselytize, temperance work was seen as unrespectable by many. The BWTA had members and leaders who were nonconformist, Methodist, and Anglican.[8] Regardless of denomination, these women felt called to speak out against the evil of drink.

CATHOLICS, JEWS, AND ATHEISTS

The next largest religious group after Protestants was the Catholic community. It comprised approximately 100,000 people in 1750; Irish immigration helped to swell the Roman Catholic population of England to 750,000 by 1851 and to more than two million by the end of our period. In Scotland, too, Catholics were an important group, who by 1914 comprised fully 15 per cent of the population and were overwhelmingly urban, working-class, and of Irish origin.[9] In Ireland, of course, Roman Catholicism was a tremendous religious, cultural, and political force. In England, Catholics were considered outsiders. Even after Catholic Emancipation in 1829 they continued to face often virulent anti-Catholic prejudice. Local authorities might make it difficult for a Catholic mission to rent rooms, and crowds would hurl stones at the windows of Catholic churches during Mass. Until 1850 the Roman Catholic hierarchy had no presence in England. During the second half of the nineteenth century, the Church served two distinct groups: wealthy converts from Anglicanism and the Irish Catholic poor. The second group was so large that 'Irish' and 'Catholic' were sometimes used interchangeably even by church leaders themselves. Wherever a group of Irish immigrants settled, the Church was likely to establish a new mission.[10]

Priests lived among their poor parishioners, often seeing several generations to adulthood, and served as sacred and secular leaders of communities that often encountered native Protestant hostility. For example, in the 1880s the women of a poor Irish Catholic congregation at St Patrick's Church in London's Soho Square, London held Monday night meetings. The priest, Father Sheridan, came regularly, to amuse the group by reading stories. Many of these were selections from a volume entitled *Irish Pleasantry and Fun* which included such anecdotes as 'The Donnybrook Spree' and 'Puss in Brogues'. Although meetings ended with the Rosary, they were more Irish and social than Catholic and theological in tone. Religion was much more than a Sunday formality.[11]

For most Catholic clergy, whether their flocks were Irish or English, immigrant or native, mixed marriages between Catholics and Protestants were a central concern, and thought to be one-quarter to one-third of all marriages celebrated in Catholic churches. Most priests would bless such unions only on condition that the couple agreed to raise their children as Catholics. Since it was generally agreed that women decided their children's religious upbringing, the size of future congregations lay in female hands. This was such an accepted truth that mixed marriages were seen as bringing potential converts and future children into the Church if the wife was Catholic, but as resulting in a net loss for the Catholic Church if the husband was. Mixed marriages were one more reason for priests and Catholic communities to nurture the faith and community spirit of the women of the congregation.[12]

England also had a small Jewish population of approximately 8,000 in 1750 and more than 20,000 a century later, most of whom lived in London. By 1830, an Anglo-Jewish elite of City and landed men had emerged to lead their community. One of these, Lionel Rothschild (1808–79), was the first Jewish MP; he was allowed to take his seat in 1858 – eleven years after he was elected – and Jews were admitted to universities in 1871. Then, in the late nineteenth and early twentieth centuries, over 120,000 immigrants fleeing anti-Semitic persecution in Russia emigrated to Britain. By 1914 there were 300,000 Jews in England, Wales, and Scotland, concentrated in London but also living in Manchester, Leeds, Liverpool, Birmingham and Glasgow. Like Irish Catholics, Jewish immigrants lived in distinct communities that were culturally as well as religiously demarcated by traditional celebrations and customs that set them apart from native English Protestants. Jewish immigrant women refrained from studying scripture, which was considered men's work, but not from earning money, which they often did so that their husbands and sons could be scholars.

Even English Judaism was affected by evangelicalism; like Christianity, it came to stress the home as a religious space and women as keepers of the family's faith. Over the course of the late nineteenth and early twentieth centuries, most Jewish immigrant families were assimilated into the English culture. At the same time they shifted away from older Eastern European patterns in which religious practice was centred on the synagogue and excluded women, to a more English and evangelical style in which some rituals were feminized and domesticated, thereby giving women a more central role in spiritual practice.[13] The domestic role of women became pivotal; for instance, the entire kitchen needed to be purified for the holiday of Passover, as in this recollection of an immigrant home in Manchester at the turn of the century:

> Everything had to be changed ... we had big cellars and all your pots had to be changed, and we had two big tea chests, that had all the Passover pots inside, that you only used for Passover. All the pots we had in the back kitchen ... had to be taken down and washed and put away in a box and taken into the cellar, and all the tables and cupboards had to be washed down, fresh white paper put inside ... We had a red rug in the back kitchen that had to be red raggled and the yard had to be whitewashed ... The oven had to be whitewashed inside, because we'd cooked ordinary food during the year.[14]

The Catholic and Jewish poor were often aided by sectarian charities. Native Catholics took responsibility for educating immigrant Catholic children, while the affluent Anglo-Jewish middle class took exclusive responsibility for their immigrant co-religionists and created charitable networks, parallel to mainstream ones, to serve them. For instance, the largest Jewish relief agency, the Jewish Board of Guardians (JBG), took its name from and modelled itself on the Poor Law's Board of Guardians. A leading Jewish philanthropist, Helen Lucas, praised the JBG for refusing to provide handouts, but also argued for using 'common sense and sympathy'[15] as well as statistics to solve the problems of poverty. The Jewish Association for the Protection of Girls and Women was established in 1885 to rescue Jewish immigrant women from prostitution. Anglo-Jews created such separate but equal agencies partly out of a sense of community, partly because they were denied access to positions of leadership in most English charities, and partly because they were embarrassed by poor foreign Jews and wanted to pre-empt English Christian contact with, and criticism of, them. They sought, through education and social services, to acculturate Jewish immigrants into English life as quickly and quietly as possible. Jewish women's relationship to English culture remained complex throughout the century, fractured by religious differences even as cultural gaps faded over time.

Not everyone in nineteenth-century England was religious. There were some avowed atheists in the middle and upper classes, such as republican and freethinker Charles Bradlaugh, who in 1866 founded the National Secular Society. Many others were irreligious: the census of 1851 suggested that about 40 per cent of the population attended no church. Evidence also suggests that men were less likely to participate in organized religion of any sort than women, and that unskilled industrial workers and the very poor were the least likely to attend church. And even in a self-consciously modern era, many remote areas maintained some form of folk religion, a mix of Christian, pagan, and traditional beliefs and practices.[16]

Women's roles

In all of these varied religions, women were more active than men during our period. Therefore a focus on religion is, almost by necessity, a focus on women and their participation, which took many forms. Perhaps the most obvious way in which women dominated religious life was the most visible: the majority of congregations (except Unitarian ones) were predominantly female. (One exception was the poorest women, who generally did not attend church regularly.) Responding to the English sociologist Charles Booth's survey of 'Religious Influences' in late-nineteenth-century London, Reverend Springett of St Matthew's Church, Brixton, commented that 'women, of course, preponderate'; his colleague at St Saviour's, Brixton Hill, admitted that nine-tenths of his congregation were women; the pastor of the Kenyon Baptist Church tried to put a positive spin on matters by explaining that fully one-fourth of his flock were men.[17] While this does not tell us very much about women's and men's spiritual lives, it does reveal that the social and institutional practice of religion was often maintained by women. Among the working population, men were especially likely to curtail church attendance when they began working full-time, so that Sunday school attendance was far more evenly balanced between the sexes than adult Church attendance. In industrial Lancashire, where so many women worked full-time in manufacturing, it was lower than anywhere else in the country.

Women did not necessarily focus on Sunday-morning services. Non-elite women might attend evening services, as it was sometimes easier for them to escape domestic responsibilities during the dinner hour. They also attended weekday services, prayer meetings and Bible classes in far greater numbers than men, and indeed many of these targeted women insofar as they were held at times when men who worked full-time could not attend. Many efforts to recruit families into the Church recognized women's church-going authority; for instance, lady church workers addressed themselves to the female, not male, head of the household.

Other non-religious factors, rather than any natural female inclination towards religion, may have conspired to make women active participants in congregational life. Women who felt isolated or subordinated in their daily domestic and working lives might have welcomed the opportunity to attend church.[18] In some areas, working-class civic and organizational life may have offered fewer opportunities for fellowship to women than to men; women might therefore have found their religious community more appealing.[19] In addition to worship, most congregations offered other services to women, ranging from children's education to social events to opportunities for material or spiritual self-improvement or the giving and receiving of charity. Women might participate in prayer meetings, sewing courses, singing classes, and holiday clubs. Many churches also offered women's gatherings such as Mothers' Meetings, to which, as one organizer explained, women could 'bring their work and babies [while] a lady reads a book to them or an address is given'.[20] Middle-class volunteers might offer to provide childcare during a weekday service, or volunteer as church visitors to poorer women; in both instances, middle- and working-class women were involved in the same church community (albeit in very different ways). Women made sure their children attended Sunday school. These examples give a sense of how important women were to organized religions, and of the broad range of church-centred activities they might participate in. All in all, while women were more likely to go to church than men, this was because of a constellation of social forces, and not because women were somehow naturally more religious.

For many women, then, religion was part of the fabric of life, shaping community networks, leisure time, and children's education as well as matters spiritual and theological. For some, religion was also their vocation and a full-time endeavour. They might be active as relatives of clergymen or in domestic or foreign missions, or they might lend their support to the missionaries whose exploits they read about. Others were, as sisters or deaconesses, professional religious women. Some very radical working-class women even claimed to be the Messiah. Some preached within their Methodist denominations to working-class followers, often addressing their spiritual and material concerns in particular. Still others worked within a more polite, middle-class evangelical tradition. Salvation Army women made urban centres their missionary targets and sought to evangelize through the medium of working-class culture. In all of these instances, female evangelizing, preaching and leadership by women, though it was unusual, was part of a larger tradition of female religious involvement that characterizes the complex interplay of belief and action in nineteenth-century English society.

CLERICAL RELATIONS AND MISSIONARIES

Clergymen's wives, daughters and sisters were sometimes referred to as the 'unpaid curates' of the clergy. While some women may have felt resentment at the responsibilities thrust on them by virtue of marriage or birth, a high proportion of clergy wives were also clergy daughters, which suggests an intergenerational sense of family vocation for some. Many used their positions to participate in the clerical profession as wives whose adult lives were subordinate but necessary to their husbands' careers.[21]

Missionary work was a crucial part of nineteenth-century life. Missionaries went into communities they perceived to be in need, both in England and abroad, to spread the Word of God, seek converts, and provide education and medical assistance. Missions were one of the most popular aspects of evangelicalism, and could be extremely fulfilling. In 1834 Mary Ann Hutchins, a missionary's wife in Jamaica, wrote home to her brother:

The thirst for knowledge amongst the blacks and coloured people is very great; many of them are asking for books to read, and the anxiety they evince, is very pleasing. I was much pleased one of the Sabbaths I was at Montego Bay, to see a Chapel pretty well filled with communicants, and instead of two – *fourteen bottles of wine* were used at the Sacrament. Oh! when in my dear native land will a scene like this be witnessed?[22]

By the turn of the nineteenth century virtually every dissenting denomination and many evangelical Anglican parish churches supported their own missionary organizations, such as the Baptist Missionary Society (1792), the Congregationalist London Missionary Society (1795), the Anglican Church Missionary Society (1799), and the Wesleyan Methodist Missionary Society (1813). Missionary involvement figured largely in evangelical autobiographies and memoirs. In the 1880s and 1890s British missionaries spent £2,000,000 per annum on their efforts, a sum equivalent to 2 per cent of annual government expenditure.[23]

Missionaries worked either in foreign missions to distant non-Christian countries including Ceylon, Persia, and Morocco, or in domestic missions to urban slums crowded with the labouring poor. While women and men across the socio-economic spectrum supported missions, most missionaries and leaders of missionary societies were middle-class and regarded themselves as different from the objects of their attention. An exception was Ellen Raynard's London Female Bible and Domestic Mission (founded in 1858), which was staffed by working-class women who reached out to their inner-city London neighbours. Significantly, for the first part of the long nineteenth century domestic and foreign missions were seen as basically alike. Both non-whites abroad and the poor at home were regarded as superficially but not spiritually different from missionaries. In both cases, missionaries were bravely leaving the comforts of home to bring Christianity to the 'uncivilized'.

Missions were omnipresent in people's lives, irrespective of age or class: children heard and read about them in Sunday school, while adults listened to sermons on them, read fiction and non-fiction on missionary life, and attended bazaars in support of the cause. Middle-class women went from door to door collecting subscriptions for the church's mission society from rich and poor alike; even a small donation allowed a working-class woman to identify herself as a supporter. Women also organized women's auxiliaries in support of missions, served refreshments at meetings, and planned, staffed, and sewed fancy goods for missionary bazaars.

During the first part of our period, foreign missions were more common and more popular with the public; in the last third of the nineteenth century, home missions to such areas as the East End of London were in the ascendent and were often better-funded by their home churches and denominations than foreign ones. Foreign missions became more inclined to emphasize racial difference and to concern themselves with general health and welfare as much as with the spiritual lives of target populations. As these changes occurred, foreign mission work became more and more the province of women. Women's involvement shifted from auxiliary and backstage forms of support to more autonomous female organizations which invited prominent female missionaries to speak at their meetings and fostered their own connections with those working abroad. This type of specifically female support for missionary efforts proved extremely popular, and by the end of the nineteenth century the major missionary organizations received 70 per cent of their contributions from British women, making foreign missions the major women's cause of the nineteenth century.[24]

Women were important abroad as well. Some of the most important missionary work in the first two-thirds of the century was done by the wives of male missionaries. Their technical status as lay people, and their practical role as wives who led by example, made them fit perfectly with accepted ideas of female leadership and virtue. Some women who wished to pursue missionary work even married male missionaries as a way of pursuing their calling; they chose to enter into unions arranged by sympathetic ministers and performed after only a few weeks' acquaintance. In the 1830s, for instance, Mary Ann Chambers originally hoped to travel overseas with her brother, who was training with the Baptist Missionary Society, and worried that he would leave her behind. She then met and married the Revd James Coultart and went to Jamaica with him instead. Rather than feeling that she had subverted the institution of marriage or wed too hastily, an 1841 biography notes that 'she regarded the whole affair as the gracious leadings of Providence.'[25]

In the 1860s and 1870s the larger missionary organizations became more interested in deploying women as missionaries in their own right. Some denominations founded associations with this sole aim, such as the Church of England Zenana Missionary Society and the Baptist Zenana Mission (*zenanas* were the separate women's quarters, to which men had no access, that were maintained in some upper-and middle-class Hindu and Muslim homes in north, north-western and eastern parts of India). By the end of the century, women had gone from comprising almost none of the official missionary population to making up almost half of the missionary force; the Church Missionary Society alone sent fewer than ten women abroad in the 1870s but over three hundred during the 1890s. Missionary work was one of the many employment opportunities that opened to unmarried middle-class women in the last few decades of the nineteenth century.

Because women were thought to be naturally moral and to have a duty to bring Christian domesticity to those who lacked it, they seemed well-suited to missionary work, especially as it became less specifically theological. Middle-class women's domestic purity qualified them for missionary work but was itself put in danger by it, rendering female missionaries simultaneously well-equipped and vulnerable. As a result, female missionaries were often depicted in the domestic press as focusing their attention on the needs of women and children, to emphasize how traditional they remained even while working overseas. Ironically, while foreign missionary work – with its emphasis on basic public health and its confrontation with unfamiliar cultures – was more physically arduous and dangerous, because of the defining difference that race had come to represent it was seen as less compromising to middle-class women's purity than missionary work at home. Mission work in the East End of London, on the other hand, seemed liable to change the women who performed it. While Ellen Raynard's Biblewomen were working-class, the middle-class women who funded her mission avoided contact with the inner-city objects of their charity. By the end of the century, lady missionaries had gained real respect for the dangerous and important work they did, and their visibility had prompted a new respect for the work of missionary wives as well.[26]

Between 1895 and 1925 missionary work at home and abroad declined in England for a variety of religious, imperial, and political reasons, including a falling-off in organized religion, a decrease in the wealth of the remaining faithful, and a change in imperial priorities following the Boer War. But for the better part of the long nineteenth century missionary work was pervasive in English society, popular with the many women who supported it from home, and a life's work to those who chose it, whether as wives or as missionaries themselves.

SISTERS

Another full-time religious commitment was sisterhood. The second half of the century saw the rise of Anglican and Roman Catholic sisterhoods, all-female communities of professional religious women. Even they, in this century of evangelical outreach, did not necessarily opt for isolation and contemplation; sisters more often than not sought to educate and assist those less fortunate than themselves. Sisters were part and parcel of this religious and evangelical century, even as they lived apart from others and dedicated themselves openly to their work and their faith in ways that were unique.

From the 1840s until the beginning of the twentieth century, England saw a sharp increase in the number, visibility, and activity of Roman Catholic and Anglican sisterhoods. In 1837, there were 3,000 Roman Catholic nuns in 235 convents in England; by 1900, there were between 8,000 and 10,000 women in 600 convents. Anglican sisterhoods began to flourish around 1850; by 1900 there were several thousand sisters in ninety communities. Most Anglican communities had between twenty-five and forty members, although some had only a handful of women, and a few had several hundred. Roman Catholic communities tended to be slightly smaller. Small communities in both faiths confined their work to a single locality, while those with more than about forty-five sisters usually opened branch houses.[27] Other denominations, including Quakers and Wesleyan Methodists, who founded the Sisters of the Poor in 1887, also attempted to make a professional religious life available to women. The Anglican Church and some evangelical churches re-established the obsolete position of 'deaconess' for women who wished to be full-time religious professionals without taking vows or living within the community.

Roman Catholic sisterhoods were spread over the country. The older convents were aristocratic, exclusive – they attracted women from older Catholic gentry families – and frequently of Continental origin. Those established in the nineteenth century, however, were distinctly non-elite. These newer sisterhoods were often founded by women who were converts to Roman Catholicism and not part of English Roman Catholic society; by the 1880s, many Anglo-Catholic converts were political radicals. Newer Catholic houses pursued an uncloistered engagement with the world and they attracted many sisters from working-class backgrounds.[28]

In an effort to avoid controversy in a nation which defined itself as separate from Catholic Europe, Anglican sisterhoods operated along deliberately different lines from traditional Roman Catholic convents. Women lived together in a community but took no vows and did not segregate themselves. Anglican sisterhoods were concentrated in London and the south. Their members tended to come from wealthier families in rural areas or market towns and their establishments maintained the social hierarchy of the outside world. Working-class women became 'lay sisters', who performed the menial domestic labour of the house, while middle-and upper-class women became higher-status 'choir sisters'.[29]

Most deaconesses, while they did not take vows and were free to leave their order at any time, did some form of domestic mission work. Anglican deaconesses were trained and sanctioned by the Church and had various roles. They focused on local issues, and usually lived in the parishes they served. In large urban parishes especially they were of crucial assistance to the local clergymen under whom they worked. Non-Anglican deaconesses, most of whom were evangelical and working-class, were especially popular in the industrial north, where they ran urban domestic missions and did work similar to that of their Anglican and Catholic counterparts. Working-class women in London could make a living and serve the Church as Biblewomen, earning ten shillings per week selling Bibles to poor families. Wealthy evangelical women usually avoided a professional religious life.

The rise of sisterhoods and deaconesses should be seen against a background of growing evangelicalism in England and America, the growth of Roman Catholicism in Western Europe, and the 'redundant' women crisis of the second half of the nineteenth century, in which there was widespread fear that there were more middle-class single women than there were eligible men to marry them. Sisterhoods were, in this context, thought to solve a social problem. Most importantly, nineteenth-century sisterhoods were one aspect of nineteenth-century female religiosity. When Jane Ellacombe entered an Anglican sisterhood, she wrote to her father:

> Do not deprive me of the blessed privilege of working for Christ with
> my brethren ... I should be then only one of many comrades, and we
> should all act together in our different parts towards one end, and my
> rashness and inexperience would be corrected and guided by the deep
> and earnest yet wise and calm spirits who would influence us.[30]

Women who chose to enter convents were not necessarily more profoundly religious than other women. Sisters responded to the same social problems as other religiously-inspired philanthropic women, focusing on the widespread poverty that followed industrialization and targeting women's specific vulnerabilities. Sisters did not retreat from the world; they engaged with it, providing welfare, education, nursing, and other forms of aid to those in need.

The attractions which convents held for many women are difficult to recapture in the present day. They gave women the opportunity to live a female-centred life, which may have been quite important for those who wished to but did not marry, those who chose not to marry, or those with strong or romantic attachments to other women. Sisterhoods provided an opportunity to transform the lonely isolation of spinsterhood into a life of community, active spirituality, and social service. In addition, some evidence suggests that sisters may have been in better health than other women, since they did not sacrifice their own needs for the welfare of husbands and children, as many wives and mothers did. Convents also allowed women to do difficult and meaningful work that was recognized as such, rather than being trivialized as a leisure activity, a hobby, or an occasion for socializing, as was so much female philanthropy. This was especially attractive to Anglican choir sisters, those from the socio-economic elite, in which work was not considered proper for women. For Anglican lay sisters and most Roman Catholic sisters, who would have worked in any case, the religious life allowed them to do that work in a supportive community. When Benedicta Bostock was asked why she wished to become a sister in the Benedictine community of St Mary's Abbey in North London, she said simply, 'The Poor Law'.[31]

Sisters seemed to their contemporaries well-suited by their celibacy to undertake rescue work, and many ran penitentiaries for 'fallen' women. Servants, and especially maids-of-all-work, were the largest occupational group to seek refuge in convent-run penitentiaries. While many were ultimately sent back to the livelihood in which they had been vulnerable, penitentiaries were often therapeutic as well as penal, and sheltered victims of incest and sexual violence, women fleeing abusive relationships, female alcoholics and prostitutes.

The existence of female communities, especially Catholic ones in Protestant England, was seen as a threat by some. This was evident in the 1869 case of *Saurin* v. *Star*, in which Sister Mary Scholastica Joseph, née Susanna Mary Saurin, a Roman Catholic Irish immigrant, sued her Mother Superior (described in court as Mrs Star) after being expelled from the convent. Although Saurin seems to have been unfitted for convent life and tolerated by her community for many years before finally being asked to leave, many newspapers and magazines – including *The Times*, the *Daily Herald*, *The Pall Mall Gazette*, and *Punch* – used the case as an occasion to criticize Roman Catholicism and convent life as 'degrading' and 'corrupting'.[32] Journalists also argued that the case revealed that women's communities were doomed to failure, as women could not govern themselves without pettiness and cruelty. The life described in court was meant to serve as a warning to fashionable young ladies who thought convent life preferable to life as a spinster. Sisterhoods declined as the twentieth century dawned and brought with it more professional options for women.

MESSIAHS

Clergy relations, missionaries, and sisters were relatively commonplace compared with a number of small and often extreme groups of religious women that were highly visible for short periods of the long nineteenth century. These believers claimed to have faith in a female Christ – a radical notion since most people took Jesus's masculinity for granted – and to understand salvation and the Messiah in a fundamentally different way. In the 1770s Ann Lee, a working woman from Manchester, claimed that she was Mother Ann the Redeemer, became the leader of the Shakers (a breakaway Quaker sect), moved to the United States, and established Shaker communities. In 1780, a Welsh woman, Mary Evans, announced that she was the bride of Christ and attracted a small group of followers. Soon afterwards a Scottish woman, Luckie Buchan, proclaimed herself Friend Mother, Christ's younger sister.

One of the most influential and interesting of the female Christs was Joanna Southcott (1750–1814). Southcott was a Methodist upholstress and domestic servant in Devonshire when, in 1792, at the age of forty-two, she heard voices that told her that she was the saviour and the 'Woman clothed with the Sun' referred to in Revelations. She was mocked by her fellow congregants but published a tract on herself in 1802 and, supported by several clerics, went to London to preach. By 1808, 14,000 people had identified themselves as Joannaites by purchasing her sealed prophecy. By the time of her death she had 100,000 followers in London alone, and thousands more in the industrializing north.

Southcott, who spoke of herself as both the bride of Christ and as Christ himself, was supported for most of her career by two wealthy believers, Jane Townley and Ann Underwood. The majority of her followers were women, many of them single and working class. Southcott appealed to them because she often spoke of her experiences as a single working woman, and many of her prophecies argued for all women's spiritual equality with men. Speaking as Christ, she reminded her listeners that women

followed Me to My Cross, and stood weeping to see Me crucified; they were the first at my sepulchre to see My resurrection . . . Let it be known unto all men, the work at first was carried on by women . . . So now suffer women to be present and forbid them not.[33]

Southcott's writings were suffused with images of weddings, marriages, sexual intercourse, adultery, and sodomy, which were rarely if ever used as expressions of faith or godliness in mainstream theologies. Her words spoke directly to the lives of many women; she wrote, for instance, about the experience of being deserted by a married lover named Wills. Such sexual vulnerability and despair were widespread problems for working women. Southcott claimed she was pregnant with a new Messiah in 1813, proposed to a man who rejected her, married a disciple, had a false pregnancy, and died in 1814. Such was its power that Southcottianism survived until the 1840s.[34]

Southcott's career and writings make clear the links between religious enthusiasm and sexual heterodoxy, both of which are central to female millenarians (those concerned with Jesus's second coming) and their followers. Her alleged pregnancy meant that she was the ultimate woman as well as redeemer, and that the two roles were intimately linked. All female millenarians claimed a central rather than a subsidiary role for themselves, and denied that they were 'mere' women; Southcott went further in insisting on the spiritual equality of women with men, as well as on her own divinity. She and her fellow Messiahs had tiny numbers of followers and short careers, but their existence demonstrates the radical gender potential of religion early in the century. By the 1840s, the working classes became more concerned with respectability than with radical politics and religion, but for the first part of the long nineteenth century many working women saw their own potential as powerful leaders rather than meek followers.

PREACHERS

This potential for leadership is also evident in female preaching, a less extreme form of female agency stemming from religion. The lay preaching that was encouraged in the various Methodist denominations constituted a radical expansion of English religious styles. Female preaching – which was almost never sanctioned and was often explicitly denounced – was an even more radical part of this revolution. The number of female preachers was small, but like the millenarians they were highly visible.

Mostly working-class, they acted as public speakers and as religious leaders, rather than operating behind the scenes as so many women did. Yet their work is perhaps best understood as part of the spectrum of female Methodist activity that included many forms of community outreach and evangelizing.

Female preachers were known for their plain and unadorned speech, their emotional fervour, and their preference for speaking to groups in an informal way about their personal relationships with God. This tendency to preach by bearing witness was distinctly Methodist in its emphasis on the personal over the theological. As a form of preaching, it was seen as more feminine and thus less threatening than more authoritative exhortations from the pulpit. When Wesleyan Methodism was first founded, its female preachers were only one aspect of its revolutionary nature. As it aged, however, opportunities for women in the Church contracted; other Methodist sects would follow similar paths.

Wesley had initially opposed female preaching, but later held that women might, in the rare case of 'an extraordinary call', speak publicly, and even supported the ministries of some individual women. Early travelling preachers, such as Ann Cutler and Mary Taft, worked on an individual ad hoc basis without achieving the respect or official status accorded to male itinerants, however, and the sanctioning of women as preachers did not long survive Wesley's death in 1791. The denomination banned women preachers in 1803 as part of a move towards propriety and polite female behaviour, but a subsequent ban in 1836 indicates that the earlier edict had not been wholly obeyed. In the late eighteenth century, *Methodist Magazine* often printed biographies of female preachers; by the early nineteenth century, these had been replaced by profiles of clerical wives. (There was a similar movement towards propriety and away from female preaching in the Quaker faith during the late seventeenth century.) A very few nineteenth-century Wesleyan Methodist women preached as late as 1860, but most were active in their churches by teaching Sunday school, organizing and participating in prayer meetings, Bible study, evangelizing, and social events, or working as deaconesses.[35]

The Wesleyan Methodist quest for respectability came into conflict with popular evangelicalism, and ensuing tensions caused some Methodists to split off from the main denomination. The largest new sects were Primitive Methodists, Independent Methodists, and Bible Christians; they, along with a smaller sect, the Female Revivalists, flaunted the new Wesleyan Methodist propriety in several ways, chief among them the continued use of female preachers. Sectarian Methodism remained popular long after Wesleyanism had become more respectable. It was strongest among cottagers and labourers in rural areas where domestic and agricultural work still thrived, and in factory-dominated areas where workers were nostalgic for the control over their working lives that they had recently lost. Considered 'true religion' by its followers, sectarian Methodism flourished during the first few decades of the nineteenth century largely without chapels or official leaders, emphasizing instead self-expression, self-government, and a priesthood of all believers. Like Quakers, sectarian Methodists believed in sexual equality before God and denied that men and women had a different spiritual status.

The Sectarian Methodists' style of worship came to be seen as lower-class and was often denigrated by middle-class observers; Primitive Methodists were derisively referred to as 'Ranters'. Believers met out-of-doors or in cottages, prayed and sang loudly (or, to unsympathetic ears, ranted), frequently reproached friends and neighbours, and emphasized personal salvation. They often held large camp meetings, which were all-day, democratic, egalitarian affairs that involved all who were present. These, like contemporaneous mass political meetings, were sometimes seen as a threat to peaceful society and government. During this period cottage religion was, in many villages and towns, a recognized working-class alternative to Anglicanism.

Sectarians allowed and even encouraged female preaching – Primitives granted it official sanction – although larger sects sometimes played down the activities of women preachers. Women were instrumental in spreading the popular evangelical message of sectarian Methodism, and itinerant female preachers mobilized working-class listeners in rural and newly industrializing areas. They would arrive in a town and speak in homes and fields about their own religious feelings; their preaching was often quiet and intimate, unlike that of sectarian male preachers. Cottage religions emphasized the primacy of the home at a time when many working people, especially working women, felt destabilized by industrialization.

Primitive Methodism spread through rural Wiltshire and Berkshire in the 1820s and 1830s, where as many as thirty women were preaching on the Brinkworth circuit that covered the area around the town of Swindon. Many women began preaching when they were quite young; Elizabeth White, Harriet Randborn, and Harriet Maslin (all born in the 1810s) started as adolescents, and the median age of women preaching on the circuit was less than twenty. Early Primitive female preachers also included

Elizabeth Gorse Gaunt of Derbyshire and Hannah Howe of Stoney Middleton in Derbyshire. The last known female Primitive itinerant preacher, Elizabeth Bultitude, retired in 1862. Female preachers were also crucial to the growth of the Bible Christian denomination in its heartland of Devon and Cornwall. Two women in particular, Mary Thorne, a married 55-year-old, and Johanna Brooks, a married 29-year-old with two children, were primarily responsible for the sect's success. Its younger itinerant preachers included Em Cottle and Elizabeth Dart.[36] Yet even as Bible Christianity depended on female preachers, it excluded women from the government of the sect.

Sectarianism also flourished in northern industrial towns. The Primitive preacher Ann Carr (1783–1841), a poor and uneducated woman whose flamboyant style and aggressive personality distressed Wesleyan officials, was at first encouraged and supported by Primitive Methodists in Nottingham and Hull, where she preached in mill yards and courtyards as well as at camp meetings. Carr, along with Elizabeth Tomlinson and Sarah Kirkland, enjoyed remarkable success in the towns and villages of Nottingham and Derby. She then moved on to Leeds, the centre of the West Riding woollen industry, where textiles were produced by home-working female labourers. Recently displaced from surrounding villages, from which they had come in search of work, these workers were Carr's audience.

Carr preached wherever and whenever the spirit moved her; this troubled the Primitive authorities in Leeds, whose denomination was, in the 1820s and 1830s, developing into a more urban, chapel-based, organized style of worship. Refusing to conform, Carr left the Primitives, and she and her followers became known as the Female Revivalists. While Wesleyans and now many sectarians were building chapels, Female Revivalists continued to preach in homes or in makeshift chapels; their theology and style appealed to women workers who were recent migrants from rural areas.

Carr resolutely rejected any challenge to her status as a preacher. She, like Joanna Southcott, positioned herself as the empathetic equal of her listeners, and was very popular among the working women of Leeds. Her prominence and independence reveal the opportunities that religion could provide for women; it is difficult to envisage a woman of Carr's social position and education attaining such a position of leadership in any secular endeavour. Her career also demonstrates the importance of female preachers to female listeners. But the Revivalist movement, which in the 1830s included an adult school, a Sunday school, and a Friendly Society, did not long outlive its leader, who died in 1841.

As older ways of life and work, and then decades of upheaval, were replaced by a definitively urban and industrialized society, cottage religion and female preaching mostly died out (although both continued to exist in isolated parts of England and Wales). Sectarian Methodism eventually followed Wesleyan Methodism and became institutionalized, respectable, and restrained. Various Methodisms continued to offer opportunities for female activity and even leadership, but as they became less radical and more respectable, they expected their female members to adhere to more middle-class styles of evangelical femininity.[37]

The next wave of female evangelical preachers, who worked in the 1860s, were of a very different order from Ann Carr and her colleagues. They came from the educated middle class and are perhaps best thought of as 'lady preachers'. Their insistence on their own subordination to their husbands, fathers, and church officials corresponded with the beliefs of many middle-class evangelicals, both Anglican and dissenting, to whom they must have seemed appealing and unthreatening. For example, while the Baptist Church offered very few opportunities for women to preach, it welcomed some lady preachers, including Matilda Bass, who left her husband to travel with a female companion and preach with 'meek gentleness'.[38] The lady preachers, then, are best seen as part of polite middle-class evangelicalism rather than in the radical tradition from which the female Messiahs and sectarian Methodist preachers derived. Their work helps to demonstrate the many meanings and forms which female preaching could take.

An 1860s revival of millenarianism also contributed to support for women preachers. This revival emphasized 'pre-millenarianism', or the belief that the second coming of Christ would precede a thousand years of peace on earth rather than following it. Many pre-millenarianists in the 1860s interpreted the biblical passage Joel 2:28–29, which states that 'your sons and your daughters shall prophesy . . . and upon the handmaids in those days will I pour out my spirit' to mean that one of the signs of the second coming of Christ was the emergence of a female ministry.

Lady preachers spoke only by invitation and only to middle-class audiences. They strove to present themselves as respectable middle-class women, dressing and speaking decorously, and arguing that women brought a peculiarly feminine quality to their preaching which was complementary, not comparable, to men's. They were true to their class as well as to their faith, conforming to middle-class evangelical beliefs about domesticity. Most argued that a married woman could not preach without her husband's consent and were opposed to women's rights. One lady preacher, Phoebe Palmer, worked only with her husband and did not publish in her own name. However, lady preachers were a temporary phenomenon; by the 1870s, they had faded from public view, although middle-class evangelical women continued to be active in many other ways, including work in visiting societies and on temperance committees.[39]

THE SALVATION ARMY

From the 1870s women's preaching and other public religiosity were visible in a new faith: William and Catherine Booth's Christian Mission, later known as the Salvation Army. Salvationists were predominantly working-class and urban. While the women of the Salvation Army were the immediate chronological followers of the lady preachers, in their beliefs, self-presentation, and willingness to appear unladylike and even unfeminine, Catherine Booth (1829–90), her daughters, and the Salvationist women who followed them – known as Hallelujah Lasses – were the spiritual inheritors of the sectarian female preaching tradition. They were as radical as the Primitive Methodists had been, but were far more numerous. Founded in 1865 as a local organization in London's poverty-stricken East End, the Salvation Army had seventy-two stations around the country by 1879. In 1886 the Army had 1,749 congregations and over 4,000 officers in Great Britain, and another 750 congregations and 2,000 officers abroad. When Catherine Booth died in 1890, fifty thousand people paid their respects.[40]

Catherine Booth and her husband William were originally Methodists; William was a minister, and Catherine sometimes preached for him when he was ill. But she was not satisfied with being a minister's wife, even an unusually active and outspoken one, and she and her husband eventually left the Methodist Church. Before founding the Salvation Army she argued fervently for women's right to preach the Gospel and became an evangelist in her own right. In her 1859 pamphlet *Female Teaching*, Booth insisted that no woman, married or single, was 'subject to man in any sense in which one man is not subject to another; both the law of God and man recognize her as an independent being.'[41]

The Booths established the Salvation Army as a domestic evangelical mission. They wore uniforms and thought of their tightly structured organization like a Christian army. That army was notable for the agency of the women who joined it, most of whom were working-class. Salvationist women learned the business skills necessary to running missions; they were also trained to write hymns, to guide penitents to Christ's mercy, and to preach to audiences of all sorts both indoors and out. Although their tactics were very gendered and even included flirting, their role in the organization was no different from men's: both sexes preached, saved souls, and ran missions. In this, the Army was quite radical. The Salvationists and especially the Hallelujah Lasses were a jubilant and disruptive presence in the poor urban areas in which they proselytized. Salvationists used popular culture for their own ends, setting Christian words to music-hall tunes. Hallelujah Lasses purposely made spectacles of themselves and created a carnivalesque atmosphere to attract attention. Some defied standards of female propriety and let their hair down when they walked the streets to announce upcoming meetings. Incorporating into their evangelizing style the urban, working-class culture of which they became part, Salvationist women cannily played on observers' perceptions of their behaviour as sexually open in the dangerous streets of the East End. They were successful in attracting new adherents to the faith, but were also hated, pelted with food and refuse and bombarded with sexually abusive insults. Their deep evangelical beliefs helped them to defy conventions of modesty and subordination in the service of Christ.

SPIRITUALISTS AND THEOSOPHISTS

Women who looked for spiritual fulfilment outside organized Judaeo-Christian institutions were, like Salvation Army women, well outside the mainstream, but became more common in the later part of our period. Spiritualists believed they could communicate with the dead. Theosophists turned eastward, hoping that their interpretations of Asian traditions could provide answers that they felt were missing from Western Christianity. Spiritualism and theosophy were both atypical belief systems. However, they were in some ways very much of their time and place. During the late nineteenth century many challenges to traditional Christianity, particularly Darwinism, led to what has been called the 'Victorian crisis of faith', from which the two movements emerged. Adherents of spiritualism and theosophy tended to be politically radical, and many were attracted by the feminism in these movements. Both movements heralded the religious heterodoxy and radicalism of the twentieth century, as well as women's increased politicization and feminist agitation.

Spiritualism originated in the United States and enjoyed its heyday in England in the 1860s, 70s, and 80s. Its followers believed that it was possible for the living to communicate with the dead through a medium, which was extremely attractive in a society in which so many people lost loved ones, including children. Women were held to be especially gifted spiritualist mediums and so were central to the movement. Female mediums led seances, spoke in public, and – while in the mediumistic trance in which they called up the dead – acted playfully or aggressively sexual, or spoke like those they communed with. At the same time, mediums insisted that they themselves were merely passive vessels or servants, who had no power of their own.

Many of the best-known mediums were young women from the upper-working- or lower-middle classes. They included Florence Cook, known for materializing a spirit named Katie King, and Mary Rosina Showers. In one case the entire middle-class Theobald family of London, plagued by long illnesses and the deaths of several children, became fervent spiritualists. When their cook, Mary, announced that she too could see spirits, she was permitted to cross class boundaries and became a trusted family friend. Such a transformation was extremely unusual in Victorian society, and demonstrates the ways in which spiritualism opened up opportunities for both elite and non-elite women. It could also be a dangerous practice. In the 1870s Louisa Lowe was incarcerated by her husband, an Anglican minister, in an insane asylum because of her spiritualist beliefs.[42]

The Theosophical Society was founded in New York City in 1875 and spread to India and Great Britain a few years later. Theosophy, a blend of spiritualism, Eastern religions, and scientific rhetoric, attracted many spiritualists; this is unsurprising since its founder, Madame Helena Blavtsky (1831–91), consciously decided to create a movement that combined these ingredients. Her books *Isis Unveiled* (1877) and *The Secret Doctrine* (1888) drew on Buddhist, Hindu, Kabbalistic, and Swedenborgian beliefs, among others.

Theosophy appealed to many women and especially to feminists because it spoke of the motherhood of God, insisted that men and women were equal, and claimed that evolution would eventually allow the human race to transcend male and female bodies. Blavatsky was the best-known female theosophist; Annie Besant, previously a member of the National

Secular Society and of the Malthusian League, was also well-known. Another prominent woman in the movement was Frances Swiney (1847–1922), a feminist, social purity activist, and eugenicist who wrote *The Awakening of Women, or Woman's Part in Evolution* (1899). Well outside the feminist mainstream, which emphasized women's roles as mothers and wives, Swiney used theosophy and eugenics theory to see women as more than biologically defined beings and to emphasize the way in which motherhood was a spiritual state, distinct from pregnancy or marriage.[43] Her life and works are good examples of the ways in which theosophy could be attractive and useful to women.

The long nineteenth century was a time in which religious beliefs, feelings, activities, and institutions pervaded society far more deeply than they do today. Religious observance often shaded into cultural practice, where women were central. Partly because they were considered the naturally more moral sex and were more religiously observant than men, women were able to accomplish a tremendous amount. Some, like female Messiahs, used spirituality to directly defy the status quo; others, such as spiritualists, posed some challenge to the evangelical Christian hegemony. For many women, middle-class notions of female domesticity and respectability were increasingly influential. This does not mean that they remained inactive or decorative; religious organizations allowed for extensive female activity, agency, and authority. But women's religious choices were framed by the larger society of which they, their religious traditionalism and their faiths were a part.

6

Education

IN THE LATE eighteenth century Mary Wollstonecraft (1759–97) claimed that only an educated woman could be a virtuous woman, but her insistence on the importance of schooling the female sex put her in the minority. In 1760 few people, with the exception of elite men, received consistent formal schooling as children, girls were virtually never as well educated as boys of their own class, and universities were closed to women. Over the long nineteenth century, education slowly became more available – and eventually free and compulsory – to children of all classes and both genders. By the time of the First World War, almost every English child went to school until the age of fourteen, and a few young women were pursuing higher education. This dramatic change had an especially profound impact on women.

Certainly improved education meant enhanced literacy and work opportunities for many. Yet this greatly expanded system of schooling retained certain key features. Most importantly, throughout the long nineteenth century education was organized to support class hierarchies; children of different classes were educated separately and prepared for their distinct stations in life. It was almost impossible for a working-class girl to get the same education as her middle- or upper-class contemporary at any point in the century. Sometimes the emphasis on class was implicit in the curriculum, as when aristocratic girls learned to sketch; drawing was not a skill they needed in their adult lives, but one they were expected to have. Sometimes schooling was explicitly tied to adult lives, as when working-class girls were taught skills thought to be needed by both domestic servants and working-class wives.

This chapter will survey the variety of educational options open to girls and women and reveal connections between women's rights and education: many leading feminists played crucial roles in the establishment of better schools for girls. Some aristocratic women also played an important part in this struggle, notably by acting as patronesses of the first university colleges for women. In 1914, English women were almost universally literate; some were even well educated. This was in dramatic contrast not only to 1760 but to 1850. All the same, girls and women were seen as a different species from boys and men, with different futures and lesser capabilities, and schools helped perpetuate those beliefs. Education changed for the better during our period, but maintained many of its limits and assumptions.

Before 1850

Until the late nineteenth century education was neither free, nor compulsory, nor state-provided. As a result, many children – and most children from working-class and poor families – were schooled haphazardly, if at all. Formal, full-time schooling was by no means a typical part of childhood for the majority of the population. Girls, even aristocratic ones, were particularly likely to receive little or no schooling, and women's literacy rates were consequently lower than men's. Historians usually use the ability to sign one's name as a marker of literacy. In 1764 59 per cent of male weavers marrying in Manchester could sign their names, but only 11 per cent of their brides could do the same.[1]

ELITE GIRLS

The education of girls varied strikingly by class. Children from wealthy families began their education at home, in the nursery as very young children and later in the family's schoolroom. Many aristocratic parents participated in their children's education; mothers were especially likely to take charge of religious instruction, and some taught their children to read as well. Children were also taught by governesses, who were (as we saw in Chapter 2) usually young middle-class women, and by male tutors. Girls were trained to be accomplished young ladies. Beyond the basics of reading, writing, and religious instruction, they learned singing or piano playing, drawing, and modern European languages. They might also learn maths, science, or classics from their brothers' tutors.

Aristocratic and gentry boys were expected to develop into the leaders of the next generation, and were sent to boarding schools at a fairly young age to prepare for this future. The classical education they received at school served as a crucial marker of class and status. The education of girls was more variable. Some ended their formal education still in the family schoolroom; others went on to spend a year or two at a girls' boarding school in their teens. These expensive finishing schools were concentrated in London and in fashionable resort towns such as Brighton and Bath.[2] They prepared students for their lives as elite wives, mothers, hostesses and philanthropists, and were more concerned with social graces than with academic achievement.

MIDDLE-CLASS GIRLS

Middle-class children, too, began their education at home, being taught reading and religion by their mothers when young. In wealthier middle-class families with an annual income over £300, older girls were taught by a governess; in the middle decades of the nineteenth century many newly wealthy professional, merchant, and manufacturing families employed governesses as a sign of status. The middle-class woman who found herself employed in a middle-class home must have been in an awkward social position. Boys were sent at a young age to all-male day or boarding schools that stressed sports and camaraderie along with academic and practical subjects. Some middle-class boys learned subjects deemed necessary to enter the family enterprise; others, from more socially ambitious families, were provided with a curriculum which, imitating aristocratic ones, stressed classical languages and literature.

Girls' training, especially before 1850, usually emphasized polite social accomplishments rather than academic or practical ones. From the age of ten, girls might be sent for four or five years to small, local, day schools privately run by middle-class ladies from their own homes. While some of these were run by women who took their profession as educators seriously, others simply provided a domestic atmosphere in which to continue an ornamental education. For girls from less affluent families, whose fathers were in shopkeeping or the civil service, this would probably complete their education. Girls from more comfortable merchant and professional families might go on to attend boarding schools modelled on upper-class ones; aspiring families might even send their daughters to the finishing schools patronized by the elite. Many wealthier middle-class families did not send their daughters to school at all, as the family home was considered a more sheltered environment than even the most carefully chosen school.

In all of these settings, the quality of the education provided was unpredictable; for example, some governesses were well-educated and good teachers, while others were simply genteel young ladies without much to offer in the way of learning. Some saw themselves as professional educators, others did not. (One important development was the establishment in 1843 of the Governesses' Benevolent Institution (GBI), which emphasized the importance of teacher training and certification for women. It was in part an attempt to improve the status and salaries of governesses, those poor middle-class women who were pitied by so many.) Jane Harrison, daughter of a timber merchant in Hull, had several governesses as a young girl in the 1860s. She remembered them teaching her 'deportment, how to come into a room, how to get into a carriage',[3] as well as fancy sewing and Bible verses. On the other hand, her favourite governess, although not especially learned herself, worked with Harrison on German, Latin, Hebrew, and the New Testament in Greek. In all of these educational settings girls were taught to read and write and instructed in religion, often some form of middle-class evangelicalism. Beyond this, girls were expected to become accomplished, though less so than elite girls, at drawing, singing, and playing a musical instrument. A few middle-class girls might learn modern languages as well. Middle-class girls were expected to be philanthropists, wives, mothers, and household managers of comfortable domestic spaces, and were trained to this station.

The only significant exceptions to this style of education before the middle of the century were in the Quaker and Unitarian communities, where girls were often provided with more academic schooling that resembled their brothers', either at home or at denominational schools. Unitarian girls were often taught Latin and Greek, like their brothers, as well as modern languages, and were the only middle-class girls who might have experienced boys' and girls' education as essentially the same.[4]

WORKING-CLASS GIRLS

Working-class families had little time or income to spend on children's education. Some rural areas, due to poverty and local indifference or hostility, had no schools at all before the Education Act of 1870, and children in such areas rarely achieved basic literacy. For those in other areas, several types of schools were available, provided by different groups. Many middle-class evangelicals believed that educating working-class children was the key to the widespread reform of society. Evangelicals also believed that every person should be able to read the Bible and thereby form a personal relationship with God. Others among the middle and upper classes feared revolt or revolution, and responded by providing an education that would, in Hannah More's words, 'train up the lower classes in habits of industry and piety'[5] in an effort to create a docile working class.

Working-class children were not educated at home, especially early in our period, because working-class mothers were too busy and often could not read themselves. Even so, they were often eager for their children to get at least some education. George Edwards remembered his mother's efforts:

> My sister and I went to bed early on Saturday nights so that my mother might be able to wash and mend our clothes and we have them tidy for Sunday. This work kept my mother up nearly all Saturday night, but she would be up early on Sunday morning to get our scanty breakfasts ready in time for us to go to Sunday school.[6]

While in the middle classes, girls and boys received very different educations, the basic structure and substance of working-class girls' education resembled that of working-class boys. Boys and girls went to the same schools and learned reading, religion, and possibly writing and arithmetic. Girls were also taught needlework and domestic skills. The average working-class child received four and a half years of schooling, but this could be cut in half by erratic attendance as a result of straitened family circumstances, unpaid school fees, housework, paid work, sickness, or inadequate clothing. In addition, girls and boys were often expected to earn wages from a young age. In 1851 a cabinet-maker told the journalist Henry Mayhew that he and his wife:

> put the children to work as soon as we can. My little girl began about six, but about eight or nine is the usual age ... She never goes to school. We can't spare her. There's schools enough about here for a penny a week, but we could not afford to keep her without working.[7]

For this family, the loss of a young girl's wages, along with the expense of school fees, made education unaffordable.

The availability of local work usually determined girls' attendance at school. In some rural areas, for example Norfolk and Suffolk, girls went to school because there was little paid work available and charity-sponsored schools did not charge fees. School could be valuable to many girls because they were taught skills of use to future servants. It might also provide an opportunity to become acquainted with local women from the middle classes, gentry, or aristocracy through whom a first situation might be obtained. In contrast, industrializing Lancashire offered much relatively well-paid work for girls and women, and there girls were less likely to be sent to school. Instead they began earning wages in the textile industry (though under the Factory Act of 1833 child workers were supposed to receive some schooling) or helped at home while their mothers earned wages.[8] In 1851, girls in rural Norfolk and Suffolk attended school far more regularly than their peers in Lancashire. Girls everywhere, however, were likely to be kept at home on occasion to mind younger children or to help with housework, especially on washday.

Dame schools

There were many different types of schools that educated the working classes before the Education Act was passed in 1870. Probably the most ubiquitous for poor girls were the working-class private schools known as 'dame' schools. These were small, private establishments for children too young to earn wages, run by one working-class woman (or 'dame') in her own home for a weekly fee of 3d to 6d per student. Dame schools were small, informal, and familial rather than institutional in tone. We cannot know exactly how many children attended them, but they were certainly widespread. They took only a few students – perhaps between five and thirty – and tended to have flexible rules regarding prompt payment of fees, student attire, and erratic attendance caused by children's duties at home. While middle-class commentators disparaged them for just these qualities, they were less crowded and more personal than most of the more formal schools described below, which to many working-class children must have seemed part of another world. At dame schools boys and girls usually learned to read and sometimes to spell; girls might also learn to sew and knit. A few schools taught writing and arithmetic, usually for an additional fee; some provided little beyond child-minding. In some rural areas, such as Bedfordshire and Buckinghamshire, where the main work available for women was in cottage industries such as straw-plaiting and glove- and lace-making, most dame schools taught only these skills. Mary Smith, born in 1822 in Oxfordshire, was sent to a dame school to learn to knit and sew; girls in her school 'had a lesson once a day in the New Testament ... but knitting and sewing occupied nearly the whole time'.[9] The popularity of dame schools declined with the rise of state-assisted schooling from 1870, but some still existed into the twentieth century.

Sunday schools

Also common were Sunday schools, which were founded in the 1780s. These were local working-class institutions supported by donations and subscriptions from the middle and upper classes. They were provided by a variety of nonconformist faiths, including Quaker, Unitarian, and many Methodist establishments, as well as the Church of England. Like dame schools, Sunday schools focused on reading, especially of the Scriptures; they also provided additional religious instruction. Some taught writing as well, though Anglicans saw this as a secular skill and refused to teach it on the Sabbath. Teachers were usually working class, although sometimes included local aristocratic women. Attendance grew even as other school options became available. In 1786 there were 200,000 children attending Sunday schools; at mid-century approximately two-thirds of all working-class children between the ages of five and fifteen attended Sunday school; and by 1861 almost two and a half million children were enrolled.[10]

Some girls supplemented their dame-school education with Sunday school; others were able to attend only Sunday school. In the late eighteenth and early nineteenth centuries, more children from working-class families attended Sunday school than any form of weekday school, partly because it was free and did not interfere with their workdays. Before 1850, for one-to three-quarters of all children who went to Sunday school, the weekly period of instruction constituted their education.[11] This limited curriculum was especially crucial to those for whom it was their entire academic experience; the average of four hours instruction per week for four years may have contributed significantly to popular literacy.

Ragged, workhouse, and factory schools

A more formal option was a charity school. These were organized principally by the Anglican Church and local middle-class leaders, flourished in the eighteenth century, and were later replaced by the voluntary National Society schools. Charity schools were intended to reform the lower classes and emphasized practical skills. Very poor children could go to free schools created specifically for them, also known as 'ragged schools'. Two hundred of these were established by Lord Shaftesbury's Ragged School Union between 1844 and 1852, and in 1870 there were three hundred and fifty. Ragged schools were run by upper- and middle-class philanthropists, many of them Unitarian, and tended to be vocational. Girls were trained for waged and unwaged work appropriate to their station in life, including domestic industry and domestic service. Children whose families were forced into workhouses by the New Poor Law Act of 1834 were educated at workhouse schools. In theory, these taught not only reading but writing, arithmetic, moral and vocational instruction, and even history and geography. In practice, however, there was much prejudice against giving workhouse children more than a 'pauper's education', and girls usually learned only how to read. What was billed as instruction in practical skills often consisted of doing the cleaning and mending for the workhouse and its governor or matron. Workhouse girls were put to work almost immediately and sent into service as soon as possible.

Working children in industrial areas sometimes went to factory schools. The Factory Act of 1833, which limited the number of hours children could work, also made education a condition of employment; part of a factory inspector's job was to make sure that children who worked were being schooled. In most cases, this meant that children produced certificates of attendance from their dame school each week. Some manufacturers agreed to set up schools, either attached to a single factory, or built and maintained jointly by several factories in the town, with children's wages reduced by a penny per week to pay for the cost of educating them. In Lancashire in 1838, 95 of 657 factories had established such schools. The quality of the education offered by factory schools varied widely. The factory school of M'Connel & Co. of Manchester was a well-appointed room staffed with qualified teachers who taught the girls reading, writing, arithmetic and needlework, but many others were simply dirty rooms overseen by barely literate instructors. The 1844 Factory Act reduced children's workdays to six and a half hours and left them free for three hours of schooling in the morning or afternoon. This was an improvement since it meant they could leave work to attend school for half-days rather than being limited to the schools attached to their workplaces.[12]

National and British schools

A small number of working-class children were educated at higher-status institutions run by two voluntary education societies. The National Society for Promoting the Education of the Poor in the Principles of the Established Church, an Anglican institution, was founded in 1811; the smaller, nonconformist British and Foreign School Society had been founded in 1808. 'National and British schools', as they were popularly known, became more widespread over the course of the century. By 1850, two-thirds of all day-school pupils in Lancashire, Norfolk, and Suffolk went to National and British schools. By 1870, National and British schools provided over 90 per cent of the places for full-time, formal, weekday schooling in England. Unlike other schools open to working-class girls before the middle of the century, National and British schools offered a structured education overseen by a centralized bureaucracy. They were considered to provide the best education available to poor children, but were attended by only a very few working-class and poor girls because their weekday schedule usually conflicted with family and work obligations. Like other schools, they taught girls reading, religious instruction, skills needed for women's paid and unpaid work, and needlework. They also taught writing, arithmetic, and a wider range of academic subjects.

The National and British Societies emphasized the importance of education for girls because women were essential conduits of morality. Girls needed to be taught Christian values so that, as adults, they could exert a civilizing influence on their husbands and children. Students were, in the words of the 1841 Annual Report of the National Society, taught 'to be sober, to love their husbands, to love their children, [and] to be discreet [and] chaste'. The schools also stressed the importance of training children to accept their station in life: a National Society report from 1862 expressed the hope 'that no desire to make girls little Newtons, little Captain Cooks ... and little Sir Joshua Reynoldses, will ever take us too low for keeping in sight the object of teaching them to make and mend shirts, to make and mend pinafores, and darn stockings and socks'.[13] While they provided girls with a curriculum that included some substantive learning, National and British schools still expected girls to become docile and able domestic workers.

Adult education

Some working-class women sought to continue or begin their education as adults. In the 1840s radical Unitarians founded the Whittington Club and Metropolitan Athenaeum, both feminist efforts at providing education for adults. Lady Charlotte Guest formed a night school for young women in 1848.[14] Women could also attend classes at mechanics' institutes, which sought to provide useful scientific knowledge, and working men's colleges, which offered a liberal arts curriculum. Both types of institutions flourished in the nineteenth century, but both were created to address the needs of skilled male workers, and as such often neglected those of their female students.[15] In spite of this, and the many other obstacles that faced them, some determined women managed to continue their education. Women employed in cotton textile factories were the most highly and consistently paid of female workers, and were best able to afford the fees of institutes and colleges. The low wages and live-in situations made it extremely difficult for domestic servants to take classes. Female agricultural labourers were most likely to be in need of literacy classes, especially during the first half of the century when many in this group, particularly older women, were illiterate. But agricultural workers throughout the century, and milliners and dressmakers in the 1830s and 1840s, were subject to low and fluctuating wages that made schooling unaffordable. Wives and mothers had even more difficulty than single women in finding the resources for further education.

All in all, while many working-class girls learned to read, education was hard to come by, haphazard, and of uneven quality until the middle of the nineteenth century. Writing and arithmetic were rare, and subjects such as history were almost unheard of. Skills pertinent to domestic labour and cottage industries were considered most valuable. Working-class girls were trained to be working-class women, wives, and mothers; it was hoped that they would make excellent servants when single, would refrain from working as wives and mothers, and act as conduits of social deference and Christian morality to their fathers, husbands, and children.

After 1850

From mid-century educational opportunities for girls (and for non-elite boys) expanded dramatically. These new opportunities took three forms: the decision on the part of the state to take responsibility for educating all of its citizens; the founding of rigorous, academically-oriented schools for middle-class girls; and the opening of universities to women. While education continued to divide children by class and gender, these new educational opportunities provided girls and women with tools that could be used to challenge cultural norms and stereotypes.

ELEMENTARY SCHOOLS

Meaningful educational change came for working-class girls through government action. From 1847, the state began to give financial support to Wesleyan Methodist and Roman Catholic schools as well as Anglican schools; from 1851, it extended the same support to Jewish schools. The biggest change came in 1870 when a major Education Act, sponsored by the Liberal reformer William Forster (1818–86), was passed. Its goal was to make sure that a basic, 'elementary' education was available in all parts of the country, suited to the working classes, for children from five to ten years old. While the Act did not immediately establish a system of state-provided education for all children, it did lay the foundation for what would become a country-wide, secular, rate-supported system providing basic education.[16]

The 1870 Act achieved this by dividing the country into over two thousand school districts. Local ratepayers elected a School Board, which was charged with assessing the elementary education provided by voluntary schools in their area (other schools were ignored). In 1871 National and British schools were educating over 260,000 children nationwide; this probably left as many again without places.[17] If there were not enough voluntary school places, the local Board was to build and maintain schools using taxpayers' money. The Boards could decide to charge a fee for these 'board schools' or to make them free, as they wished, and had discretion as to whether attendance was required or not; elementary schooling was made compulsory in London from 1871. The 1870 Act also allowed women to vote and run for School Board positions; many feminists, including Emily Davies (1830–1921) and Elizabeth Garrett Anderson, were elected to School Boards. They used this opportunity to show that women could be capable public servants.[18]

Since the 1870 Education Act asked local School Boards to fill in gaps rather than create a state system of education, schools remained of uneven quality. In addition, the fact that some local board schools charged fees limited access to education for many children. Yet the 1870 Act was an important step forward. A decade later, the Education Act of 1880 made school attendance across the country compulsory to the age of ten; later Acts raised the age to twelve in 1899 and to fourteen in 1918, and elementary education was free for all from 1891.[19] In 1902, another major Education Act abolished local School Boards and gave their responsibilities to local education authorities, which continued to develop elem-

entary education by organizing schools into infants', girls', and boys'
sections and establishing state-run grammar and technical schools. From
1906 some schools provided children with meals and medical check-ups.[20]
By the start of the First World War, children spent more time in school
than had ever been the case, and were provided with a range of services
that went beyond the strictly educational.

In spite of increased opportunities, many families still needed girls'
help at home and treated their education as less necessary than that of
boys. A Mrs Layton, born in 1866, recalled that: 'My fourth sister and
I always stayed away from school on washing day to mind the
babies ... everybody had large families and generally kept the elder
girls, and sometimes boys, at home to mind the little ones'.[21] School
officials seemed to share families' priorities in this instance. In London
between 1870 and 1914, for instance, most girls missed two or three
half-days each week, and the authorities seemed to find this compromise
acceptable.

The elementary education provided by the state after 1870 was by no
means gender-neutral. After the infant level (age seven or so), more than
half of elementary schools had separate classrooms, playgrounds, and
even entrances for girls and boys. Many middle-class observers and School
Board officials thought that state elementary schools, like charity schools
and workhouse schools, should train girls to be good domestic servants,
and later wives and mothers. During the 1880s and 1890s the education
of working-class girls became weighted down with special subjects, while
academic courses became harder to squeeze in. Needlework, in particular,
figured largely in the curriculum, to the annoyance of many teachers.
(These requirements varied from place to place; the London School Board
required domestic economy from 1883, while poorer rural boards and
many voluntary schools often lagged behind in establishing domestic
science courses.[22])

The state encouraged girls to study needlework, domestic economy,
cookery, laundry, and practical housewifery, and huge numbers of girls
enrolled in these courses. After the state provided financial incentives for
doing so, the number of girls at Board Schools who enrolled in domestic
economy jumped from 844 in 1874 to 59,812 in 1882. For those who passed,
cooking, laundry, and housewifery became grant-earning subjects soon
afterwards. Courses taught the moral as well as practical necessity of such
skills. In 1894, one participant in an essay competition on temperance
wrote that

People do not drink so much if there are light and comfort at home. It is necessary for girls to learn to cook so that their husbands and friends may not have to go out to get a good meal.[23]

At this time, anxieties about high infant mortality rates also led to the introduction of courses on infant and child care, as working-class mothers were held accountable for the unhealthy homes they lived in and the inadequate meals they fed their children. These curricular examples demonstrate how the state continued to reflect and promote normative ideas about working girls and women. In addition, working-class motherhood was put into a national, imperial and racial context at the turn of the century as the Boer War and the growing popularity of eugenics – the specious science of breeding for human excellence – fostered anxieties about the unfitness of recruits. Elementary schools tried to promote in working-class girls a sense of national duty as wives and mothers to the English race.[24]

The new state-sponsored system of schooling did little to narrow the divide between working-class and middle-class girls' education since it was almost impossible for working-class girls to receive any post-elementary education before the early twentieth century. However, the importance of the provision of universal – if rudimentary – education cannot be denied, and an increasing number of working-class girls were able to attend state grammar schools by the end of our period. Most girls who stayed at school until they were twelve or fourteen were under enormous pressure from parents and school administrators to justify their schooling by taking practical courses. At the same time, many elementary-school teachers, who were themselves of modest origins, encouraged their students to pursue a broader range of academic subjects.[25] As we have seen, most of the new white-collar jobs, such as clerking and elementary-school teaching, were only open to those who had continued in education until the age of sixteen, a commitment not all families were willing to make. But even elementary education brought class and cultural aspirations to some that would not have been possible in previous generations, and literate working-class girls and women were crucial members of the burgeoning lower-middle-class. They were a key feature differentiating England on the eve of the First World War from the England of King George III, in which far fewer than half of adult working-class women were able to read.

GRAMMAR SCHOOLS

Formalized middle-class girls' education came about largely as the result of the work of a few impassioned feminist reformers. It began at mid-century with two new schools, North London Collegiate School (in London) and Cheltenham Ladies' College (in Gloucestershire). These schools, and those that followed them in the next decades, were distinguished from many earlier girls' schools by their intellectual standards: they provided less socially oriented, more academically rigorous curricula. They were also differently organized. Rather than being privately owned by an individual or a family, they were owned and governed by trustees, as were boys' public schools. Few aristocratic girls chose to attend these schools, but girls from all ranks of the middle classes did.

North London Collegiate School was a day school founded in 1850 by Mary Frances Buss (1827–94). Buss was a committed educational reformer and feminist; she gave evidence to the 1856 Schools Enquiry Commission on gender inequalities in education, worked with Emily Davies on the campaign to open the Oxford and Cambridge examinations to girls, was a founding member of the Kensington Society and the London Suffrage Committee, and assisted Josephine Butler (1828–1906) with her campaigns against the white slave trade and the Contagious Diseases Act. Most of Buss's students came from professional middle-class families of limited means; the fathers of many were clerks or tradesmen. Molly Hughes, a pupil who moved from a fashionable day school to North London Collegiate in the 1880s gratefully remembered that 'at North London I sensed at once a different atmosphere. No one asked you where you lived, how much pocket-money you had, or what your father was – he might be a bishop or rat-catcher.'[26] Unusually for the time, North London employed only trained and qualified teachers, and sought to give girls a liberal education based on religious principles. It aimed to produce academically accomplished students who none the less adhered to traditional standards of femininity. North London became the prototype for new girls' day schools, and its model of compulsory academic subjects being studied all morning became the norm. In 1872 North London Collegiate also inspired the foundation (by Lady Stanley of Alderley, sisters Maria Grey and Emily Shirriff, and Mary Gurney) of the Girls' Public Day School Trust, which by 1898 had established thirty-four schools in places such as Blackheath, Clapham, Bath, Norwich, Nottingham, Wimbledon, and York.

Cheltenham Ladies' College, which opened in 1854, was a boarding school, established by a small group of local professional men who modelled it on a local boys' institution, the Cheltenham College for Boys. Under Dorothea Beale (1831–1906), who was principal from 1858 until her death in 1906, Cheltenham became known for its academic rigour. Like Buss, Beale was an academic reformer and a feminist who was active in bringing the suffrage movement to English women living outside London. In the 1890s, Beale purchased the house that would become St Hilda's College, Oxford, one of the first women's colleges. Cheltenham Ladies' – perhaps not surprisingly, given that it was a boarding school – catered deliberately to a more socially elite clientele than North London Collegiate, as did the new boarding schools that followed it, including St Leonard's (in Scotland), Roedean and Wycombe Abbey; Beale did not accept students whose parents were in trade.[27] The school intended to provide

> an education based upon religious principles which, preserving the modesty and gentleness of the female character, should so far cultivate [a girl's] intellectual powers as to fit her for the discharge of those responsible duties which devolve upon her as a wife, mother, mistress and friend, the natural companion and helpmate for men.[28]

The school expected the excellent education it provided to be used in the service of students' roles as wives and mothers. Annabel Jackson, a student in the 1870s, remembered a teacher, Miss Soulsby:

> She could make us cry and she could make us laugh ... She drummed English literature into us willy-nilly ... Miss Soulsby rammed into my head, once and for all, that every woman should know about housekeeping, the direction of a household, needlework, cooking, catering and enough of public affairs to be able to discuss them with her menfolk.[29]

Cheltenham so promoted ladylike behaviour that it discouraged sports, although later boarding schools for girls followed boys' schools in promoting fresh air and athletic competition. At Wycombe Abbey in the 1890s Winifred Peck enjoyed athletic opportunities that had been unavailable at the small private girls' schools she had previously attended: '[W]hat freedom, what glory, to scamper about after one ball or another in sun or rain or wind as one of a team, as part of the school, on an equality, I felt, with my brothers at last.'[30]

These new schools educated only a minority of middle-class girls; in 1900, 70 per cent of middle-class girls who received any schooling outside of their homes were educated in the more old-fashioned, privately owned, socially oriented schools. After the passage of the 1902 Education Act, though, the number of grammar schools grew to over 1,000 by 1913, and the number of less affluent middle-class girls who could receive an academically oriented education increased.[31]

By the start of the First World War, educational systems were not so aware of class and gender as they had been. Teachers had long opposed efforts to keep more advanced education unavailable to the working classes, and more and more local governments had reorganized their school systems to focus on students' ages and abilities rather than on their gender and class. Although education beyond the elementary level was neither free nor compulsory, by 1914 over half the places in grant-earning, state-supported grammar schools were filled by children from working-class families.[32]

UNIVERSITIES

Like grammar-school education, university education was for the most part the preserve of the middle classes at first; aristocratic women eschewed it while working-class women could rarely hope to attain it. Like the first grammar schools, women's colleges were founded by feminists. Acceptance of the idea of women students, by the general public as well as by universities, was a slow process, because most saw the higher education of women as a direct challenge to the status quo. In an attempt to seem less revolutionary, many of the educational reformers who struggled to make higher learning possible for women claimed that 'sweet girl graduates' were being trained primarily to be better wives and mothers.

University education began at mid-century with the opening of two colleges for women. Queen's College, founded in London in 1848 by the Christian Socialist F. D. Maurice, with the support of the Governesses' Benevolent Institution, was an Anglican institution linked to King's College. A fairly conservative establishment, the college was governed entirely by men and was founded to educate middle-class women to become qualified governesses and teachers. This was considered necessary because, until the 1860s, these were the only respectable professions open to middle-class women who needed to earn a living. As a result, Queen's College posed no great challenge to ideas about women and education. However, discomfort with the notion of professional training for middle-class women led it to adopt a less vocational curriculum.

Bedford College, founded the following year by the wealthy Unitarian abolitionist Elizabeth Jesser Reid (1789–1866), was more liberal. It was non-denominational, included women in its governing body, and offered a full liberal arts curriculum rather than a limited teacher training programme. In practice, however, it too catered mostly to middle-class students who expected to earn a living by teaching. In 1878, the University of London opened its degrees to women, and Bedford became one of its colleges, as did Westfield College in 1882 and Royal Holloway in 1887. All three were non-residential institutions for women that grew steadily.

While Queen's and Bedford Colleges were important first steps, the places most English people thought of in connection with university education were the elite institutions, Oxford and Cambridge. The founding of women's colleges at Oxford and Cambridge was a great milestone and was fiercely resisted by many. In the mid-nineteenth century, women were permitted to take the Local Examinations for entrance to Oxford and Cambridge (tests that had been designed to help non-elite men qualify for admittance). They were not, however, permitted to matriculate or even to attend classes at first. Both universities resisted accepting female students long after other institutions had done so. Women did not become full members of Oxford until 1919, and of Cambridge (which began granting them titular degrees in 1921) until 1948.

Oxford and Cambridge carried great symbolic weight among the country's elite. The campaigns to make them, and other institutions of higher education, accessible to women were led by such feminists as Barbara Bodichon, Emily Davies, Mary Frances Buss, Dorothea Beale and Elizabeth Garrett Anderson. These women – who did not always agree on the shape that women's higher education should take – and other members of the Langham Place circle also founded the North of England Council for Promoting the Higher Education of Women, the London National Society for Women's Suffrage, the Society for Promoting the Employment of Women, and *The Englishwoman's Journal*. Almost all were from the professional middle classes, although some came from northern commercial and industrial families; many northern Unitarian families in particular provided financial support for the first women's colleges at Cambridge and Oxford. Local organizations also supported women's pursuit of university education. Many towns had Ladies' Educational Associations and other local organizations that supervised girls and women who took the Oxford and Cambridge and other Local Examinations, created support groups for women teachers, organized local classes and lecture series, sponsored scholarships, and lobbied local institutions of higher education for women's access to classes and facilities. The campaign for women's inclusion in higher education was part of a larger movement to make Oxford and Cambridge modern research and teaching institutions rather than bastions of the gentlemanly study of classical writings.

Emily Davies and Barbara Bodichon worked together to raise money for the establishment of the first women's college at Cambridge, and in the late 1860s purchased a house outside town that in 1873 opened as Girton College. (Davies had hoped for £30,000 from donors and twenty-five students, but was forced to settle for a more modest £7,000 and only six students.[33]) At the same time, the educational reformer Henry Sidgwick (1838–1900) founded the Association for the Promotion of the Higher Education of Women in Cambridge, and Anne Jemima Clough successfully campaigned for Cambridge to institute a new public Higher Local Examination, which served as a qualifying exam for schoolteachers and was the first post-secondary certification women could achieve. In 1871 Sidgwick and Clough opened a second women's college at Cambridge, Newnham, which was at first a hall of residence for women who attended lectures at Cambridge University, but by the late 1870s, like Girton, had its own tutorial staff. Most university professors gave Girton and Newnham students formal permission to attend lectures; as mentioned earlier, the medical faculty was an important exception.[34] Some lecturers would not speak to mixed audiences but gave separate lectures for women. By 1881, Girton and Newnham were both fully established women's colleges, whose students took the university's degree examinations and received official certification of that fact.[35] In 1879 Oxford followed Cambridge's lead, opening two women's colleges: Lady Margaret Hall, which was Anglican-affiliated, and Somerville College which was non-denominational.

Opposition to higher education for women profoundly shaped the first women's colleges. Opponents claimed that advanced study was irrelevant or even harmful for women, as it would render them discontent and unfit for lives as wives and mothers. They sought to demonstrate, using economic data, anatomical observation, religious doctrine, and notions of social propriety, that universities were best left as the preserve of men. Critics also used economics to argue that women with degrees would seek employment and thereby drive down wages and salaries and take jobs from men who needed to support wives and children. What might be good for individual women was bad for the larger society. Those more scientifically inclined held that close examination of human and primate skulls conclusively proved that Europeans were the most evolved of all humans, but that European men were more advanced than European women. Women who wanted to progress to further education were physiologically mannish and therefore objects of suspicion.[36]

Medically, education put women in danger; proponents of this argument included Henry Maudsley, Professor of Medical Jurisprudence at University College, London, John Thorburn, Professor of Obstetrics at Owen's College, Manchester, and Dr Matthews Duncan, who was the president of the London Obstetrical Society in 1881 and the author of *On Sterility in Women* (1884). Thorburn published his lectures on 'Female Education from a Physiological Point of View' in 1884 and held that the death of Annie Eastwood, one of the first female university students, from tuberculosis was brought on by 'over-education'. Matthews Duncan claimed that since the female form was not designed to withstand the rigours of sustained intellectual endeavour, higher education induced in women '[a]menorrhoea and chlorosis ... development of great nervousness ... destruction of sensuality of a proper commendable kind, [with] consequent personal and social evils'.[37] Social Darwinists argued that any energy spent on scholarship was better conserved for maternal duties, and that learning threatened education-hungry women with sterility, brain damage, or nervous collapse and therefore led to racial decline.[38] In any case, it was further argued, the education of women was useless since menstruation incapacitated them one week out of every four. Of course, as Elizabeth Garrett Anderson pointed out in an essay of 1874, all those who invoked this argument had female servants who were required to provide them with service all month every month.[39]

Some of the most conservative critics of higher education for women were those who used religiously-based arguments. Evangelical opponents claimed that learning destroyed women's faith and modesty and distracted them from the Christian duty of motherhood. Of course, many clerics also supported women's entrance into higher education and Queen's College was also Anglican. Male students' reservations about female colleagues are evident in the nervous jokes that appeared in student magazines, where female students were referred to as 'bejantinas' (in Scotland), 'doves' (in Durham) or 'sweet girl graduates' elsewhere, and were depicted as either socialites more concerned with dress than books or as humourless 'goody-goodies'.[40]

While advocates of women's education overcame all these arguments, their approach to higher education and the presentation of it to the public was shaped by these concerns. They hoped to prove the worthiness of their cause by emphasizing the ladylike virtue of female students, a protected domestic setting, and the production of educated wives, not competitive professional harpies. Most leaders in women's education, especially in its first decades, were determined that faculty and students alike should maintain proper feminine decorum at all times; to this end, they provided a domestic and sheltered life within the college. College doors closed in the early evening and students were only allowed to stay out later with special permission. Many colleges encouraged their students to take some appropriate form of exercise (riding and callisthenics were encouraged) to combat any harmful effects of mental exertion.

Opinions varied as to how best to organize women's university education. Emily Davies and Elizabeth Garrett Anderson wanted Girton's students to study the traditional male curriculum which emphasized the classics; they believed that any separately devised women's education would always be an inferior one. Davies also insisted that the college be affiliated with the Church of England, and imposed a very strict regime with regard to student behaviour and discipline. The more radical Barbara Bodichon championed a departure from the traditional curriculum, which she saw as outmoded, and a more relaxed approach to student behaviour. Henry Sidgwick, who was a Cambridge professor, wished to revamp the university's entire system of education; as part of this he wanted to provide a separate, less rigorous curriculum for women. In this he was assisted by Anne Clough and Josephine Butler.

The debate over whether women should pursue an identical course of study to men or a separate one, would continue to plague women's university education. Some educationalists felt that allowing women to compete with men on already established terms was advisable; others wished to redefine curricula or maintained that women were too delicate for certain types of study. Some felt that strict standards of decorum would guarantee that students were demure and ladylike, and would therefore help win support for the cause; others rejected polite standards of female decorum. Most were agreed that femininity was essential to the cause, and that the gradual achievement of full status in the university was an acceptable strategy.

Of course, the perspective of the first women students was different from that of the older women who organized, funded, and staffed the first colleges. Young women who went to university were seeking further education for a variety of reasons. Many, especially early on, sought learning without pursuing a degree of any sort. Some sought a degree unrelated to any expectations of gainful employment. Still others pursued a career, usually grammar-school or university teaching; a few went on to train for social work or to study medicine. Most faced some obstacles to higher education, including fees of £50 to £100 per annum, resistance or opposition from parents, domestic duties that conflicted with study away from home, and extensive studying for entrance exams as a result of an inadequate previous education. For those from comfortable homes, college life was physically inferior to home life; rooms were cramped and housework was a shared responsibility.

Life outside the classroom could be both enriching and limiting. Colleges and halls of residence at Oxford, Cambridge and elsewhere provided space and community for women, and could be places of vigorous social and communal life. Women were able to live in communities of like-minded women who took learning and each other seriously. But college life could also be very traditional and replicate middle-class domesticity. For instance, many of the earliest university societies formed by female students were devoted to philanthropy, the standard preserve of middle-class women. Students in Manchester worked with local mill girls or helped at the Clarendon Street Girls' Club before the university established its own settlement in 1895. Such activities were encouraged by faculty and staff, who wanted women's colleges to be models of female decorum and virtue.

Women's colleges tried to act as substitute families and homes, shelters from the outside world; college heads tried to reassure parents and critical onlookers that students would act correctly and retain their femininity. Mary Paley, one of the first students at Newnham College, remembered residential life as protective and domestic:

> We lived very much the life of a family; we studied together, we had our meals at one table, and in the evening we usually sat with Miss Clough in her sitting-room. We did our best to keep down household expenses: our food was very simple; we all, including Miss Clough, not

only made our beds and dusted our rooms, but we helped to wash up
after meals, and we did the domestic sewing in the evening ... I believe
we were all hard-working and well-intentioned, but during that first
year there was a good deal of friction between Miss Clough and some
of us ... The venture of women's education in Cambridge was a new
one: she was, I think, a little afraid of us, and did not know what we
might do next.[41]

Female faculty and staff tried to counter the radical nature of their
work by living exemplary lives of feminine selflessness and service.
Though same-sex relationships flourished in women's colleges and halls
of residence, sexual radicals could be made unwelcome: when the well-
known birth-control advocates Annie Besant and Alice Bradlaugh applied
to attend classes at University College, London, in 1883, they were turned
away. Another early Newnham student recalled that Anne Clough was,
in the college's early days,

always nervous lest the students should attract attention and criticism
by any eccentricity in dress or conduct, for her great desire was to be
unnoticed, and to make it clear that this little colony of women was
harmless and inoffensive.[42]

While students were not all revolutionaries, many chafed under the
socially restrictive rules imposed on them. Looking back on her days as a
student at Girton before the First World War, Margaret Cole remembered:

We were not allowed to go to meetings unchaperoned, so that before
the closing of the debate or whatever it might be we had to rise and go
home with our nurse, as it were, in order to get in before the Lodge
gates closed.[43]

Gradually these rules relaxed, especially with regard to constant chap-
eroning and sports; by 1914 Lady Margaret Hall and Somerville College
had dropped their bans on hockey, cricket and bicycling, and most
women's colleges had made sport part of their community lives.

While in the last quarter of the nineteenth century many women,
referred to as 'lady' students, had attended selected university lectures in
the pursuit of general knowledge, by 1911 their 'debutante attendance' had
been replaced by the degree-seeking seriousness of registered 'women'

students. And while university education for women was at first seen as radical and irrelevant to normal women's lives, by the end of the century many held that university-educated women were the fittest wives and mothers. This was a limited vision of the transforming potential of higher education but it signalled an acceptance of women's learning. Of course, some graduates never married. Higher education also created a new role for them, that of the celibate career woman, and made this fate far more attractive than it had been a generation earlier. People accepted that unmarried women could achieve meaningful adult lives through education and a career. Until the First World War, there was a formal or informal marriage bar to most educated or white-collar professions, including that of university tutor or professor. But by the end of the war students attended university with the intention of getting a degree and using it professionally before, if not instead of, marriage.

In 1900, only 15 per cent of university students in Britain were women, but by 1939 this had risen to 23 per cent. Many of those who used their education professionally did so in traditionally female, low-paid or unpaid positions. Teaching remained the most common work for female graduates. On the other hand, by the start of the Second World War many more female graduates married, suggesting that fewer saw education and work as irreconcilable with becoming wives and mothers.[44]

The educational landscape for English girls and women was remarkably different in 1914 from 1760. For the first half of our period, girls' schooling had been difficult to obtain, difficult to afford and make time for, and uneven in quality. Some girls never went to school; others went to Sunday school for a few years, or attended ragged, dame, workhouse, or factory schools. Only a very few received any sustained education. Even girls of the more elite ranks of life, who were carefully schooled, were scarcely educated.

After mid-century, much of this changed. The state sought to ensure that all children could attend school regularly and could get at least a basic education. More meaningful academic opportunities for middle-class girls were pioneered by determined feminists. As had been the case earlier, most if not all of these opportunities were still shaped by the assumption that girls and women would not and should not challenge their class and gender status. At the same time, new educational opportunities did provide the possibility of change. Girls whose mothers had been domestic servants, sweated labourers or factory workers could become clerks or even elementary-school teachers. Middle- and upper-class girls could also do white-collar work; a few even entered male-dominated professions such as university teaching and medicine. Even women who pursued marriage and children rather than careers saw education as integral to, rather than at odds with, proper female adulthood. Mary Wollstonecraft's radical insistence that women needed education had become almost a commonplace.

PART THREE

Politics in the Imperial Nation

7

Imperialism

IT WAS OFTEN said that the sun never set on the British Empire. The pride that later-nineteenth-century schoolchildren were encouraged to feel when they saw how much of the map was coloured red (to indicate British domination) tells us how important imperialism – the political, military, cultural and economic fact of Britain's dominance over much of the world, and the significance of the Empire in Britons' world-view – was in English society. Historians once saw English and imperial history as two very separate stories, with the latter a military and therefore an exclusively male history. Over the past twenty years, however, a new picture has emerged, one which looks beyond narrow military concerns to show women's importance to the history of imperialism and imperialism's importance to the history of women. It stresses the ways in which an attention to gender and sexuality can help us to understand British imperialism. This new approach also foregrounds the interdependence of 'home' and empire.

Empire played a key role in the ways that English people, at home or abroad, understood themselves. Anglo-Indians who had never seen England were proud of being British; Britons who had never met an Asian or African were proud of being white; reformers who had never been outside Europe spent their lives trying to improve the lives of Indian women. An understanding of England and its Empire was fashioned in both the 'metropole' (the dominant polity, England) and in its colonies (the subordinate polities).

By 1760 Britain was already a colonizing nation, and during the nine-teenth century it would come to be the largest Empire on earth. By the 1890s Britain controlled one-quarter of the world's land and ruled one-fifth of its people. When the First World War began, the population of the British Empire included 1.7 million people in the Caribbean, 30 million in Africa, and 315 million in India. Millions of colonial troops, including almost one and a half million Indians, 600,000 Canadians, 322,000 Australians, 124,000 New Zealanders, 55,000 Africans, and 10,400 Jamaicans fought for Britain, though of course women could not demonstrate their devotion to empire in this particular way.

This chapter will begin by noting the pervasiveness of imperialism in English popular culture. It will then explore the ideas of race, sexual danger, and motherhood that structured relations between English women and the Empire, taking note of the web of relationships between the 'metropole' and its colonies, before turning to women's various imperial roles. Because there is still a need for more research into the lives of poorer English women and their work in empire, the chapter focuses on that of the upper portions of society, aristocratic and upper-middle-class women, though there are some important exceptions.

IMPERIALISM IN POPULAR CULTURE

Empire was everywhere in English culture. The capital, London, was an imperial city, dominated by signs of Britain's military victories and imperial status. The Colonial Office was in Whitehall. Imperial goods were unloaded at the docks and railways every day. A statue of Field Marshal Hugh Rose, conqueror of India, stood in Knightsbridge. Empire was a constant presence in the visual arts, high and low literature, and periodicals. For example, the well-known explorer Captain Cook's death in Hawaii in 1779 was commemorated in poems, paintings and engravings. Photographs of India, Burma, China and North Africa were available in England from the 1850s. India was a popular subject in melodramatic plays and imperial dramas from the early nineteenth century.

After about 1870 empire saturated popular culture. The new title which Queen Victoria acquired in 1877, 'Empress of India', meant little in political practice, but festivities that year served as a celebration of empire and royalty, and the ceremony that was coming to characterize both; so did Victoria's Golden and Diamond Jubilees in 1887 and 1897. Coins, stamps, and letter-boxes across the Empire bore the royal image or cipher. Many places were named in honour of the Queen: although she never visited her dominions, across the Empire there were the Victoria Range, Bay, Strait, Fjord, Gap, Harbour and Hill, six Lake Victorias, two Cape Victorias, the Victoria Colony in Australia and the Victoria Nile in Uganda; other streets, squares and crescents had names such as Queen, Empress, Jubilee, Edward (after Edward VII) or George (after George V). Statues of Victoria and later monarchs were erected in city squares and in front of government buildings all over the Empire.

Displays of exotic colonial peoples and animals, painted panoramas and dioramas, and museums were other ways of creating imperial knowledge for the English public. So too were official exhibitions, such as the Colonial and Indian Exhibition of 1886, where attendees could purchase booklets on the 'History, Products, and Natural Resources' of all the colonies and dominions for 6d. Many of these resources were available in England during the late nineteenth and twentieth centuries: when English women went shopping they bought Indian tea, Nigerian chocolate, New Zealand lamb and butter, and South African apples, grapes and pears. In the twentieth century, cinema newsreels covered colonial events like the Boer War in a new and dramatic medium.

Empire was a subject of celebration in music halls, which offered an evening of short entertainments and were incredibly popular across a wide social spectrum throughout Victoria's reign. By the 1870s there was at least one music hall in almost every town in England, including five hundred in London alone; in the 1890s, the largest music halls had audiences of 45,000 people every night. Evening programmes that expressed imperialist-nationalist sentiments had titles like 'Indianationality', 'Britannia', and 'Grand Military Spectacle'. Popular songs such as 'Soldiers of the Queen', and 'Sons of the Sea', and 'By Jingo!' celebrated imperial military exploits abroad.

Children were especially inundated with empire. Its importance to England, and vice versa, was emphasized in textbooks; for example, *A Student's History of England* assured readers that 'England cannot but perceive that many things are done by the natives of India which are in their nature hurtful, unjust, or even cruel, and they are naturally impatient to remove evils that are evident to them.'[1] Extracurricular activities, like the celebration of Empire Day from 1904, also encouraged an awareness of, and pride in, the Empire. Popular periodicals such as *Boy's Own Magazine* (1855–75) and *Boy's Own Paper* (1879–1967) depicted empire as a place of adventure and conquest throughout the Victorian period and as a site of character formation during the Edwardian era. Boys and girls could also swap or send inexpensive picture postcards featuring scenes from the Empire, including new buildings, royal visits, frontier warfare, dramatic depictions of imperial heroism, and indigenous peoples. 'Cigarette cards' issued by tobacco, tea and confectionery companies had similar scenes, as did commemorative plates, mugs and tins put out by chocolate and biscuit companies, which might be decorated with a map of the Empire, population figures, lists of imports and exports, pictures of the Queen, and the motto 'The Empire on which the Sun never Sets'. Children could read imperial adventure stories in *Boy's Own Paper* and *Girl's Own Paper*, or play with imperially-themed toy soldiers, board games, and jigsaw puzzles.[2]

RACE

Imperialism created many ways of interpreting the world. Perhaps the most important was the idea of race. While social and natural scientists alike now see race as a fictive category without biological reality, for much of the eighteenth, nineteenth, and twentieth centuries it was understood to be a real and fundamental human difference. However, racial difference was not always defined by skin colour or other physical characteristics, and was not always as fixed as it later became. Before the late eighteenth century, race was a fluid category that was judged by such criteria as religion and manners. For example, the English often characterized the French as a separate race from themselves, in part because they were Catholic. Conversely, in Bartholomew Stibbs's 1723 *Journal of a Voyage up the Gambia*, he noted that black Africans living along the Gambia River who were Christian 'account[ed] themselves White Men', a judgement with which he concurred. Even in the late 1700s, as skin colour took on more significance, white Britons' reactions to non-white skin varied widely.[3] As the nineteenth century progressed, the idea that skin colour and other external physical characteristics determined race, and that the different human races should remain separate from one another, took firmer hold. Racial thinking was enforced by its status as a scientifically proven, objective set of differences. By the late nineteenth century eugenics also contributed to racist (and class-driven) ways of thinking.

Race was especially important with regard to Britain's Caribbean possessions which were, in the second half of the eighteenth century, the most valuable part of the Empire (especially after the loss of the American colonies). The English had first settled several Caribbean islands in the early seventeenth century, and by 1760 controlled many islands including Barbados. Jamaica was the most valuable of the islands because of its huge sugar production. It was seen as a place where fortunes could be made, but not a spot for putting down roots or raising a family. At the end of the eighteenth century Jamaica's population was made up of 30,000 white people (mostly men of English descent but also people who were Jewish, Irish and Scottish), 12,000 freed black and 'coloured' or mixed-race people, and a quarter of a million slaves. By 1830 the European population had shrunk by half, while the number of slaves and free non-whites rose. White Jamaican culture was a colonial culture: West Indian whites called England home, but were considered by those in England to be West Indian. From the 1780s, however, the anti-slavery movement challenged the permanence of Jamaica's plantation economy and culture, and the island became more and more a source of strife for colonial authorities.[4] The abolition of the slave trade in 1807 and of slavery in 1833 exacerbated the problem: by the 1860s it seemed clear that sugar would not be as profitable an industry when its labourers were free blacks rather than slaves. Ironically, calls for separation of the races intensified after the abolition of slavery. While slavery had once served as a marker of racial difference, emancipation threatened this stability and provoked new ways of imposing racial difference.[5]

EFFEMINACY

Race was also shaped by other categories and approaches to difference. The European tendency to glorify non-Western cultures as pleasingly exotic while disparaging them for being uncivilized is termed 'Orientalism' by some scholars. Many British writings on India especially, in which its noble past was praised while its lack of Christianity and representative government were faulted, had Orientalist leanings. Gender also shaped the understanding of empire. In Jamaica black, English, Creole, and settler femininity were all seen as different. Across the Empire non-white men were often accused of effeminacy.[6] The importance of gender in imperialism was especially apparent in late-eighteenth-century India, where travel writers, military memoirists and others were eager to justify the East India Company's hegemony by depicting Indian men (particularly Hindus) as effeminate and in need of British rulers. The East India Company was portrayed as virile, in contrast to the passivity of Indians; critics also claimed that India enervated and effeminized English men. In the late nineteenth century Indian masculinity was again politicized and attacked, as middle-class Hindu Bengali men were disparaged by the English as effeminate.[7]

SEXUAL DANGER

The Empire and racial difference were often discussed in terms of sexuality and sexual danger. The threat of sexual assaults on white women by non-white men helped shape imperial lifestyles and policies. These images emerged particularly sharply in India during the 1857 Rebellion and the 1883 Ilbert Bill controversy, discussed below, in Jamaica during the Morant Bay Rebellion of 1865, and in South Africa after the Boer War. While the panics were unfounded, their power was pervasive.[8]

During the early nineteenth century, in part because of the loss of the American colonies, the focus of the British Empire turned from the Caribbean to the Indian subcontinent. Until India gained its independence in 1947 it was the most prized part of the Empire, the 'jewel in the crown'. Until the mid-nineteenth century the British government did not rule the continent directly. Instead the East India Company, which had been a commercial presence on the coasts of Madras, Bombay and Calcutta since 1600, operated as a governmental presence. From 1765, Bengal was the capital of the East India Company's administration, which by 1840 ruled much of India, from Calcutta to beyond Delhi. By 1800 the Company (having finally defeated the Sultans of Mysore, who had resisted encroaching British authority in southern India in four Mysore wars waged between 1769 and 1799) began to act more confidently and more imperially. This confidence – accompanied by a growing chasm between whites and Indians – was shattered in 1857, when Indian soldiers in the Bengal Army staged a mutiny that quickly developed into a much larger rebellion in the north and north-west. Although the rebellion was put down by the end of 1858, it had lasting consequences. It was soon followed by the Maori Wars in New Zealand, from 1861 to 1865, and the Morant Bay riot in Jamaica in 1865; taken together, these were seen as evidence that natives were naturally rebellious. In the second half of the nineteenth century India was ruled directly by the Crown and Anglo-Indian society became quite stable but also far more racially divided. In 1885, the Indian National Congress was founded by professional, middle-class, high-caste Hindus; this organization eventually led to the call for Indian independence, promised in a 1917 Declaration but not achieved until 1947.

The Indian Rebellion of 1857 – once called the Indian or Sepoy Mutiny – was marked by looting and killing on both sides. The British public at home was kept well-informed about Indian atrocities but it heard little or nothing of comparable acts committed by the British, such as the brutal mistreatment of almost three hundred rebels at Ajnala, where over two hundred were shot and forty-five died of crowding and exhaustion awaiting the same fate. The Indian act considered most horrific by the British was the massacre at Cawnpore (now Kanpur), in which prisoners –

including women and children – were thrown down a well and left to die. That women in particular were subjected to such treatment enraged the British. In addition, there were many rumours of Indian men raping and torturing English women at Cawnpore and elsewhere. The popular British press was full of allusions to 'unspeakable' and 'atrocious' acts – clearly meant to be understood as rapes – even though no official or personal accounts of rape survive. Even though the most exaggerated reports were later discredited by official inquiries, the images remained in popular narratives and visual representations and became a key part of the collective imperial memory. English women were considered to be in danger from Indian lasciviousness, and the 1857 Rebellion was used as a way of casting white women as helpless and passive, and as a reason for British men to exert close control over British women and over all Indians.

Over fifty memsahibs, or middle-class English wives of British officials, wrote accounts of their experiences in 1857. They included Katherine Bartrum, whose diary, published in 1858, recounts her capture and her grief at the deaths of her husband and infant son, and Elizabeth McMullin Muter, whose work *My Recollections of the Sepoy Revolt, 1857–1858* was published in 1911. Women's memoirs of the Rebellion give no indication that English women saw Indian men as potential rapists. Most accounts emphasize the women's determination to act courageously in the face of danger; they also reveal the creation of strong female communities while under siege and deprived of male protectors. Most accounts differentiate between rebel strangers and Indians whom the authors knew personally and who they could not believe would ever harm them. Their disbelief is a testament both to their political and cultural naiveté and to the depth of their intimacies with some Indians. Accounts published decades after the event tend to exhibit more in the way of racial contempt, with Muter's 1911 memoir describing 'yelling fiends with dripping swords and hands red with blood'.[9]

White women living in South Africa were also warned of, and controlled by, fears of the 'black peril'. Laura Ridding's diary of her 1908 stay in South Africa records her fears:

Col. Fortescue warned us that we should not walk alone on any part of Table Mountain out of reach of houses because of the bad number of assaults on white women by coloured or black people that had recently taken place ... He says nowadays white people will have one servant, a 'black boy', who will bang on their bedroom door – bring in their cup

of coffee to them in bed – bang again to come in to clear it away and
be allowed to come in even if they were in their baths – (women or
men) – so 'familiarity breeds contempt' . . .'[10]

Ridding seems to have quickly absorbed the values in the colonel's
warning, and to have believed that barriers between the races were necessary to avoid sexual assault.

MOTHERHOOD AND SISTERHOOD

While white women were restrained by the threat of sexual assault, they
could also use their gender to advantage. This is apparent in the centrality
of motherhood, and images of motherhood, to empire. England was
described as the mother of colonial white communities and indigenous
peoples. Alfred Milner wrote of 'the Mother Country'; the Colonial Secretary Joseph Chamberlain described England as a 'vigorous and fruitful'
mother.[11] Feminists used maternal rhetoric to argue that women were
necessary to the proper governing of empire.

Colonial white women were described as 'sisters' by white English
women, who actually saw them as daughters. Indigenous peoples were
seen as the charges of these white colonists, and so doubly infantilized.
The philanthropist Mary Carpenter, who spent many years there, said,
'[i]n India I am regarded as "the old Mother", and I am proud of the
title.'[12] Imperial motherhood could also be a duty and another way of
controlling women. In the late nineteenth and early twentieth centuries,
the relationship between imperialism and motherhood took on new
resonances as imperialism became increasingly racialized and as eugenics
became popular across the political spectrum. Imperial propaganda
encouraged women to see themselves as 'the future nursing mothers of
the English race to be'.[13] Upper-class female imperialists exhorted
working-class women to emigrate, marry, and bear English children in
the colonies. Missionary wives (who were usually from the lower middle
classes) often stressed their roles as mothers both of their own children
and of the natives with whom they came in contact. The English saw
themselves as threatened by native races and competing European powers,
so the bearing of white children at home, as soldiers and workers of the
future, was another aspect of women's duty to race as well as to nation.
Sometimes motherhood was seen as metaphorical, with single women

being encouraged through their careers to make maternal contributions to race, nation, and empire.

Critics scolded middle-class women for 'shirking' motherhood in favour of education or career, or by limiting family size. They chastized working-class women for their ignorance, which had contributed to the poor health of army recruits, seeing the mothers' lack of education as more responsible for this than the poverty and unsanitary conditions in which they were forced to bring up their children. As a result of this criticism, classes on mothering for poor women sprang up all over England during the first two decades of the twentieth century.[14]

ENGLISH BLACKS, COLONIAL WHITES

As these examples show, there were many connections between the nation and the Empire. Additionally, there were many non-white imperial subjects of African and Asian descent in England. In 1770, the English population (which together with the Welsh population numbered somewhere just under 8 million) included between 15,000 and 20,000 non-whites, mostly Africans and West Indians, with some South and East Asians. Many were African or Afro-Caribbean men who were former slaves, former servants, or sailors; they often married English working-class women, who were thought to find African men particularly virile and desirable. Others were bi-racial, children of white Caribbean planters and their black concubines or of white East India Company officials and their Indian companions. Most lived in London or in port cities that had dealings with Africa or plantation colonies, such as Bristol, Liverpool, Chester, Dartmouth and Plymouth, and had developed a black urban culture.

During the nineteenth century, as transportation improved, an increasing number of Africans and Asians came to England (where they probably remained concentrated in urban port areas). In addition to sailors and servants, there was a steady stream of travellers, students and others, arriving, settling, or departing.[15] These included men and women, rich and poor, although elite men were the most likely to come to England and the poor were least likely to leave traces of their presence. A former slave, Mary Prince, was well-known on the lecture circuit in the early 1830s; prominent Indian visitors included reformer Rammohun Roy, a leader of the Brahmo Samaj (a Hindu reform movement) who also travelled to England during this period and promoted the cause of Indian social reform, and Pandita Ramabai, a social reformer who came to England in the 1880s to train as a doctor. While such elite Indian men and women often enjoyed the friendship and support of many individuals and groups, they were also aware of themselves as spectacles at whom many white people gawked.

Not all imperial subjects were coloured: England also received a steady stream of white colonials – Canadians, New Zealanders and Australians – who often referred to the country as 'home' even before they arrived. As an Australian woman, Alice Grant Rosman, remarked in 1913, 'Australia is much farther from England than England from Australia.' White colonials have been referred to as 'fictive Europeans'.[16] They could move across the English landscape more freely than coloured people, but their colonial status – apparent from their accents and other cultural traits – marked them as socially subordinate to 'true' English people. As a result, white colonials had an ambiguous status that gave them certain freedoms but also imposed limitations.

The so-called 'settler colonies' – Australia, Canada, New Zealand and South Africa – had a different place in the Empire from other colonies. There the English preferred to ignore the indigenous populations entirely, often speaking of newly visited continents as 'empty'. The first Briton to encounter Australia and New Zealand (in 1769 and 1770) was the explorer Captain Cook (1728–79); the first British settlements in Australia were penal colonies established on Tasmania and the east coast of Australia in the late 1780s. Other settlements followed, populated at first by European sheep and convicts. In 1815 Australia had 15,000 whites and half a million Aboriginals, but by 1860 the indigenous population had been decimated (largely by smallpox and venereal disease) and swamped by British immigrants. The separate colonies established legislatures in 1850 and united to become the Commonwealth of Australia in 1901. New Zealand was visited by sailors, whalers, traders and missionaries in the late eighteenth and early nineteenth centuries; it was formally annexed by Britain in 1840. Europeans emigrated, first with assistance and later seeking gold; they soon numerically overwhelmed the native Maori population. In 1870 a central government replaced provincial councils, and by the First World War New Zealand was governed as an autonomous dominion of the British Empire.

Europeans first encountered Canada in the sixteenth century, and the British conquered New France, subsequently the province of Quebec, in 1763. By 1815 the British had several territories on the Atlantic seaboard, but while demonstrating some respect for Canadians of French origin (who were allowed to practise Roman Catholicism) they showed very little for the Native Americans, who constituted 20 per cent of the population in 1815 but only one per cent (100,000 people) in 1911. In 1818, a border between the United States and Canada was established (it was extended to the Pacific Ocean in 1849). In 1867, the Canadian colonies became provinces and underwent confederation to become a dominion of the British Empire. Canada became fully autonomous in 1931.

The British government considered South Africa important because of its place on the only existing trade route to India. When the British seized the Cape of Good Hope from the Dutch in 1795, its population included 20,000 Boers or Afrikaaners (whites of Dutch origin) and about 45,000 black Africans, of whom 25,000 were slaves. European-controlled South Africa doubled in size in the mid-nineteenth century. Tensions came to a head with the Boer War (1899–1902), in which 450,000 British troops took over two years to defeat 45,000 Boers. The British ultimately won, but they were nevertheless humiliated. In 1910, several South African states united to form the Union of South Africa, an independent state that remained a dominion of the Empire until 1961. Its history of racial segregation was legally enforced under the 'apartheid' system from 1948 until 1994.

White colonizers abroad did not necessarily share common interests and were not a unified group because of the importance attached to class and gender. They included elite officials, civil servants, soldiers, missionaries, entrepreneurs, and the wives and children of many of them. Middle- and upper-class governors and their families were concerned with maintaining their dominance over poorer whites as well as over coloured people. They were also concerned to present a unified white front; their horror of white prostitutes who served brown or black customers is evidence of this. Later in the 1908 diary quoted above, Laura Ridding described 'the lowest type of white prostitute, who prefers soliciting coloured men because they pay better' as an 'awful cancer'.[17]

White domesticity

One of women's most important imperial tasks was to make possible a regime of white domesticity. In most places this meant that an eighteenth-century imperial culture of white men and their native concubines was replaced by a nineteenth-century emphasis on white marriages, families, and domestic habits. Although white men in the Caribbean rarely married women of African descent, they often maintained free black women as companions and had ongoing sexual relations with slave women. Men went to the islands of the West Indies to make huge fortunes as planters but not to settle down; as one historian has recently remarked, 'In this situation, England was for families, Jamaica was for sex.'[18] Maria, Lady Nugent, who lived in Jamaica from 1801 until 1805 as the wife of the Governor, was struck by how isolated she felt as one of the few white women on the island. She also criticized the behaviour of white men there because she felt that their example rendered black Jamaican society immoral:

> White men of all descriptions, married or single, live in a state of licentiousness with their female slaves; and until a great reformation takes place on their part, neither religion, decency, nor morality, can be established among the negroes. An answer that was made to Mr Shirley, a Member of the Assembly (and a profligate character, as far as I can understand), who advised one of his slaves to marry, is a strong proof of this – 'Hi, Massa, you telly me marry one wife, which is no good! You no tinky I see you buckra no content wid one, two, tree, or four wives; no more poor negro.' The overseers, &c. too, are in general needy adventurers, without either principle, religion, or morality. Of course, their example must be the worst possible to these poor creatures.[19]

From the early nineteenth century all this changed. In the West Indies the push for white domesticity was shaped by the slavery debate. Both pro- and anti-slavery forces in England became determined to distinguish between black and white women's femininity and sexual morals. Interestingly, both sides maintained that non-marital and interracial sexual union revealed the immorality of plantation culture, though they differed about what this meant and what the solution might be. Opponents of slavery held that the lasciviousness of slave-holding plantation society, rife with non-marital interracial unions, demonstrated that it was incompatible with British domestic virtue. Advocates of slavery relied on white women to solve the problem by encouraging men to settle into domesticity on the islands, and by bearing many children so as to increase the domesticated white population. Stable white marriages, pro-slavery forces maintained, would render plantation and slave-holding society stable, virtuous and domestic; therefore white women and domesticity both had a place in the slave-holding West Indies.[20] While the white population in Jamaica remained small, pro-slavery groups increasingly stressed the importance of permanently settled white families.

In the settler colonies, as mentioned, the English tried not to recognize the existence of native peoples but they were none the less worried about interracial sex and procreation. They were anxious that white marriages should replace white men's relationships with Aboriginal women in Australia and with native American women in Canada. The white population's gender imbalance in Australia was thought to lead to prostitution, illegitimacy, and homosexuality. While in the late eighteenth century soldiers were encouraged to form relationships with indigenous Australian women, so that they would be sexually satisfied and remain unmarried, by the nineteenth century virtuous English women were needed to populate, domesticate and render the colonies socially and sexually respectable.

Later in the century many Canadian promoters of female emigration hoped that the presence of white women, especially in the less densely settled west, would dissuade white men from forming relationships with native women. The Anglican Bishop of the mission to British Columbia warned that 'the mixture of different bloods is all against the new colony' and saw large-scale immigration by white women as the only way to stop such mixing.[21] In both Australia and Canada, white women were seen to have a special responsibility, since they brought civilization to an untamed region. Feminists often took this duty quite seriously. For instance, temperance was an important part of Australian feminism, which sought to curb the drinking and wildness of the masculine frontier.[22]

A similar dynamic pertained in India until the 1790s. Before then, many white male employees of the East Indian Company had native companions with whom they produced mixed-race children. High-ranking British men often formed relationships with elite Indian women. The Company explicitly encouraged interracial relationships, seeing white wives and children as expensive encumbrances, and in fact prohibited its officers from marrying. Novels depicting interracial sex and marriage, such as James Annesley's *Memoirs of an Unfortunate Nobleman* (1743) and Henry Brooke's *Fool of Quality* (1767–70), were popular in the mid-eighteenth century. In them (while white English women and non-European men were invisible) high-ranking native women – in spite of their different colour and religion – married white men, the forgers of empire.[23]

All this is not to claim that British India enjoyed racial equality before the 1790s. Most men did not marry their native companions, thereby denying them legal rights and social power. Many European men kept these relationships, and their mixed-race offspring, secret, revealing them only after death in their wills.[24] Some men with native companions married white women – simultaneously or later, in England or India – thereby allowing themselves both native and 'respectable' wives, the latter of whom might bring wealth as well as prestige to their husbands. Inter-racial relationships were part of Anglo-Indian society, but native companions were denied public recognition and respect.

Around 1790, Anglo-Indian society changed, just as Jamaican and settler societies did. Accusations of mismanagement and corruption led to various Acts of Parliament that regulated the East India Company's doings. Prime Minister William Pitt's India Act of 1784 separated the Company's civil service and military from its trading wing, and raised salaries. The Act's goals were to curb corruption by separating the East India Company's two conflicting functions – that of trading and that of governing the subcontinent – and to give the government a more direct role in ruling India. The Company's racial policies also changed. While it had once hired many mixed-race people, from 1793 Eurasians (those of mixed European and Indian ancestry) were declared ineligible for such posts. Elite officials were now discouraged from keeping Indian companions; lower-ranking men (soldiers and civil servants) were provided with prostitutes, thought to be necessary since the tropical heat intensified men's sexual appetites. In spite of these new policies and prohibitions, interracial relationships continued to flourish.

As it did in England, the government passed the Contagious Diseases Acts and introduced other legislation intended to regulate prostitution in India and all over the Empire, including Jamaica, Hong Kong, and parts of Australia. Officials were empowered to inspect native prostitutes to make sure they were 'clean' so that soldiers and other men could remain healthy while patronizing them. In general these laws, particularly those in India, were far more coercive than domestic ones, and were in force throughout the nineteenth century rather than for just a few decades as in England. This was in part because the problem of venereal disease was thought to be worse in India, but largely because racial and imperial thinking inclined officials to treat Indian women poorly. Venereal disease was indeed a serious problem among the imperial armed forces. Infection rates in the Indian Army usually hovered between 20 and 30 per cent, but could be as high as 50 per cent. White prostitutes, especially those who served Asian men, were considered a separate problem; the British authorities were relieved to report that most white prostitutes in India were Central European Roman Catholics and Jews, not Protestant English girls.[25]

From the middle of the nineteenth century more white men were encouraged to bring their wives and children to India. As English women started to arrive in large numbers, a culture of native companions and bi-racial children was replaced by English domesticity and social and cultural distance from Indians. For example, from the 1850s the families of white men who worked for Indian railway companies lived in protected communities built by their employers, which were meant to encourage white middle-class domesticity and shield inhabitants from the Indian culture. Because white women's presence was accompanied by a growing racial divide, many contemporaries (and historians) have claimed that white women were more racist than white men and were responsible for increasing racial tensions during the second half of the century. In reality – though most white women certainly believed in white superiority, just as most white men did – the presence of English women was merely a symptom of the larger shift. (Of course, many Indians were as disapproving of interracial marriages as Europeans were. While Eurasian women were often eager to marry white men, few Indians from the *bhadralok* (Hindu gentry) or *ashraf* (Muslim gentry) were eager to have European husbands or sons-in-law.)[26]

By mid-century the push for white domesticity abroad had succeeded, and white women lived in most of the colonies (Canada experienced the shift slightly later), where they were expected to provide homes which definitively marked off white society. However, this project was always threatened by the natives around them, especially since women and children were considered vulnerable to such influences. Many observers complained that white Jamaican children learned African 'behaviour' and 'Vices'.[27] Lady Nugent believed that all Caribbean whites adopted African habits, and wrote:

> It is extraordinary to witness the immediate effect that the climate and habit of living in this country have upon the minds and manners of Europeans, particularly of the lower orders. In the upper ranks, they

become indolent and inactive, regardless of everything but eating, drinking, and indulging themselves, and are almost entirely under the domination of their mulatto favourites. In the lower orders they are the same, with the addition of conceit and tyranny.[28]

A similar problem was observed in India: memsahibs usually hired low-caste Hindu or Muslim *amahs* (wet-nurses) because white doctors claimed that English women could not nurse in the Indian heat. However, parents worried that *amahs* would somehow racially contaminate the babies they nursed (much as women in England who used poor wet-nurses worried about the possibility of moral contagion). As their children got older, memsahibs worried that they would pick up native habits and language from their *ayahs* (nannies). In 1839, Julia Thomas Maitland wrote in a letter about her baby daughter that she intended 'as much as possible, to prevent her learning the native language though it is rather difficult ... most English children do learn them [native languages] and all sorts of mischief with them, and grow like little Hindoos',[29] a fate she clearly considered undesirable.

Middle-class women were particularly important in India. We know that in the nineteenth century there were many white women from the working or lower middle classes living in British India, including nannies, soldiers' wives, and prostitutes. However, little is known about these women's lives (other than that soldiers' wives were thought to be ill-intentioned gossips, and that soldiers' and missionaries' widows often had difficulty making claims for state and church pensions after their husbands' deaths[30]). The white women in India about whom we have the most information are memsahibs, who were in India because of family obligations and did not necessarily have any interest in, or sympathy with, the Indian culture. Memsahibs were usually dismissed as frivolous housewives, with more servants than most people of a similar status could have afforded in England. In many ways the stereotype of the idle, pleasure-loving memsahib was quite the opposite of the moral and domestic wife and mother most praised by the Victorians, encouraging fears that India sapped English women of their female virtue (just as it was sometimes accused of effeminizing English men). While memsahibs led lives of relative leisure, they also faced many difficulties, leaving behind their families and friends and the comforts of home. In India, their social lives were quite different from what they would have been in England; for

instance, they were expected to entertain travelling Britons and to treat
family celebrations as public ceremonials.

Bearing and raising children was difficult, especially as Anglo-Indians
suffered from a high rate of infant and maternal death in childbirth. One
family tombstone in Benares bears the inscription:

John died 11 March, 1834 aged 7 months
Jesse died 18 August, 1835 aged 8 months
Henrietta died 3 June, 1838 aged 6 months
Oliver died 14 August, 1839 aged 13 months
Arnold died November, 1841 aged 5 months
Joseph died 29 May, 1842 aged 5 months[31]

Most women found it especially hard having to give birth without the
support of their mothers. And new communities were few and far
between, since Anglo-Indian society was as classbound as English society
but much smaller, and women formed female networks only with neighbours of the same social status. Women whose husbands were in the civil
service or the armed services found friends more easily than the wives of
higher-ranking officers or civil servants.

Women could not even rely on their husbands for companionship,
as Anglo-Indian families were frequently separated. After giving birth,
women and their infants often left for hill stations, which were considered
healthier, but which meant being apart from their husbands for several
months of the year. Children were sent back to England at a very young
age, both to attend school and to prevent enervation caused by the Indian
climate and culture. Memsahibs were constantly faced with the choice of
deciding whether to stay with their husbands or accompany their children.
Most remained in India when their children went to school; the long
distance meant that some mothers did not see their children for years at
a time. Soldiers' wives often suffered the same separation from their
children.[32]

Of course memsahibs were also involved in the world beyond the
family, and could certainly make their opinions known in Anglo-Indian
politics. One episode, the Ilbert Bill controversy, reminds us of how fully
complicit white women were in the racial privilege they enjoyed. From
the 1850s Indians and Eurasians were once again eligible to compete for
various government positions. In 1883, a government official, Courtenay
Ilbert, introduced a bill that would have allowed Indian judges to try

white Britons on criminal charges. Though at the time there were only two Indian judges senior enough to have been eligible, Anglo-Indians – including an unprecedented number of women – were outraged at this challenge to white racial superiority. Indian men were held to be unfit to serve as judges because they did not treat their own women well; in contrast, white English men were seen as the protectors of both white and native women. Opponents of the Ilbert Bill focused on the spectre of an Indian man (as judge) having control over a white woman (as defendant), and of acquittals of Indian rapists that would lead to an increase in rapes of white women. In the end the bill was withdrawn.[33]

White women were involved in the Ilbert Bill controversy in several ways. They flooded the Anglo-Indian press with letters opposing the bill, participated in various organizations that formed in opposition to the bill, and socially boycotted supporters of the bill in Calcutta. The wives of non-officials eschewed all Government House social events in Calcutta for two seasons, to great effect. One lady opponent, Flora MacDonald, wrote a letter to a local paper in which she invoked the image of:

> an English girl in all her maidenly dignity ... accused by her *ayah* ... of a loathsome crime, a crime that is common among native women; the Court is crowded with natives of all castes who have flocked to ... laugh and jeer, and stare that English girl in the face ... the most irrelevant questions are asked, questions that only a native would dare to ask.[34]

Annette Akroyd Beveridge (1842–1929) wrote that 'to subject us [white women] to the jurisdiction of native judges [is] an insult. It is not pride of race which dictates this feeling – it is the pride of womanhood.'[35] However, as the womanhood to which she referred was a specifically white one, the pride she felt was both racial and gendered.

Consuming the Empire's goods

In addition to establishing white domesticity throughout the Empire, English women also linked England and its empire through their role as consumers. Many foods, clothes, items in homes, and flowers in gardens, came from the empire. Women were seen as the chief consumers in society, and their engagement with the material products of empire was

evident in many ways. In the 1790s Caribbean sugar, which had become
a staple of the British diet, was a symbol of the relationship between
Britain and its slave-holding Caribbean colonies. Abolitionists and advocates of slavery differed over whether this relationship, and the sugary
foods and drinks it made possible – chief among them a proper cup of
tea and the puddings for which the English were becoming known – was
natural and beneficial or ungodly and destructive, but both sides saw
women and femininity as crucial to the debate. Women were thought to
be especially fond of sweet foods, and sugar was depicted in ways that
linked it closely to the female body. Pro-slavery advocates of Caribbean
sugar often compared it to breast milk to emphasize how sweet and
nourishing it was and how proper for human consumption. They also
emphasized how good sugar was for slave children as a way of depicting
British imperialism as benevolent. Opponents of slavery, in contrast, saw
the slave's body and the sugar produced by its labour as one and the same,
and compared eating sugar to cannibalism: one 1791 pamphlet argued
that the slave who was forcibly fed by his masters 'cannot account for
their brutal kindness; he concludes that they mean to fatten him, in order
to feast upon him at a convenient season.'[36] Here those who ate slave-
grown sugar were also consuming the slaves who were forced to stay alive
so that they could grow sugar for English consumers.

In the 1790s, anti-slavery women boycotted slave-grown sugar. These
boycotts were highly charged political acts. Some scholars have seen
boycotts as humanitarian attempts to use women's role as consumers in
a positive way. Others viewed those who participated in them as no
less racist than pro-slavery groups, because they sought to cleanse their
English homes of African blood, sweat and tears. While it is certainly true
that the boycotters did not see slaves or other Afro-Caribbean women as
their equals, their anti-slavery stance must be seen as less racist than
support for slavery.[37]

Women were also conduits of Indian goods. When in England, whether
for visits or permanently, memsahibs functioned as crucial purveyors of
imperial products. True, when in India they eschewed all things Indian,
insisting on English foods, clothing, jewellery, and interior decorations;
this is no surprise given that it was their responsibility as middle-class
women to create and maintain ethnocentric home environments. But in
England it was quite a different story, as memsahibs helped to shape
material expressions of imperialism. During the first half of the nineteenth
century, Indian items appealed only to the upper and upper middle

classes, but from about 1860 the diffusion became more widespread. Memsahibs helped to popularize many items, notably Kashmir shawls and curry and rice dishes: Eliza Acton's *Modern Cookery* (in its thirteenth edition of 1853) and Mrs Beeton's *Book of Household Management* (1861) both provided recipes for curries and rice.

Indian shawls were preferred to similarly styled ones made elsewhere; in 1867 the *Ladies' Treasury* remarked that in England 'nobody but provincials buy French Kashmeres ... the shawl must be undeniably and manifestly, Indian.' Imported Indian curry powders were much preferred in England even when large department stores (such as Fortnum & Mason's) began selling their own blends. This meant that memsahibs were in a position of economic strength; for instance, imported Kashmir shawls were too expensive for most English women (they cost somewhere between £25 and £100, depending on the shawl and the decade), and memsahibs often sold or bartered theirs while in England. Both *The Englishwoman's Domestic Magazine*, founded in the 1850s for middle-class women, and *Queen*, aimed at the wealthy, had exchange columns full of advertisements from memsahibs offering to sell or trade shawls and other goods. Less affluent Anglo-Indian women, too, could barter. In one advertisement a woman – probably the wife or widow of a soldier who needed to earn her living upon her return to England – sought a sewing machine in exchange for a shawl.[38]

Travel narratives

Female travel writers were unusual, and not all women travelled out of their own desire; some were accompanying male relatives on official business. Others – mainly from the middle and upper classes – travelled with a view to writing about their experiences. Because travel narratives were often widely read in England by those who never went abroad, they were key shapers of the English understanding of empire. While offering valuable descriptions of the colonies, they were also part and parcel of the British domination of them. These popular works purported to give readers a taste of the experience of being in a foreign culture. Many travel accounts depicted their authors living among the natives, and so seemed to transcend colonialism, but they also reaffirmed it by portraying natives and their habitats as exotic and different. Women's travel writings also reveal their ambivalent role as the subordinate gender in the dominant race. Many positioned themselves specifically as female contributors to the library of travel writings; they paid much attention to landscape and to native women, and especially offered accounts of life in *zenanas*, or segregated women's quarters in north, north-western, and eastern India.

The relatively elite status of travellers thoroughly shaped their experiences and perceptions. In India, travel was quite a luxurious affair. One of the wealthiest travellers was Emily Eden, whose *Up the Country* (1866) was probably the most widely-read travel account by a woman in the nineteenth century. She was part of a distinguished and politically active Whig family, and an adviser to prime ministers Melbourne and Palmerston. Eden, accompanying her unmarried brother, the new Governor-General of India, travelled in magnificent style, with a party that included 12,000 attendants. But even those much further down the social scale travelled in a style almost unimaginable today: they were accompanied by servants including cook, waiter, valet, maid, and luggage-bearers. At each stop large tents, completely furnished with tables, chairs, and rugs, were set up, and multi-course meals were served. Other English travel writers about India included Maria Graham (later Lady Callcott), who travelled with her father to India, met her husband there, and wrote *Journal of a Residence in India* (1812); Fanny Parkes, author of *Wanderings of a Pilgrim* (1850); Amelia Falkland, wife of the governor of Bombay, who wrote *Chow-Chow: Being Selections from a Journal kept in India, Egypt, and Syria* (1857); and Mrs Colin Mackenzie, author of *Six Years in India* (1857).

Like most travel writing on India, the accounts of Englishwomen were shaped by an Orientalist tendency to privilege and sentimentalize Indian culture (especially that of ancient India); by the belief that it was the responsibility of white English people to improve the condition of India; and by the notion of the picturesque, which emphasized an imaginative appreciation of, and detachment from, things foreign and exotic. The search for an Indian picturesque was very important to many female travellers' perceptions. 'What bits to sketch! What effects here! What colouring here!' Lady Amelia Falkland observed delightedly, noting with disapproval that 'the natives very rarely have an eye for the picturesque, or any admiration for nature.'[39] Many felt that the glory of India's past could best be seen in ruins and tombs, which writers viewed with nostalgia. Fanny Parkes's *Wanderings of a Pilgrim in Search of the Picturesque*, for instance, is full of descriptions of ruins interspersed with retellings of ancient Indian myths. Mrs Mackenzie was dismayed by the Indians' lack of appreciation for their picturesque country:

> The Hindustanis are very apathetic to scenery. I have never known one to stop to admire anything. My husband cross-questioned a chaprassi (from Delhi I think) to find if he had any appreciation for the beauties which surrounded him. Not in the least. He said the pain in his legs in running up and down hill with messages was not to be expressed, and that if it were not for the wants of his stomach he would not stay here a day.[40]

Not all observers were as insensitive as Mrs Mackenzie; Emily Eden, describing an English dance held in the hills at which European foods were served, and at which several thousand Indians waited on one hundred Europeans, remarked: 'I sometimes wonder they do not cut all our heads off, and say nothing more about it.'[41]

The obsession which many female travellers had with the *zenana* was partly because it was a female space and so afforded English women access to Indian culture that was denied to English men and also because this allowed them to claim intimacy with, and authority over, some aspects of India. Most descriptions of the *zenana* stressed how little privacy the inmates enjoyed, though Fanny Parkes found the first *zenana* she saw quite sensual and described one woman in it as 'the loveliest creature in existence'.[42] However, by the later nineteenth century, with racial segregation of colonial society firmly in place, women travellers' interpretations of the *zenana* changed. Few of the later travel writers ever saw one; most simply included second-hand descriptions in their books. They tended to see the *zenana* not as a site of female sexuality but as a place in which female potential was stunted and women were rendered childlike, jealous, and petty. Isabella Bird, a member of the Church of England Zenana Missionary Society who travelled to India, Persia, China and Morocco, claimed in 1893 that she visited *zenanas* frequently, and was almost always 'asked for drugs with which to disfigure the favourite wife, or to take away the life of the favourite wife's infant son'.[43] At the very end of the century some conservative women saw Indian women as embodying feminine virtues that were threatened in England by feminism; they praised traditional Indian society, including the *zenana*, and criticized the attempts of British reformers and missionaries to modernize it. But, in their varying commentaries, all of these writers were using

Indian women and the *zenana* as a foil against which English women could define themselves and their liberties.

Women also travelled to Africa. The most famous English woman to do so was Mary Kingsley (1862–1900), a middle-class woman who travelled to West Africa twice and was the first European person to reach many parts of the region. She was the author of the enormously popular *Travels in West Africa* (1897), which made her in high demand as a lecturer in London. Kingsley was well-known for her defence of African culture, including polygamy and alcohol consumption, and for her criticisms of most European interventions into African society, especially by missionaries, for whom she had little use. These opinions made her a controversial if respected figure; the Colonial Secretary Joseph Chamberlain sought her advice on governing Africa but asked her to keep their meetings secret. Kingsley died of typhoid after volunteering as a nurse in South Africa during the Boer War.

By then, women's travel was becoming more common. Mary Hall, in her book *A Woman's Trek from the Cape to Cairo* (1907), was concerned to emphasize that ordinary travellers, including women like herself, could and should travel in Africa. Hall's contemporary Helen Caddick's book *A White Woman in Central Africa* (1900) describes her encounters with Africans, whom Caddick claimed to love although she saw them as childlike and inferior to Europeans. She also preferred Africans who were unspoiled by contact with missionaries. Like many female authors, Caddick claimed to feel an affinity for the African women she met, although as she spoke no African languages most of her interpretations were conjectural. In some ways Caddick's book is most remarkable for its unadventurous qualities; she worries about accommodation and travel connections, and sees herself not as an adventurer like Kingsley but as a tourist.[44] By 1900, then, even an unremarkable Englishwoman could feel quite safe travelling in Africa.

Missionary work

One of the most important ways in which the British experienced, engaged with, and thought about its empire was through foreign missionary activity. Missionary work brought the Empire to life at home through its prominence in literature and in the weekly services of most Protestant denominations and their fundraising efforts. Most working- and middle-class churchgoers regularly donated small sums of money to mission funds; as we saw in Chapter 5, taken together these made foreign missionary work an enormous endeavour. Such acts of giving were ways of participating in empire. So, too, was reading: the writings of missionaries were the primary source of information about the Empire for many people. These included biographies, fiction, and anecdotes and articles in general periodicals like *The Leisure Hour* and in denominational periodicals such as *The Church Missionary Gleaner*.

Early in the nineteenth century, missionaries saw natives as sinners not unlike the poor at home. In the second half of the century, when a stark contrast was drawn between whites and non-whites, natives were seen as different from all white people (though still in need of salvation). While British imperial possessions were technically Christian, and most had some Anglican presence, missionary efforts before the early nineteenth century were mainly focused on white settlers, not on native populations. The first Baptist Missionary Society (BMS) workers intent on converting black slaves arrived in Jamaica in 1813. Especially active in the 1830s, BMS missionaries were a sort of imperial loyal opposition, who were fiercely opposed to slavery and to what they saw as the immorality of planter culture in general.

Before mid-century, women worked as missionary wives. They were cultural as well as religious proselytizers, who sought to make natives more English in their style of dress and methods of housekeeping as well as in their beliefs. Their work was varied and endless – one missionary wife, Hannah Philippo, ran a school with her husband, taught the girls' classes in it, presided over her household, bore nine children (and buried five of them), and visited the sick and the poor, all while suffering from ill health herself.[45] From the 1860s onwards, various denominations began training and sending women overseas as missionaries in their own right, until, by 1899, nearly as many women as men worked in foreign missions. Overall, female missionaries did much the same work as missionary wives had done, focusing on women, children, family life, domesticity and education. But although missions enjoyed extensive support and popularity at home, they were generally unsuccessful in the field. Missionaries were only ever able to convince a very small minority of Indians to convert to Christianity; they were marginally more successful in the West Indies, the South Pacific, and Africa (a popular destination for single evangelical mission women), but not until the twentieth century. Lady missionaries were sent where missions were least successful – India, the Middle East, and the Far East. In Asian or Islamic areas, women could enter restricted female-only spaces and preach the Gospel. In India, while many lower-caste people in the south had become Christians, higher-caste conversions remained rare, so missionary women began visiting elite women during this period. Yet native converts, however elite, were never considered the equals of whites; even in India they were always referred to as 'native' teachers, nurses, and so on; elite converts were called 'native ladies'.[46]

Low success rates meant that although missionaries might be popular at home, they were often lonely and rejected abroad. This was not only because the natives were unreceptive to their message; many missionaries were from the lower middle class and were themselves looked down upon by the colonial officials and ruling elites, including the planters of the West Indies and the administrators and memsahibs of India. Flora Annie Steel, for instance, was highly critical of missionary women for their 'lack of dignity in dealing with their clientele'.[47] In India, missionaries (though they wore European clothes and ate European food) maintained close relationships with Christian Indians, and were kept on the social margins of white colonial life.[48]

Reformers and feminists

Similar in impulse to missionary work was reform work, an aspect of the philanthropy and social work so central to middle-class women's lives. Some educated middle-class reformers travelled to the colonies. Like missionaries, and unlike the wives of officials, they arrived not as part of the formal imperial establishment but on its margins, brought not by family obligations but by their own interest. Others worked for colonial causes but remained in England. Like domestic philanthropists reformers focused their attentions on women – not the poor white women on whom their counterparts at home concentrated, though these certainly existed, but on indigenous women.

Reformers used images of colonial women, and their own interest in them, both as a means of doing good and of establishing themselves as imperialists. One reformer, Mary Carpenter, described Indian women as trapped in the 'sunless, airless' rooms of the *zenana*, and most reformers saw Indian women as passive, silent victims of Indian men and Indian culture. Reforming women wanted to help Indian women, but were also intent on contrasting Indian and English women so as to establish themselves as active citizens.

Two of the crucial mechanisms of oppression, according to reformers, were *purdah* (the practice of secluding women) and the *zenana* (the space to which they were confined), and *sati* (the act in which a widowed woman threw herself on her husband's funeral pyre and was burned with his body). Since Indian men oppressed their women, reformers argued, it was the responsibility of English men and women to set them free. Although the criticized practices were restricted to small areas of the country or to small elites (none were widespread, and none were engaged in by poor Indians, the vast majority of the population), reformers focused on these as illustrative of the difficulties Indian women faced.

The *zenana* was to English reformers not just the organization of household space, but a symbol of Indian women's oppression and segregation. Their interpretations of the *zenana* differed over time. The *zenana* was variously seen as a site of potential conversion of Indian women to Christianity; as a site for female education; as a symbol of how Indians lived in the past, mired in tradition; as a site of potential female solidarity and power; and as a site of stubborn resistance to the British civilizing project. All of these overlapping interpretations were based on the reformers' views of Indian culture, which were deeply coloured by their own beliefs in the superiority of English culture and especially of Christianity.[49]

The campaign against *sati*, waged from 1813 (when the practice first received British legal attention) until 1829 (when it was made illegal in British India), was the first organized political intervention by female reformers. It was not limited to women, but their participation was crucial as part of an imperially oriented feminism. Reformers protested against *sati* by supporting missionary efforts to outlaw the practice and by working to improve the education of girls and women in India. They also petitioned Parliament on the subject, appropriating a widely recognized tool for intervening in national politics.

The *sati* debate in India focused on how to interpret Hindu Scriptures correctly and who was authorized to do so; Indian women were the grounds of the debate rather than its subject. In England, the debate was framed as an issue of Indian women's welfare and of English women's mission to colonial women. It was an evangelical as well as an imperial matter: *sati* was opposed by Christian missionaries to India, and the matter was discussed in the English press – especially the widely-read missionary press – in an evangelical context. If Indians could be converted to Christianity, they would surely discontinue the practice. British legislation and Christian education were, it was thought, the keys to this transformation. From the beginning, then, the possibilities for Indian women's emancipation were structured by English women's beliefs in the superiority of British civilization and Christianity. While English women laboured under many legal oppressions of their own, anti-*sati* reformers did not compare these limitations to those faced by Indian women; they contrasted their own lives – as English, Christian, and civilized – with those of Indian women. Yet in the process of challenging other women's subordination, they began indirectly to challenge their own.[50]

The anti-*sati* campaign was accompanied by the anti-slavery campaign, another movement of imperial reform, this one focusing on Africa and the Caribbean. The latter was far larger than the former, but in some aspects proceeded along very similar lines, especially regarding the focus on colonial women, petitions to Parliament, and a tendency to contrast rather than compare English and other women's oppressions. Women of all classes were important participants in the fight to end the slave trade (abolished in 1807) and slavery (abolished in 1838) in the British Empire and elsewhere. (In Scotland, though, slavery had been illegal since 1778.) Conservative Hannah More (1745–1883) and radical Mary Wollstonecraft were both active and early opponents of slavery.

Before the 1820s the anti-slavery movement was relatively unorganized. Mary Wollstonecraft included a number of abolitionist writings in her educational anthology *The Female Reader* (1789). Other less prominent women who were active opponents of slavery showed their opposition to it by boycotting sugar and by wearing bracelets and hairpins decorated with a popular Wedgwood cameo depicting a kneeling slave over the motto: 'Am I not a man and a brother?' Late-eighteenth-century women also saw it as their duty to read all they could about slaves. Because women were considered more emotional and more moral than men, they were able, it was thought, to empathize with them and to feel their pain. Many anti-slavery women in the late eighteenth and early nineteenth centuries understood the reading, and dissemination, of texts depicting the horrors of slavery as an important political gesture, one that was the sole province of women.

In the 1820s, female opposition to slavery became more widespread, more organized, and more focused on female slaves. A new cameo appeared that said: 'Am I not a woman and a sister?' In this organized phase the anti-slavery movement was modelled on the anti-*sati* campaign. While the Society for the Mitigation and Gradual Abolition of Slavery throughout the British Dominions (known as the Anti-Slavery Society), formed in 1823, excluded women from all national committees, women organized self-governing local organizations. From these, they made significant contributions to the fight against slavery, focusing on aid to women and on the family lives of slaves. In 1825, the first women's anti-slavery society, the Female Society for Birmingham, was established. It was soon part of a large network of ladies' anti-slavery associations; seventy-three of these were active in Britain between 1825 and 1833, and hundreds of thousands of women signed anti-slavery petitions, indicating that the movement had extensive support from large numbers of women who never formally joined associations. Many societies sponsored women-only debates in private homes, thereby rendering the domestic and female political. Most female anti-slavery leaders in the 1820s and 1830s were middle-class, the wives and daughters of wealthy industrialists, tradesmen, farmers, clergymen, and schoolmasters. Supporters, however, came from all classes and included many Unitarians (some of whom were radical Unitarians), Quakers, and Anglican and nonconformist evangelicals.

Anti-slavery women were not anti-imperialist as a group; indeed, many wished to end slavery precisely because they saw it as uncharacteristic and unworthy of the British Empire. Nor were they free of racial prejudice, as is apparent in their representations of white and black women. Anti-slavery activists called white American abolitionists their 'sisters', but usually represented black women as passive, silent, sexually oppressed victims, obscuring their long history of resistance. Although the former slave and autobiographer Mary Prince was welcomed into the movement, it was more as an exhibit than as a fellow campaigner, and she was never asked to join any ladies' anti-slavery associations.

Women's financial gifts to the national Society's funds were significant; in 1829 contributions from local women's societies made up 21 per cent of the total amount of donations and subscriptions (local men's societies gave only 14 per cent). In keeping with earlier strategies, women's societies spent much of the rest of the money they raised on producing and distributing anti-slavery information locally, believing that one of their primary roles was to turn public opinion against slavery. Female anti-slavery reformers sewed workbags from East Indian fabric not made by slave labour, put anti-slavery tracts into them, and gave them away. Such feminine and domestic efforts enabled women to be politically active and suitably feminine at the same time. Most anti-slavery women emphasized the ways in which their work was domestic, religiously – often evangelically – inspired, and therefore appropriate for women. They depicted anti-slavery as a moral concern, not as a political issue, which therefore fell under women's purview.

Like anti-*sati* women, anti-slavery women contrasted their own happiness with the miseries of wives and mothers who were slaves. In so doing they overlooked their own social and legal subordination, accepting and even celebrating their position, which they saw as an explicitly Christian one. For instance, anti-slavery women from Oxford sent a petition to Parliament in which they stated that they were grateful for:

> the distinguished privileges which in the several characters of daughter, wife, mother, Christian, they enjoy under the benign influence of the principles of Christianity, and by the administration of the enlightened and paternal Government of this happy land.[51]

Through such petitions women brought their softening feminine influence to the public sphere.

One woman, Elizabeth Heyrick, led the movement to drop its original commitment to the gradual abolition of slavery in the British colonies in favour of a demand for the total and immediate abolition of slavery. Heyrick was a Quaker abolitionist from Leicester who was, unlike many anti-slavery women, politically radical. In 1824, she anonymously published the pamphlet *Immediate, Not Gradual Abolition; or, an Inquiry into the Shortest, Safest, and Most Effectual Means of Getting Rid of West-Indian Slavery*. It was an attack on the principles and priorities of the national Anti-Slavery Society, which worked first to ameliorate the living and working conditions for slaves and second to free them from slavery via a period of indentured service. Heyrick's 'immediatism' changed the goals of the national Society. In 1830 it adopted her plan, voting to drop the words 'mitigation and gradual abolition' from its official title and goals. Heyrick and the local women's associations that supported her were instrumental in this crucial policy shift.

Between 1833 and 1838 slavery was entirely abolished in Britain and its empire, and abolitionist women turned their attention to slavery elsewhere in the world. British women's anti-slavery groups were important moral, financial, and tactical sources of support for female abolitionists in the United States. This was especially necessary because while many, or most, Britons actively or passively opposed slavery, American abolitionists were a tiny and vilified minority. They relied heavily on the aid of British and Irish anti-slavery groups in the 1840s and 1850s. British women's societies, which now outnumbered men's, donated money to American and Canadian groups which hid and aided runaway slaves; they also donated money to American anti-slavery bazaars and expanded their own boycotts to include slave-grown American cotton. Two prominent English anti-slavery advocates, Anne Knight and Elizabeth Pease, both also Quakers and radicals, were important figures in the American campaign for abolition, as was the Unitarian author Harriet Martineau.[52]

Imperial reformers often represented themselves as mothers in their work. In India, for example, so many reformers saw themselves as mothers of India or Indians that their interventions have been termed 'maternal imperialism' in reference to their feminized patriarchal attitudes. Leading female reformers, like Mary Carpenter and Annette Akroyd Beveridge, also adopted a maternal approach to the reform of Indian society. Carpenter, a prominent education reformer in England, visited India four times in the 1860s and 1870s. Her book *Six Months in India* (1868) made her a celebrity, transformed feminist imperialism into action in India, and shaped the approaches and concerns of the generation of female reformers who followed her. Carpenter was committed to the cause of improving women's education in India, but rather than empowering Indian women by working with them as colleagues, her relationships there were with elite Indian male reformers, with whom she shared a determination to care for Indian women as if they were children in her charge. Carpenter focused on training teachers as the key to improving education and was especially concerned with Hindu women of the educated classes. While she had originally hoped to train Indian women as teachers, her visits to India convinced her that white teachers were necessary to instill the proper Victorian values into young girls; Indian women were not yet, she thought, up to the task. In her writing on education, Indian women are presented as daughters who have an as yet unrealized potential to become adults controlling their own destinies. Carpenter cared deeply for them but did not trust them to take proper care of themselves.[53]

Annette Akroyd was a liberal who, in 1872, inspired by the Bengali reformer Keshub Chandra Sen, travelled to Calcutta to set up a school for

Hindu girls. The project failed, but Akroyd married the liberal Indian civil service administrator Henry Beveridge and remained in India for most of her life. Akroyd Beveridge disapproved of British Indian racism, at least at first. Yet she was repulsed by Indian women's clothes and jewellery, which she found overtly sexual. She was interested in reforming the dress codes and domestic styles of *bhadramahila*, or middle-class women, and especially wanted to get Bengali women to wear shoes and stockings. She also wanted them to establish English Victorian house-holds, which she saw as the proper places for modest adult women. She saw all of these steps as necessary to preparing Indian society for eventual self-government.[54]

Carpenter and Akroyd Beveridge both did valuable work on behalf of Indian women, but failed to establish organizations or networks that could continue their work. Both claimed some gender solidarity with Indian women, yet also saw race, religion, and rank as fundamental divides. And both can be thought of as 'maternal imperialists' in that they saw Indians as childlike, and themselves as mothers to Indians and to India itself.

One reformer who was less maternal and less imperialist than many was Annie Besant, the well-known birth-control advocate and radical who spent the last forty years of her life in India. She first defended traditional Indian patriarchy against English reformers and others, but from 1913 called for reforms including the end of *purdah*.[55]

Many but not all of these reformers were feminists, and it is difficult to separate the history of imperial reform from that of feminism. It is sometimes assumed that, because feminism challenged many fundamental cultural assumptions and social hierarchies, feminists as a group were anti-imperialist. In fact the opposite was true; many feminists proclaimed women's place in, and allegiance to, empire and celebrated feminism as an agent of imperial progress.[56] But while most female anti-*sati* and anti-slavery reformers contrasted their own lives with those of colonial and enslaved women, feminist reformers emphasized the similarities between non-white and white women's oppressions. They called English marriage another form of slavery. In other words, some feminists were not only interested in empire but used descriptions of colonial women to argue for their own emancipation.

This feminist interest in empire was most visible and explicit after 1865. Between then and 1914, when British imperialism was at its most evident and most powerful, feminism became an organized movement. Feminists sought to associate their cause with nation and empire and to assert that the Empire, which seemed a male preserve, was in dire need of women as moral authorities and a softening influence. In identifying themselves with the imperial project, feminists helped to reinforce the notion that Indian women were passive and in need of rescue by English women. For instance, the feminist *Englishwomen's Review* played down the role of Indians in establishing medical aids funds for poor Indian women, emphasizing instead that of the London School of Medicine for Women, which was directed and supported by the feminist sisters Elizabeth Garrett Anderson and Millicent Garrett Fawcett.[57] Much feminist rhetoric relied on the image of the passive, disenfranchised, colonized Indian woman as a pointed contrast to Englishwomen, who as part of the ruling race were active, reforming, civilizing people deserving of enfranchisement and other political rights – more rights than women of colour and as much say as white men in ruling the Empire.

Emigration

Women also had a profound effect on empire via emigration to the settler colonies. They emigrated first to Australia and New Zealand, and later on to Canada and South Africa. Exact figures are scattered, but between 1788 and 1899 over two million Britons emigrated to Canada and Australia, around 400,000 of whom were single women, and between 1899 and 1911 another 156,000 women emigrated to all the settler colonies.[58]

Colonial governments and societies, emigrators (promoters of emigration), and female emigrants themselves, all had different goals. Emigrants usually wanted jobs, husbands, or both. Some women were aided by friends who had already emigrated; others used the services of emigration agents, who worked for colonial governments or large shipping companies. Settler colonies wanted women as workers and as wives and mothers who could help domesticate and 'whiten' settler society. Emigrators wanted to strengthen the white English presence in the settler colonies, with whom they felt England had a racial bond, and to help the native women. One of these, Maria Rye (1829–1903), felt that female emigrants had to be:

> ... of a certain stamp. – women who dislike work, or who are not very steady in their principles – are a thousand fold better off at home ...

Queen Charlotte by Benjamin West, *c.* 1782. This painting of Charlotte, with her many children in the background, was part of the Queen's public portrayal of herself as both glamorously royal and virtuously maternal.

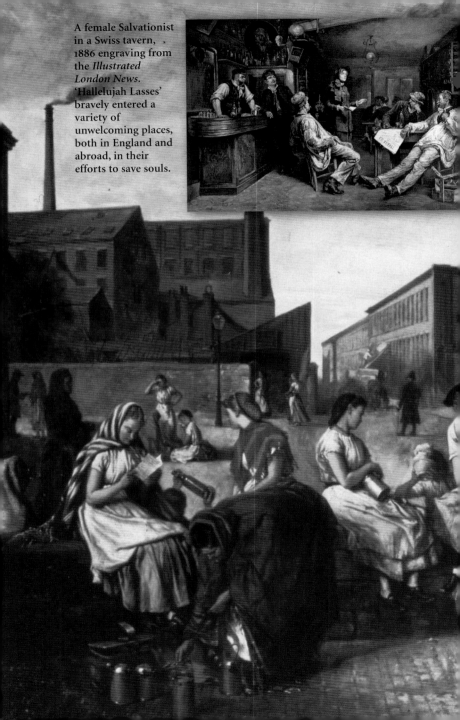

A female Salvationist in a Swiss tavern, 1886 engraving from the *Illustrated London News*. 'Hallelujah Lasses' bravely entered a variety of unwelcoming places, both in England and abroad, in their efforts to save souls.

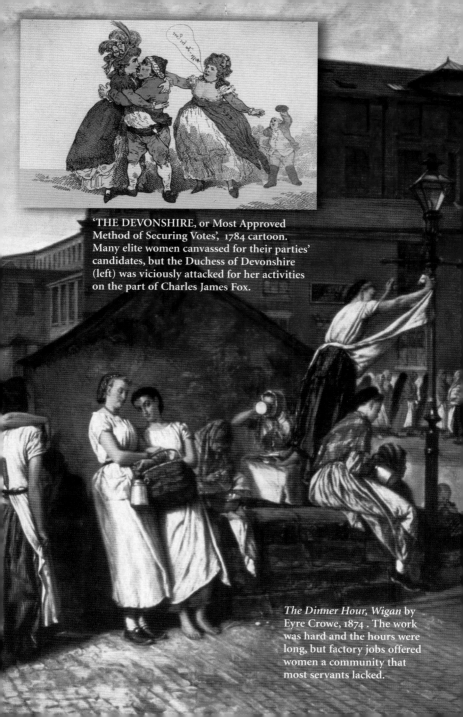

'THE DEVONSHIRE, or Most Approved Method of Securing Votes', 1784 cartoon. Many elite women canvassed for their parties' candidates, but the Duchess of Devonshire (left) was viciously attacked for her activities on the part of Charles James Fox.

The Dinner Hour, Wigan by Eyre Crowe, 1874 . The work was hard and the hours were long, but factory jobs offered women a community that most servants lacked.

Miss Fay and her pupils at a Christian missionary school in Shanghai, photograph *c.* 1855. Missionary women often focused on educating and civilizing their charges, as well as on preaching the Christian gospel.

Notice in *The Christian Herald* of 1898 that four missionaries, three of whom were women, had been murdered in Sierra Leone. From the mid-nineteenth century women worked as missionaries in their own right; it was dangerous work and many died abroad.

A Women's Rights meeting in Hanover Square, from *The Graphic*, 1872. Champions of moderation and respectability Lydia Becker and Millicent Garrett Fawcett are in the front row.

The Empty Purse by James Collinson, *c.* 1857. A wide variety of trinkets and decorative objects were available at the charity bazaars run and frequented by well-off middle-class women.

Abolitionist seals, amber and clear glass, *c.* 1825. The motto 'Am I not a woman and a sister?' on these seals reveals English women's growing interest in the condition of female slaves.

Mrs Pankhurst arrested in Victoria Street, 1908 postcard. Diminutive but charismatic, Emmeline Pankhurst maintained her commitment to ladylike delicacy in unlikely circumstances.

'The Appeal of Womanhood,' 1909 postcard. Suffrage women argued that they would use the vote to help those in need and would add feminine sympathy to politics.

Poster for a play, *The New Woman*, 1896. The 'new woman' was equal parts cultural creation and actual phenomenon.

An Anti-Suffrage League meeting in Manchester, 1909. Women against suffrage argued that advising men was preferable to having a vote themselves.

Ten suffragettes, 1912. Scotland Yard detectives circulated photographs like these to keep many suffragettes under surveillance.

WSPU bazaar at Bexleyheath, Kent, 1911 postcard. Bazaars were a common way for middle-class women to raise money for their church or favourite charity. Here WSPU members hold one to support 'the Cause'. Note how respectable these radicals look.

the colonies like the testing fire of the apostle tries every man's work and every man's character to the very core.[59]

Women's emigration was heavily promoted by emigration societies which sprang up in the 1830s, lasted well into the twentieth century, and helped approximately 20,000 women to emigrate. This was only a small proportion of the total number of women who emigrated, but the societies' public prominence meant that they were disproportionately influential. Many emigration societies focused on working-class women. Some were devoted entirely to female emigration. Others, including the Salvation Army, took it as only part of their mission (the Army became the largest emigration agency in the Empire). Several societies were narrowly focused: the philanthropist Angela Burdett-Coutts founded (in collaboration with Charles Dickens) a rescue home called Urania Cottage in west London to rehabilitate former prostitutes and send them abroad to begin new lives. In its six-year existence (1847–53) it accepted fifty-six women and sent thirty abroad.[60]

Some emigration societies were especially interested in middle-class or 'gentlewomen's' emigration. The prominent emigrator Edward Wakefield declared that 'a colony that is not attractive to women, is an unattractive colony';[61] his schemes to settle women in New Zealand in the 1850s helped to make emigration more appealing to potential middle-class female emigrants, as did some of the emigration societies that were modelled on traditional female philanthropic societies. These included the Family Colonialisation Loan Society, founded in the 1850s by the upper-middle-class Caroline Chisholm. Chisholm instituted the practice of having matrons travel with single women to Australia and pioneered the use of loans to help families and single women with the costs of emigration.[62]

There was one feminist emigration society, the Female Middle-Class Emigration Society (FMCES), founded in 1862. The FMCES strove to promote middle-class female emigration as part of a larger, and a permanent, shift of public recognition of the fact that marriage was not all women's destiny and that women needed marketable skills and meaningful paid employment. Although well-intentioned, the FMCES helped only 302 women to emigrate in its more than two decades of existence.

During the late-nineteenth and early-twentieth centuries, emigration was also promoted by some elite women who have been called 'lady imperialists' by one historian. They tended to see the Empire in racialized and eugenicist terms, believing that whites were superior, the natural leaders of empire and the best hope for its future. Working through a number of organizations (notably the Girls' Friendly Society, the Primrose League, the British Women's Emigration Association (BWEA) and the Victoria League), lady imperialists saw emigration as key to establishing British mothers and families all over the settled Empire and worked with like-minded women in the colonies who could receive and superintend new immigrants. They saw the proper management of female emigration as a vital part of ensuring the planting of British culture and virtuous British families on colonial soil.[63]

As a result of these varied and competing priorities, many different sorts of women emigrated from England to the settler colonies. Female emigrants were for the most part poor and working-class women seeking work. The voyage took several months and cost between £11 and £20, but most were assisted in their passage and settlement by the English or colonial governments, clergy, gentry, landlords, colonial employers and emigration societies. Upon arrival they were greeted, housed, and placed in their first jobs, usually by middle-class philanthropists eager to provide superintendence. Working-class women generally found work in domestic service, for which there was a huge demand in all the settler colonies. In the later nineteenth and earlier twentieth centuries, working-class and lower-middle-class women also found positions as nurses, governesses, teachers and factory workers.

The earliest female emigrants to Australia were convicts, as already mentioned, sent there forcibly during the late eighteenth and early nineteenth centuries because they had been convicted of crimes – mostly petty theft – for which the punishment was transportation. While English and colonial populations disapproved of them, local colonial governments saw convict women as desirable because domestic servants were in such short supply. Between 1788 and 1853 25,000 women were transported to Australia; until the 1830s, most white women in New South Wales were convicts. Unlike male convicts, female convicts were not allowed to take their spouses or children with them except for breast-feeding babies. Elizabeth Coltman, a thirty-year-old servant and ribbon weaver, Hannah Buttledoor, a thirty-six-year-old laundress, and Caroline Humphries, a seventeen-year-old servant, were all transported in 1828. Humphries was unmarried and had no children, but Coltman left behind a husband, and Buttledoor, a widow, had to leave her two children in England. Transportation fragmented many families and left many children as wards of the state.[64] Most female convicts settled permanently and went on to become Australian workers, spouses, mothers, colonists, and finally citizens. Australian women gained the right to vote sixteen years earlier than English women.

Other working-class women chose to emigrate. From the 1830s promotional material on emigration appeared in the form of posters, newspaper advertisements, tracts, pamphlets, books, articles in popular papers like *The Illustrated London News*, guides such as *The Emigrant Gazette and Colonial Settler's Guide*, and newspapers such as *The Emigrant and Colonial Gazette*. Many females appear to have been quite well-informed about emigration and applied for assistance from several sources.[65] On their arrival, they were often dissatisfied with conditions at the depots in which they were housed. One immigrant woman, whose name has been lost to history, complained: 'We are not allowed to go outside the doors, and we are like so many prisoners caged in'; another, Isabella Maugham, wrote that at the depot in Brisbane 'there were 32 beds for 132 girls, but the worst of it was they drove us in like so many cattle and locked us up'; Rosamond Smith remarked, 'We ought not to be used worse than thieves; but I suppose the Government considers that in giving us a free passage it buys and pays for us and has a right to do as it pleases with us.'[66]

The two most important qualifications for female emigrants applying for assistance were domestic skills and a good character. Women were told that servants could name their own salaries, but were often forced to take their first jobs before they knew the local market and so worked for less than the going rate at the start. Advertisements encouraging female emigration to Australia stressed that 'None but women of pure and unexceptionable character should be assisted in coming to the colony.'[67] As in England, the middle and working classes had conflicting notions of female virtue, and the behaviour and expectations of emigrants often clashed with those of sponsoring emigration societies and colonial governments and communities. Girls' Friendly Society leaders in Australia lamented the fact that emigrants often did not 'in any way report themselves to the society' and seemed 'careless whether they remain members of the Society or not'; around the same time one new arrival, Agnes Stokes, was indeed avoiding GFS members and meetings:

> Mrs Glennie was determined to get me into the Girls' Friendly Society but I was just as determined not to go. She reminded me too much of the people at the Great House. Here I'd got away from all my relations and from people giving me advice and I didn't want it starting again . . .

I told Mrs Glennie I was going down to see my friend the quartermaster [from the ship Agnes had arrived on]. She disapproved.[68]

Familiar class conflicts were often played out in new colonial contexts.

From 1851 the relationship between women and empire was in many ways structured by the so-called 'redundancy crisis'. The census of that year seemed to indicate that there were between half a million and over a million more women than men in England; of particular concern was the apparent fact that many of these women were between the ages of twenty and thirty-five. The census figures were taken to mean that these 'surplus' women would never marry and were therefore destined for lives of misery. Although there was no evidence to support this, 'redundancy' was always framed as a middle-class problem, largely because there were so few respectable options outside marriage for middle-class women.

Of course, single women were not new to English society. While they faced economic, social, and cultural challenges that married women did not, we should resist nineteenth-century descriptions of them as 'excess' or otherwise useless. The statistics were shaky – well-known social commentator W. R. Greg claimed that 1,248,000 English women between the ages of twenty and forty would never marry, while journalist George Sala found only 350,000 excess women of all ages.[69] The interpretation of what they predicted was even more subjective. At most, 'surplus' women constituted only 2 to 3 per cent of the population (and no more than a quarter of these could have been middle-class), and so might not seem too much of a cause for alarm. Yet the redundancy crisis was accepted as fact and acted upon for almost seventy years, from the 1851 census until the start of the First World War.

Many people tied the redundancy crisis to the British Empire. Noting that most settler colonies had many more English men than women living in them, the emigration of surplus women seemed to offer the solution. As a result, emigration was heavily promoted for middle-class women, even though most colonies were in need of domestic servants and nurses. Calls for female emigration came from non-feminist and feminist camps alike. The most famous opinion was voiced by W. R. Greg in an essay entitled 'Why Are Women Redundant?', first published in the *National Review* in 1862. Greg described the gender imbalance, which he blamed on male emigration, as 'abnormal [and] unwholesome', and saw female emigration aimed at marriage in the colonies as the way to restore balance both at home and abroad. Greg's essay was extremely influential; it was frequently cited and was reprinted as a pamphlet in 1868 and 1869. While feminists took exception to Greg's tone and to his reliance on marriage – whether in England or in the colonies – as women's only profession, many of them accepted Greg's figures and agreed with him that emigration could be part of the solution.

Although middle-class women were a small minority of the women who chose to settle abroad, their emigration was an important topic of public discussion and one that helped shape changing ideas about the capabilities of middle-class women. Many of these women were eager for new opportunities but in two minds as to whether emigration was respectable. The colonies offered middle-class women the opportunity to work for wages, as they could not at home. Colonial employment usually involved heavy domestic labour even for those hired as governesses rather than servants. One middle-class emigrant to Melbourne, a Miss Barlow, boasted in 1863 that:

> I am getting quite a Colonial woman, and fear I should not easily fit into English ideas again, can scrub a floor with anyone, and bake my own bread and many other things an English Governess and School-mistress would be horrified at.

But another middle-class transplant to Melbourne, Rosa Phayne, wrote in 1869:

> I do not use too strong a language when I say *no one* with the tastes, habits, or feelings of a lady should ever come out to Australia, it may do for [those] who can put up with roughness, or I should rather say vulgarity of mind and great want of intellect but I would never advise a lady to try it. I hate Australia and the Australians. I shall be with them but never of them . . .[70]

Clearly some women adapted better than others. Emigration societies tried to make domestic service in the colonies seem genteel by calling middle-class women who did domestic service 'lady helps'; complaints that they were more 'lady' than 'help' reveal how difficult the transition to a life that included manual labour must have been for many.

Few female emigrants returned to England. Most went in search of work and found it; in addition, most found husbands as well. For example, Jean Burns emigrated to Ontario in 1913, at the age of eighteen; she 'talked

it over with mother and she said, "If you think you're going to better
yourself by going out to Canada I'll no keep you back." ' But work as a
rural domestic servant was more difficult than Burns had anticipated.
She was never treated as part of the family, as she had expected she would
be on a farm, and she complained that 'I had no idea I had to get up at
5 a.m. and besides looking after the baby was expected to work, work
from morning till night.' Resolving that she was 'not going to be in jail
for the rest of my life', she gave notice and took work in a carpet factory.
When it closed she went back into service, this time in town, where she
could meet more people. This position was better than her first, but still
involved hard work, no regular days off, and clear social distinctions
between maid and mistress. When her employer asked her to wear a
uniform, Burns refused:

> I think they're just afraid, you know, that you might be taken for the
> lady of the house and that wouldn't do. That's your distinction, you're
> the maid. You have to wear this cap.[71]

After three years in Canada, Jean Burns left her job, married a Canadian
farmer, and raised a family. In doing so, she was a typical female emigrant.
Marriage was common because of the gender imbalance in the white
communities of settler colonies; for instance, at the turn of the twentieth
century, in Queensland, Australia, there were 171 men for every 100
women. This imbalance led to high rates of marriage for female emigrants.
Whether poor, working class, or middle class, whether convicts or voluntary emigrants, most British women who moved to the settler colonies
stayed permanently, and became part of the vast imperial population.

Imperialism significantly shaped English women's lives. Stories of sexual
danger helped to define white female virtue; official encouragement of
white domesticity created a role for white women in the Empire, especially
in the Caribbean and India. (English masculinity was also defined in an
imperial context, and was contrasted to the effeminacy, laziness, and
otherwise insufficient virility of men of colour.) The use of familial meta-
phors in imperial discourse helped to shape English women's motherhood
and philanthropy. Even if they never went abroad themselves, most
women experienced empire through a variety of consumer goods, travel
and missionary stories, and projects relating to reform and emigration.

Women also moulded the British Empire. Their presence in the Caribbean, India, and elsewhere was necessary to creating the white domesticity that was such an important feature of English society abroad after the early nineteenth century. Their work as missionary wives and missionaries brought English education, medicine, and Christianity to places that would otherwise never have had them. Their campaigns against *sati* and slavery changed the Empire's laws, economy, and ethics. The work they performed and the families they raised, in Australia, New Zealand, Canada, and South Africa, changed those societies. Looking at the many interconnections between women and the British Empire, it is less remarkable that gender and imperialism are now studied together than that they were ever studied separately.

8

Domestic Politics

DURING THE LONG nineteenth century, women of all classes and political dispositions involved themselves in politics, in spite of the fact that they could not vote or hold office. Women engaged in extra-parliamentary politics, using a variety of means and joining with men to effect change. Although most men of the middle classes received the vote in 1832, urban working-class men did not do so until 1867, and rural working-class men until 1884. Yet the relationship between women and politics was a problematic one, given that most areas of politics were not only male-dominated but patriarchal, and that many mocked – even as they feared – the spectre of 'petticoat government'. It was complicated by the use of accusations of 'effeminacy' – often associated with the aris-tocracy, with the French and with non-white men, especially Hindus – as synonymous with incompetence. Equally vexatious was the equation of femininity with apolitical domesticity, which intensified from the late eighteenth until the mid-nineteenth century and then only slowly sub-sided as it was challenged by feminists.

The questions of why women could not vote, and what it meant for them to act politically when they were denied the franchise, persisted throughout our period. They became increasingly germane as feminist agitation for the vote intensified and as more people came to support their cause. From about 1850 some women challenged their exclusion from politics by using both established and new political tactics and strategies in feminist campaigns that specifically targeted women's legal, sexual, and political subordination. In this chapter we will examine women's engagements in a variety of political movements and activities, including party organizations and electoral politics, and how English politics was changed by feminism. The impact of gender on the political realm was complex: attention to it alters the terms by which we judge politics.

Throughout the long nineteenth century, women worked politically. However, more often than not, the work they did was subordinate or

ancillary to men's. Women were often active in organizing the social
aspects of a political movement; they were also valued as political daughters, wives, and mothers. It was rare for a political party or movement to
welcome women as true equals or to give priority to issues that specifically
impacted on women's lives. Sometimes women accepted these restrictions. Other times, as in the temperance movement and the anti-*sati* and
anti-slavery campaigns, explored in previous chapters, they used male-
oriented or male-dominated movements to work on matters of interest
to them – usually those involving morality or family life – or to insist
on women's political abilities. This chapter will first consider women's
relationship to a variety of traditional, male-dominated political groups
and movements. It will then turn to feminism, which was the attempt by
some women to remap the English political landscape by making women's
work, marriage, the sexual double standard, venereal disease, and the
possibility of women's free sexual expression political, rather than personal, issues.

Women and politics

CONSERVATIVES, LIBERALS, AND RADICALS

Various camps across the political spectrum offered different things to
women. Conservatives held that gender and class hierarchies were natural
and beneficial. This might not seem to bode well for women, and tensions
did surface. On the other hand, in conservative circles women could
flourish. Conservative ideology actively celebrated women's particular
contributions, especially their domestic abilities. The Conservative or
Tory Party supported the Anglican Church and more generally glorified
women's special moral qualities. Tory Party leader Benjamin Disraeli even
favoured granting the vote to women. All of this gave women many
opportunities so long as they denied that they were acting politically and
insisted that they were simply softening the public realm by feminizing
it. The life of the conservative Hannah More – who wrote extensively and
oversaw a large number of schools, all the while asserting the importance
of female submission and insisting that women should not participate in
public life – is perhaps the best example of this. Many women acted
publicly and politically while claiming not to do so.

Liberals held quite different political beliefs from Conservatives. They were more open to change, favoured individual freedoms and greater democratic representation, and believed that the government ought to be responsive to 'public opinion'. Economically, they supported free trade and opposed any intervention that hindered it. But both the party and liberal theory itself tended to give women and gender short shrift. As a result, the relationships between women and liberalism and especially between feminism and liberalism were fraught. Most of the feminists working in the mid-nineteenth century were from Liberal families and relied on liberal principles, but they also struggled with the party, with the personal opposition to women's rights of Prime Ministers William Gladstone and Herbert Asquith, and with liberalism's inadequate attention to gender.

Radical politics, which challenged the political status quo and sought to empower the common people in a variety of ways, are where we might expect to find women most engaged. Radicalism did hold potential for some women, who, as champions of 'the People',[1] confronted long-held political assumptions. It might have been expected to challenge women's social and political subordination and to attract women, yet this was rarely the case with popular or working-class radicalism which was at heart patriarchal. Most working-class radicals championed the rights of the skilled male worker and head of household and identified political power with masculinity. As a result, popular radicalism rarely addressed women's oppression, and from the mid-1830s emphasized respectability, which held some appeal for working-class women but restricted them by emphasizing chastity and domesticity. Middle-class radicals paid more attention to women's subordination and sought to end it.

The tenuous relationship between women and conventional political labels becomes evident if we try to contrast two women who wrote on the subject of women's abilities early in our period: Mary Wollstonecraft and Hannah More. Wollstonecraft was a radical, More a conservative; the perhaps surprising correspondences between their work suggest that gender helped to constitute political involvement and complicate the political spectrum in fundamental ways.

Mary Wollstonecraft was a radical and feminist writer of the late eighteenth century. Born in 1759 to a lower-middle-class family in Spitalfields, Wollstonecraft spent most of her short adult life as a writer and a member of the Anglo-French radical intelligentsia. She was fiercely intelligent and wrote a number of important feminist texts, including *The Female Reader* (1789), an educational anthology, and *Maria, or the Wrongs of Woman*

(1796), a novel, as well as her most famous work, *A Vindication of the Rights of Woman* (1792), which historian Barbara Caine calls the ' "founding text" of Anglo-American feminism'.[2] She was disliked by many for her unfeminine interventions into politics; Horace Walpole called her 'that hyena in petticoats'.[3] She was a passionate person who defied convention by helping her sister to escape an unhappy marriage, and a politically curious and courageous woman who survived the Terror in revolutionary France. In other words, her radicalism was personal and sexual as well as political; this would inflect the reception of her work for decades to come.

Wollstonecraft's romantic life, though accepted in the radical intellectual circles in which she moved, was by most contemporary standards quite scandalous. Before she died at the age of thirty-eight she had several lovers, including the Romantic painter Henry Fuseli, and the American businessman Gilbert Imlay. Wollstonecraft lived with Imlay in Paris as his wife, calling herself Mrs Imlay, although they were not married. The couple had a daughter, Fanny, in 1794; soon afterwards, Imlay's neglect and infidelity led Wollstonecraft to attempt suicide. In 1796 she began a relationship with her last lover, the writer William Godwin. Though both rejected the institution of marriage on political grounds, when Wollstonecraft became pregnant they married for the sake of their child's social status. Wollstonecraft died in 1797 soon after giving birth to a daughter, Mary (later Mary Shelley, author of *Frankenstein* (1818)).

Wollstonecraft protested against contemporary gender hierarchies, insisting that training and tradition, not nature, had rendered women frivolous. Her writings help us to see how some radical women, influenced by the French Revolution and the Enlightenment, attempted to rethink English class and gender hierarchies. In *A Vindication of the Rights of Woman*, Wollstonecraft's central preoccupation is women's different and inferior status in society. To correct the social ills that currently render women uneducated, irrational, and downtrodden, she stresses four areas in which women's oppression was most obvious, and which most demanded reform: education, marriage, motherhood, and work. By connecting these and placing them in the context of public and civic as well as private life, she made a claim for them as political issues. Inadequate education made women frivolous creatures and prevented them from being good helpmates (let alone equals) to their husbands. Women were encouraged, even required to marry, because marriage was the only profession open to them; women needed education and paid work as alternatives to marriage. She also stressed the idea that motherhood was an important and honourable profession that deserved to be considered as such (and required an educated and rational woman to do it justice). Thus all four areas were intimately related and equally in need of serious reform for the good of society as well as the individual woman and her family.

That the *Vindication of the Rights of Woman* encompasses a wide range of issues is perhaps its greatest contribution. Wollstonecraft did not separate marriage from citizenship or women's rights from social justice; by insisting on their intimate connections, she attempted to redefine the political and women's relationship to it. Wollstonecraft's broadly conceived political sphere, which encompassed sexuality, family life, and virtue as well as education, print culture, constitutions and suffrage, was one that some radicals would embrace early in the nineteenth century. By mid-century they had retreated from this position to focus on male enfranchisement and employment, excluding domestic, marital, and sexual issues from politics and economics. Soon after her death, Wollstonecraft's works became overshadowed by details of her notorious life, and by a more general rejection of revolutionary principles. While scattered feminist and radical women read her books during the nineteenth century, radicals rejected her ideas in favour of domestic respectability, and the feminist movement – while deeply influenced by it – did not acknowledge her until almost the start of the twentieth century.

Hannah More, in contrast, embraced existing social and gender norms and endorsed a conservative outlook. She was a devout evangelical Christian who lived a long and celibate life and insisted that her work was concerned with moral – not political – reform. More detested Wollstonecraft's work, and wrote to a friend:

> I have been pestered to read *Rights of Women*, but I am invincibly resolved not to do it. Of all jargon, I hate metaphysical jargon; besides there is something fantastic and absurd in the very title. How many ways there are of being ridiculous! ... So many women are fond of government, I suppose, because they are not fit for it.[4]

Hannah More wrote on many of the same issues as Mary Wollstonecraft, but denied that they were political, arguing that women were meant for their families and the private realm.

More was the second of five daughters of a gentleman headmaster, and she was brought up in a comfortable but downwardly mobile middle-class home. Intelligent and well-educated, she never married but lived as an adult with her sisters. She was a popular and famous writer of numerous works including *Strictures on the Modern System of Female Education with a View to the Principles and Conduct of Women of Rank and Fortune* (1799), and *Hints Towards Forming the Character of a Young Princess* (1805). Her extremely popular novel *Coelebs in Search of a Wife: Comprehending Observations on Domestic Habits and Manners, Religion and Morals* (1809) portrayed virtuous elite women as society's chief models of charitable domesticity and sparked a rush of philanthropic activity among such evangelical women.[5] In addition to writing, More was an enthusiastic educator of the poor, and she and her sisters founded and ran a number of Sunday and day schools that served the rural poor of Somerset. She worked relentlessly, writing into the 1820s and dying in 1833 at the age of eighty-seven.

More believed strongly in social hierarchies and gender restrictions. She felt that it was the task of the elite to lead moral lives and she wrote and published the *Cheap Repository Tracts* (1795–8) to convince the masses also to live sober and Christian lives. Modelled on popular literature, the *Tracts* warned against idleness, gambling, drink, and striving to better oneself socially, and preached the virtues of thrift, industriousness, and humility. They condemned community pleasures and exalted family life and social hierarchy. The *Tracts* sold well but may have been more successful in convincing the elite of their role as examplars than in infiltrating popular culture.[6]

Unlike Wollstonecraft, More believed that the gender hierarchy was natural and good. She maintained that women had valuable and explicitly feminine skills, but that they should always remain subordinate to their fathers and husbands. In *Strictures on the Modern System of Female Education* she argued that women should be educated so that they could exert themselves in a feminine manner for the public good. More stressed how influential women could be in society and how important women – particularly elite women – were to the project of morally regenerating England. Women should focus on religion and charitable works, at which they were naturally adept, and not on entering the political realm. They should evangelize, but discreetly. Their most important role was as mothers; here they needed to eschew luxury and embrace religion so that they could be proper examples to their children. Where Wollstonecraft saw this as a social issue, More claimed that it was familial; where Wollstonecraft tried to expand women's role, More tightly defined it. More's insistence that women remain in the domestic and feminine world of apolitical good works stands in sharp contrast to Wollstonecraft's attempt to redefine women as political.

In practice, however, More's feminine and domestic good works bear a strong resemblance to Wollstonecraft's political action. For all their supposed differences, Wollstonecraft and More seem to have agreed on many points. Both were concerned with women's education and with motherhood. Both had great faith in women's intellectual capacities, and both argued that women should be better educated to serve their families and the wider world. While Wollstonecraft argued for women's rights, a radical demand, her call for women to embrace responsible mothering and reject fashion and idle frivolity was being sounded by men and women of many political stripes. While More denied that women had a place outside the home, needed rights, or were fitted for politics, she spent her life convincing middle- and upper-class women that they were crucial examples to those around them and had a responsibility to the public. More participated in politics by aiding Edmund Burke's campaign for election to Parliament in Bristol in 1774, by supporting William Wilberforce's parliamentary efforts for over twenty years (she donated £50 to his campaign in 1807), and by petitioning Parliament to open India to Anglican missionaries.[7] While Wollstonecraft and More's differences were and are important, their similarities are suggestive of the problematic relationship between women and political labels.

Throughout the long nineteenth century the question of political orientation – which could often be as much a matter of temperament as of a specific position – was a vexed one for women, especially since most political labels did not take into account beliefs about proper gender roles. To call a woman 'conservative' could mean that she aligned herself with the Conservative or Tory Party, or came from a family that did; that she favoured conservative political thinkers such as Edmund Burke (1729–97); or simply that her political temperament was conservative in the sense that she supported tradition, approached new ideas with caution, or preferred gradual to sudden change. The same held for liberal and radical women. Later in the century, when applied to feminist political thought, the labels of 'conservative', 'liberal', and 'radical' still did not translate particularly well. For instance, Emily Davies, the founder of Girton College, Cambridge, was socially and politically quite conservative and a committed Tory. But her feminism was quite radical: she insisted that there were no inherent differences between men and women and that the Cambridge curriculum for women should be identical to that for men. The feminist Frances Power Cobbe (1822–1904) favoured the Conservative Party even though it supported the Anglican Church, which Cobbe rejected, and opposed women's rights, which Cobbe favoured. She too was personally conservative, believing deeply in the rightness of social hierarchies and decorum and resisting sudden change. Millicent Garrett Fawcett came from a Liberal family, and even after she broke with the party over Home Rule she continued to consider herself a Liberal and to believe in basic liberal principles such as the notion of free trade and the importance of individuals' rights.

ELECTORAL POLITICS

The lack of the vote did not necessarily mean that women had no input into elections or party politics. They did not set party agendas and of course could not sit in Parliament but, as we saw in Chapter 3, throughout the nineteenth century elite women worked quite actively for their parties. Hostesses such as the Whig Lady Holland and the Tory Lady Jersey supported their parties via social politics. Some lesser elite or gentry women could also influence electoral politics in other ways. Anne Lister of Halifax is one example. Best known to historians for her diaries that detail her sexual relationships with other women (which were discussed in Chapter 4), she was unmarried and from 1826 the mistress of Shibden Hall in Halifax, in the West Riding of Yorkshire. She was from a genteel but not particularly wealthy family, and although she was opposed to women's rights, she was an active Tory all her life. She suggested candidates to the party's local election committee and sought out Tory voters, canvassing her tenants to ensure that they voted for the Tory candidate, and later, as properties became vacant, filling them with tenants who voted with her (she threatened those who did not with eviction). She wrote letters to newspaper editors about local elections and used an extensive network of female friends and lovers to advance her political agenda.[8]

Less elite women may also have been part of electoral political ritual. Many middle-class women wore a rosette or ribbon in their party's colours as a show of support on polling day, and some working-class women dressed entirely in party colours.[9] Many candidates, recognizing women's influence over their husbands, courted voters' wives as energetically as male voters themselves. Canvassers often visited during the day, though they knew that only wives were likely to be at home, which implies that women were seen as partners in their husbands' election decisions. After 1832, wives of newly enfranchised shopkeepers and skilled tradesmen could sometimes use bribery; for instance, in 1859 Mrs Elizabeth Graham of Carlisle asked a candidate for a spirit licence for her husband's beer-house in exchange for his vote. It seems that votes were a sort of family property, in whose use both wives and husbands had a say.[10]

PATRIOTISM AND PROTEST

Women were involved in politics far beyond elections. The late eighteenth and early nineteenth centuries saw a surge of loyalism (or patriotism) from women of all classes, partly as a response to the Napoleonic wars. They celebrated Britain and its liberties, collecting clothes for the troops, making flags and banners to present publicly to soldiers, and giving money to public and private subscriptions in support of the war effort. While seeming to adhere to a traditional domestic role by engaging in sewing and charity, patriotic women were also using war work to create a public civic role for women's support of the state.[11]

During the same period, working-class women used protest as politics. In the eighteenth and early nineteenth centuries crowd actions were an important part of high politics, with disenfranchised people entering the formal political realm. During this time women were prominent in food riots – planned responses to high prices or scant supplies of bread or grain – regularly taking part in and occasionally leading them. While female food riots remained effective in some communities into the 1840s, from the turn of the century, as industrialization came to towns in the Midlands and the north, working men began to reject rioting as a political tool and started using newer forms of protest such as strikes.[12]

PATRIARCHAL WORKING-CLASS RADICALISM

Women participated in a variety of ongoing radical movements as well. In these they often tried to use the tradition of the women's auxiliary group to suggest a role both supportive and equal, but they more often succeeded only at the former. Nineteenth-century popular radicalism included small, underground groups such as the Spenceans, also called ultra-radicals. Spenceans were followers of Thomas Spence (1750–1815), a radical bookseller who from the 1770s began to argue that all land should be nationalised and in 1792 was arrested for selling a copy of Thomas

Paine's *Rights of Man*. In the nineteenth century the Spenceans sought the reorganization of the ownership of land through popular insurrection. There were also larger radical groups who, after the Napoleonic wars, demanded universal male suffrage. In these groups, women were both crucial and subordinate. Janet Evans, for example, wife of Spencean leader Thomas Evans, worked closely with her husband in underground politics, and was imprisoned in 1798 for her radical activity even though she was pregnant and nursing an infant son. She and other women earned money to support their children when their husbands were in prison, wrote letters to the government pleading for their freedom and educated their children into their political beliefs. Richard Carlile, editor of the radical periodical *The Republican* and leader of the freethinking 'zetetic' movement (the term denoted the pursuit of knowledge) which aimed for both respectability and radicalism, enjoyed the support of various women over the course of his political career, including his sister Mary-Ann, his wife Jane, and after his separation from her, his paramour Eliza Sharples. Sharples, who aspired to be a reform leader, claimed that her 'moral marriage' with Carlile was an equal relationship; she was in fact as much disciple as lover.[13] Ultra-radicalism was, as these examples make clear, a movement of male radicals and their long-suffering wives or devoted younger sweethearts.

Women were somewhat more integral to the mass radical platform movement, which from 1815 demanded universal male suffrage, annual parliaments, and a secret ballot. Women formed their own reform associations, wrote pamphlets, and submitted addresses to Crown and Parliament. The leader of the Manchester Female Reformers, Mary Fildes (?–1875), was one of the best-known female reformers of her day; she sold books on birth control – a radical and unrespectable cause – and named her sons after the radical leaders John Cartwright and Henry Hunt. Women were an important part of the spectacle of large celebratory public meetings where, amidst a festive, carnivalesque atmosphere and a copious array of rituals and symbols, they appeared dressed in their best white clothes carrying caps of liberty, defiant symbols of reform.[14] For instance, in July 1819, a representative of the Blackburn Female Reform Society 'ascended the hustings ... step[ped] forwards towards the chairman ... [and] presented him with a most beautiful Cap of Liberty'.[15] However, here, too, women were prominent but subordinate, supporting men of their class in highly gendered ways. A female reform society might present an address to the crowd, but it was read by the chairman of the meeting;

in it, they might call for 'universal suffrage', but they meant universal male suffrage. They justified their participation in politics by invoking their roles as mothers, not as citizens. The movement came to an end in 1819, at a meeting at St Peter's Field, Manchester, which turned violent when local magistrates tried to impose order. Eleven people were killed, including two women, and the incident came to be known as the Peterloo Massacre. Overall, while the presence, actions, and work of women were all key parts of mass platform reformism, women were ultimately symbolic and subsidiary.

THE QUEEN CAROLINE AFFAIR

Not so in the Queen Caroline Affair of 1820, in which the Queen was symbolic but the women who supported her were hardly subordinate. The affair was a political moment in which class, gender, melodrama, and competing notions of female virtue came to the forefront of public debate and engaged women of all classes because it brought the problem of women's power in marriage to centre stage. Caroline of Brunswick (1768–1821) and George, Prince of Wales, were unhappily married. They had lived separately since shortly after their wedding in 1795, and Caroline had lived in exile on the Continent from 1814. In 1820, when her husband was to be crowned King George IV, she returned to England to claim her title as his queen. The King, who had been unpopular with the English people even before the Peterloo Massacre, was determined to stop her and, accusing her of committing adultery with her Italian manservant Bartolomeo Bergami, tried to obtain a divorce. The House of Lords, however, acquitted the Queen of any wrongdoing, which was seen by the Queen's supporters as a great victory. Although triumphant, the Queen was still barred from the King's coronation, quickly lost popular support when she accepted an annuity from Parliament, and died a year later. However, huge numbers of people waited in pouring rain to pay their final respects as her funeral procession, diverted from its planned route by her supporters, became a final pro-Caroline, anti-government protest.[16]

The Queen Caroline Affair was famous throughout England. The goings-on 'obsessed all levels of English society for a year';[17] the political journalist William Hazlitt called it 'the only question I have ever known that excited a thoroughly popular feeling. It struck its roots in the heart of the nation.'[18] The divorce trial was accompanied by a proliferation of addresses, articles, ballads, chapbooks and political cartoons, and the whole affair inspired more political caricatures than any previous event of the nineteenth century. The celebrations that followed Caroline's acquittal by Parliament included fireworks, bonfires at Seven Dials and St Giles, and the illumination of much of London for three successive nights.[19]

The affair drew a new and unprecedented number of women into the political life of the nation. Newspaper reports claimed that women outnumbered men among Caroline's supporters. She received addresses signed by thousands of women, including one from the 'Ladies of Edinburgh' and one from the 'Females of Bristol' which was signed by 11,047 women. The longest came from 'the married ladies' of London, of whom 17,652 sent their greetings to the Queen.[20]

Women of various classes empathized with Caroline as a wronged wife who could do little to defend herself from her husband's moral slurs and legal and economical assaults. In their address to the Queen, the 'Ladies of Edinburgh' wrote:

[The] principles and doctrines now advanced by your accusers do not apply to your case alone but if made a part of the law of the land, may hereafter be applied as precedent by every careless and dissipated husband to rid himself of his wife however good and innocent she may be ... Such being the consequence of these principles and doctrines, your Majesty's case becomes a common cause with all the females in this kingdom.[21]

Caroline was a queen, but she was also a married woman whose virtue was being impugned by a husband whose own behaviour would not pass close scrutiny, but who could nevertheless lock her out of his house if he wished. It was on this level that many women identified with her and supported her cause.

In the Queen Caroline Affair, we see the category of the political broadened to include the institution of marriage and the issue of female virtue, topics of compelling interest to many women. Working-class women used the Queen Caroline Affair to bring their own issues to the popular radical agenda. The strength of their support for Caroline was such that male radicals took notice and tried to appeal to women, as, for instance, with the publication of a pro-Caroline pamphlet which depicted Britannia wearing a banner inscribed: 'To assert the Rights of Man / To Avenge the Wrongs of Woman', thereby establishing a connection between the two goals. Middle-class women supported the Queen as a way of celebrating their class's rejection of lax aristocratic morality and its endorsement of the value of home and family.

Recent work on the Queen Caroline Affair has emphasized not only the nature of the expressions of support for the Queen – attacks on the King as an oppressive husband and corrupt monarch, demands for parliamentary reform, or sympathy for Caroline as a wronged wife – but also the form these took. The Queen Caroline Affair was most often represented as a melodrama, in which the King became the vicious aristocratic villain and the Queen an innocent and wronged woman.

Historians differ over how to interpret the use of melodrama in the Queen Caroline Affair. Thomas Laqueur argues that the affair was 'overwhelmed' by the melodramatic narrative, which drained it of its radical potential. The historian Anna Clark disagrees, pointing out that melodrama was a highly politicized art form which depicted innocent maidens whose virtue was endangered by vicious aristocrats. Melodramatic representations of the affair, she argues, simultaneously politicized the affair and brought it to a wider audience than it otherwise might have reached. While the lasting effects of the Queen Caroline Affair are unclear – in some ways its importance seemed to end with the death of the Queen in 1821 – it allowed women publicly to protest the inequality of the sexes before the law and in marriage, decades before the laws on marriage were actually changed.

OWENISM

Inequality in marriage was the subject of other political critiques as well. Owenism was a small, radical, working-class movement that was actively concerned with sex and gender as political issues. The movement was begun by Robert Owen (1771–1858), a prosperous and philanthropic factory owner who came to oppose capitalism and, in the early 1820s, began espousing, in writings and lectures, a 'new social order' which was to be based on co-operative communities free of all class and gender inequalities. In pursuit of this objective, the Owenites founded sixteen communities in the United States and ten in Britain. In the 1830s and 1840s Owenites pursued a vision of a world free of class- and sex-based oppression through a commitment to communal life and a focus on religious free thought, women's rights, marriage reform, and popular education.[22]

The feminist Owenite analysis of society was developed by Anna Wheeler and William Thompson and articulated by Thompson in his *Appeal to One-Half the Human Race, Women, against the Pretensions of the Other Half, Men, to Retain Them in Political, and Thence, in Civil and Domestic Slavery* (1825). In it, Thompson acknowledged that the current subjugation of women had economic causes, but emphasized the role of marriage in women's subordination to men.

Unlike many other radical political groups, Owenites critiqued marriage as well as private property and saw women's emancipation as integral to social progress. Fanny Wright (1795–1852) declared that the goal of Nashoba, an Owenite community she helped to found, was to create a place where

> No woman can forfeit her individual rights or independent existence, and no man assert over her any rights of power whatsoever beyond what he may exercise over her free and voluntary affection. Nor on the other hand, may any woman assert claims to the society or peculiar protection of any individual of the other sex, beyond what mutual inclination dictates and sanctions; while to every individual member of either sex is secured the protection and friendly aid of all . . .[23]

Owenites believed that social justice required the abolition of the marital family, which would be replaced by communalized family life and free love. The existence of private property and the fact that women were treated as their husbands' property were linked; the only way to end oppression in marriage was to abolish private property.

Yet although Owenism sustained a feminist critique of society, there were few feminist or female leaders in the movement. Many unionized Owenite men resented wage-earning women who wanted to be union members; in a letter to the working-class newspaper *The Pioneer* one Owenite wrote that the only women who wanted to go to union meetings were 'lazy, gossiping, drunken wives'.[24] Most Owenite men and women presumed that women would participate in the community as wives and mothers. As regards marriage, Owenite men were far more enthusiastic about free love than Owenite women, who saw the potential abuses of such a system. Private housework was to be abolished in Owenite communities, but only by having women do it together. As the historian Barbara Taylor drily observes, 'No doubt shared housework lightened [women's] overall workload, but it hardly revolutionized their existence.'[25]

CHARTISM AND ANTI-POOR LAW AGITATION

While Owenism was small, another contemporaneous movement, Chartism, attracted thousands of people. After the Great Reform Act of 1832 gave middle-class but not working-class men the vote (it was also the occasion of the first explicit statement that the vote was for men only), the most important political and social response was Chartism. Chartists agitated in the 1830s and 1840s for the passage of their six-point Charter into law; it included demands for universal male suffrage, annual parliaments, and a secret ballot, and until its demise in 1848 the National Chartist Association served as the main political voice of the working class.

There were many thriving female Chartist associations, in which Chartist women represented their support of the Charter and of popular rights as an extension of their domestic duties, thereby recasting themselves as both respectable women and political beings.[26] Women were the main organizers of local Chartist social events, which were integral to the movement and included tea parties, theatre visits, concerts, and boat and rail trips. They played an important role collecting money for local organizations and were active in local protests. Chartist mothers were expected to educate their children into Chartist thinking: they (and other radical women) used their role as political mothers to promote themselves as self-taught teachers. Many expressed their Chartist sentiments by participating in 'exclusive dealing' schemes in which they patronized only those shops whose (usually middle-class) owners supported the Charter, often after a local female Chartist association had passed a resolution calling on them to do so. (Women otherwise politically inclined often used the same strategy; in 1834 G. W. Norman, a leading Liberal from Kent, received a letter from a supporter who complained that Tory ladies too often used their custom and the threat of its withdrawal as a political tool.[27]) Others might support the movement informally from home, attend Chartist meetings, work as leaders of the movement, or speak publicly at meetings.

Surviving pamphlets and speeches reveal that female Chartists were often concerned with women's rights. Chartist newspaper advertisements for inexpensive editions of Mary Wollstonecraft's *Vindication of the Rights of Woman* suggest that at least some Chartists were reading her work, and many female Chartists invoked Wollstonecraft in their speeches and writings. Yet there were only a handful of female Chartist speakers, who described themselves as drawn into the movement by fathers or husbands. For instance, the Nottingham Female Political Union's first address, issued in December 1838, claimed that female Chartists needed to act 'in aid of those measures in which our husbands, fathers, brothers, and children are now so actively and zealously engaged'.[28] As the years went on, Chartist strategies became more difficult for women to participate in, and Chartist ideology relied more heavily on notions of sexual difference. Early informal, local, and confrontational actions were replaced by centralized, formal events that focused on London and national politics and so marginalized women, especially those with young children, who could not travel easily or often. And while the first draft of the Charter included a demand for female suffrage, this disappeared from the final version, as Chartists argued simultaneously that men deserved the franchise (because they were skilled workers), whereas women deserved to remain in the home (as their paid work was unskilled and degrading). At the same time, Chartists began to emphasize the respectability and domesticity of the working-class family and the demand for a breadwinner's wage. These they melodramatically contrasted with an image of female workers in need of rescue from the horrors of factory work. As the 1840s progressed, the rhetoric of domesticity (which some Chartist women had used to justify their own public political work) and melodrama together silenced female Chartists.[29]

The one exception to this pattern of the masculinization of popular politics was the opposition to the New Poor Law. In 1834, the system by which the British government provided assistance to those in need changed radically. Since the sixteenth century every parish had been responsible for its own poor (including the elderly and the physically and mentally ill), and aid was dispensed parochially and deemed a customary right. By the early nineteenth century, many non-poor Britons perceived the poor as lazy and poor relief as encouraging their indolence. The New Poor Law of 1834 was enacted to solve these problems. Poor relief was to a large degree nationally organized, though still locally distributed, and wage supplements were abolished. Those able-bodied poor who needed government aid were required to leave their homes and enter a parish workhouse; 'outdoor' government relief (i.e., outside the workhouse) became illegal (although it persisted in some places). Poor Law Guardians in each parish (usually prominent citizens) collected compulsory Poor Law taxes, supervised the workhouse and reported to the Central Poor Law Commission.

Conditions in the workhouses were deliberately made harsh and unpleasant. Food was often scant and usually of poor quality, work was arduous, and families were separated from one another upon admission. The new law, which was supported by middle-class groups as disparate as Benthamites and Evangelicals, still assumed that poverty was the fault of the individual and tried to distinguish between the 'deserving' and 'undeserving' poor, the latter being those who were able-bodied and therefore simply lazy. It also tended to assume that the typical pauper was the male head of a household, even though the majority of the poor were women and children.[30] The first chapters of Dickens's *Oliver Twist* (1838) are an attack on these ideas and the grim workhouse life they produced.

Working-class women, many of whom joined the Chartist movement, were vociferous opponents of the New Poor Law. Its implementation provoked widespread agitations all over England and Wales. The largest anti-Poor Law meeting took place in Yorkshire, on Hartshead Moor, in May 1837; it was attended by 100,000 to 250,000 people, and forced the local commissioners to postpone the implementation of the law for a full year. In Huddersfield, in June 1837, the local workhouse was wrecked by a crowd of several thousand, and throughout that summer and autumn meetings of local Poor Law Guardians were disrupted by crowds burning them in effigy. Anti-Poor Law demonstrations and rhetoric utilized older and newer styles of political expression. The protesters threatened (and sometimes resorted to) popular violence, but also made shrewd use of pamphlet literature, the press, and speaking opportunities.

Women were vocal and often violent participants in anti-Poor Law agitations; historians describe them as 'notoriously defiant of authority in the crowd politics of ... the anti-Poor-Law movement', 'demonstrat[ing] with vehemence against the New Poor Law', and 'mobiliz[ing] to defend their families against ... the punitive operation of the New Poor Law'.[31] Describing an agitation in Mansfield, Nottinghamshire, the *Nottingham Journal* claimed that 'the infuriated females' in the crowd surrounded an assistant commissioner of the new law and vowed 'to tear him to pieces'.[32] Women used other political tools besides crowd action. Thousands of women from Elland, Middleton, Barnsley, Stalybridge, and Northampton sent petitions to the new Queen and to Parliament denouncing the New Poor Law.

The separation of husbands from wives and mothers from children in workhouses outraged working-class women, most of whom were responsible for child-rearing and housekeeping in their families and many of whom considered themselves mothers and wives above all. The workhouse policy on families in the New Poor Law was understood not only as a hardship but as an assertion that the poor were to be deprived of the family lives to which they had no right. Working women were vigorous opponents of such an ideology. The female Chartists of Newcastle wrote in the *Northern Star* in February 1839:

> We have seen ... a law enacted to treat poverty as a crime ... to drive the poor from their homes ... to separate those whom God has joined together, and tear the children from their parents' care ... We tell the wealthy ... that our homes shall no longer be destitute of comfort, that in sickness, want, and old age, we will not be separated from them, that our children are near and dear to us and shall not be torn from us.[33]

These women refused to accept the notion that the poor could be forced to give up their children, even temporarily, or that poverty made women unfit to be mothers.

Working-class women were also firmly against the bastardy clause of the New Poor Law. This section of the law made an illegitimate child the sole responsibility of his or her mother, whereas under earlier laws the child's father had also been accountable. The New Poor Law, then, imposed unequal burdens on unmarried mothers and fathers, and blamed women but not men for their sexual activity. The bastardy clause infuriated the working classes, whose morality did not equate female virtue with perfect physical chastity. As we saw in Chapter 4, working-class women with illegitimate children were not necessarily pariahs in their communities. Most working-class women understood the precarious position they were in with regard to sex and marriage, and refused to reject other women whose virtue was, by narrowing middle-class standards, irretrievably damaged.

Chartist women were (after 1838) important anti-Poor Law agitators. Indeed, the issue seems to have drawn many women to Chartism. Many female Chartists such as Mary Ann Walker of London and the Birmingham Chartist we know only as 'Sophia' gave speeches and wrote articles denouncing the new law in the Chartist press. Most female Chartist associations were founded in 1838 and 1839 in direct response to the New Poor Law, and women were most active in the movement between then and about 1843. In other words, women were often Chartists because they opposed the new law.[34]

Like Chartism, anti-Poor Law agitations ultimately failed. By 1839 the campaign had dissipated, and by 1859 60 per cent of the country, including the south, east, industrial north, Wales, the West Country and London had new workhouses. Yet the relationship between Chartism and anti-Poor Law demonstrations is revealing. Women supported a movement aimed at securing working men's political privileges in part because it provided a space from which they could work politically on what they cared about – the state's treatment of families, especially women and children.

MIDDLE-CLASS RADICALISM

Among the middle classes, radical groups included rational dissenters and the Ham Common Concordium (also called the First Concordium), a group who ran an experimental school called Alcott House, practised 'harmonic' or vegan cookery, and promoted animal rights. Another group of middle-class radicals were the Ashurst circle, which was centred around lawyer William Ashurst's four prominent radical daughters: Caroline, Emilie, Matilda, and Eliza. The Ashursts were part of a larger group, the radical Unitarians (centred around William Fox's ministry at the South Place Chapel in London, with important provincial associates) who were active in the 1830s and 1840s and whose politics were informed by their sympathies with the working classes and their own class status. Radical Unitarians were principally interested in the problems of the working classes and with the position of women in society. They read Wollstonecraft, promoted associated housing schemes and other forms of cooperative living, supported the Chartist movement (but took issue with the exclusion of women's suffrage from the Charter, and even staged confrontations on the issue at Chartist meetings), and castigated the legal inequalities of husband and wife.[35]

Many radical Unitarians came from literary circles and believed that literature could serve social and political functions. Eliza Ashurst (?–1850) and Matilda Hays (1822–66) collaborated on a project to translate all of George Sand's novels into English in the belief that these contributed to women's liberation. One of the most prominent radical Unitarians was Mary Leman Grimstone (1800–1866), a novelist from a gentry family who worked for such causes as co-operative housing arrangements. Her contributions to the *Monthly Repository* (which was edited by William

Fox and had a small, educated readership) included some 'Sketches of Domestic Life', which sought to illustrate how cultural mores had produced undesirable feminine traits. In one typical sketch from 1835, a woman raised to be concerned with beauty rather than intellect proves a disastrously bad wife.

Radical Unitarians emphasized how inferior women's current position was in both the middle and the working classes. They pointed out the oppression of idleness (under which so many middle-class women chafed) as well as lamenting the oppression of having to work (as working-class women did). This led to radical Unitarian demands for more forms of female employment for women of all classes, so that those who wished to work could choose from a wider field and those who had to work could find employment.

All of this is not to say that male and female middle-class radicals had an identical understanding of women's subordination. In the second half of the nineteenth century, tensions between men and women in the radical middle class pushed women to articulate a sense of solidarity with working-class women. The radical suffragist Lydia Becker (1827–90) once commented that aristocratic and working women were at least on equal terms with the men of their own classes, whereas middle-class women were 'nobodies [who] if they act for themselves lose caste'.[36] After mid-century, working-class women were most notable by their absence from radical politics, but middle-class women continued to flourish in radical circles. They were enthusiastic supporters of Italian unification; Caroline Ashurst Stansfeld named her son after Mazzini, the leader of the unification movement, and her sister Emilie declared her religion to be 'Mazzinian'.[37]

THE ANTI-CORN LAW LEAGUE

Contemporaneous with Chartism, anti-Poor Law agitation, and radical Unitarian activism – but far more successful – was the Anti-Corn Law League (ACLL), in which middle-class liberal and radical women played crucial roles in turning a local agitation into a national movement. Here too women were most important on the social side of things. Yet the Anti-Corn Law League was invaluable as a political training ground; many women who worked for feminist causes later in the century cited their family's involvement in the ACLL as critical to their own political development.

The Anti-Corn Law League opposed protectionist tariffs on foreign grain, which favoured aristocratic landowners and rural interests over manufacturing and urban ones. Founded in the late 1830s, it became a national movement and in 1846 succeeded in seeing the hated tariffs repealed. Supported by both liberals and radicals, it claimed to bring the middle and working classes together but was largely a middle-class movement. Attempting to remain above partisan politics, which were often seen as unfit for women, the ACLL appealed to women to support the cause as wives and mothers who knew the value of cheap bread. The League also presented the issue as social and economic rather than political, part of women's mission to the poor, who needed affordable food. The use of such rhetoric freed middle-class women to act politically. Thousands of women discussed and debated the issue of the Corn Laws, signed petitions to the Queen, attended meetings, and went from door to door to raise money for the cause. They also organized two major bazaars, one in Manchester in 1842 which raised £10,000, and one in Covent Garden in 1845 that raised £25,000. The ACLL provided a space in which women could construct a political identity based on women's mission and on linking feminized domestic economy to the state's economic policy.[38]

LOCAL POLITICS

From 1869 single-women ratepayers were able to vote locally, first in municipal elections, later in county and district elections. From 1894 married-women ratepayers were extended the same right. By 1900 one million women had the local government vote; they made up one-fifth of local voters nationwide, and were as much as one-quarter of the electorate in some cities. Women were also able to run for local offices. Many middle-and upper-class women, often inspired by their philanthropic work, by their involvement in various causes, notably temperance, and by the women's rights and suffrage movements, voted and ran for office. Between 1870 and 1914 almost three thousand women held various positions on parish, rural and urban district councils, London vestries, and school and Poor Law boards. Organizations such as the Women's Local Government Society were founded to encourage their participation.

As we saw in Chapter 2, women served on School Boards and as Poor Law Guardians, and in both instances stressed their feminine contribution to the work, their special interest in women and children, and their philanthropically-inspired approach. Women served as councillors in rural government, where they were thought to be more familiar than men with the cottages and lives of the poor. They also served in urban government, where they tended to join committees on education, health and housing, leaving finance and public works to male councillors.

From 1869, then, local government not only provided services for women but also employed them, offered them opportunities to help make public policy, and gave them the chance to enter into politics in some of the ways men did. Local politics were seen by most people as an appropriate sphere for women's energies because they were somehow domestic, housekeeping on a larger scale. As we shall see in Chapter 9, local politics came to be seen as a testing ground for women's fitness for national politics, and so became part of the women's suffrage debate.

PARTIES AND AUXILIARIES

Towards the end of the nineteenth century women were welcomed into party politics as never before, thanks to the passage of the 1883 Corrupt Practices Act which made paid electioneering illegal and women attractive as volunteer workers. The Act led to the formation of the Primrose League, a social and political organization that was an unofficial wing of the Conservative (Tory) Party. It welcomed men and women of all classes into a single organization, and most local branches, called habitations, were mixed. Although members were distinguished by rank (elite men and women were Knights and Dames, others were Associates), they socialized across class lines. Local branches varied in size and composition. The League was most successful in rural areas, but had habitations in urban areas too; members in Brighton were mostly middle class, while those in the northern industrial towns were factory workers. Promoting imperialism, welcoming Catholics as well as Protestants, non-elite men and women as well as aristocrats, and sponsoring many respectable social events, by 1900 the League claimed one and a half million members.

Women were important and valued in the Primrose League. Probably half of its members, that is hundreds of thousands of them, were women. While technically only honorary members, they played key roles. Women led one in four mixed habitations, and female deputies (seconds-in-command) led many that, on paper, had male Ruling Councillors. As well as offering many social opportunities, the Primrose League also provided political ones. Primrose League women gave speeches to female audiences.

While election canvassing was at first done by aristocratic women, whose political and philanthropic experience made them comfortable with door-to-door work, soon dozens of non-elite women were joining them. The Primrose League even educated many women about politics so that they would feel able to canvass. Female members often seemed to feel some tension between the political message they heard and promoted, which emphasized women's traditional place, and their own political work, which was at odds with this message. Many members sought to justify their political work as part of their roles as wives and mothers, rather than claiming it as boundary-breaking. However, while the Primrose League did not champion the rights of women, it did much to normalize the idea that average women might make a practical contribution to political life.

The Liberal Party had a number of women's associations that, like the Primrose League, offered women electoral work and tried to bring them into the party mechanism. Women's Liberal Associations (WLAs) appeared in about 1880; the Women's Liberal Federation (WLF) was formed in 1887 as a national umbrella for them. (Other liberal groups included the Women's National Liberal Association, which declined to support suffrage, and the Women's Liberal Unionist Association, which opposed Home Rule.) The WLF was known for its politically involved women and its commitment to women's suffrage on equal terms with men. However, lack of party support for women's suffrage created tensions, and WLF membership declined in the years immediately preceding the First World War. Many radical suffragists became very involved with their local WLAs, seeing them as important political opportunities, and many WLAs affiliated with the Central National Society for Women's Suffrage (better known as the Parliament Street Society) in the 1880s. Unlike the Primrose League, these liberal associations were all-female and often feminist political spaces, but had far less impact on their party. Nor were they anywhere near as large as the Primrose League, with only 10,000 members in 1888 and 133,000 at their peak in 1912. Overall they tended to be more political and less social than the Primrose League, which they mocked for its frivolous paraphernalia even as they envied its success.[39]

WLF pamphlets sought to reassure women that politics was well within the sphere of womanly influence.[40] As with the Primrose League, liberal women's groups attempted to educate their members, and were very organized about their canvassing efforts. They emphasized the moral contribution women could make to politics and encouraged members to do door-to-door canvassing for the party. They also acted as pressure groups, writing letters to MPs, ministers, and newspapers.

Left-leaning working-class women who joined political groups gravitated towards socialist ones, leaving Women's Liberal Associations largely middle-class affairs (WLF leaders often failed to understand how difficult it was for women without servants to escape domestic and childcare responsibilities in order to attend meetings). However, English socialism did not welcome women or questions about gender into its analysis of society. The Social Democratic Federation (SDF), a socialist group active from 1884 until 1911, had no separate women's group, but it was an important organization in which many women participated. It was strongest in Lancashire, Northampton, and London, small (with a membership of only two or three thousand) and largely working class. While individual SDF women often held feminist views and tried to incorporate women's issues and an analysis of gender oppression into socialism, the party was equivocal on gender issues. In general it saw socialism as economic, and therefore held that gender was irrelevant to its critique of society. As a result, the SDF marginalized both female members and issues concerning women, and SDF women were expected to subordinate their feminist convictions to their socialism.[41] The SDF's successor, the British Socialist Party (BSP), had a Women's Council, organized by Margaretta Hicks, which tried to organize women to put their role as consumers to political use by opposing rising food prices. However, with the start of the First World War this issue was taken up by male socialists and ceased to be a women's concern.[42] Another group, the Women's Labour League (WLL), was the women's auxiliary of the Labour Party (which took that name in 1906), and had only a few thousand members.[43] It, too, gave priority to class as the most important social organizing principle, and tended to ignore sex-based oppression. The Primrose League, the various Liberal organizations, and the WLL all tried to bring women into politics while keeping them in auxiliary groups doing gendered work, while the SDF was led by men and discouraged feminism in its members.

Overall, during the long nineteenth century women were active in a variety of political movements which, though they might inspire women and improve their lives as members of a class or political circle, failed to recognize their specific political needs. Indeed, very different political groups often resembled each other only in their similar disregard for gender as a political category. Women were expected to participate as political mothers and wives rather than as individuals. They were given tasks related to political socializing rather than politicking. Such partisan political experiences and involvement had their value but also their very clear limitations. In spite of all of this, many women were clearly keenly interested, active participants in the political movements they cared about. They insisted on their own political presence as workers, thinkers, wives, and mothers.

Feminist politics

From the middle of the nineteenth century women's involvement in domestic politics took a new and important turn that would change English politics dramatically. That turn was the development of feminism, a politics which focused on women. While the term 'feminism' did not exist until late in the century, we use it here because contemporary descriptions of 'women's rights women' and the like are so cumbersome, and because it accurately describes what preceded its use. Feminists challenged women's disabilities and disadvantages in education, occupation, sexual practices, and marriage, among other things; they agitated for both access to public life and justice in private life, and were especially concerned about sexual relations as a site of oppression. Feminists also challenged a set of deeply entrenched beliefs about women: that they were more emotional and less capable of rational thought than men; that they were moral not political beings; and that marriage and family were their only destiny. Feminist thought and activism demonstrated that many inequalities experienced by women – especially in the areas of marriage and politics – were in fact intertwined and based on long-held and, they argued, incorrect assumptions about women's abilities.

MID-VICTORIAN FEMINISM

Organized feminism began as a movement of mostly middle-class women in London and Manchester. Feminists employed a liberal critique of politics and a female middle-class style of activism, in which small groups of respectable women would form committees, hold meetings, and circulate petitions to submit to Parliament. They developed a separate women's culture, with most feminists accepting and even celebrating differences between men and women. They began by focusing on the plight of single women who needed to support themselves and on trying to reform marriage laws. Later in the nineteenth century feminism developed a broader class base, a keener interest in the lives of working-class women, and a more direct approach to sexual issues. Some gravitated towards socialism.

Feminism was not a unified practice and is perhaps better thought of as feminisms. Among its leaders, Emily Davies believed that women and men were innately equal; Josephine Butler was certain that they were not, and that women were more moral than men. Millicent Garrett Fawcett valued respectability, while Elizabeth Wolstenholme (1834–1913) was willing to jettison it for the sake of change. That feminists often disagreed with one another is no surprise, as feminism had connections to Conservative, Liberal, and radical politics as well as with religion, philanthropy, the social purity movement, and imperialism. On the other hand, a focus on women's legal, political, and sexual subordination united these women and allowed them to work together despite their areas of disagreement.

The London campaigns were based around the Langham Place circle, which began with Barbara Leigh Smith (from 1857 Barbara Leigh Smith Bodichon) and her friend Bessie Rayner Parkes, both from radical Unitarian families. Bodichon had a private income and in 1854 had written a pamphlet, *A Brief Summary in Plain Language of the Most Important Laws of England Concerning Women*. The same year Parkes had written *Some Remarks on the Education of Girls*. The two began by working together on a petition to reform laws about married women, and on the first feminist periodical, *The Englishwoman's Journal* (Bodichon financed it while Parkes acted as editor). These two projects led them to make the acquaintance of other women of similar class status also seeking to improve women's position. The group needed rooms to work in, and from 1859 rented property at 19 Langham Place that could house their already widely varying and interconnected activities, including the Kensington Society, an all-female debating club. With offices, rooms for holding classes, a library, and a dining room, the, space was ideal for a fledgling reform group; it offered social and work spaces in central London, and was perfect for recruiting and networking.

During the 1860s the early London feminists came to include Maria Rye, who worked on female emigration and opening the legal profession to women; Jessie Boucherett (1825–1905, who was from the gentry) and Adelaide Proctor (1825–64), who helped find employment for unmarried middle-class women who needed to support themselves; Emily Faithfull (1835–95), who established the Victoria Press, which trained women in printing, maintained humane working conditions, and became the leading feminist publisher of the day; and Emily Davies, founder of Girton College, the first women's college at Cambridge.

Also crucial were North of England feminists who worked out of Manchester. They organized a variety of campaigns and societies, including the North of England Council for Promoting the Higher Education of Women and the Manchester wing of the suffrage movement, which was consistently more radical than the London branch throughout the nineteenth century. They also tended to be more personally radical than the Langham Place group. One Manchester feminist was Elizabeth Wolstenholme, a prominent radical suffragist, secularist, and free-lover who lived with Ben Elmy before they married, and who encouraged Josephine Butler to lead the campaigns against the Contagious Diseases Acts. Others included Jacob Bright (1821–99), a radical MP for Manchester (and the brother of the better-known John Bright, also a radical MP but an opponent of women's suffrage), Ursula Mellors Bright (1835–1915, his wife and an important fundraiser and politicker for married women's property reform), Lydia Becker (editor of the *Women's Suffrage Journal* and a leader of the suffrage movement), and Richard Pankhurst (whose future wife Emmeline and daughters Christabel and Sylvia Pankhurst led the militant suffragette movement). Younger feminists included Millicent Garrett Fawcett, another suffrage leader, and Caroline Ashurst Stansfeld of the prominent radical Unitarian family.

Overall feminists were a well-integrated group who carried out a series of interlocking campaigns against the sexual double standard, for women's access to the public sphere, and for the improvement of women's domestic, family, marital and sexual lives. Many families worked together; the Garretts are the most famous example, with six active sisters including Elizabeth, who became the first woman doctor and a co-founder of the London School of Medicine for Women, and Millicent, national leader of the suffragists. Others drew strength from their friendships with fellow activists; still others had passionate relationships with one another or lived together. Many worked on a range of campaigns; a woman might lead one campaign, work on another, and contribute to a third. Most leaders structured their lives around their commitment to these causes. This may help to explain how incredibly productive these hard-working women (of the 'leisured class') were.

Feminists saw a variety of oppressions as interrelated. They saw connections between education and work, marriage and prostitution, politics and sexuality; although they came to focus on the vote, they also saw lesser public and political victories as equally important. While exclusion from the franchise was a major problem, the story of English feminism is more complex than simply the fight for the vote and has deeper roots. Indeed, one might say that nineteenth-century feminists focused their efforts on suffrage because it was the one battle they were losing; from the 1850s to the end of the century they won astonishing victories in almost every other area.

As radical as feminist politics were, and as unconventional as the personal lives of many, most feminists presented a modest and decorous face to the world. As we have seen, early feminist thinkers included Mary Wollstonecraft, Owenites, and radical Unitarians; however, most post-1850 feminists were extremely concerned with respectability. They ignored Mary Wollstonecraft because of her notorious personal life, in spite of her early calls for education and work for women, two of their key demands. This emphasis on decorum could be a strength, since respectable middle-class women were more likely to be listened to than those who seemed beyond the pale; yet it could also undermine the movement's credibility. The insistence on the value of respectability remained a feature of nineteenth-century feminism and especially of London feminists; women based in the north, and those of the next generation, were as a rule far more radical, personally as well as politically.

It would be impossible to do justice here to the achievements of nineteenth-century feminists. We have already seen the results of their work because so many changes in the conditions of women's lives were effected by feminists. Clerking, teaching, and other lines of work were opened to women in large part because of the efforts of Jessie Boucherett and Adelaide Proctor to change notions of what work women could and should do. The campaigns to gain entrance to various professions for middle-class women were led by feminists. Louisa Twining, who helped professionalize workhouse visiting by opening Poor Law Guardianships to women, was a feminist. Mary Frances Buss and Dorothea Beale, who opened the first academically-oriented secondary schools for girls, were feminists, as were Emily Davies and Barbara Leigh Smith Bodichon who, together with Buss, Beale, Garrett and others, paved the way for university education for women.

Single women and work

Organized feminism's first struggles were to change expectations about, and improve the lives of, single middle-class women, to change the laws regarding marriage, and to repeal the Contagious Diseases Acts. As we saw in the last chapter, the 1851 census seemed to indicate a gender imbalance in the population which meant that many women would never marry. This information sparked what became known as the 'redundancy crisis'; because the prevailing belief was that marriage was a woman's destiny, women who could not marry would be 'surplus' or 'redundant'. As middle-class women could not work, for reasons of propriety, they would be destined to poverty as well as misery. These assumptions infuriated many women, who argued that there was nothing inherently unacceptable about respectable middle-class women remaining unmarried, finding paid employment and leading fulfilling lives. They set out not only to solve an economic problem but to challenge long-held beliefs.

Feminists argued that all middle-class women should train for some occupation at which they could work until, or instead of, marriage, depending on their romantic fortunes. This involved opening new occupations to women: clearly not every redundant woman could be employed as a dressmaker or a governess, the only two positions considered respectable for middle-class women. In some ways, then, feminists used the redundancy crisis as an opportunity to insist on women's abilities to work. Langham Place feminists Jessie Boucherett and Adelaide Proctor founded the Society for the Promotion of the Employment of Women (SPEW) in 1859. Millicent Garrett Fawcett and Frances Buss sat on the committee; the Queen herself, who was certainly no feminist and who in 1870 would describe the cause of women's rights as a 'mad, wicked folly', was a patron. Members persuaded employers to consider hiring young women in several key fields previously considered to be the territory of men. SPEW's most important contribution was ideological rather than practical. While the number of women for whom SPEW secured employment was not high, by the end of the nineteenth century over half a million women – at least three times the number of middle-class women who had been earning money when the organization was founded – were working as teachers, nurses, shop assistants, clerks, or civil servants.[44]

A related effort was the Female Middle-Class Emigration Society (FMCES), mentioned in the previous chapter. While other groups promoted female emigration because surplus women would find husbands in the colonies, the FMCES saw emigration as a road to work, not marriage. Like SPEW, the FMCES was not terribly successful on a practical level, but the feminist movement was able to use the emigration and redundancy issues to its own advantage, moving gradually from cautious suggestions that some women might need to work to firm insistences that all women should work, before or in place of marriage.

Marriage and divorce

Just as these efforts to aid unmarried women went beyond sympathy, charity, or even practical assistance in seeking to change society's understanding of women's abilities and proper roles, so too did efforts to change the laws regarding married women. The act of marriage had profound social, economic, and legal consequences, because wives had no legal or economic identity apart from that of their husbands. If the marriage was a happy one, this might remain a theoretical problem, but if there was any conflict between the spouses, the difficulties soon became all too apparent. Husband and wife became 'one person in law', but that person was the husband; the legal theorist William Blackstone (1723–80) explained that 'the very being or legal existence of the woman is suspended during the marriage'.[45]

The technical term for this idea was the doctrine of 'coverture', under which married women were called *femes covert* (unmarried women were *femes sole*). Coverture dictated that a married woman could not own property. When a woman married, everything she had became her husband's; any wages his wife earned belonged to him as well, even if he had agreed not to take them, raped her (a possibility the law did not even recognize), treated her badly, deserted her, or kept her from seeing her own children. With her legal personhood in suspension, a married woman could not incur her own debts or sign contracts (making it difficult to run her own business), could not write her own will, and could not contradict her husband's desires in financial matters.

In practice, the laws of coverture were not always strictly followed, and in some cases were honoured mostly in the breach; wives were allowed to pledge their husbands' credit to buy household 'necessaries', and their frequent appearance in small claims courts indicates that shopkeepers, judges, and juries alike saw them and not their husbands as the true consumers and debtors. Yet the laws remained, and restricted women's economic activities, especially those unrelated to household consumption. The problem weighed especially heavily on poor and working-class women. Women from the affluent middle and upper classes could often use a special form of law called equity law to put their property in trusts, out of their husbands' control. Even then the trusts were controlled by other men, usually relatives, since married women could not technically control any property. But such complex legal instruments were out of the reach of most women.

While couples across a broad social range often agreed on informal separations, few women pursued divorce. Suing for divorce was difficult and expensive. Divorce also carried a tremendous social stigma (at least among the polite classes). If the marriage was so unhappy that the spouses could not live together, divorce was extremely difficult to obtain even if husband and wife both agreed to it, and nearly impossible to get, especially for women, in the face of a husband's resistance. To pursue a divorce before 1857, one needed to go through the ecclesiastical courts. Couples could get a divorce *a menso et thoro*, the equivalent of a separation, which enabled them to live apart but did not end their interest in each other's property or allow them to remarry. More rarely they could get a divorce *a vinculo matrimonii*, which was akin to an annulment; this entirely ended the marriage but was difficult to get and made the children illegitimate. Another route was a divorce by private act of Parliament. Here a husband (for it was almost always he) obtained a divorce *a menso et thoro* from the church courts, then sued his wife's lover (if she had one) for damages resulting from adultery, and then had a divorce bill introduced into Parliament. The marriage was ended and the children remained legitimate. In all cases a divorce cost at least £300 to £1,000, and could incur many thousands of pounds more. In a famous exchange, a judge sentencing a working-class man for bigamy asked why he had not divorced his first wife before marrying his second. 'The whole proceeding would not have cost you more than £1,000.' 'Ah, my lord,' replied the defendant, 'I was never worth a thousand pence in all my life.'[46] Due in part to the high cost, divorces of any sort remained rare, and parliamentary divorces were in practice almost impossible for women to obtain; during the eighteenth and nineteenth centuries (the procedure was abolished in 1857) only four were obtained by women.[47]

Marriage and divorce laws were an obvious problem for women, who were under enormous social and economic pressure to marry, under tremendous legal disadvantages once they did, and trapped if their marriages were not tenable. The situation was even worse when the couple had children: fathers had all rights to the custody of their children. The fear of being separated from their children was a tremendous disincentive to divorce for most women.

A notorious marriage that brought many of these problems to public attention was that of Caroline Norton (1808–77). Born Caroline Sheridan, she was from a well-known family (her grandfather was the playwright Richard Brinsley Sheridan), but had little money. In 1827 Caroline, nineteen, married George Norton, who was twenty-six and heir to his older brother, Lord Grantly. While it produced three sons, the marriage was a disaster from the start. Norton was less intelligent and less social than Caroline, refused to earn money, and resented her when she did (by writing poems and novels). He pressured her to find him a government appointment through her friend, the Home Secretary, Lord Melbourne; Melbourne managed to get Norton a position as a magistrate, with an annual income of £1,000. Norton also drank and abused his wife, and they separated several times.

In 1836 George Norton hid his sons from their mother and barred her from the family home. He demanded a legal separation but refused to grant Caroline any allowance. When she refused these terms, he sued her for divorce, claiming she was having an affair with Lord Melbourne. His flimsy case was quickly dismissed, but Caroline was enraged. Seeking redress, she soon discovered that the law was of no help to her in regaining access to, let alone custody of, her children. In protest, Caroline Norton published a number of pieces protesting the injustice of English custody laws, including *Observations on the Natural Claim of a Mother to the Custody of her Children as Affected by the Common Law Right of the Father* (1837). Although a Custody of Children Act was passed in 1839, George Norton still kept the children from Caroline. He only allowed them to live with their mother in 1842 when the youngest child fell ill and he died before his mother could see him.[48]

Norton was an extremely effective writer who used a number of genres, notably melodrama, in her work, as for instance when she appealed to readers to

> think what it must be to spend all one's youth, as I have spent mine, in a series of vain struggles to obtain any legal justice! ... let my part in this, be only as a voice borne by the wind – as a cry coming over the waves from a shipwreck, to where you stand safe on the shore – and which you turn and listen to, not for the sake of those who call, – you do not know them – but because it is a cry for HELP.[49]

Norton's sad story and affecting style made her famous and helped to promote the cause of legal reform.

Norton also wrote on marriage laws, most famously in the privately circulated essay *English Laws for Women in the Nineteenth Century* (1854), which made her a heroine to many advocates of women's rights. Norton was not affiliated with the women's rights movement. She always maintained that she believed in men's natural superiority and rejected the idea that women could claim any right but the right to men's protection. She insisted on traditional gender roles, and sought rights for married women only because some husbands, like her own, did not fulfil their obligations to protect and care for their wives. The problem with coverture, she believed, was that it could cause hardship in these cases.

Though her approach differed from theirs, Norton's life and writing moved many feminists, including Barbara Leigh Smith, who wrote her *Brief Summary . . . Concerning Women* in the same year that Norton wrote *English Laws for Women*. Smith, in contrast to Norton, saw legal difficulties beyond unhappy marriages. She and her feminist colleagues argued that even happily married women were adults and so, like other adults, had a right to own property of their own. Coverture, they argued, was unjust, as were child custody and divorce laws.

Inspired by Norton, as well as by her own radical heritage and her feminist principles, Smith began a campaign to change the laws regarding married women. She formed a Married Women's Property Committee that in 1856 circulated and submitted to the House of Commons a petition demanding for married women the same rights over property that were enjoyed by *femes sole* and men. Prominent signatories included the expatriate poet Elizabeth Barrett Browning (1806–61), the novelist Elizabeth Gaskell, the radical writer on political economy Harriet Martineau (a heroine of the mid-Victorian feminists), and Marian Evans (soon to achieve fame under her pen name, George Eliot). At the same time, the House of Lords was debating a bill that would create a civil Divorce Court. When it became clear that the married women's property petition would not soon meet with success in the House of Commons, the committee worked to insert provisions favourable to married women into the divorce bill. In this way the notions of married women's property and of divorce became linked.[50]

In the end the committee – aided by Lord Brougham (1768–1868), a champion of legal reform, and by Matthew Davenport Hill (1792–1872), a prominent reformer – was partly successful. Under the 1857 Divorce

Act, proceedings became simpler (though not simple) and cheaper (though out of the range of many working-class people; working-class women and those who lived far from London, site of the only Divorce Court, found it hardest to bring suits). Legally separated as well as divorced women attained the rights of *femes sole*. Women could sue their husbands for divorce, but had to prove adultery plus some aggravating factor (such as incest), while men needed only to demonstrate their wives' adultery. For example, in 1861 Elizabeth Lander was able to divorce her husband only after he threatened her with a razor and a gun and struck her with an iron rod, in addition to committing repeated acts of adultery. The same year, William Pettit Dawes was able to divorce his wife for adultery alone. Charlotte Coleman's emotions are evident in her 1865 petition for divorce, which describes how her husband

> vehemently urged her to obtain money by prostitution, and threatened her with personal violence if she persisted in refusing to do so. He also argued ... that other married women did the same thing and there was no harm in it ... [he] reduced [her] to a state of great bodily fear ...[51]

Coleman eventually went to live with her brother. She was granted a divorce in July 1866, but her husband never paid her legal costs of £35 5s. as he had been ordered to do.

While these advances were more than Parliament had ever intended to concede to women, they did not constitute a feminist victory. Women had gained some rights, and used them: in the first decade of the new court's existence, women filed 40 per cent of the petitions for divorce and 92 per cent of the judicial separation proceedings, and they were as successful as men in winning their cases.[52] However, the law still treated them differently from men. Indeed the new Divorce Law reinforced, rather than challenged, the sexual double standard. A husband's adultery (unless accompanied by some other failing) was a dismissable dalliance; Lord Chancellor Cranworth was opposed to punishing husbands merely for being 'a little profligate'. A wife's adultery was unforgivable. One historian describes the Act's effects as 'tinkerings with patriarchal authority in marriage'[53] which feminists had been trying to overturn; women were not able to sue for divorce on the same terms as men until 1923.

Feminists continued to debate and publish on the legal problems faced by married women, and in 1867 Manchester feminists Elizabeth Wolstenholme and Elizabeth Gloyne, joined by Josephine Butler (from

Liverpool) and Jessie Boucherett (from London), organized a new Married Women's Property Committee (MWPC) to reform the laws that governed married women's control of their property and their children. While its leaders were from Manchester and the north, the campaign attracted supporters from all over the country and included Henry and Millicent Garrett Fawcett, the prominent radical Unitarians Clementia and Peter Taylor and Emilie Ashurst Venturi (1826–93) and the Irish feminist Isabela Tod (1836–96). Overall it was a larger and more varied group than Bodichon's first committee had been. Not by coincidence, this was the same year that the demand for women's suffrage took organized form, and that the Manchester Women's Suffrage Society was founded; leading Manchester suffragist Lydia Becker was also the secretary of the MWPC. Many people were members of both groups, and feminists insisted on the connection, arguing that coverture and the lack of the vote together kept women unjustly subordinated in private and in public. Radical suffragists were particularly outraged by coverture and saw its end as equally important to achieving the franchise since, under it, married women were denied the vote twice, by sex and by coverture. By the mid-1870s supporters and opponents alike saw married women's property and suffrage as connected issues.[54]

The committee promoted and publicized its views in a variety of places. The National Association for the Promotion of Social Science, a social reforming group, invited members to speak on the issue. Frances Power Cobbe wrote a witty and memorable attack on the common law entitled 'Criminals, Idiots, Women and Minors: Is the Classification Sound?' The MWPC pressured Parliament, invoking the plight of working-class wives (who were particularly oppressed by the current laws) as well as the issue of injustice to further their cause. The first result of these efforts, the Married Women's Property Act of 1870, was a defeatist victory much like the Divorce Act had been. It improved women's situation slightly, principally by allowing married women to retain control of any wages they earned while they were married. Members of Parliament had focused on the fact that a working-class man could desert his family, and then return and take from his wife the wages she had earned to support herself and her children in his absence. Such abuse was now illegal. However, married women still could not own any of the property they brought to a marriage, and the bill was of almost no use to middle- and upper-class women who did not earn money during their married lives. Members of Parliament, who were middle and upper class, seemed more willing to help the wives of other men than their own. Even the wages earned by the deserted working-class wife were referred to in the Act as her 'separate' property, not her 'own' property, as if MPs could not bear the notion of a married woman owning anything outright.

In 1874 the secretary Lydia Becker urged the Married Women's Property Committee to suspend their campaign until women's suffrage had been won, a victory she expected imminently (but would not live the necessary forty-four years to see). But the larger part of the committee fought on, seeking to change public opinion while pressuring MPs. They were aided from 1875 by the committee's treasurer Ursula Mellors Bright, who was an excellent fundraiser and networker; her husband, brothers-in-law and nephews were all MPs at various times, and she moved confidently among politicians. When a Liberal government was returned to power in 1880 it agreed to amend the 1870 Act, and so the 1882 Married Women's Property Act, now a government bill, passed without fanfare.[55] While it preserved the notion of coverture and fell short of making marriage irrelevant to women's legal status, it allowed married women to act more independently of their husbands. They still were not responsible for their debts and could not act in the same way as single women and men, but they could control several forms of separate property and make contracts and wills. As with the 1870 Act, Parliament was willing to adjust laws, making it more difficult for husbands to mistreat their wives, but refused to grant married women *femes sole* status and denied all women the vote. Similarly, amendments to custody laws passed in 1878 and 1886 gave mothers (especially legally separated or widowed ones) greater control over and access to their children but did not give them the same rights and responsibilities as fathers. In spite of these ideological shortcomings, such changes made a material difference to many women's lives and would not have happened without intense feminist effort.

Repealing the Contagious Diseases Acts

During this same period, the 1860s, 1870s, and 1880s, feminists – together with philanthropists, left-leaning liberals, and working-class men – waged a campaign to repeal the Contagious Diseases Acts. These Acts, passed in 1864 and extended in 1866 because of rampant venereal disease in the military, empowered the police in eighteen port and garrison towns to stop women they believed were prostitutes on the street, subject them to a physical examination, bring them before a magistrate, and hospitalize them if they found evidence of venereal disease. The Acts were preceded by similar but harsher colonial systems, used in India since 1805 and in Hong Kong from 1857, and were modelled on regulations already in use in the Ionian islands and Malta. The Contagious Diseases Acts aroused the ire of social purity feminists, who saw in them government-sanctioned vice that made clear the connections between women's sexual and political subordination. Becker and other suffrage women put their faith in the vote, claiming that once the political battle was won marital and sexual rights would follow. Repealers, in contrast, attempted to address sexuality first and foremost. The campaign was extremely successful, and the Contagious Diseases Acts were repealed in 1886.

We know that the figure of the prostitute occupied a central psychic space in Victorian culture, so it is no surprise that so much legislative pressure was brought to bear on this supposed source of contagion and uncleanness. What is surprising is how middle-class feminists reached across barriers of class and sexual respectability and declared themselves in solidarity with (as well as rescuers of) prostitutes. For example, in a letter of 1870 to Prime Minister William Gladstone, Mary Hume-Rothery of the Ladies' National Association wrote:

> ... there is not one of us – no, Gentlemen, there is not one of the mothers, wives, sisters, or daughters whom you cherish with proud affection – who dare safely assert that, had she been born in the same unprotected, unfenced position, in the very jaws of poverty and vice ... she, too, in the innocent ignorance of her unfledged girlhood, might not have slipped, like them, into that awful gulf from which society at large has long done its best to make escape hopeless.[56]

Repealers insisted on the vulnerability of all women. They also astutely analysed the Acts to reveal the pervasiveness and oppressiveness of the double standard: the separate expectations about men's and women's sexual behaviour that rendered the same actions, such as extramarital sex, regrettable for men but wholly unacceptable for women. The campaign to repeal the Contagious Diseases Acts was also aimed at eradicating the sexual double standard of which the Acts were the most glaring effect.

Feminist repealers were led by the prominent feminist Josephine Butler. She came from a middle-class Liberal family that had been active in the anti-slavery and Anti-Corn Law campaigns and was connected with the Liberal Party all her life. Beautiful and devoutly religious – Butler was evangelical and said that she was called by God to do her work – she was a compelling figure and a charismatic leader for whom the repeal of the Acts was as much a transformative moral crusade as it was an episode of political agitation. While active in the fights for higher education for women and reform of the married women's property laws, she was most concerned with the sexual double standard and its part in the oppression of women. She saw prostitutes as victims of male lust, of the sexual double standard, and of the laws that inscribed these as public policy. Rather than seeing middle-class women as different from prostitutes and therefore immune from these indignities, Josephine Butler argued that the laws made all women vulnerable because they empowered the police to judge whether a woman was a prostitute. Butler's radical attack on the double standard and stance of solidarity was based on conservative notions of sexual difference; she believed that all women were naturally more moral than men and that prostitutes needed to be returned to that state. She blamed male clients, not female prostitutes, for prostitution.

Led by Butler, social purity feminists formed the Ladies' National Association (LNA) in 1869. Technically the ladies' auxiliary of the larger national organization, from which women were excluded, in practice the LNA was separate from, and more active and more effective than, the men's group. By 1871 it had fifty-seven local branches, a central organizing committee, and a periodical, *The Shield*. Most feminists supported the LNA's position and work, actively or tacitly. Ursula Bright, Lydia Becker, Elizabeth Wolstenholme, and Emilie Ashurst Venturi all signed its first petition along with Josephine Butler. LNA members were mostly educated women from progressive middle-class families, and like their leader were often involved in other progressive or reforming causes.

As feminists pointed out, the Contagious Diseases Acts and the assumptions behind them made the sexual double standard at work in Victorian society especially evident. Although military men were found to be diseased, it was women who were subjected to examinations. The problem was not that they were infected but that they would infect soldiers. Women were imprisoned even though soliciting was not illegal and no effective treatments for venereal disease existed. Perhaps most infuriatingly, the state took responsibility for ensuring that the men – including husbands – could hire prostitutes, without becoming infected. The assumption was that men needed sexual outlets and that fallen women existed to provide them. Yet a single act of adultery by a wife was grounds for her husband to divorce her and prevent her from seeing her children. And even though

supporters claimed that the Acts were aimed in part at reducing prostitution, they did the opposite. Most women who engaged in it, who
were poor and in their teens and twenties, worked in prostitution only
temporarily. The Acts forced them to register with the local police as
prostitutes, which made it more difficult for them to leave the field and
reintegrate into the local working-class community.[57]

Feminists wielded a variety of arguments. They protested against the
right of the state to seize and imprison its citizens, and argued that
the Acts deprived women of their personal liberty (especially galling as
the clients of prostitutes were subject to no such accostment). Repealers
also challenged the government's assertion that prostitutes were not delicate enough to be troubled by forced examinations, which feminists
referred to as 'instrumental' or 'specular rape'. That the military and
medical men who supported the Acts were, like the clients of prostitutes,
all men, did not escape the repealers' notice and made the oppression of
prostitutes – and by extension of all women – even more glaring. Yet
barriers and hierarchies remained; the LNA never invited any prostitute,
active or rescued, to join the Association, and was clearly acting on behalf
of prostitutes rather than empowering them to help themselves.

The LNA employed a range of tactics to publicize the cause. Like
other feminist campaigners they published in the general press, lobbied
individual MPs, and petitioned Parliament. Their periodical *The Shield*
publicized the miseries perpetrated under the Act.[58] Members also worked
in alliance with working-class men, appealing to them to protect their
women from these harmful laws. In addition, inspired in part by the
American temperance movement, another social purity campaign, they
held prayer meetings and vigils and spoke publicly on the topic. The idea
of well-dressed, respectable, middle-class women speaking about such
unmentionable topics as sex, venereal disease, and prostitution brought
the movement much publicity and notoriety. The repeal of the Act in
1886 was seen as a great victory, after which Josephine Butler turned
her attention towards ending organized prostitution, repealing the 1868
Contagious Diseases Act and the 1889 Cantonment Act in India, and
stamping out the perceived white slave trade in Europe. Other social
purity campaigners who followed in Butler's footsteps included Laura
Ormiston Chant (1848–1923), a member of the LNA and of the National
Vigilance Association (NVA), England's main purity organization. In the
1880s, Chant worked to abolish brothels in England. She became well
known in the 1890s for her efforts to regulate music halls (efforts Butler

opposed as oppressive); she was appalled by both the indecency she saw on the stage and the prostitutes soliciting in the audience.[59]

LATE NINETEENTH- AND EARLY TWENTIETH-CENTURY FEMINISM

Taken together, these campaigns for better lives for women demonstrate the breadth and depth of the first burst of nineteenth-century feminist activism. During the late nineteenth and early twentieth centuries, as women's rights became more publicly, broadly, and fervently debated, feminists continued their work in a different context. The new concern for women's rights developed in part because of feminists' own work publicizing women's subjugation, in part because of the attention that militant suffragettes received from about 1906, and in part because, as time went on, more women and men became sympathetic at least to some feminist principles. Feminism itself continued to develop. The next generation took a more direct approach to sexuality, had a socialist bent, and encouraged the participation of working-class women. All of these developments would also inflect the ongoing campaigns for the vote. Leading feminists of this period include writers Cicely Hamilton, Mona Caird (1854–1932) and Olive Schreiner (1855–1920), trade union enthusiast Lady Emilia Dilke, social investigators Clementina Black and Clara Collet, and Women's Co-operative Guild secretary Margaret Llewelyn Davies (1861–1943), who was Emily Davies's niece.

Notions about the British nation and Empire continued to mould feminists' ideas as motherhood became the subject of state attention. During the Boer War and the First World War especially, fears about the physical health of the nation led to an understanding of motherhood as a national and imperial responsibility (rather than a private one), since only fit mothers could bear and raise strong soldiers and citizens. Feminists gave their own edge to this new message by emphasizing how politically important the demands of motherhood made women. Other imperial ideas about racial theory also helped to shape feminism. Many feminists were attracted to eugenics theory, with its promise of progress in human nature and its glorification of the responsibilities of mothers.

One measure of how much feminism changed around the beginning of the twentieth century is the rise in Mary Wollstonecraft's reputation. While she had been disdained by mid-Victorian feminists, who rejected her sexual and political radicalism, now a number of biographies of

Wollstonecraft, critical studies of her work, and new editions of her *Vindication of the Rights of Woman* appeared. Many women began to acknowledge her as an influence and to take her work seriously. Her personal choices were now often seen as courageous, and she was applauded for following her own moral code rather than pursuing respectability. The shift was so pronounced that even the more decorous feminists of the previous generation could not disregard her any longer; Millicent Garrett Fawcett wrote the introduction to an 1891 edition of the *Vindication*, though in it she still ignored Wollstonecraft's personal life.[60]

Feminists continued to address sexual issues in public, began addressing the question of sex within marriage, and were particularly forceful on the subject of venereal disease, which was still widespread. The militant suffragette Christabel Pankhurst (1880–1958) wrote a pamphlet on the topic called *The Great Scourge*, which gave rise to the famous motto, 'Votes for Women, Chastity for Men!' In it she argued that English men were so riddled with venereal disease that happy marriage was an impossibility for women. Even those who did not go so far sustained a more open discussion of venereal disease and a pointed criticism of the institution of marriage.

While the focus on venereal disease emphasized the dangers of sex, and many feminists insisted on women's right to refrain from it, other feminists explored the positive sides of sexuality. Influenced by the new field of sexology, they recognized women as sexual beings and insisted that they needed the freedom to desire and willingly engage in non-procreative sex (with men or women) as well as the freedom not to. Many of these women contributed to the new journal *Shafts* (founded in 1892), which ran pieces that favoured birth control and were critical of conventional marriage. The views of readers were also printed and the editors announced classes and meetings on these and similar issues, suggesting a larger community of discussion.

The 'new woman'

One of the questions which *Shafts* posed to readers in 1895 was: 'Does the modern type of novel help or retard the cause of woman?' The sorts of novels under discussion were those that depicted the 'new woman', who became a trope of the late nineteenth and early twentieth centuries. The focus on the 'new woman' recalled the attention paid in the late 1860s and 1870s to the 'girl of the period', who was described by anti-feminist Eliza

Lynn Linton (1822–98) in an essay that appeared in *The Saturday Review* in March of 1868 as:

> a creature who dyes her hair and paints her face ... who lives to please herself ... [who along with] purity of taste ... has lost also that far more precious purity and delicacy of perception ... [Her] imitation of the *demi-monde* ... leads to slang, bold talk and general fastness.[61]

While Linton deplored the immodesty of such a woman, others applauded her independence. The 'new woman' was endlessly described and debated (*Shafts* approved of her, while the older-style *Woman's Signal* did not), and seems to have been a literary and journalistic construction that had some basis in reality. The 'new woman' was a young woman of principle, middle-class, independent and financially self-reliant, reflecting her class's increased opportunities for education, work, career, and feminist activism. She rejected the spiritual slavery and physical dangers of marriage, sometimes in favour of freer unions, at other times arguing for celibacy. 'New woman' was not a synonym for 'feminist', but women who thought the label applied to them probably held some feminist convictions.[62]

'New woman' novels explored their characters' experiences of higher education, work, sex, and sexual unions of all kinds, including marriage, and in so doing were able to dramatize contemporary debates on the topics. They included Mona Caird's *The Daughters of Danaus*, Emma Brooke's *A Superfluous Woman*, Sarah Grand's *The Beth Book* and *The Heavenly Twins*, and Olive Schreiner's *Story of an African Farm*. While 'new women', both in reality and in novels, were seen as sexually transgressive, most of these authors overlooked women's sexual desire and supported heterosexual marriage and eugenics theory. *The Heavenly Twins*, for example, features a baby born with syphilis and centres on the importance of sexual purity, motherhood, and racial fitness. On the other hand, all of these authors were themselves outspoken and financially independent, living examples of 'new women' and proof that the image was not entirely chimerical.

These writers also wrote in many other genres that had wide audiences. Mona Caird's 1888 essay 'Marriage' in *The Westminster Review* criticized marriage as a 'vexatious failure',[63] and argued that, along with prostitution, it was a system of institutionalized violence against women. The piece set off a debate that went far beyond the educated elite; the *Daily Telegraph* invited correspondence on the issue and received over 25,000 letters in two months. Clearly Caird had touched a nerve, and not just among fellow writers or 'new women'. She remained notorious into the twentieth century for her radical views on marriage, sex, motherhood, civil rights, and animal rights. Cicely Hamilton wrote the play *How the Vote Was Won* with Christopher St John, was a founder of the Women Writers' Suffrage League, and most famously the author of the widely-read book *Marriage as a Trade* (1909). Oliver Schreiner published *Women and Labour* (1911) and was a friend of the sexologist Havelock Ellis (they both approved of free love and birth control).[64] All of these works inspired public debate about the proper relationship of women to marriage, politics and sexuality.

Socialism and working-class women

While the 'new woman' debate centred on young middle-class women, feminists also turned to workplace issues for poorer women. At the same time feminism ceased to be a middle-class liberal movement. Many middle-class feminists active in this period were socialist, rather than liberal, thinkers; in addition, working-class women themselves, many with socialist sympathies, became involved with women's issues. Socialist feminists contributed a new emphasis on the material basis of the oppression of women, especially of working-class women. Furthermore, from the 1880s socialists treated the 'woman question' seriously, debating how to place sexual oppression within the socialist critique. Tensions often arose as feminist and socialist groups competed for the loyalty of working-class women; the conflict between the feminist campaign for women's suffrage and the socialist campaign for adult suffrage is one example of this. There were also tensions between liberal and socialist feminists. For example, older liberal feminists such as Millicent Garrett Fawcett opposed any protective legislation for women workers as unjust and an affront to the free market; socialist feminists saw such measures as necessary and endorsed them because they would improve working conditions for women.

One of the best-known socialist feminists of this period (who favoured both women's and adult suffrage) was Lady Emilia Dilke. She was a member of England's cultural and political elite, friendly with John Ruskin, Walter Pater, George Eliot (she was said to be the model for Dorothea Brooke in *Middlemarch*), Robert Browning and Herbert Asquith (who was Prime Minister in 1918 when women were finally granted the vote). Dilke was a member of the Women's Trade Union League (WTUL) from its inception in 1874 and was president from 1886 until her death in 1904. She believed strongly in the ability of middle- and working-class women to recognize their differences and yet work together in gendered solidarity, and felt that feminist trade unionism would bring women together; to that end, she recruited middle-class women to the WTUL. She also worked for the WTUL by going on speaking tours, contributing money, and writing articles for the League's journal and the general press, and helped to forge better relations between the women's unions represented by the WTUL and the men's unions of the Trades Union Congress (TUC).[65] In the 1890s, she put pressure on Asquith, then Home Secretary, to create a women's branch of the Factory Department, so that lady inspectors could investigate the women's workplace issues so often overlooked by male inspectors.

Clementina Black, who as a young woman was a protégée of Lady Dilke, was a middle-class socialist feminist and suffragist who led a variety of organizations that aimed at improving wages and employment conditions for working women. These included the Consumers' League, which encouraged middle-class women to use their power as consumers to put pressure on low-paying employers (their successful campaign against the Bryant & May match firm included the famous 1888 matchgirl strike); the Women's Trade Union League; the Anti-Sweating League; and the Women's Industrial Council (WIC). At the latter she helped collect and publicize information about the conditions under which so many women worked, and served as president for twenty years. Towards the same end she also wrote *Sweated Industry and the Minimum Wage* (1907) and *A Case for Trade Boards* (1909). Clara Collet, another social investigator and feminist, did similar work for the Royal Commission on Labour and the Board of Trade. Dilke, Black and Collet, in contrast to the previous generation of feminists, were all socialists and were all more concerned with the material conditions of poor women's lives than with abstract injustices.

The end of the nineteenth century and start of the twentieth also saw more interest in feminism on the part of working-class women themselves. Having been conspicuously absent from radical politics from the middle of the century, they now – strengthened by their own labour organizations and by middle-class socialist suffragists – began to assert themselves. Many working-class women were members of the WTUL, working for the improvement of their own lives. Through the WTUL they lobbied for government legislation on working hours and conditions and represented their interests to the larger TUC. Most working-class feminists favoured protective legislation, unsurprisingly given that it offered them some control over their working conditions. Working women also became involved in the suffrage movement; for example Jessie Craigen (c.1835–99), who had experience in the temperance movement, worked as a paid employee of the suffrage and repeal campaigns in the 1880s.

Another important venue for working-class feminists was the Women's Co-operative Guild (WCG), founded in 1883 as part of the consumers' co-operative movement. It had 30,000 members in the early twentieth century. Linked to no party, the WCG was officially politically neutral (members ranged from socialists to Conservatives, with an apolitical majority) but devoted to the advancement of the working classes. Many thought of the WCG as, in the words of one member, Rosalind Nash, 'a trade union for married women'.[66] It was led from 1889 until 1921 by its general secretary Margaret Llewelyn Davies (who was herself middle-class). Under Llewelyn Davies the Guild grew quickly, from 51 branches and 1,700 members in 1889 to 1,800 branches and 88,000 members in 1938. Llewelyn Davies reshaped the WCG, originally founded to provide a venue for education and socializing, into a political campaigning organization that took women's rights as central. She aimed to make the Guild a feminist, progressive, and autonomous part of the working-class socialist movement. By 1900 most Guild members agreed on the importance of female trade unions, protective legislation for women workers, and political rights for women.

The WCG not only promoted its members' interests but gave them political confidence. Before women won the vote, working-class women were marginal in the Labour Party and in most aspects of the socialist movement. As we saw previously in this chapter, the Women's Labour League (the Labour Party's auxiliary) remained small and mostly supportive of male leaders' positions (although between 1918 and 1922 100,000 women joined women's sections of local Labour Party organizations, revealing their strong interest in class-specific party politics[67]). The WCG, on the other hand, argued that working women were valuable and indeed necessary participants in politics, who had public as well as private duties. It offered members political training and in spite of their lack of education encouraged them to believe in their own vast but untapped potential. It also challenged the notion that home was a safe haven for working-class women by exposing the many forms of domestic sexual oppression to which they were vulnerable; a 1913 Guild publication emphasized the need for 'parity to begin at home',[68] thereby applying the language of demands for workplace equality to the domestic sphere.

Llewelyn Davies focused Guild work on investigating various aspects of working women's lives and publicizing the results. After a study of working conditions for women in co-operative stores, the WCG advocated a minimum wage, which by 1912 was honoured by the Co-operative Wholesale Society and other stores. The Guild's most famous campaign was for reform of the divorce laws. The Royal Commission on Divorce (created in 1909) asked the WCG for information on working-class women's opinions on divorce. Guild branches sent out questionnaires to members and the results were collected, submitted to the Commission, and also published as *Working Women and Divorce* (1911). The responses were testimony to a number of serious marital problems, including the withholding of housekeeping money, infidelity, domestic violence, and enforced intercourse, the last of which led to the transmission of venereal diseases and to unwanted pregnancies, despair, and desperate abortion attempts. Llewelyn Davies, who appeared before the Commission, presented her evidence along with the WCG's recommendation that divorce should be legalized if by mutual consent and following two years of separation, that divorce proceedings should be made more affordable, and that men and women should be granted divorces on the same terms; WCG members felt especially strongly about the last point.

The notion of working-class women demanding an egalitarian divorce procedure from the government would have been unthinkable sixty years earlier. The fact of the demand itself reveals how much feminism had changed England. Women were now participants in the political debates of the day.

Throughout the long nineteenth century women's relationship to politics was a complex one. Although they were technically excluded from the formal political realm and from national electoral politics for the entire period, they often made their presence felt in elections none the less. They also participated in a variety of political moments and movements. Food riots were a traditional form of protest; mass platforms were carnivalesque; the Anti-Corn Law League allowed women to make domestically-oriented contributions to politics. Though certain events, such as the Queen Caroline Affair and the anti-Poor Law agitations, were exceptions, most political movements marginalized women and their concerns. So too did the major political parties, even after they sought women's contributions as volunteers after 1883. While women were active in local government, many women and men insisted that such work was housekeeping on a large scale rather than parliamentary politics on a small one.

One of the most important changes in women's lives and in English politics was the advent of organized feminism. Feminists campaigned for society to value women who did not marry and for the granting of legal rights to women who did, for women's intellectual and professional capacities to be respected, for sexuality and sexual health to be treated as political issues, and to bring working-class women into the movement. By the early twentieth century, demands for women's sexual and legal equality with men, and for equal opportunities for education and employment, were commonplace; many problems had even been addressed, if inadequately, by Parliament. The one change for which 'women's rights women' worked, and for which they did not see at least some victory until after the First World War, was inclusion in the parliamentary franchise. It is to that famous fight that we now turn.

9

Suffrage

IN 1866 THE Langham Place feminists Barbara Bodichon and Helen Taylor asked John Stuart Mill (1806–73) to bring a Ladies' Petition for women's suffrage to the House of Commons. The House was debating a bill to widen the male franchise; Mill was a radical MP, a renowned philosopher, and Taylor's stepfather. He agreed on the condition that they collect at least one hundred signatures. Putting their penchant for organizing to work, Bodichon and several Langham Place friends quickly formed a Women's Suffrage Committee in London; Elizabeth Wolstenholme did the same in Manchester. Together they collected 1,500 signatures in a few weeks. Mill and a fellow MP Henry Fawcett presented them in Parliament and introduced a women's suffrage amendment to the 1867 Reform Bill which, when passed, enfranchised most urban working-class men. The amendment was defeated by 123 votes, but the suffrage movement had begun.

Early campaigns

Though the radical Mary Wollstonecraft, Owenites Anna Wheeler and William Thompson, and some early Chartists had argued that the parliamentary vote should be extended to women, this first strike by London and Manchester feminists was the beginning of the formal political campaign. While the notion of votes for women was a radical one, the first suffrage society, in London, was fairly moderate in its methods. It was dominated by its president, John Stuart Mill, whose fame was a great asset but who was also firmly fixed on a very conservative approach. Mill was a feminist but also (until his death in 1873) the patriarch of women's suffrage; he was manipulative, domineering, extremely concerned with respectability, committed to a gradualist strategy, and willing to work only with 'womanly' women. He cautioned supporters never to 'underrate the value of "a pretty face" in a lecturer on women's rights' and argued that such a face was important not for its effects on men but

> for the influence it has on the younger women. It shows them that the championship of women's cause is not confined to women who have no qualifications for success in the more beaten track.[1]

This insistence that the suffrage movement prove that its adherents were not simply women unable to attract husbands clearly demonstrates Mill's limits as a leader.

The London suffragists led by Mill included Millicent Garrett Fawcett, a liberal feminist who became the head of the National Union of Women's Suffrage Societies (NUWSS). Fawcett was from a comfortable middle-class family that included many impressive women, and was well-educated for a girl of her time. A famous, probably apocryphal story holds that one evening, when Millicent was only eight, her sister Elizabeth and their friend Emily Davies (both in their twenties) stated their goals: Emily was to open higher education to women and Elizabeth to do the same for the professions (both were successful). The two then turned to young Millicent and told her that she would have to win the vote for women. Millicent's husband Henry was a Cambridge professor, a Liberal MP for Brighton, an ally of Mill's in the House of Commons, and a supporter of his wife's suffrage work. She was a devoted follower of Mill, endorsed his moderation, and always supported his policy decisions for the London Suffrage Committee. A skilful politician herself (she was a good speaker and a better organizer), Millicent always wanted the women's movement to appeal to a wide public and as a result was prepared to accept small, incremental gains. She was younger than many of her suffrage colleagues but, ideologically, remained part of the first generation of cautious London suffragists all her life.

In Manchester, the suffrage fight was led by radical men and women of various generations, including Jacob Bright and Ursula Bright and the historian Alice Clark (1874–1934). Its most famous member, Emmeline Pankhurst, would go on to become the charismatic leader of the militant Women's Social and Political Union (WSPU) in the twentieth century. Manchester suffrage had ties to the Anti-Corn Law League, anti-slavery agitations, male radicals who sought a larger male franchise, and dissenting Quaker and Unitarian traditions. Throughout the nineteenth century Manchester suffragists tended to be more radical and more democratically inclined than many in London. They were also more drawn to socialism and had links with working-class movements.

The women's vote was at first pursued only by these small groups, but as the nineteenth century progressed various provincial suffrage societies sprang up. The Liverpool society was headed in 1894 by Mrs Alfred Booth, Mrs Allan Bright and Nessie Egerton Stewart Brown, women from wealthy shipowning families who were previously active in Liberal politics and organizations that promoted the welfare of working-class women. In contrast, the Bath society was formed by women who had never done any political work before. In Lancashire, politically radical women textile workers organized themselves to work for issues that affected working-class women's lives and kept suffrage vital during the difficult 1890s, when the movement seemed in danger of stagnating. And in the twentieth century, the cause grew quickly and attracted the interest and support of many previously apolitical women, some of whom became devoted to suffrage as to a calling or religion.[2]

The meanings of the vote

As the franchise broadened to include middle-class men in 1832 and working-class men in 1867 and 1884, it came to take on a larger significance in English political life. Once the province of elite men only, the vote became synonymous with citizenship, even adulthood, and women's exclusion from it became more pointed. But that women would eventually win the vote was anything but a foregone conclusion. The issue of voting women was one not only of a larger franchise but of an 'alternate sexual order'[3] that many found horrifying. It was such a direct challenge to the status quo that it was either condescendingly dismissed or vociferously opposed by men of all classes for decades. Members of Parliament expressed their resistance by voting against it, while men working as police and prison wardens were often physically and sexually violent with suffrage women. It was only through the untiring work of thousands of suffrage workers that the vote was eventually won.

Of course, the suffrage movement was never monolithic, and different women approached and experienced the campaign in different ways. Individual experiences were marked by level of commitment, marital status, party affiliation, geographical location, religion, employment, and class. Many married women joined suffrage organizations, donated money, and worked for the cause. But women with households to run and children to raise found it difficult to carve out time to contribute to the movement. Husbands, although they did not generally require as much care as children, sometimes disapproved of any activism that interfered with their domestic lives. The women who gave the most time and energy to the cause were usually single and childless (this is not to say that every unmarried or childless woman was without domestic obligations). Unmarried activist Mary Richardson (1889–1961) wrote:

> What brought me relief, personally, was the knowledge that I belonged nowhere; I had no home, and so there was nobody who would worry over me and over whom I need worry.[4]

As was the case with feminists generally, most suffragists had some party affiliation or sympathy, and these could cause conflicts. Many suffragists were middle-class and Liberal. There were also Conservative suffragists, whose influence in the movement has been underestimated. Many radical middle-class and working-class suffrage women were drawn to the socialist movement and later to the Labour Party. Working-class women often found themselves torn between a class affiliation with socialism, which emphasized fighting for the vote for working men, and a gender affiliation with the suffrage movement, which all too often assumed that all women were middle-class.

As the movement became more national in scope it also became more centred on London, but few women had the time or money to travel to London, let alone to travel there frequently. Local groups were their main site of suffrage activity, from which they could assert both their local identities and pride in their participation in a national movement. The local level was often more flexible than the national, with branches of sparring national organizations, in Portsmouth for example, working together. In addition to local suffrage groups, many women belonged to smaller ones organized around religious or professional affiliations, such as the Clerks' Women's Social and Political Union, the Women Writers' Suffrage League, the Actresses' Franchise League (members of which wrote and performed many pro-suffrage plays), the Church League for Women's Suffrage, the Catholic Women's Suffrage Society, and the Jewish League for Woman Suffrage (whose members wore items coloured purple for suffrage and blue for Judaism). Here women filtered their politics through religious or other identities important to them.

Finally, the suffrage movement was often divided by class. Suffrage was once seen by historians as the province of mainly middle-class women. Some aristocratic women felt that their influence made the formality of suffrage unnecessary. Others, including Lady Knightley and the Duchess of Sutherland, thought that elite women's de facto involvement in politics made their lack of voting privileges ridiculous. Many suffragists from the middle and upper classes resented the fact that they could not vote when working-class men could. The turn-of-the-century feminist Margaret Llewelyn Davies once remarked of her feminist aunt, Emily Davies, that she wanted the vote largely because she resented the notion of 'an employing lady not [having] a Vote when her gardener did'.[5]

Working-class women, it was once thought, had little time and even less interest in agitating for an abstract political right when they had so many pressing economic and legal disadvantages to contend with. But in fact many working-class women cared a great deal about women's suffrage and supported the cause in a variety of ways. In Lancashire's textile districts, women were well-organized, but here women enjoyed workplace communities and skilled work, both of which probably contributed to their political confidence. No other localities have been found where working women similarly organized themselves for the suffrage cause. Outside Lancashire it is difficult to know precisely how many working women participated in the struggle for suffrage, and in what ways. Many signed petitions, gave money, or participated in marches and demonstrations. Others worked (as volunteers or for pay) distributing leaflets, selling newspapers, or providing administrative support at local or national societies.

Some working-class suffrage women were paid 'organizers', and these were usually women who were very committed to suffrage. They needed to support themselves and were willing to work hard for the cause for low pay. Sarah Reddish worked as an organizer for the North of England Suffrage Society in 1899 and 1900; she helped collect signatures from Lancashire cotton workers. In 1904 the newly formed National Union of Women's Suffrage Societies (NUWSS) hired two national organizers, who were paid about £75 per annum, and by 1909 they employed ten organizers; the larger NUWSS societies employed their own organizers, such as Helga Gill, who in 1914 worked for the Oxford NUWSS for £120 per annum. The WSPU also paid organizers, including Minnie Baldock, Ada Nield Chew (1870–1945), and teacher Mary Gawthorpe (1881–1973); by 1909, the WSPU had thirty women in its employ. Middle-class women who needed a salary worked as paid secretaries to local societies. In the nineteenth century, when pay for middle-class women still carried a stigma, the suffragist Lydia Becker always stressed that she volunteered her services, though she had little money and allowed her expenses to be paid. By the twentieth century, this stigma was gone; in the next generation Esther Roper took the paid position of secretary to the Manchester society without any qualms.[6]

A very few working women, such as Annie Kenney, Mary Richardson, and Jessie Craigen, were well-known speakers. Craigen was a freelance speaker and not employed by societies. The daughter of a Scottish sailor and an Italian actress, she had experience as a stage actress and a temperance activist when she began a career as a paid suffrage speaker, which lasted from 1870 to 1884 (from 1880 to 1883 she was also a paid lecturer for the campaign to repeal the Contagious Diseases Acts). She had an impressive voice that Helen Blackburn compared to 'a mighty melodious bell'. On her travels around the country she spoke tirelessly and her speeches were often reprinted. Like most women who were paid suffrage workers, Craigen's life was a precarious one, and she sometimes felt that wealthier suffrage women treated her as an employee rather than a fellow agitator. She was aided by several radical suffragists, especially the Quaker sisters Anna Maria and Mary Priestman, who saw her as crucial to the important task of attracting the working classes to suffrage. They helped her financially when she was no longer in demand as a speaker, by organizing the 'Jessie Craigen Lecture Fund' which supplied her with a small income.[7]

In general, though, suffrage leaders, speakers, and activists came from the middle and upper classes and were not paid. Middle-class women had the time, education, and social confidence to be willing and able to contribute in these prominent roles. But their priorities were often different from those of working-class women, and this could cause conflicts.

THE CASE FOR SUFFRAGE

In the last part of the nineteenth century, women who once fought a variety of forms of female oppression – political, legal, sexual, cultural – came to concern themselves only with the vote, claiming that once won it would lead to other rights. This focus is understandable given the many infuriating cultural assumptions that were used to explain why women could not possibly be responsible parliamentary voters – that women were overly emotional, unable to judge impartially, or to put the common good ahead of that of their own families – or why, if they did win the vote, it would ruin England, as babies would be left hungry and families uncared for while women neglected the domestic sphere for the public one. Some have argued that this intense focus on the vote impoverished feminism. But this is a misunderstanding of nineteenth- and twentieth-century women's appreciation of the vote. While the vote was a single political privilege, feminists saw it as both real and symbolic. Real benefits might be limited – parties, governments, and connections might matter at least as much as the franchise – but suffragists also wanted the emblematic value of full citizenship for women.

Suffragists did not see the vote as entirely separate from other issues, although they often pursued it this way. While Emily Davies focused on higher education, and Josephine Butler on the sexual double standard, Millicent Garrett Fawcett saw the vote as a means of ending women's disabilities in education, as wives, and as victims of sexual exploitation. Many women explicitly connected their determination to win the vote to women's subordination: Fawcett often recounted the experience of having her purse snatched in the 1870s and discovering that the thief stood accused of stealing from her person 'the property of Henry Fawcett'; in her autobiography she said, 'I felt as if I had been charged with theft myself.'[8] Many others emphasized memories of sexual subordination. This is evident if we look at memoirs and autobiographies. Mary Gaw-thorpe, who was from a working-class neighbourhood in Leeds, said that seeing her mother's sexual oppression at the hands of her father made her pro-suffrage. She described her parents' relationship as a 'battle of the beds', and on many nights would invite her mother into her own bed when her father came home from an evening of drinking. Helena Swan-wick (1864–1939), who came from a middle-class bohemian family, hated her mother's willing subordination to her father; Mrs Swanwick had her own separate income but insisted on turning it over to her husband and then begging him for household money to demonstrate his power and her own helplessness. Swanwick later wrote that her active suffrage career (she was the editor of the suffrage journal *Common Cause*) began with her frustration over these domestic sexual politics.[9]

Suffragists used a variety of arguments to justify women's inclusion in the franchise. These generally divided between equality-based arguments and difference-based arguments. Equality arguments grew out of the humanist tradition and Enlightenment thought (Mary Wollstonecraft's work relied on them). They stated that women were, like men, fully human, so it was intrinsically unjust to deny them rights, political or otherwise, that were granted to men. Difference arguments grew out of nineteenth-century ideas about gender roles (especially middle-class evangelical domestic ideology). Suffrage advocates agreed with the general public that women were, indeed, quite different from men, but denied that they were in any way men's inferiors. Rather, they argued that it was precisely the unique potential contributions of women that made them necessary in the nation's political life. As early as 1870 the suffragist Helen Taylor (1831–1907) drily asked:

> Have any of the members [of Parliament] who think that women ought by no means to have the suffrage, but ought to be properly protected by the lawgivers, have any of these lawgivers brought a bill for flogging men who ill-treat women? Not one.[10]

Such comments attacked the myth that men would protect women; women needed the vote to protect themselves.

While feminists working in other areas often stressed the injustice of inequality, in the suffrage movement arguments based on difference predominated. Most suffrage writers emphasized the benefits of the specific contributions women would make to political culture. Women were domestic and would therefore provide a softening element to the hard world of Westminster; women were more moral than men and so would bring morality to politics; women were anxious about the welfare of women, children, and the poor, and would bring those concerns to Parliament. Difference arguments must have resonated with many women, as those from varied class backgrounds and with opposing party sympathies were surprisingly ideologically united by a shared understanding of women as different from men.[11] The most emphatic version of the difference argument was articulated in the twentieth century by Emmeline Pankhurst and Christabel Pankhurst, who saw the fight for suffrage not simply as a demand for women's inclusion in the political world but as a sex war in which women battled against men's dominance over them. They used difference arguments to justify their political strategies and to insist on women's moral and political superiority.

Suffrage work was never just political work; it always had other social and cultural aspects, and for some very dedicated women it became a lifestyle. Women wore distinctive brooches, scarves, or other accessories that indicated their support for suffrage. They subscribed to suffrage journals and read suffrage pamphlets. They enjoyed suffrage plays (*The Case in a Nutshell: a Dramatic Dialogue on Woman's Franchise* (c. 1890), *How the Vote was Won* (1909), *Helping the Cause* (1912)), poems ('What the Widow Thinks', 1882), and novels (*Daughters of the City* (1899), *Suffragette Sally* (1911)). Some of these argued for the vote; others portrayed suffragist heroines in a variety of situations. Suffrage pervaded supporters' lives, and all of Britain in the early twentieth century, as pro- and anti-suffrage images flooded public spaces.[12]

Suffrage also had a crucial imperial context. Women's suffrage was debated and slowly and unevenly granted not in England but across the British Empire before the female vote was won in England. Female householders on the tiny Isle of Man won the vote in 1881. In New Zealand both European and indigenous women could vote from 1893. Nine years later Australia – now the Australian commonwealth – granted white women the vote; most Aboriginal women could not vote until 1963. Imperialism played an important role in suffrage discourse in England itself. As was typical of nineteenth- and early twentieth-century thinkers, many suffrage supporters believed in the idea of the progress of civilizations, with England the most advanced and most rapidly progressing nation on earth. Elizabeth Wolstenholme-Elmy wrote that the accomplishments of the English women's movement would soon spread over the globe, and that 'such a higher social and political morality is vital to the well-being of the race, and essential to its upward and onward progress'.[13] Many suffragists were, like many feminists and other white Britons, racist and eugenicist. They justified women's claim to the vote by asserting their moral superiority and civilized status as white Christian Westerners, just as many invoked their superior class status and education compared to enfranchised working-class men. White Christian women, once granted the vote, would lead non-Christian Eastern women of colour, particularly Indian women, to freedom. Helena Swanwick wrote in 1913:

> If it were only for the sake of India, women here in Great Britain would be bound to demand the vote. The knowledge of that vast multitude of silent and too suffering women weighs on us always . . .[14]

British imperial responsibility was a privilege which suffragists wished to take on.

The writings of prominent nineteenth-century suffragists relied on racial and imperial notions. Millicent Garrett Fawcett, who was a patriot and an imperialist all her life, published an essay entitled 'England' in 1884. It was a history of England that argued for women's suffrage by celebrating a largely invented ancient Saxon past in which women enjoyed legal and constitutional rights that needed to be restored to them. More militant suffrage women writing in the twentieth century approached history from a different angle. Though also nationalistic and racial thinkers, they celebrated the struggle for the vote as a break with the British past rather than as a restoration of its best features, and were more willing to acknowledge foreign ideas – notably those of the French Revolution – as valuable.[15]

THE CASE AGAINST SUFFRAGE

Of course not all women were in favour of women's suffrage, and some were actively opposed to it. Women who opposed suffrage agreed with suffragists about women's essentially different nature, but saw this as the basis for a different political future. The most famous anti-suffrage woman was novelist Mrs Humphry Ward (1851–1920), who frequently wrote and spoke publicly on the topic; her essay 'An Appeal Against Female Suffrage' was signed by many prominent women and published in the periodical The Nineteenth Century in 1889. Other women who opposed suffrage included Violet Markham and Lady Jersey. Beatrice Webb, the socialist and social investigator who preferred to be thought of as a professional first and a woman second, signed Ward's petition, but she came to see the gesture as a mistake: she entitled the section of her memoir in which she recounted the event 'A False Step'. Seventeen years later she became a supporter of women's suffrage (though never an avid one), and even wrote to Millicent Garrett Fawcett that she now believed that women's 'social obligations compel them to claim a share in the conduct of political affairs'.[16]

Anti-suffragists, who were mostly upper and middle class, promoted what they called the 'Forward Policy', which emphasized not just their opposition to the parliamentary franchise but a positive view of women's involvement in government which stressed their fitness for local politics and their potential to advise male politicians on matters such as education and maternity care. Organized anti-suffrage activity by women developed in 1908 into the founding of the Women's National Anti-Suffrage League (which later joined with the men's league to become the National League for Opposing Woman Suffrage). By 1910 they had over a hundred branches, 16,000 members and 400,000 signatures on petitions; they promoted the idea of a Women's National Council or Advisory Committee that would advise and influence Parliament.[17]

The irony of women campaigning to be excluded from politics and speaking publicly about women's unfitness for public life was not lost on suffrage women; Millicent Garrett Fawcett remarked of Mrs Ward that 'she really does us more good than harm ... She is so amusingly and delightfully inconsistent – we love her for it.'[18] Yet in some ways anti-suffrage was, like suffrage, part of the growing national debate on gender and citizenship. Suffragists and anti-suffragists agreed on many points, especially regarding women's special nature and abilities. (They were not, of course, united on all points; anti-suffragists detested the 'new woman' and the individualism and the sexual rebelliousness she stood for, while many suffragists, especially those born after 1870, applauded and emulated the image.) Louise Creighton (1850–1936, whose husband Mandell Creighton was made Bishop of London in 1896) worked with Mrs Ward opposing suffrage from 1889. But in 1906 Creighton decided to support the suffrage movement. In her memoirs, she claimed that she had originally joined the anti-suffrage movement only at the prompting of Mrs Ward, who 'opposed [women's suffrage] from a very different point of view to mine'. While Creighton would have preferred women not to get involved in party politics:

> As time went on & women joined the Primrose League & Liberal & other political Associations, & took an active part in elections & political work generally, I came to see that as they insisted on doing this they had better have the responsibility of the vote.

Creighton claimed that the suffrage and anti-suffrage movements were not necessarily opposed, and for many years worked to build alliances between them.[19]

Of course there was much anti-suffrage feeling among the male population as well, including many Members of Parliament. Some anti-suffrage arguments were based on women's supposed mental differences from men: women were generally less intelligent, as evidenced by the fact that there were almost no female geniuses in the arts or politics; women lacked common sense; women were unable to use logic, and instead were overly swayed in their thinking by emotion and by the influence of others. Other arguments pointed to women's physiological shortcomings as compared to men, claiming that women were politically incapacitated by menstruation, pregnancy, childbirth, and breast-feeding.

These mental and physical shortcomings were also invoked as political and diplomatic problems. Opponents of suffrage were tenacious in arguing that it would be unjust to allow women to vote to send men to war, when they themselves could not serve as soldiers. The maintenance of Britain's position in the world required, insisted suffrage opponents, that every vote represented a potential soldier. In particular, governing the Empire required virility; Lord Curzon explained that 'For the discharge of great responsibilities in the dependencies of the Empire you want the qualities not of the feminine but of the masculine mind,'[20] and others claimed that imperial subjects would not respect a ruling country where women voted.

Of course many people felt that the very notion of women voting was so absurd that it required no response. While the number of MPs that voted for Mill's amendment to include women in the 1867 Reform Bill, seventy-three, was surprisingly high, the condescending tone of anti-suffrage speeches in Parliament reveals that women's suffrage was never a serious consideration for most members. As the House of Commons debated the 1867 bill to widen the male franchise, one MP called the debate over the women's suffrage amendment a 'pleasant interlude ... interposed with the grave and somewhat sombre discussions on the subject of Reform'.[21] Reforming the male franchise was serious business; the very idea of a female franchise was a diverting fantasy.

Working for the vote

The basic strategy of the suffrage movement was to persuade politicians and the public of the rightness of its cause, and to introduce women's suffrage into Parliament. In the latter endeavour, the suffrage movement was quite successful in the nineteenth century. During the same years that feminists achieved the repeal of the Contagious Diseases Acts, reform of the laws relating to married women's property, and changes in child custody laws, they also made strides in introducing suffrage debates into parliamentary discourse. Between 1867 and 1884 (the dates of the second and third Reform Acts) suffrage bills and amendments were introduced and debated almost every year, and several more were introduced between 1884 and 1897.

Following the failure of Mill's first parliamentary amendment, some suffragists thought the best thing might be simply to demonstrate that women could vote. This cautious strategy was introduced by suffragist Lydia Becker. Becker was an unmarried woman from an industrialist family. Originally part of the radical circle led by Jacob Bright, she became an advocate of political moderation and compromise and as a result became alienated from the Manchester suffragists. She was the editor and principal writer of the *Women's Suffrage Journal* (1870–90), which was the voice of the movement in those years, and her combination of personal dynamism and political caution marked the movement until her death in 1890. These qualities were both in evidence in her campaign to demonstrate that some women were already enfranchised. In 1867 the name of Lily Maxwell, the owner of a small shop in Manchester, mistakenly appeared on the list of qualified voters. Hoping that a successful female elector would advance the cause, Becker encouraged Maxwell to cast her vote (which she did). Becker argued that women who paid taxes had already been granted the vote because the 1867 Reform Act used the term 'man' (not 'male person'), which in legal terminology normally referred to both men and women. In 1868 Becker and several colleagues registered as many female ratepayers as they could on the electoral roll. Some local parish overseers, as in Salford, accepted female names; others, as in Manchester, refused. But when the issue was brought before the Court of Common Pleas, in the case of *Chorlton* v. *Lings* (1868), the court ruled that while 'man' might mean 'person' in most legal contexts, in the context of voting it meant male persons only. In other words, women could not vote because they were women; that they were unqualified to participate in politics at the national level went without saying.

So women could not simply slip into the franchise. But the future was not altogether grim: in 1869 single women who had sufficient property were granted the right to vote on the same terms as men in some municipal elections, as the result of a bill introduced by the suffrage supporter Jacob Bright. (This privilege was extended to county councils in 1888 and to district councils in 1894.) In 1870 the Education Act allowed women to vote for, and sit on, school boards. In the decades following the Acts of 1869 and 1870, many people would insist on a clear distinction between local politics (as domesticity writ large) and national ones (as true politics). Even anti-suffrage women, including Mrs Ward, supported women's involvement in local politics; Ward herself was active in them. Anti-suffrage women believed that the same special qualities that fitted women for local work made them poor candidates for national involvement.

But it was increasingly clear that local politics were a testing ground for the national scene. We have already seen the many opportunities women had to gain experience with budgeting and public speaking in domestic, religious, philanthropic, and political venues. Suffrage women were especially eager to take on elected responsibilities on school boards and as Poor Law Guardians in order to demonstrate how fit women were for public life. Early School Board representatives included the suffragist Helen Taylor. Early Poor Law Guardians included suffrage supporters Louisa Twining, Emmeline Pankhurst, and Charlotte Despard (1844–1939), a political radical, novelist, and pacifist.

Yet the suffrage cause had few supporters in Parliament. Most importantly, it had no party willing to champion it. Among Conservatives, several leaders (including Benjamin Disraeli) were sympathetic, but the rank and file of the party were not. In the Liberal Party the situation was reversed, with a sympathetic rank and file but hostile leaders, notably Prime Ministers Gladstone and Asquith (who, like many Liberals, feared that middle-class women would vote for Conservative candidates). This meant that whichever of the two major parties was in power, suffrage was never a priority and never introduced as a government-sponsored bill. This was a very serious disability at a time when governments were so busy that they tended to ignore those bills they had not themselves introduced.

As a result, suffragists had only two options in Parliament: amendments offered to existing franchise reform bills, and private member's bills, introduced by individual MPs on their own initiative. Without party support, suffragists pursued what they called the 'best friends' strategy: they supported candidates who were in favour of votes for women, irrespective of party. Some suffragists advocated moving away from a non-party stance as early as the 1880s, but most continued to believe in it. This strategy seemed the soundest one available, but the reality was that any cause without party (and therefore government) support was doomed. And so it was: while suffrage amendments and bills were offered and debated frequently, none had any serious chance of passing into law. Until 1897 none even got as far as a second reading (of the necessary three). Because parties and suffragists did not work together, suffrage was unable to move forward during the nineteenth century. In contrast, the Married Women's Property Act of 1882 passed easily because it was adopted as a government bill.

In addition to this parliamentary problem the movement was often internally divided. As suffrage societies sprang up all over the country after 1867, they joined together as a loose confederation called the National Society for Women's Suffrage (NSWS), led by its secretary Lydia Becker. Yet not everyone was as given to compromise as Becker, and differences remained in spite of the formation of a national group. The major debate was over whether to demand the vote for all women, or to begin by asking for the vote only for unmarried women. The choices were framed by the doctrine of coverture, which (as we saw in the previous chapter) feminists also confronted in their fights over married women's property. Since married women were *femes covert* who did not own any property, and the English franchise qualification was based on the amount of property an individual owned, married women were under a double disadvantage – of sex and of property disqualification – and no matter how wealthy they seemed, they could never technically qualify to vote given the laws as they stood. Single women, a much smaller group, were *femes sole*; they could legally own property and therefore, if there were no sex bar, qualify for the vote. Demanding the vote for single women, then, meant asking for the sex bar to be lowered. Demanding the vote for married women also meant addressing marriage law and the whole notion that a male head of household was the political representative of his family. The idea that a wife might want a political voice separate from her husband's challenged many people's idea of what marriage ought to be.

Suffragists were unsure whether to use a 'widows and spinsters' approach and pursue only the *feme sole* vote first. Most suffragists believed that all women, married and unmarried, should have the vote. More radical suffragists insisted that the central injustice of coverture could not be overlooked even temporarily. Moderates pointed out that the 'widows and spinsters' strategy, while less satisfying, was likely to succeed sooner. This strategic question also revealed differences of opinion about how intimately connected were disparate aspects of women's subordination.

The 'widows and spinsters' issue first split the movement in 1874. More moderate and politically cautious suffragists in the London branch of NSWS, including Millicent Garrett Fawcett, stressed the importance of moderation and endorsed a *feme sole*-first approach. They argued that a principle was at stake – their opposition to the sex bar in the franchise –

and that therefore it was necessary to win some female votes but not to win the vote for large numbers of women immediately. A few pioneers could demonstrate women's ability to vote responsibly, and the public would be converted. The more radical Manchester suffragists insisted that married women be explicitly included in any suffrage amendment. They refused to consider the issue of coverture separately from the vote, feeling that the two had to be opposed simultaneously. In addition, they argued that since most adult women were married, it was hardly helpful to win the vote for a tiny minority. And since suffragists claimed that voting women would extend their caretaking role to the nation, the franchise had to include married women, who were more typical and were the domestic caretakers of most households. Anti-suffrage MP E. A. Leatham protested against the 'widows and spinsters' approach when he asked, in an 1875 debate, whether it was 'any proof, because a woman happens to have failed, from one cause or another, in the role of her own sex, that she can adequately discharge the more difficult and less congenial part of man?' Other anti-suffrage commentators pointed out how absurd it would be if only single women could vote: a woman might lose the right to vote when she married and regain it when widowed, or might actually seek a divorce so as to vote again; an unmarried prostitute might be entitled to vote when a respectable married women could not.[22]

The schism among suffragists over the question of married women was healed by way of a compromise – the decision to pursue votes for women on 'equal terms with men'. In practice, this formulation could mean that married women would be denied the vote; since they owned no property of their own, they could not – when the strategy was adopted in the late 1860s – qualify for the franchise. However, the 'equal terms' formulation did not explicitly exclude married women from future demands for the vote, so that suffragists were only acknowledging current law rather than tacitly endorsing it. The compromise allowed suffragists of various opinions to work together.

Suffragists disagreed over other core issues. On the topic of sexual respectability, they debated whether suffrage societies could associate themselves with Josephine Butler's Ladies' National Association and its fight to repeal the Contagious Diseases Acts in the 1870s. As we saw in Chapter 8, repealers spoke openly about sex, prostitution and venereal disease – atypical topics of conversation for middle-class ladies. Again, the question was one of both strategy and principle. Although most members of suffrage societies opposed the Acts, opinion was bitterly divided as to whether or not the cause of women's suffrage should be publicly linked to a campaign in which respectable women spoke out on unrespectable issues and defended the civil rights of prostitutes. John Stuart Mill, although publicly opposed to the Acts himself, insisted that the London branch of the NSWS hold itself aloof from repeal. Millicent Garrett Fawcett supported him. Many others disagreed, and in 1872 formed the Central Committee of the National Society for Women's Suffrage as a protest. The Central Committee allowed its member societies to speak out against the Acts, as the NSWS did not, and many provincial societies allied themselves with it and against the previously dominant London faction. The more conservative London branch worked alone until this schism was healed in 1878 and the NSWS acted as one large umbrella once more.

Respectability, propriety, and middle-class femininity remained problematic issues. In 1875 Millicent Garrett Fawcett asked the prominent suffragist Elizabeth Wolstenholme-Elmy to step down as secretary of a committee because of 'circumstances connected with your marriage' – Wolstenholme had practised free love by living with Benjamin Elmy before her marriage and had been pregnant at her wedding – that would, in someone so prominently placed, cause 'great injury to the cause of women'.[23] Throughout the suffrage years most societies demanded that their speakers dress and act in a ladylike manner (working-class Annie Kenney (1879–1953) complained about the hat and gloves she had to wear when speaking publicly), believing that conforming to (rather than challenging) these norms would help the cause.

Suffrage opinion about sex itself varied but was less divisive than coverture or respectability. Most advocated a system of 'voluntary motherhood' in which women were able to choose, even within marriage, when they had intercourse and when they had children. But there were also extremes. Some, mostly older women, practised and advocated celibacy; at the other end of the spectrum were sexual radicals who sought an end to monogamy and marriage, including some self-styled 'new women'. Frances Power Cobbe had a lifelong female companion. Many women were unable to agree on the subject of sexual politics but had in common their attempts to defy current sexual conventions and assumptions in order to achieve a world in which women had power over their own bodies.[24]

Suffrage suffered a huge disappointment in 1884, when in spite of much lobbying, the Reform Act enfranchised two million rural working-class men but no women. (This still left one-third of adult men, mostly younger men from the working classes, voteless as well.) This was seen as a great injustice, and to some middle- and upper-class women the notion of uneducated working-class men voting when they could not was highly insulting. Suffragists with connections to Liberal politicians were distressed that their families and friends in Parliament remained unpersuaded. Millicent Garrett Fawcett came to hate Gladstone (for the 1884 defeat and for his championing of Irish Home Rule, which she opposed) and broke with the Liberal Party, though most Liberal suffragists continued to support it. Worst, it was clear that another major Reform Act would not be passed in the foreseeable future. Between 1867 and 1884 women's suffrage had been debated in Parliament every year but one, but in the twenty years after 1884 there would be only three parliamentary debates on the subject.

The problem of party politics plagued the suffrage movement after the passage of the 1884 Reform Act. Some suffragists wanted partisan political societies that supported women's suffrage to be able to affiliate with the National Society for Women's Suffrage. Others disagreed, insisting that only suffrage societies could be part of the NSWS. The fight was really about the various political groups open to women that had sprung up since 1883, such as the Primrose League, which was closely aligned with the Conservative Party, and the Women's Liberal Associations (WLAs) that made up the Women's Liberal Federation (WLF), many of which favoured affiliation. While some suffragists welcomed such support, others rejected it, worried that the cause of women's suffrage would be swallowed up and reduced to one of many Liberal Party issues, and that feminism would be lost in a more general Liberal platform. Allowing broad affiliation was also resisted by Conservative suffragists, because Primrose League chapters were not permitted to affiliate with any other groups; they feared an unbalanced organization to which WLAs had affiliated but Primrose League branches had not. As a result of all this, in 1888 the NSWS divided into two societies (whose almost identical names made it easiest to refer to them by the addresses of their new headquarters). The Great College Street Society, which included Millicent Garrett Fawcett and Lydia Becker, refused affiliation to political societies. It was also more moderate, supporting only parliamentary amendments and bills that excluded married women. The Parliament Street Society adopted the new and less restrictive rules that the Great College Street Society rejected and allowed political societies to affiliate. It supported both bills that specifically excluded married women, and 'equal rights' bills that would have had the effect of excluding them from the franchise. However, it did not approve of more radical bills that explicitly included married women.

Yet for some of the more radical suffragists neither of these positions sufficiently challenged the oppressive status quo under which women lived. Because neither Great College Street nor Parliament Street would support the most radical formulation, an explicit demand for votes for married women, a third society, the Women's Franchise League (WFL), was formed in 1889 by a group that included many Manchester radicals such as Elizabeth Wolstenholme-Elmy and Richard and Emmeline Pankhurst. The WFL only supported bills that explicitly included married women. It saw itself as an organization of Liberal women but it had a broad vision, working against many legal disabilities faced by women, and formed links with the developing labour and socialist movements and international (especially American) feminist movements. The WFL dissolved in 1899, but its principled radicalism continued to inflect the movement.

In spite of these splits and the disappointment of 1884, suffragists continued to work together and to try to move forward. In 1892 and 1893 the Great College Street Society, Parliament Street Society, and Women's Franchise League collaborated on a Special Appeals campaign and collected almost 250,000 signatures in support of votes for women which they submitted to Parliament as the Appeal from Women of All Parties and All Classes. The issue of suffrage was not dead, even if it seemed so in Parliament.

In 1894, an important victory came with the passage of the Local Government Act which allowed married women to vote in local elections just as single women did (provided they owned sufficient property). By 1900 women made up 13.7 per cent of voters in local elections. This development, along with the passage of the 1882 Married Women's Property Act, meant that married women had fewer legal disadvantages than ever before. As regarded the vote, the issue of coverture was now irrelevant: if women were granted the vote, married women would be as able to vote as unmarried ones.

Partly as a result of this, in 1897 the Great College Street and Parliament Street Societies reunited to form the National Union of Women's Suffrage Societies. The NUWSS became the principal suffrage organization, a voice of moderation that worked within accepted political channels.

Following Lydia Becker's death in 1890, the now-widowed Millicent Garrett Fawcett had become the leader of the suffragists; she was prominent in the NUWSS and its president from 1907. NUWSS members were largely middle-class and supporters of the Liberal Party. Radically and democratically inclined suffragists found themselves more and more marginalized.

As the twentieth century began, the suffrage movement seemed to have done well in many ways. The 1897 bill for women's suffrage had not become law, but it received more support and progressed further in the parliamentary process than similar bills brought in previous years. While the NUWSS had halted its work during the Boer War, the movement had grown in size, unity, and power. From 1902 to 1910 the NUWSS expanded and became a national movement with a cross-class membership and some degree of ethnic and religious diversity. Suffrage culture had developed a striking visual component, and billboards and posters deluged public spaces, especially in the capital, reached a general audience, and made suffrage a constant presence. One typical poster from 1912, 'The Appeal of Womanhood', depicted a woman in classical garb in front of the smaller figures of a mother, a laundress, a prostitute, and a chainmaker, all arrayed against the background of Westminster, while the banner she held high proclaimed, 'We want the vote to stop the white slave traffic, sweated labour, and to save the children.' Anti-suffrage groups posted their own images, so that debate was in the air. 'The Appeal of Womanhood' was a reply to an anti-suffrage poster, 'No Votes Thank You', which it resembled, and which portrayed an anti-suffrage woman as feminine and a suffrage women behind her as a gangly harridan.[25] Yet suffragists' efforts had as yet failed to achieve the main result. Although membership of the suffrage movement had grown, and leaders had become more politically astute, women seemed no closer to the parliamentary ballot than they had in 1866.

Militancy and the founding of the WSPU

In 1903 an entirely new kind of suffrage group came into being, one that would change the movement significantly. This was the Women's Social and Political Union (WSPU) which Emmeline Pankhurst, the Manchester radical, formed with her daughters Christabel and Sylvia (1882–1960). Characterized by a new set of tactics and by members' dedication to their leaders, their cause, and each other – a loyalty so fierce that the WSPU was often described as a kind of army or secular religion – the WSPU changed the suffrage movement dramatically. The WSPU was – and, among historians, is – a polarizing force. While many argued that WSPU tactics ultimately delayed victory by making a political issue into a spectacle and by turning public opinion against suffrage women, members claimed that they resuscitated a dying movement and single-handedly won the vote.

The Women's Social and Political Union was originally committed to a broad agenda (as its name would indicate). However, it soon moved its headquarters from Manchester to London, where its national leaders focused exclusively on the vote. Many local branches and members, however, maintained a commitment to socialism and some affiliation with the Independent Labour Party (ILP). Most importantly, the WSPU espoused a wide range of non-traditional, attention-grabbing tactics that are collectively referred to as suffrage militancy. The emergence of a militant tendency, under the umbrella of the WSPU, was so important that it spawned new terms and new debates. The term 'suffragettes' (coined by the *Daily Mail*) was used to refer to militants. 'Suffragists' was reserved for the anti-militant NUWSS and to individuals who did not subscribe to militancy; non-militants preferred the term 'con-stitutionalist', which emphasized their continued faith in the value of engaging in the existing political process.

While suffrage militancy is often thought of as violent – and much of it was, especially in the years immediately before the Great War – its purpose was broader than that. Many women engaged in militancy but rejected violence, and many worked in both militant and constitutionalist organizations. Militancy was a set of highly public actions – some violent, some not, but all, in the words of one historian, 'performative and spec-tacular'[26] – that called attention to the cause of suffrage. Much militancy emerged from the WSPU's creative use of established tactics of political disruption, used by men in other contexts but intended here to feminize male politics.[27] Militants rejected the policy of making gradual inroads into the political system in favour of dramatic actions that served as a commentary on politics from without.

The NUWSS and the WSPU had different styles but similar beliefs: while the WSPU used more extreme tactics, and was more interested in pursuing a vision of a woman-centred politics, the two groups shared an understanding of gender roles. Both groups stressed notions of difference and emphasized women's special contribution to politics. Like other suffrage leaders, Emmeline Pankhurst insisted that militants dress according to middle-class standards of propriety even as they set out to be arrested. She always tried to make sure that the WSPU representatives who faced a crowd were pretty ones. In general suffragists, though they might engage in spectacular public acts, continued to focus on women's right to citizenship, while suffragettes were more interested in asserting women's right to resist the government and its laws until they were recognized as citizens.[28] In other words, constitutionalists remained focused on the franchise, while militants were concerned with protesting the lack of it. Locally, the different political styles of the NUWSS and WSPU attracted women of different classes. In most provincial cities the NUWSS branch was dominated by middle-class women, and meetings were genteel, often held over tea in private homes. Working-class women were more comfortable at the more informal and more spirited WSPU meetings: Lancashire, where textile women for suffrage aligned themselves with the NUWSS, was an exception to this rule.

The WSPU revolved around its leaders, Emmeline Pankhurst and her daughter Christabel (who expelled her sister Sylvia from the WSPU in 1913 for being insufficiently focused on the vote as the sole political goal). Both women were clever strategists, brilliant speakers, and charismatic leaders who inspired the devotion of their followers. Both were committed to woman-centred politics and all-female political groups and communities, which attracted many women to the WSPU. An early militant, Theresa Billington-Greig (1877–1964), described the atmosphere of the Pankhursts' home as 'reformist, rebellious, revolutionary' and Emmeline as:

> very beautiful, very gracious, very persuasive ... She was ruthless in using the followers who gathered around her as she was ruthless with herself ... a dictator without mercy.[29]

It was Emmeline's conviction that women were being under-served by the socialist movement as well as her dissatisfaction with NUWSS tactics, which she saw as ceremonial and ineffective, that led her to found the WSPU. She was deeply committed to suffragette activism: because of it she gave up paid employment as a local Registrar General, the income from which she badly needed, in 1907. Thereafter she had no home of her own. She was watched by the police and frequently imprisoned; the physical toll of militancy made her an invalid by the start of the First World War.[30]

Christabel Pankhurst was her mother's favourite child; Elizabeth Wolstenholme-Elmy wrote of her 'force and originality'.[31] She was a confident woman who believed that only she could adequately lead the WSPU. In 1912 her belief that her leadership was irreplaceable led her to move to Paris, escaping in disguise to avoid arrest so that she could continue as the WSPU's principal strategist.

The WSPU had few mechanisms for member input or shared governance. In November 1907 a faction led by active militants Theresa Billington-Greig and Charlotte Despard left the WSPU to found the Women's Freedom League, a more democratically organized group committed to non-violent militancy and to a wider feminist agenda than the WSPU. But many women were devoted to the Pankhursts and to the fellowship of the WSPU, which simultaneously encouraged group loyalty to the cause and individual acts in support of it. A member, Annie Kenney, compared life as a militant to life in a convent. She remembered that:

> It was an unwritten rule that there must be no concerts, no theatres, no smoking; work, and sleep to prepare us for more work, was the unwritten order of the day. These rules were good, and the more I look back on those early days the more clearly I see the necessity for such discipline. The changed life into which most of us entered was a revolution in itself.[32]

The WSPU was, for its most involved members, a radically new way of life that symbolized the intensity of their commitment.

The WSPU's motto was 'Deeds, not Words!' and members consistently rejected discussion, compromise, and slow progress in favour of symbolic and highly visible actions. Militants in both the WSPU and the Women's Freedom League argued that traditional political methods had clearly failed the suffrage movement and that a new approach was needed, one that called attention to the cause and attacked the political system that ignored women. Emmeline Pankhurst believed strongly in the importance of passion over reason and in the ability of individuals to bring about dramatic social change through spiritual greatness. Joan of Arc was a frequently invoked WSPU heroine; many posters featured her, and many marches were led by women dressed as her, wearing armour and riding white horses.[33] The militant movement placed great emphasis on individuals and their actions and on transgressive acts in particular. These acts progressed from asking questions at public meetings to destroying property and suffering imprisonment and forcible feeding. In spite of the Pankhursts' autocratic style, many members planned and executed new militant actions on their own initiative; only later would the Pankhursts publicly endorse the new strategy, which often became a widely followed precedent. The more democratic, process-oriented Women's Freedom League endorsed new forms of militancy much more slowly.

NON-VIOLENT MILITANCY

Early suffrage militancy was non-violent, though it challenged notions of appropriate feminine behaviour. It had its roots in Quaker traditions of civil disobedience and passive resistance. It was performed in a world full of political protest: Irish nationalists and members of Josephine Butler's Ladies' National Association had both used similar tactics.[34] The first militant suffragette action came in October 1905 at a Liberal Party rally in Manchester. Christabel Pankhurst held up a flag that read 'Votes for Women' while Annie Kenney demanded to know whether, if the Liberal Party remained in power, it would take up the cause. They were ejected from the meeting. Determined to be arrested, Christabel Pankhurst spat on a police officer and she and Kenney were briefly imprisoned, attracting much press attention; even the respectable *Times* reported it. (Defending her status as a lady, Christabel later wrote that 'it was not a real spit, but only ... a perfectly dry purse of the mouth. I could not *really* have done it, even to get the vote, I think.'[35]) This episode was characteristic of early militancy as an attack on the existing system, in which two women invaded a male political space and insisted on their right to be there. Harassing Liberal politicians during public appearances was a key militant action. Others included poster displays, bicycle parades, street-corner meetings, refusing to co-operate with the police and prison authorities, and resisting paying taxes. The Women's Tax Resistance League (WTRL) was founded in 1909 and attracted suffrage women of all stripes.[36]

Early militancy was often extremely creative. One excellent example is the grille protest. Women could listen to House of Commons debates only from the Ladies' Gallery, which was covered by a metal grille that made women invisible spectators. In October of 1908 Women's Freedom League members Helen Fox and Muriel Matters (1877–1969) chained themselves to the grille while Violet Tillard threw leaflets demanding women's suffrage from the Ladies' Gallery down to the floor of the House (male supporters of the League threw leaflets from the Strangers' Gallery). More Women's Freedom League members protested outside the House. Since Fox and Matters refused to hand over the keys to their chains, the whole grille had to be removed and the women's chains filed off (they were arrested and the Ladies' and Strangers' Galleries were temporarily closed). The grille was never replaced. This well-planned, well-executed and imaginative protest did not succeed in stopping the House's debate that day, but it did call attention to the suffragettes' demands and to the grille that symbolized the exclusion of women from politics.[37] Suffragettes did not simply invade male political spaces; once there they made cogent, symbolic political critiques.

Another non-violent militant moment was the 1908 'Rush the Commons' protest. In October 1908 Christabel Pankhurst, Emmeline Pankhurst, and another WSPU member were summoned to appear in court and explain themselves after having distributed flyers calling on the public to 'rush' the House of Commons demanding votes for women. The day before the proposed action the Pankhursts were arrested (for conduct likely to provoke a breach of the peace). Christabel represented herself in court, and her defence was a more central act of suffrage militancy than the abortive 'rush'. Although she lost the case, her performance was a brilliant piece of political spectacle. She subpoenaed Chancellor David Lloyd George, placed suffrage in the English tradition of popular radical constitutionalism, and cast doubt on the Liberal government's commitment to liberalism and to the constitution itself.[38]

THE MOVEMENT REINVIGORATED

The formation of the WSPU and its early actions invigorated the suffrage movement immeasurably, although not always by strengthening the WSPU itself. Many previously politically inactive women became aware of suffrage because of WSPU militancy, but chose to join the much larger NUWSS because they were more sympathetic to its methods and policies. Between 1907 and 1910 the NUWSS membership increased by over 50,000 women and four hundred new societies, and its income quadrupled. At the same time the WSPU celebrated its small size as indicative of the purity of members' commitment.[39] The two groups worked together for several years in a symbiotic and productive relationship. Many women were members of both their local WSPU and NUWSS chapters, or participated in events sponsored by either group. Many in the WSPU (though not the Pankhursts themselves) conceded that the NUWSS had been crucial in educating the public and creating a national suffrage movement. Many in the NUWSS respected militants even if they did not join them. NUWSS leader Millicent Garrett Fawcett admitted that the huge growth of membership from 1906 was due in large part to the publicity which the WSPU brought to women's suffrage, and she admired the militants' courage. In December 1906 she even organized a banquet in honour of WSPU members who had been recently released from Holloway Prison. This helped to legitimate WSPU militancy in the eyes of many middle-class NUWSS members; its journal *The Common Cause* reported that Fawcett 'did homage to the selfless cause of these women'. Privately Fawcett went even further, telling her friend Lady Balfour that:

> The physical courage of it all is intensely moving. It stirs people as nothing else can. I don't feel it is the right thing and yet the spectacle of so much self-sacrifice moves people to activity who would otherwise sit still and do nothing.[40]

As this comment makes clear, Fawcett chose to interpret WSPU militancy as feminine by seeing suffragettes as self-sacrificing.

In 1907 and 1908 joint militant–constitutionalist demonstrations were held in several provincial cities. Also from about 1908 suffragists and suffragettes were supported by men's auxiliaries like the Men's League for Women's Suffrage, which was affiliated with the Women's Freedom League, and the Men's Social and Political Union, which supported the Women's Social and Political Union. Between 1907 and 1913 the NUWSS and WSPU each executed large public demonstrations in London that drew attention to suffrage and impressed the public and the government by demonstrating the mass support which suffrage enjoyed. These events included the Mud March of February 1907, in which over three thousand women from forty suffrage organizations marched through London's streets to Hyde Park. In June 1908 the NUWSS and WSPU both held rallies in response to the claim of the new Liberal Prime Minister Herbert Asquith that if he were convinced that women really wanted the vote he would support the cause. In the NUWSS demonstration, thousands of people watched over ten thousand women walk from the Embankment to the Albert Hall carrying signs indicating their provincial origins ('Leeds for Liberty'), their work (over one hundred lady doctors marched, as did many clerical workers), their education (university graduates from Royal Holloway, Newnham, and Girton all marched), or their party affiliations (Liberal and Conservative banners were waved). The Women's Freedom League was there, though the WSPU was not. Crowds of spectators looked on and the press coverage, which was extensive, emphasized how organized the event was, how effective as a spectacle, and how dignified and socially diverse its participants.[41]

In the WSPU's 'Women's Sunday', held a week later, a far larger crowd gathered – the WSPU estimated that 500,000 women were there. The WSPU had spent many months and pounds planning and advertising the event: handbills were distributed, sidewalks were chalked, buses were covered with posters, and canvassers visited factories, shops and hospitals calling on women to join them. The WSPU colours of purple, white and green (said to represent justice, purity, and hope) were chosen for this occasion and used widely from that day onwards. Again the press coverage was extensive and positive; *The Times* observed that the occasion was less dignified than the NUWSS rally but displayed 'a high-spirited energy ... not to be found on the earlier occasion'.[42]

VIOLENCE AND IMPRISONMENT

Although many WSPU members continued to choose non-violent forms of militancy such as demonstrations and outdoor meetings, in 1909 some began engaging in acts of violence. They did not hurt other people but they damaged government and private property, setting off hundreds of false fire alarms and throwing stones through the windows of government offices. They also suffered themselves, risking or sacrificing their physical and mental health for the cause.

Suffragettes were frequently arrested and indeed courted imprisonment as a further act of militancy. For a core group of very active WSPU militants, most of whom were middle or upper class, constant arrest became part of a way of life organized around the cause. Seeking to distinguish themselves as political prisoners rather than common criminals, and continuing the process of using their bodies to oppose government actions, they went on hunger strikes in prison. The government retaliated by forcibly feeding them. Prison and force-feeding were difficult experiences that, at least in hindsight (in memoirs written after the war), suffragettes saw as unifying. Descriptions of force-feeding make clear how violating it was. Many suffragettes compared it to rape, just as Contagious

Diseases repealers had done with the internal examination of prostitutes. Suffragette Mary Leigh (1885–1978) described her experience this way:

> The sensation is most painful – the drums of the ears seem to be bursting, a horrible pain in the throat and breast. The tube is pushed down 20 inches. I have to lie on a bed, pinned down by wardresses, one doctor stands up on a chair holding the funnel at arm's length, so as to have the funnel end above the level, and then the other doctor who is behind, forces the other end up the nostrils.
>
> The one holding the funnel end pours the liquid down ... The after effects are a feeling of faintness, a sense of great pain in the diaphragm or breast bone, in the nose and in the ears ...
>
> I have used no violence, though having provocation in being fed by force. I resist and am overcome by weight of numbers.[43]

Mary Richardson emphasized that the physical pain was only one aspect of the unpleasantness; she held that the worst part of being forcibly fed was the 'moral humiliation'.[44]

Force-feeding could be dangerous to militants. The upper-class suffragette Constance Lytton (her father was the first Earl of Lytton and Viceroy of India when Constance was born) was first imprisoned in 1908 but was treated more gently than other suffragettes because of her status and because prison officials knew of her delicate health (she had a weak heart). Enraged by this, Lytton assumed the identity of a working-class woman, Jane Wharton, when she was imprisoned again. This time she was treated the same as all the other suffragettes; the forcible feeding she endured was so violent that it caused a stroke which left her a semi-invalid until her death in 1923 at the age of fifty-four.

The Women's Freedom League and the NUWSS repudiated the use of violence, and began working more independently from the WSPU than before. But these new tactics were empowering for the WSPU members who pursued them. WSPU violence spiralled ever higher, in part because members believed that violence demonstrated greater loyalty to the cause.

THE CONCILIATION BILL

A turning point for suffragists and suffragettes alike came in 1911. Suffragists were losing patience with the Liberal Party and with their own 'best friends' strategy. The Liberal Party, meanwhile, was also struggling to deal with the question of Irish Home Rule and with labour unrest. Prime Minister Asquith was personally hostile and at best politically lukewarm towards women's suffrage. By 1910, however, it was no longer easy for a Prime Minister to dismiss women's suffrage, as opinion had shifted and a majority of Members of Parliament now supported it, while they remained divided over what form it should take. Conservatives had historically favoured granting women the vote on the same terms as men, which would have meant that most enfranchised women would be propertied and therefore, they thought, most likely to vote Conservative. Liberals had wanted to expand the male electorate and at the same time enfranchise all women, a move which would have resulted in most new voters being poor or working-class men and women who were most likely to vote Liberal or Labour. In 1910 a Conciliation Committee was formed to draft a compromise that both sides would accept; the resulting bill would have given the parliamentary vote to women who were already local voters (totalling about one million, mostly unmarried). Called the Conciliation Bill, it (like previous women's suffrage bills) was a private member's bill, but pro-suffrage MPs of all parties were united behind it – as was the NUWSS, albeit with misgivings. As a result, Asquith's government promised to support its passage. The WSPU called a halt to militant actions while the bill was in Parliament. However, in the end Asquith (along with the Chancellor David Lloyd George), undermined the coalition of pro-suffrage MPs and effectively killed the Conciliation Bill.

The betrayal and failure of the Conciliation Bill was the last straw. The NUWSS and WSPU both revised their campaigning strategies, but so differently that from 1912 the schism between them could no longer be countenanced. The NUWSS, furious at Asquith, the Liberal Party, and its alleged supporters in Parliament, abandoned its long-held 'best friends' strategy. NUWSS leaders studied the Conciliation Bill vote carefully and realized that Irish nationalists had not as a group supported women's suffrage. Labour MPs, however, had. The NUWSS decided on a dramatic shift in policy: it formally allied itself with the Labour Party, the only party that had women's suffrage as part of its platform. The NUWSS committed itself to supporting Labour candidates in all elections, regardless of the candidates' individual records on suffrage, even if they ran against Liberals who personally supported it. By backing the Labour Party in this way, the NUWSS hoped to bring pressure to bear on the Liberal government. Many democratically and radically inclined suffragists were delighted with the new policy. No longer would constitutional suffragists try to convince politicians of the justice of their cause; from now on they would simply make it less pleasant for them to resist than to concede. The main tool of this strategy was the newly developed Election Fighting Fund (EFF), a pool of money dedicated to Labour candidates. Its effects were soon felt by Liberal candidates all over the country.

The failure of the Conciliation Bill changed WSPU policies as well. Some WSPU members became more violent and began smashing the windows of stores and churches and pouring acid on golf courses.[45] In December 1911, Emily Wilding Davison set fire to three post-boxes, and by 1914 suffragettes had damaged five thousand letters in this way. In 1914, suffragettes mutilated eleven works of art, most famously the Rokeby Venus in the National Gallery. The slasher was Mary Richardson, who explained that she had

> tried to destroy the picture of the most beautiful woman in mytho-logical history as a protest against the Government destroying Mrs [Emmeline] Pankhurst, who is the most beautiful character in modern history.[46]

Her description of her motives is a reminder of how devoted WSPU militants were to the Pankhursts, how politically symbolic even the most violent militant acts were, and how individually motivated was WSPU militance.

The WSPU also intensified its commitment to women-centred politics as it became more disgusted with male politicians. WSPU rhetoric became markedly anti-male (leaving the auxiliary Men's Social and Political Union in an awkward position). It also emphasized the notion of women as a sex class (stressing that the oppression all women suffered because they were women united them across economic class lines) and the struggle for the vote as a sex war. The most shocking incident of suffragette violence came in the summer of 1913, when Emily Wilding Davison attended Derby Day carrying two pro-suffrage flags and, during a race, rushed at the King's horse. She collided with horse and jockey and died several days later. Although it is unclear whether she intended to commit suicide or died in militant action, the episode shocked the nation; Davison's funeral was a spectacular militant event in itself. The same year the government, tired of the negative publicity it received for forcibly feeding suffragettes, passed the Prisoners' Temporary Discharge for Ill

Health Act, popularly known as the Cat and Mouse Act. It allowed hunger-striking suffragettes to be released and then reimprisoned to complete their sentences when they had regained their physical strength. Emmeline Pankhurst was the first to be released under this Act, which ended force-feeding and is indicative of the uncomfortable position into which militants had put the government.

By the summer of 1914 WSPU members had become so focused on their protests that engaging in the struggle for the vote seemed more important than the vote itself. As the WSPU became more extreme, it grew smaller and more tightly bound; by 1914 the group was so small, so financially strapped, and so violent that it no longer seemed a politically credible body (the fact that Christabel Pankhurst insisted on leading the organization from exile in Paris did not help matters). Meanwhile the NUWSS's new Labour-affiliated strategy and EFF seemed to be effective; the campaign had reached a point where no politician or government could fail to have an opinion on, and plan for, women's suffrage. By the end of the summer of 1914, with an election coming up, suffragists were hopeful that a new Liberal government would (and a new Conservative government might) back women's suffrage.

Then, in August 1914, Britain entered the First World War. This changed the work and actions of suffrage women significantly. The Pankhursts adopted a nationalistic and patriotic stance, declaring an end to all suffragette militancy for the duration of the war and devoting themselves to pro-war activities. (This did not sit well with the many radical and democratic women in the WSPU, who were less supportive of the war.) In response, the government released all imprisoned suffragettes. The WSPU's suffrage militancy thereby ended with a whimper. The NUWSS also declared that it would cease its political activities during the war, though it defined politics quite narrowly and continued with many of its efforts. A newer society, the United Suffragists (founded in February 1914), continued to press for the vote in their publications.

By 1916 it was clear that the next government would pass a new reform bill in which women would be included, and on 6 February 1918 (after much compromise and wrangling) the Representation of the People Act finally enfranchised women over thirty who were on the local government register or who were wives of men who were, who occupied property that had an annual rent of at least £5, or who were graduates of British universities. Obstacles still remained: the age limit was set because older women were thought to be less radical than younger women; many women teachers, who were active in the movement, lived with parents or in lodgings and so were denied the vote; the local government requirement excluded many working-class women. But the sex barrier had been broken and 8.4 million women were enfranchised, comprising almost 40 per cent of the new electorate. Millicent Garrett Fawcett considered the day of its passage the greatest of her life. (Ten years later, on 2 July 1928, another Act gave women and men aged twenty-one or over the vote on equal terms. At this point women had won full parliamentary voting rights.)

Many have argued that the vote was a recompense for women's war work. But while the war may have provided a comfortable excuse for many politicians who finally acquiesced after years of resistance to women's suffrage, most war workers were younger than thirty and so remained unrewarded. However, it must be said that the radical dislocations of the First World War, including the prominence of women in many critical war-related fields, had changed the terms of the debate over women's contributions to the nation. While the war was one factor, it is also true that suffrage women won the vote, after years of campaigning, through their own political efforts. In European countries without well-developed suffrage movements (such as France and Italy), women remained unenfranchised.

The winning of the vote for women was the culmination of years of work by generations of suffrage women. They were not a unified group: their different political beliefs, strategic approaches, socio-economic backgrounds, and personal lives made the movement for women's suffrage diverse and sometimes bitterly divided. That women were denied the vote for so long reveals the degree to which parliamentary politics, even as it became more democratized, was still seen by most as an inherently male preserve. That such a large and varied group of women were all working towards the same goal tells us much about how important the vote had become in English politics. Winning the vote was a great victory.

CONCLUSION

THE GOAL OF this book has been to demonstrate the wide range of English women's activities during the long nineteenth century, in spite of the serious constraints under which they lived. The tension between the restrictions imposed upon women and women's response to them was a key feature of English society.

Limits on women's actions were variously imposed by forces including custom, law, religion, and science, and meant that women had different experiences from men in every aspect of life. Girls were not as well-educated as boys, and women were considered less rational than men. Throughout their lives women needed to protect their reputations to remain respectable. Sexually, they were seen as passionless (or suffered the consequences if they acted otherwise). For young women, courting meant risking an illegitimate pregnancy that could lead to poverty or disgrace. Even if they had no children, those who did not marry were seen as a burden to society; some emigrated to parts of the British Empire to find jobs and husbands. For the majority of women, who did marry (in England, India, or another part of the Empire), pregnancies were frequent and life-threatening. As wives, women lost many of their legal rights, and they were less able than men to initiate divorce or to maintain custody of their children. As adults, they were expected to run their households, act as the main consumers for their families, and care for their children. As employees, they were key players in industrialization and the growth of white-collar tasks, but were never valued or respected for their work. They had fewer employment opportunities and earned less than men. In old age, they were at greater risk of poverty. They were excluded from formal politics.

Yet women led full and fulfilling lives. Throughout the long nineteenth century they worked, went to church, raised (and sometimes buried) their children, and cared for their families; they read and wrote pamphlets, essays, and books; they gave money to charities they cared about, and political energy to issues they thought important, in England and in the

British Empire. They worked to ameliorate suffering, especially that of women and children, in places as disparate as Jamaican slave-holding plantations, English workhouses, and Indian zenanas.

The long nineteenth century witnessed important changes. Girls and women of all classes saw their educational opportunities expand; by 1914 almost all English women were literate, many were educated, and a few even attended university. Partly as a result of this, occupational choices expanded too. Working-class women could choose work other than manual labour; middle-class women could earn money without compromising their respectability. Women could act as individuals rather than as men's assistants, as, for example, in the shift from missionary wives to female missionaries. Thousands of women were active in the campaign for women's suffrage. Sexual options, too, had broadened, to include celibacy, non-marital sex, and lesbianism; none were considered wholly womanly, but all were at least acceptable in certain circles.

As I hope has been made clear, many of the positive changes in women's social and economic standing came about as the result of feminism. From the 1850s, prolific feminist writing helped to change attitudes about women and gender. Feminists were instrumental in opening new schools, jobs and professions to women. They worked to improve the lives of disadvantaged women in England and the British Empire and served their communities in a variety of positions – as did many women who were not feminists. Feminist political action, particularly their lobbying of Parliament, improved women's lives enormously. Feminists were not wholly admirable: many of their beliefs and practices were shaped by racial and class biases that excluded some women and mistreated others. But their work did more to improve women's lives than any other force during the long nineteenth century.

Other forces, too, combined to transform women's lives. The process of industrialization and the growth of white-collar and bureaucratic work expanded women's employment opportunities. So too did changes in education, especially the establishment of state elementary schools and academic grammar schools. Developments in public health led to safer homes and healthier families, even in the poorest urban areas. Changes in public policy led to safety nets, such as national health insurance, that made many women's lives easier. Religion was, throughout our period, an area in which women could express themselves and exert some authority. The Empire was of interest to many women, who variously promoted it, purchased its products, protested against its policies, sought to manage it, or lived in it. Various movements and institutions, from small fringe groups to the Conservative, Liberal, and Labour Parties, provided ways for women to work politically. As with feminism, many women not only benefited from these opportunities but were instrumental in creating them.

Most importantly, women were neither passive victims nor spectators. They were active participants who helped to create the society in which they lived. The history of England during the long nineteenth century is, to a large extent, the history of English women.

APPENDIX

English Money during the Long Nineteenth Century

Between 1760 and 1914 English currency was a bit different from that of today. While today a pound has one hundred pence in it, then a pound had two hundred and forty pence. The pound sign was '£'; shillings were 's.' and pence were 'd.'. The most common units, in addition to those three, were the crown and the half-crown. Neither florins nor double florins were ever very popular. The system worked as follows:

Coin/note	Value	Written and described as
Guinea	21 shillings (one pound, one shilling)	1 g. or 1 gn.; not minted after 1813; used mostly for luxury goods
Sovereign (or £1 note, rare)	1 pound (20 shillings)	£1 (there were also £5, £10, £20, and £50 notes; these were more common than £1 notes)
Half-sovereign coin (or half-£ note)	10 shillings (120 pence)	10s. or 10/-
Crown	5 shillings (60 pence)	5s.
Half-crown	2½ shillings (30 pence)	2s. 6d. Very popular currency
Florin (or 2 shilling piece)	2 shillings (24 pence)	2s. or 2/-(introduced in 1849; there was also a double florin from 1887)
shilling	1 shilling (12 pence)	1s. (= 12d.) (also called a 'bob')
sixpence	6 pence	6d.
groat	4 pence	4d.
threepence	3 pence	3d. ('thruppence')
twopence	2 pence	2d. ('tuppence')

Coin/note	Value	Written and described as
penny	1 penny	1d. ('copper')
halfpenny	½ penny	
farthing	¼ penny	
half-farthing	⅛ penny	

Sums of money were written out in their value in pounds, shillings and pence; £5 2s. 3d. was five pounds, two shillings and threepence. Amounts under a pound were also written using slashes; 6s. 3d. could be written as 6/3d (pronounced 'six and three').

NOTES

Introduction

1 See for example Kelly Boyd, *Manliness and the Boys' Story Paper in Britain: A Cultural History, 1855–1940* (Palgrave, Basingstoke, 2003); Tim Hitchcock and Michele Cohen, eds., *English Masculinities, 1660–1800* (Addison-Wesley, London, 1999); Michael Roper and John Tosh, eds., *Manful Assertions: Masculinities in Britain since 1800* (Routledge, London, 1991).

2 See for example Esther Breitenbach and Eleanor Gordon, eds., *Out of Bounds: Women in Scottish Society, 1800–1945* (Edinburgh UP, Edinburgh, 1992); Angela V. John, ed., *Our Mothers' Land: Chapters in Welsh Women's History, 1830–1939* (U. Wales P, Cardiff, 1991); Margaret Kelleher and James H. Murphy, eds., *Gender Perspectives in Nineteenth-Century Ireland: Public and Private Spheres* (Irish Academic Press, Dublin, 1997).

3 Mike Savage and Andrew Miles, *The Remaking of the British Working Class 1840–1940* (Routledge, London, 1994), p. 59.

4 *New York Times*, 20 May 2003, p. B2.

5 Stella Tillyard, *Aristocrats: Caroline, Emily, Louisa, and Sarah Lennox, 1740–1832* (Noonday Press, New York, 1994), p. 76.

6 Simon Sretzer, *Fertility, Class and Gender in Britain, 1860–1940* (CUP, Cambridge, 1996), p. 1.

7 Robert Millward and Frances Bell, 'Infant Mortality in Victorian Britain: The Mother as Medium', *Economic History Review* 54.4 (2001), p. 699; Sretzer, p. 295.

8 Robert Woods, *The Demography of Victorian England and Wales* (CUP, Cambridge, 2000), p. 116; Sretzer, pp. 1, 295; Millward and Bell, p. 727.

1 Working-class Women

1 Mike Savage and Andrew Miles, *The Remaking of the British Working Class 1840–1940* (Routledge, London, 1994), pp. 39–40.

2 Peter Earle, 'The Female Labour Market in London in the Late Seventeenth and Early Eighteenth Centuries', *Economic History Review* 42.3 (1989), pp. 339–42.

3 Jane Humphries, 'Women and Paid Work', in June Purvis, ed., *Women's History: Britain, 1850–1945, An Introduction* (2000; Routledge, London, 1995), p. 91.

4 Joyce Burnette, 'An Investigation of the Female-Male Wage Gap During the

Industrial Revolution in Britain', *Economic History Review* 50.2 (1997), pp. 264–5.

5 Eric J. Evans, *The Forging of the Modern State: Early Industrial Britain 1783–1870* (Longman, New York, 1996), pp. 129–130; Nicola Verdon, ' " Physically a splendid race" or "hardened and brutalised by unsuitable toil"?: Unravelling the Position of Women Workers in Rural England during the Golden Age of Agriculture', in Ian Inkster, ed., *The Golden Age: Essays in British Social and Economic History, 1850–1870* (Ashgate, Aldershot, 2000), p. 231.

6 Carol E. Morgan, *Women Workers and Gender Identities, 1835–1913: The Cotton and Metal Industries in England* (Routledge, London, 2001), p. 139; Deborah Valenze, *The First Industrial Woman* (OUP, New York, 1995), pp. 48–67.

7 Katrina Honeyman, *Women, Gender, and Industrialisation in England, 1700–1870* (Macmillan, London, 2000), p. 73; Joanna Bourke, 'Housewifery in Working-Class England 1860–1914', *Past and Present* 143.2 (May 1994), p. 168; Maxine Berg, 'What Difference Did Women's Work Make to the Industrial Revolution?', in Pamela Sharpe, ed., *Women's Work: The English Experience 1650–1914* (Edward Arnold, London, 1998), p. 168.

8 Trevor May, *An Economic and Social History of Britain 1760–1970* (Longman, Harlow, 1987), pp. 53, 56.

9 Ellen Ross, *Love and Toil: Motherhood in Outcast London 1870–1918* (OUP, Oxford, 1993), pp. 50–1.

10 Ross, p. 58.

11 Ross, pp. 12, 63; Ellen Ross, ' "Not the Sort that Would Sit on the Doorstep": Respectability in Pre-World War I London Neighborhoods', *International Labor and Working-Class History* 27 (1985), pp. 42–6; Anna Davin, *Growing Up Poor: Home, School, and Street in London, 1870–1914* (Oram Rivers Press, London, 1996), pp. 69–72.

12 Quoted in Bourke, pp. 173–4.

13 Evans, p. 162; Pamela Sharpe, 'The Female Labour Market in English Agriculture During the Industrial Revolution: Expansion or Contraction?', *Agricultural History Review* 47.2 (1999), p. 168; Nicola Verdon, 'The Employment of Women and Children in Agriculture: A Reassessment of Agricultural Gangs in Nineteenth-Century Norfolk', *Agricultural History Review* 49.1 (2001), p. 44; Nicola Verdon, 'The Rural Labour Market in the Early Nineteenth Century: Women's and Children's Employment, Family Income, and the 1834 Poor Law Report', *Economic History Review* 55.2 (2002), pp. 304, 314; Verdon in Inkster, ed., p. 234.

14 Verdon in Inkster, ed., K. D. M. Snell, 'Agricultural Seasonal Unemployment, the Standard of Living, and Women's Work, 1690–1860', in Sharpe, ed., *Women's Work*, p. 54; Verdon, 'The Rural Labour Market', p. 304.

15 Verdon, 'The Employment of Women and Children', p. 41.

16 Evans, p. 149; Verdon in Inkster, ed., p. 229; Snell, pp. 78 90.

17 Verdon in Inkster, ed., p. 230.

18 Flora Thompson, *Lark Rise to Candleford* (3 vols., originally published in 1939, 1941, 1943; trilogy published in 1945, reprinted OUP, London, 1946), pp. 148–49.

19 Valenze, p. 169; Cecillie Swaisland, *Servants and Gentlewomen to the Golden Land: The Emigration of Single Women from Britain to Southern Africa, 1820–1939* (U Natal P, Berg, 1993), p. 13.

20 Mrs Isabella Beeton, *The Book of Household Management* (S. O. Beeton, London, 1861; fascimile edn, Jonathan Cape, London, 1986), p. 8; Donald Read, *The Age of Urban Democracy: England 1868–1914, rev. edn* (Longman, London, 1994), p. 237.

21 Quoted in *The Diaries of Hannah Cullwick, Victorian Maidservant,* ed. Liz Stanley (Rutgers UP, New Brunswick, NJ, 1984), p. 114.

22 Quoted in Lucia Zedner, *Women, Crime, and Custody in Victorian England* (Clarendon Press, Oxford, 1991), p. 67.

23 I am grateful to Marjorie Levine-Clark for supplying me with these quotes from her work, *Beyond the Reproductive Body: The Politics of Women's Health and Work in Early Victorian England* (Ohio State UP, Columbus, 2004), before its publication.

24 Quoted in Judith R. Walkowitz, *Prostitution and Victorian Society: Women, Class, and the State* (CUP, Cambridge, 1980), p. 194.

25 From the Bethnal Green police report from 7 Sept. 1888 on the Mary Ann (Polly) Nichols murder, reprinted in Stewart P. Evans and Keith Skinner, eds., *The Ultimate Jack the Ripper Sourcebook* (Robinson, London, 2000), p. 24. I am grateful to Rohan McWilliam for this anecdote and citation.

26 Kathryn Gleadle, *British Women in the Nineteenth Century* (Palgrave, Basingstoke, 2001), p. 100.

27 Quoted in Morgan, p. 34.

28 A. B., *Observations on the detriment that it is supposed must arise to the family of every cottager throughout the kingdom from the loss of woollen spinning by the introduction of machines for that work* (1794), p. 7. Italics are in the original.

29 From *The Manufacturing Population of England* (1833), p. 147, quoted in Jane Rendall, *The Origins of Modern Feminism: Women in Britain, France, and the United States, 1780–1860* (Schocken Books, New York, 1984), pp. 195–6.

30 Ivy Pinchbeck, *Women Workers and the Industrial Revolution 1750–1850* (originally published in 1930; Virago, London, 1981), pp. 191–3; Sonya O. Rose, *Limited Livelihoods: Gender and Class in Nineteenth-Century England* (U California P, Berkeley, 1992), pp. 32, 158, 244–5.

31 Pinchbeck, p. 187.

32 Quoted from the *Report of the Select Committee on Factory Children's Labour,* Parliamentary Papers, vol. XV, 1831–1832, pp. 195, 197.

33 Sophie Hamilton, 'Images of Femininity in the Royal Commissions of the

1830s and 1840s', in Eileen Janes Yeo, ed., *Radical Femininity: Women's Self-Representation in the Public Sphere* (Manchester UP, Manchester, 1998), p. 82.

34 Quoted in Harriet Bradley, 'Frames of Reference: Skill, Gender and New Technology in the Hosiery Industry', in Gertjan de Groot and Marlou Schrover, eds., *Women Workers and Technological Change in Europe in the Nineteenth and Twentieth Centuries* (Taylor & Francis, London, 1995), p. 26.

35 Morgan, pp. 21–43.

36 Morgan, p. 70.

37 Anna Clark, *The Struggle for the Breeches: Gender and the Making of the British Working Class* (U California P, Berkeley, 1995), p. 177.

38 Pinchbeck, pp. 113–14. Crompton's memories are quoted from Gilbert James French, *The Life and Times of Samuel Crompton* (London, 1859).

39 Quoted in Eileen Yeo and E. P. Thompson, *The Unknown Mayhew* (Pantheon, New York, 1971), pp. 120–2.

40 Quoted in Judy Lown, *Women and Industrialization: Gender at Work in Nineteenth-Century England* (U Minnesota P, Minneapolis, 1990), p. 13.

41 Quoted in Sally Alexander, 'Women's Work in Nineteenth-Century London: A Study of the Years 1820–50', in Elizabeth Whitelegg et al., eds., *The Changing Experience of Women* (Martin Robertson, Oxford, 1982), p. 37.

42 Quoted in *The Unknown Mayhew*, p. 148.

43 Quoted in *The Unknown Mayhew*, pp. 149–51.

44 From the Staffordshire Record Office, Stourbridge Union, Kingswinford District, Application and Report Books, 16, 23, and 30 July, 1891, D585/1/5/73; I am grateful to Marjorie Levine-Clark for providing me with this citation.

45 Peter Bailey, 'White Collars, Gray Lives? The Lower Middle Class Revisited', *Journal of British Studies* 38.3 (July 1999), p. 284.

46 Lee Holcombe, *Victorian Ladies at Work: Middle-Class Working Women in England and Wales 1850–1914* (Archon Books, Hamden, CT, 1973), pp. 19–20.

47 Dina M. Copelman, *London's Women Teachers: Gender, Class and Feminism 1870–1930* (Routledge, London, 1996), p. 152; Susan D. Pennybacker, *A Vision For London 1889–1914: Labour, Everyday Life and the LCC Experiment* (Routledge, London, 1995), p. 47.

48 Copelman, pp. 76–7.

49 Gregory Anderson, 'The White-Blouse Revolution', in Gregory Anderson, ed., *The White-Blouse Revolution: Female Office Workers since 1870* (Manchester UP, Manchester, 1988), p. 9.

50 Meta Zimmeck, 'Jobs for the Girls: the Expansion of Clerical Work for Women, 1850–1914', in Angela V. John, ed., *Unequal Opportunities: Women's Employment in England 1800–1918* (Basil Blackwell, Oxford, 1986), p. 158.

51 Susanne Dohrn, 'Pioneers in a Dead-End Profession: The First Women Clerks in Banks and Insurance Companies', in Gregory Anderson, ed., p. 57.

52 Zimmeck, p. 169; Anderson, 'The White-Blouse Revolution', p. 4; Samuel

Cohn, *The Process of Occupational Sex-Typing: The Feminization of Clerical Labor in Great Britain* (Temple UP, Philadelphia, 1985), p. 26.

53 Ellen Jordan, 'The Lady Clerks at the Prudential: The Beginnings of Vertical Segregation by Sex in Clerical Work in Nineteenth-Century Britain', *Gender and History* 8.1 (April 1996), p. 66; Anderson, 'The White-Blouse Revolution', p. 9; Copelman, pp. 76–7.

54 Jane E. Lewis, 'Women Clerical Workers in the Late Nineteenth and Early Twentieth Centuries', in Gregory Anderson, ed., p. 43; Zimmeck, p. 164.

55 Copelman, p. 32.

56 Copelman, pp. 143–4; Holcombe, p. 36.

57 Copelman, pp. 105, 157.

58 Holcombe, p. 43; Copelman, pp. 77, 199.

59 Copelman, pp. 153, 185.

2 Middle-class Women

1 Margaret R. Hunt, *The Middling Sort: Commerce, Gender, and the Family in England, 1680–1780* (U California P, Berkeley, 1996), p. 17.

2 Gladys Carnaffan, 'Commercial education and the Female Office Worker', in Gregory Anderson, ed., *The White-Blouse Revolution: Female Office Workers since 1870* (Manchester UP, Manchester, 1988), p. 82.

3 Hunt, p. 15.

4 Quoted in Dorice Williams Elliott, ' "The Care of the Poor is her Profession": Hannah More and Women's Philanthropic Work', *Nineteenth-Century Contexts* 19 (1995), p. 195.

5 Julia Bush, *Edwardian Ladies and Imperial Power* (Leicester UP, London, 2000), p. 73.

6 Patricia Branca, *Silent Sisterhood: Middle-Class Women in the Victorian Home* (Carnegie-Mellon UP, Pittsburgh, 1975), p. 22.

7 Branca, p. 47.

8 Branca, pp. 48–51.

9 Mrs Isabella Beeton, *The Book of Household Management* (S.O. Beeton, London, 1861; fascimile edn, Jonathan Cape, London, 1986), pp. 5, 6, 37.

10 Quoted in Leonore Davidoff and Catherine Hall, *Family Fortunes: Men and Women of the English Middle Class, 1780–1850* (U Chicago P, Chicago, 1987), p. 339.

11 Elizabeth Gurney Fry, *The Memoir of the Life of Elizabeth Fry, with extracts from her journal and letters. Edited by two of her daughters* (J.W. Moore, Philadelphia, 1847), vol. 1, pp. 17–18.

12 Fry, p. 16.

13 Davidoff and Hall, pp. 281–3.

14 Quoted in Davidoff and Hall, p. 304.

15 Mary Poovey, *The Proper Lady and the Woman Writer: Ideology as Style in the*

Works of Mary Wollstonecraft, Mary Shelley, and Jane Austen (U Chicago P, Chicago, 1984), p. 210.

16 Marlene Tromp, Pamela K. Gilbert, Aeron Haynie, 'Introduction', in Marlene Tromp, Pamela K. Gilbert, Aeron Haynie, eds., *Beyond Sensation: Mary Elizabeth Braddon in Context* (State U of NY P, Albany, 2000), pp. xv, xviii, xxii; Marlene Tromp, 'The Dangerous Woman', in Tromp, Gilbert, Haynie, eds., pp. 94–5.

17 Poovey, pp. 35–7, 39, 241.

18 Quoted in Elsie B. Michie, *Outside the Pale: Cultural Exclusion, Gender Difference, and the Victorian Woman Writer* (Cornell UP, Ithaca and London, 1993), p. 83.

19 Sally Mitchell, *Dinah Mulock Craik* (Twayne, Boston, 1983), pp. 7–8.

20 Quoted in Olive Banks, *Faces of Feminism: A Study of Feminism as a Social Movement* (Basil Blackwell, Oxford, 1981), p. 14.

21 Alex Tyrell, ' "Woman's Mission" and Pressure Group Politics in Britain (1825–60)', *Bulletin of the John Rylands University Library of Manchester*, 63.1 (1980), p. 205.

22 F. K. Prochaska, *Women and Philanthropy in Nineteenth-Century England* (Clarendon Press, Oxford, 1980), pp. 21–7.

23 Prochaska, pp. 47–71.

24 Quoted in F. K. Prochaska, 'Charity Bazaars in Nineteenth-Century England', *Journal of British Studies* 16.2 (Spring 1977), pp. 80, 82.

25 Quoted in Emma Curtin, 'Gentility Afloat: Gentlewomen's Diaries and the Voyage to Australia, 1830–80', *Australian Historical Studies* 105 (1995), p. 640.

26 Paula Bartley, *Prostitution: Prevention and Reform in England, 1860–1914* (Routledge, London, 2000), pp. 27–8.

27 Prochaska, *Women and Philanthropy*, pp. 140–71.

28 Prochaska, *Women and Philanthropy*, pp. 175–80; Theresa Deane, 'Late Nineteenth-Century Philanthropy: The Case of Louisa Twining', in Anne Digby and John Stewart, eds., *Gender, Health and Welfare* (Routledge, London, 1996), pp. 122–42.

29 Louisa Twining, 'Workhouse Cruelties', *Nineteenth Century* (Dec. 1890), p. 709.

30 Ann B. Shteir, *Cultivating Women, Cultivating Science: Flora's Daughters and Botany in England 1760 to 1860* (Johns Hopkins UP, Baltimore, 1996).

31 Ellen Jordan, *The Women's Movement and Women's Employment in Nineteenth Century Britain* (Routledge, London, 1999), p. 84.

32 Deane, p. 126.

33 Jordan, p. 168.

34 Ellen Jordan, 'The Lady Clerks at the Prudential: The Beginnings of Vertical Segregation by Sex in Clerical Work in Nineteenth-Century Britain', *Gender and History* 8.1 (April 1996), p. 66.

35 Ellen Jordan, ' "Suitable and Remunerative Employment": The Feminization of Hospital Dispensing in Late Nineteenth-Century England', *Social History of Medicine* 15.3 (2002), pp. 429–56.

36 Anne Summers, 'The Costs and Benefits of Caring: Nursing Charities, *c.* 1830–1860', in Jonathan Barry and Colin Jones, eds., *Medicine and Charity Before the Welfare State* (Routledge, London, 1991), p. 134.

37 Quoted in Martha Vicinus, *Independent Women: Work and Community for Single Women 1850–1920* (U Chicago P, Chicago, 1985), p. 114.

38 Jordan, *The Women's Movement*, p. 136.

39 Quoted in Judith Moore, *A Zeal for Responsibility: The Struggle for Professional Nursing in Victorian England, 1868–1883* (U Georgia P, Athens, 1988), p. 171.

40 Vicinus, p. 90.

41 Quoted in Carol Helmstadter, 'Old Nurses and New: Nursing in the London Teaching Hospitals Before and After the Mid-c19 Reforms', *Nursing History Review* 1 (1993), p. 64.

42 Dina M. Copelman, *London's Women Teachers: Gender, Class and Feminism 1870–1930* (Routledge, London, 1996), p. 18.

43 Quoted in Vicinus, p. 175.

44 Fernanda Perrone, 'Women Academics in England, 1870–1930,' *History of Universities* 12 (1993), p. 348.

45 Perrone, p. 360.

46 Quoted in Copelman, p. 10.

47 Copelman, p. 74.

48 Copelman, p. 161.

49 Quoted in Jane Martin, *Women and the Politics of Schooling in Victorian and Edwardian England* (Leicester UP, London, 1999), p. 1.

50 Louisa Twining, 'Women as Public Servants', *Nineteenth Century* (November 1886), pp. 952–3.

51 Emmeline Pankhurst, *My Own Story* (1971 rpt, Kraus Reprint Co.; Hearst's International Library, New York, 1914), pp. 24–7.

52 Ronald G. Walton, *Women in Social Work* (Routledge, London, 1975), p. 30.

53 Martin, pp. 26–8; Jane Lewis, *Women in England 1870–1950: Sexual Divisions and Social Change* (Wheatsheaf, Brighton, Sussex, 1984), p. 94.

54 Quoted in Caroline Morrell, 'Octavia Hill and Women's Networks in Housing', in Anne Digby and John Stewart, eds., p. 95.

55 Quoted in Katharine Bentley Beauman, *Women and the Settlement Movement* (Radcliffe Press, Cambridge, Mass., 1996), p. 61.

56 Quoted in Mary Drake McFeely, *Lady Inspectors: the Campaign for a Better Workplace, 1893–1921* (U Georgia P, Athens, 1991), p. 8.

57 Quoted in McFeely, p. 36.

58 Carol Dyhouse, 'Driving Ambitions: Women in Pursuit of a Medical Education, 1890–1939', *Women's History Review* 7.3 (1998), p. 321.

59 Quoted in Jo Manton, *Elizabeth Garrett Anderson* (E. P. Dutton, New York, 1965), p. 147.

60 I am grateful to Geraldine Forbes for making a version of her forthcoming *Dictionary of National Biography* entry on Fanny Butler available to me prior to publication via personal communication, December 2003.

61 Nan H. Dreher, 'Redundancy and Emigration: The "Woman Question" in Mid-Victorian Britain', *Victorian Periodicals Review* 26 (1993), p. 6.

3 Elite Women

 1 Trevor May, *An Economic and Social History of Britain 1760–1970* (Longman, Harlow, 1987), p. 71.

 2 Judith S. Lewis, *In the Family Way: Childbearing in the British Aristocracy, 1760–1860* (Rutgers UP, New Brunswick, NJ, 1986), p. 71; David Cannadine, *The Decline and Fall of the British Aristocracy* (Yale UP, New Haven, 1990), p. xiv; Lawrence E. Klein, 'Politeness and the Interpretation of the British Eighteenth Century', *Historical Journal* 45.4 (Dec. 2002), pp. 869–98.

 3 Elaine Chalus, 'Elite Women, Social Politics, and the Political World of Late Eighteenth-Century England', *Historical Journal* 43.3 (2000), p. 669.

 4 Lewis, p. 61.

 5 Pat Jalland, *Women, Marriage and Politics, 1860–1914* (Clarendon Press, Oxford, 1986), p. 175.

 6 Lewis, pp. 124–7, 209.

 7 Jessica Gerard, *Country House Life: Family and Servants, 1815–1914* (Basil Blackwell, Oxford, 1994), pp. 66, 76.

 8 Lady Maud Leconfield, ed., *Three Howard Sisters: Selections From the Writings of Lady Caroline Lascelles, Lady Dover and Countess Gower 1825 to 1833* (John Murray, London, 1955), p. 41.

 9 K. D. Reynolds, *Aristocratic Women and Political Society in Victorian Britain* (Clarendon Press, Oxford, 1998), p. 32.

10 Pamela Sharpe, 'Gender in the Economy: Female Merchants and Family Businesses in the British Isles, 1600–1850', *Histoire Sociale/Social History*, 34 (2001), p. 304.

11 Consuelo Vanderbilt Balsan, *The Glitter and the Gold* (Harper and Brothers, New York, 1952), p. 87; Gerard, pp. 123, 126–7.

12 Peter Mandler 'From Almack's to Willis's: Aristocratic Women and Politics, 1815–1867', in Amanda Vickery, ed., *Women, Privilege, and Power: British Politics, 1750 to the Present* (Stanford UP, Stanford, 2001), pp. 161, 165.

13 Reynolds, p. 91.

14 Quoted in Maurice J. Quinlan, *Victorian Prelude: A History of English Manners 1700–1830* (Columbia UP, New York, 1941), p. 157.

15 Dorice Williams Elliott, ' "The Care of the Poor is her Profession": Hannah

More and Women's Philanthropic Work', *Nineteenth-Century Contexts* 19 (1995), p. 181.

16 Quoted in Quinlan, p. 156.

17 Quoted in Reynolds, p. 90.

18 Mandler, p. 165.

19 Elaine Chalus, 'Women, Electoral Privilege and Practice in the Eighteenth Century', in Kathryn Gleadle and Sarah Richardson, eds., *Women in British Politics, 1760–1860: The Power of the Petticoat* (Macmillan Press, Basingstoke, 2000), pp. 20, 21, 34.

20 Quoted in Matthew Cragoe, ' "Jenny Rules the Roost": Women and Electoral Politics 1832–1868', Gleadle and Richardson, eds., pp. 155–6, italics in original. The second example comes from the borough of Brecon, in Wales.

21 Chalus, 'Elite Women', pp. 677, 683, 687.

22 Quoted in Revel Guest and Angela V. John, *Lady Charlotte: A Biography of the Nineteenth Century* (Weidenfeld & Nicolson, London, 1989), p. 80.

23 Quoted in K. D. Reynolds, 'Politics Without Feminism: The Victorian Political Hostess', in Clarissa Campbell Orr, ed., *Wollstonecraft's Daughters: Womanhood in England and France 1780–1920* (Manchester UP, Manchester, 1996), p. 102.

24 Quoted in Jonathan Schneer, *London 1900: The Imperial Metropolis* (Yale UP, London (7:1), 1999), p. 125.

25 Julia Bush, *Edwardian Ladies and Imperial Power* (Leicester UP, London, 2000), p. 18.

26 Nancy Ellenberger, 'The Transformation of London "Society" at the End of Victoria's Reign: Evidence from the Court Presentation Records', *Albion* 22.4 (Winter 1990), p. 637.

27 Martin Pugh, *The Tories and the People 1880–1935* (Basil Blackwell, Oxford, 1985), p. 47; Linda Walker, 'Party Political Women: A Comparative Study of Liberal Women and the Primrose League, 1890–1914', in Jane Rendall, ed., *Equal or Different: Women's Politics 1800–1914* (Basil Blackwell, Oxford, 1987), p. 172.

28 Linda Colley, 'The Apotheosis of George III: Loyalty, Royalty, and the British Nation 1760–1820', *Past and Present* 102 (1984), p. 125; O. Hedley, 'George III and Life at Windsor', *History Today* 25 (1975), pp. 749–60.

29 Quoted in Colley, 'The Apotheosis of George III', p. 125.

30 Linda Colley, *Britons: Forging the Nation 1707–1837* (Yale UP, New Haven, 1992), pp. 268–70.

31 Stephen C. Behrendt, *Royal Mourning and Regency Culture: Elegies and Memorials of Princess Charlotte* (Macmillan, Basingstoke, 1997), p. 38.

32 Letters dated 8 and 16 Nov. 1817, from Virginia Surtees, ed., *A Second Self: The Letters of Harriet Granville 1810–1845* (Michael Russell Ltd., The Chantry, Wilton, 1990), pp. 118–19.

33 Lewis, *In the Family Way*, p. 187.

34 Colley, *Britons*, p. 272.

35 Behrendt, pp. 90, 120, 236.

36 Margaret Homans, *Royal Representations: Queen Victoria and British Culture, 1837–1876* (U Chicago P, Chicago, 1998), p. 227.

37 Quoted in Richard Hough, *Victoria and Albert* (St Martin's Press, New York, 1996), p. 33; italics in original.

38 Quoted in Dorothy Thompson, *Queen Victoria: The Woman, The Monarchy, The People* (Pantheon, New York, 1990), p. 38.

39 F. K. Prochaska, *Royal Bounty: The Making of a Welfare Monarchy* (Yale UP, New Haven, 1995), pp. 77–80.

40 Lewis, *In the Family Way*, p. 211.

41 Homans, pp. 3–4.

42 William Kuhn, *Democratic Royalism: The Transformation of the British Monarchy, 1861–1914* (Macmillan, Basingstoke, 1996), p. 29.

43 Reynolds, *Aristocratic Women*, pp. 190–220.

44 Reynolds, *Aristocratic Women*, p. 209.

45 Richard Williams, *The Contentious Crown: Public Discussion of the British Monarchy in the Reign of Queen Victoria* (Ashgate, Aldershot, 1997), p. 31.

46 Homans, p. 163.

47 Homans, p. 101.

48 Thomas Richards, 'The Image of Victoria in the Year of Jubilee', *Victorian Studies* 31.1 (Autumn 1987), pp. 17, 19.

49 David Cannadine, 'The Context, Performance and Meaning of Ritual: The British Monarchy and the "Invention of Tradition", c. 1820–1977', in Eric Hobsbawm and Terence Ranger, eds., *The Invention of Tradition* (Cambridge UP, Cambridge, 1983), p. 134.

4 Sexuality

1 Thomas W. Laqueur, 'Orgasm, Generation, and the Politics of Reproductive Biology', *Representations* 14 (Spring 1986), p. 1.

2 Quoted in Laqueur, p. 2.

3 Quoted in Laqueur, p. 2.

4 Quoted in Pat Jalland and John Hooper, *Women from Birth to Death: The Female Life Cycle in Britain 1830–1914* (Humanities Press International, Atlantic Highlands, NJ, 1986), p. 21.

5 Quoted in Jalland and Hooper, p. 22.

6 Nancy F. Cott, 'Passionlessness: An Interpretation of Victorian Sexual Ideology, 1790–1850', in Nancy F. Cott and Elizabeth H. Pleck, eds., *A Heritage of Her Own: Toward a New Social History of American Women* (Simon & Schuster, New York, 1979).

7 Douglas M. Peers, 'Privates off Parade: Regimenting Sexuality in the

Nineteenth-Century Indian Empire', *International History Review* 20.4 (1998), p. 841.

8 Quoted in Mary Thale, ed., *The Autobiography of Francis Place* (Cambridge UP, Cambridge, 1972), pp. 75–6; see also Tim Hitchcock, *English Sexualities, 1700–1800* (St Martin's Press, New York, 1997), p. 39.

9 Quoted in Roy Porter and Lesley Hall, *The Facts of Life: The Creation of Sexual Knowledge in Britain, 1650–1950* (Yale UP, New Haven, 1995), pp. 42, 44.

10 Quoted in Porter and Hall, p. 130.

11 Quoted in Michael Mason, *The Making of Victorian Sexuality* (OUP, Oxford, 1994), p. 195.

12 Quoted in Lucy Bland and Laura Doan, eds., *Sexology Uncensored: the documents of sexual science* (U Chicago P, Chicago, 1998), p. 13.

13 Lucy Bland, 'Introduction to Gender and Sexual Difference', in Bland and Doan, eds., p. 13; Lesley Hall, 'Introduction to Other Sexual Proclivities', in Bland and Doan, eds., p. 233; Porter and Hall, p. 166.

14 Quoted in Porter and Hall, p. 156.

15 Quoted in Porter and Hall, p. 172.

16 Quoted in the *Taunton Courier*, 18 April 1827, p. 3.

17 Susie I. Steinbach, 'The Melodramatic Contract: Breach of Promise and the Performance of Virtue', *Nineteenth Century Studies* 14 (2000), p. 1.

18 Barry Reay, 'Sexuality in Nineteenth-Century England: The Social Context of Illegitimacy in Rural Kent', *Rural History* 1.2 (1990), 228, 239.

19 Quoted in John Gillis, 'Servants, Sexual Relations and the Risks of Illegitimacy in London, 1801–1900', in Judith L. Newton, Mary P. Ryan, and Judith R. Walkowitz, eds., *Sex and Class in Women's History* (Routledge & Kegan Paul, London, 1983), p. 127.

20 Amanda Foreman, *Georgiana, Duchess of Devonshire* (Random House, New York, 2000), pp. 244–7.

21 Hitchcock, p. 86.

22 Martha Vicinus, Introduction to Martha Vicinus, ed., *Lesbian Subjects: A Feminist Studies Reader* (Indiana UP, Bloomington, 1996), p. 7; Lisa Moore, 'Something More Tender Still Than Friendship: Romantic Friendship in Early-Nineteenth Century England', in Vicinus, ed., p. 39; Martha Vicinus, ' "They Wonder to Which Sex I Belong": The Historical Roots of the Modern Lesbian Identity', in Vicinus, ed., p. 243.

23 Anna Clark, 'Anne Lister's Construction of Lesbian Identity', *Journal of the History of Sexuality* 7.1 (1996), pp. 23–50.

24 Vicinus, ' "They Wonder to Which Sex I Belong"', p. 242; Moore, pp. 33–4; Camilla Townsend, ' "I Am the Woman for Spirit": A Working Woman's Gender Transgression in Victorian London', in Andrew H. Miller and James Elie Adams, eds., *Sexualities in Victorian Britain* (Indiana UP, Bloomington, 1996), pp. 214–34.

25 BL. Add. MS, 27,828, Place Papers, vol. XL: Manners and Morals vol. IV fo. 119. I am grateful to Tim Hitchcock for this example.

26 Thale, ed., p. 92; I am indebted to Tim Hitchcock for directing me to this example.

27 Hitchcock, p. 33.

28 A. James Hammerton, *Cruelty and Companionship: Conflict in Nineteenth-Century Married Life* (Routledge, London, 1992), p. 45; Shani D'Cruze, *Crimes of Outrage: Sex, Violence and Victorian Working Women* (UCL Press, London, 1998), p. 72.

29 Quoted in Ellen Ross, *Love and Toil: Motherhood in Outcast London 1870–1918* (OUP, New York, 1993), p. 108.

30 Ross, pp. 112, 118–20.

31 Quoted in Elizabeth Roberts, *A Woman's Place: An Oral History of Working-Class Women, 1890–1940* (Basil Blackwell, Oxford, 1984).

32 Simon Sretzer, *Fertility, Class and Gender in Britain, 1860–1940* (CUP, Cambridge, 1996).

33 Quoted in Hammerton, p. 110.

34 Angus McLaren, *A History of Contraception from Antiquity to the Present Day* (Basil Blackwell, Oxford, 1990), p. 191.

35 McLaren, p. 179.

36 Mason, pp. 54–5.

37 Marjorie Levine-Clark, ' "Being Syphilitic": Experiences of Disease Among Poor Women in Early Victorian England', unpublished paper presented at the Social Science History Association Conference, Oct. 2000; Hammerton, p. 109.

38 Linda E. Merians, 'The London Lock Hospital and the Lock Asylum for Women', in Linda E. Merians, ed., *The Secret Malady: Venereal Disease in Eighteenth-Century Britain and France* (UP Kentucky, Lexington, 1996), pp. 128–45.

39 Porter and Hall, p. 108.

40 Hammerton, p. 50.

41 Lesley A. Hall, 'Venereal Diseases and Society in Britain, from the Contagious Diseases Act to the National Health Service', in Roger Davidson and Lesley A. Hall, eds., *Sex, Sin and Suffering: Venereal Disease and European Society since 1870* (Routledge, London, 2001), p. 126.

42 Sally Ledger, *The New Woman: Fiction and Feminism at the Fin de Siècle* (Manchester UP, Manchester, 1997), pp. 69–70.

43 Lucy Bland, *Banishing the Beast: English Feminism and Sexual Morality 1885–1914* (Penguin, London, 1995), pp. 256–65, 278–80; Judy Greenway, 'It's What You Do With It That Counts: Interpretations of Otto Weininger', in Bland and Doan, eds., pp. 27–43.

5 Religion

1 Frances Knight, *The Nineteenth-Century Church and English Society* (CUP, Cambridge, 1995), p. 63.

2 Paula Bartley, *Prostitution: Prevention and Reform in England, 1860–1914* (Routledge, London, 2000), p. 78.

3 Quoted in Knight, p. 26.

4 Joyce Goodman and Camilla Leach, ' "At the Center of a Circle Whose Circumference Spans All Nations": Quaker Women and the Ladies Committee of the British and Foreign School Society, 1813–1837', in Sue Morgan, ed., *Women, Religion, and Feminism in Britain, 1750–1900* (Palgrave, London, 2002), pp. 53–69.

5 Anthony Fletcher, 'Beyond the Church: Women's Spiritual Experience at Home and in the Community 1600–1900', in R. N. Swanson, ed., *Gender and Christian Religion* (Boydell Press, Woodbridge, Suffolk, 1998), p. 197.

6 Linda Wilson, ' "She Succeeds With Cloudless Brow ..." How Active was the Spirituality of Nonconformist Women in the Home during the Period 1825–75?' in Swanson, ed., pp. 352–3.

7 Hugh McLeod, *Religion and Irreligion in Victorian England: How Secular was the Working Class?* (Headstart History, Bangor, 1993), p. 37.

8 Lilian Lewis Shiman, *Women and Leadership in Nineteenth-Century England* (St Martin's Press, London, 1992), pp. 54, 98, 108, 157.

9 James Obelkevich, 'Religion', in F. M. L. Thompson, ed., *The Cambridge Social History of Britain 1750–1950*, vol. 3: *Social Agencies and Institutions* (CUP, Cambridge, 1990), pp. 317, 335.

10 Raphael Samuel, 'The Roman Catholic Church and the Irish Poor', in Roger Swift and Sheridan Gilley, eds., *The Irish in the Victorian City* (Croom Helm, London, 1985), pp. 271–2, 279.

11 Samuel, pp. 267–8, 275, 277.

12 Rosemary O'Day, 'Women in Victorian Religion', in David Englander and Rosemary O'Day, eds., *Retrieved Riches: Social Investigation in Britain 1840–1914* (Scolar Press, Aldershot, 1995), p. 344.

13 Frances Knight, ' "Male and Female He Created Them": Men, Women and the Questions of Gender', John Wolffe, ed., *Religion in Victorian Britain*, vol. V: *Culture and Empire* (Manchester UP, Manchester, 1997), p. 30.

14 Quoted in Ricki Burman, 'Jewish Women and the Household Economy in Manchester, c. 1890–1920', in David Cesarini, ed., *The Making of Modern Anglo-Jewry* (Basil Blackwell, Oxford, 1990), p. 47.

15 Quoted in Susan L. Tananbaum, 'Philanthropy and Identity: Gender and Ethnicity in London', *Journal of Social History* 30.4 (1996), p. 946.

16 Obelkevich, pp. 318, 336.

17 O'Day, pp. 340, 344.

18 O'Day, pp. 341–3.

19 Susan Thorne, *Congregational Missions and the Making of an Imperial Culture in Nineteenth-Century England* (Stanford UP, Stanford, 1999), p. 160.

20 Quoted in O'Day, p. 347.

21 O'Day, p. 354; Jeremy Gregory, 'Gender and the Clerical Profession in England, 1660–1850;, in Swanson, ed., pp. 235–71.

22 Quoted in Catherine Hall, *White, Male and Middle Class: Explorations in Feminism and History* (Routledge, London, 1992), p. 218.

23 T. Thomas, 'Foreign Missions and Missionaries in Victorian Britain', in Wolffe, ed., p. 104.

24 Thorne, p. 94.

25 Quoted in Hall, p. 223.

26 Judith Rowbotham, ' "Soldiers of Christ"? Images of Female Missionaries in Late Nineteenth-Century Britain: Issues of Heroism and Martyrdom', *Gender and History* 12.1 (April 2000), p. 102.

27 Figures on the sizes of sisterhoods come from Susan Mumm and Carmen Mangion, personal communication, October 2003. I am grateful for their assistance.

28 Susan O'Brien, 'Terra Incognita: the Nun in Nineteenth-Century England', *Past and Present* 121 (Nov. 1988), pp. 110–40.

29 Susan Mumm, *Stolen Daughters, Virgin Mothers: Anglican Sisterhoods in Victorian Britain* (Leicester UP, London, 1999).

30 Quoted in Martha Vicinus, *Independent Women: Work and Community for Single Women 1850–1920* (U Chicago P, Chicago, 1985), p. 52.

31 Quoted in Mumm, p. 15.

32 Quoted in Walter L. Arnstein, *Protestant versus Catholic in Mid-Victorian England: Mr Newdegate and the Nuns* (U Missouri P, Columbia, 1982), p. 121.

33 Joanna Southcott, *The Answer of the Lord to the Powers of Darkness* (1802), quoted in Barbara Taylor, *Eve and the New Jerusalem* (Pantheon, New York, 1983), p. 163.

34 Taylor, pp. 161–72.

35 Kenneth D. Brown, *A Social History of the Nonconformist Ministry in England and Wales 1800–1930* (Clarendon Press, Oxford, 1988), p. 17.

36 David Shorney, ' "Women May Preach But Men Must Govern": Gender Roles in the Growth and Development of the Bible Christian Denomination', in Swanson, ed., pp. 309–22.

37 Deborah Valenze, 'Pilgrims and Progress in Nineteenth-Century England', in Raphael Samuel and Gareth Stedman Jones, eds., *Culture, Ideology and Politics: Essays for Eric Hobsbawm* (History Workshop Series, Routledge & Kegan Paul, 1982), pp. 113–26; Deborah Valenze, *Prophetic Sons and Daughters: Female Preaching and Popular Religion in Industrial England* (Princeton UP, Princeton, 1985); Deborah Valenze, 'Cottage Religion and the Polities of Survival', in Jane

Rendall, ed., *Equal or Different: Women's Politics 1800–1914* (Basil Blackwell, Oxford, 1987), pp. 31–56.

38 Quoted in Linda Wilson, ' "Constrained by Zeal": Women in Mid-Nineteenth Century Nonconformist Churches', *Journal of Religious History* 23.2 (June 1999), p. 201.

39 Olive Anderson, 'Women Preachers in Mid-Victorian Britain: Some Reflections on Feminism, Popular Religion and Social Change', *Historical Journal* 12.3 (1969), pp. 467–84.

40 Pamela J. Walker, *Pulling the Devil's Kingdom Down: The Salvation Army in Victorian Britain* (U California P, Berkeley, 2001), pp. 42, 235.

41 Quoted in Walker, p. 27.

42 Alex Owen, *The Darkened Room: Women, Power and Spiritualism in Late Victorian England* (U Pennsylvania P, Philadelphia, 1990).

43 George Robb, 'Eugenics, Spirituality, and Sex Differentiation in Edwardian England: The Case of Frances Swiney', *Journal of Women's History* 10.3 (Autumn 1998), pp. 97–117.

6 Education

1 Meg Gomersall, *Working-Class Girls in Nineteenth-Century England: Life, Work and Schooling* (Macmillan, Basingstoke, 1997), p. 157 n. 5.

2 June Purvis, *A History of Women's Education in England* (Open UP, Milton Keynes, 1991), p. 68.

3 Quoted in Purvis, p. 67.

4 Ruth Watts, *Gender, Power and the Unitarians in England 1760–1860* (Longman, London, 1998), pp. 123–4, 140.

5 Quoted in Gomersall, p. 47.

6 Quoted in Thomas W. Laqueur, *Religion and Respectability: Sunday Schools and Working-Class Culture 1780–1850* (Yale UP, New Haven, 1976), p. 171.

7 Quoted in June Purvis, *Hard Lessons: the Lives and Education of Working-Class Women in Nineteenth-Century England* (U Minnesota, Minneapolis, 1989), p. 78.

8 Gomersall, p. 60.

9 From *The Autobiography of Mary Smith, Schoolmistress and Nonconformist* (1892), pp. 24–5, quoted in Purvis, *Hard Lessons*, p. 81.

10 Purvis, *Hard Lessons*, p. 82.

11 Laqueur, p. 100.

12 Maurice Walton Thomas, *The Early Factory Legislation: A Study in Legislative and Administrative Evolution* (1948; Greenwood Press, Westport, CT, 1970), pp. 161–74.

13 Quoted in Purvis, *Hard Lessons*, pp. 87–8.

14 Kathryn Gleadle, *The Early Feminists: Radical Unitarians and the Emergence of*

the Women's Rights Movement, 1831–51 (Macmillan, London, 1995), p. 140; K. D. Reynolds, *Aristocratic Women and Political Society in Victorian Britain* (Clarendon Press, Oxford, 1998), p. 93.

15 Purvis, *Hard Lessons*, p. 2.

16 Dina M. Copelman, *London's Women Teachers: Gender, Class and Feminism 1870–1930* (Routledge, London, 1996), p. xiii.

17 Copelman, p. 65.

18 Patricia Hollis, *Ladies Elect: Women in English Local Government 1865–1914* (Clarendon Press, Oxford, 1987), pp. 71–90.

19 Felicity Hunt, ed., *Lessons for Life: The Schooling of Girls and Women, 1850–1950* (Basil Blackwell, Oxford, 1987), p. xvii.

20 Peter Gordon, Richard Aldrich, and Dennis Dean, *Education and Policy in England in the Twentieth Century* (Woburn Press, London, 1991), pp. 8, 16–32, 123–40, 157–69.

21 Quoted in Anna Davin, *Growing Up Poor: Home, School, and Street in London, 1870–1914* (Oram Rivers Press, London, 1996), p. 89.

22 Stephen Heathorn, *For Home, Country, and Race: Constructing Gender, Class, and Englishness in the Elementary School, 1880–1914* (U Toronto P, Toronto, 2000), pp. 165–6.

23 Quoted in Davin, p. 50.

24 Heathorn, p. 22.

25 Diana E. St John, 'Educate or Domesticate?: early twentieth century pressures on older girls in elementary school', *Women's History Review* 3.2 (1994), pp. 191–218.

26 Quoted in Purvis, *A History of Women's Education*, p. 79.

27 Martha Vicinus, *Independent Women: Work and Community for Single Women 1850–1920* (U Chicago P, Chicago, 1985), p. 167.

28 Quoted in Elizabeth Raikes, *Dorothea Beale of Cheltenham* (Archibald Constable & Co., London, 1908), p. 87.

29 Quoted in Purvis, *A History of Women's Education*, p. 87.

30 Quoted in Purvis, *A History of Women's Education*, p. 88.

31 Felicity Hunt, 'Social Class and the Grading of Schools, Realities in Girls' Secondary Education 1880–1940', in June Purvis, ed., *The Education of Girls and Women: Proceedings of the 1984 Annual Conference of the History of Education Society of Great Britain* (History of Education Society, Evington, Leicester, 1985), p. 34; Purvis, *A History of Women's Education*, p. 76.

32 Copelman, p. 122; Lee Holcombe, *Victorian Ladies at Work: Middle-Class Working Women in England and Wales 1850–1914* (Archon Books, Hamden, CT, 1973), p. 32.

33 Vicinus, p. 125.

34 Carol Dyhouse, *No Distinction of Sex? Women in British Universities, 1870–1939* (UCL Press, London, 1995), p. 13.

35 Perry Williams, 'Pioneer Women Students at Cambridge 1869–1881', in Hunt, ed., p. 171.
36 Joan N. Burstyn, *Victorian Education and the Ideal of Womanhood* (1980; Rutgers UP, New Brunswick, NJ, 1984), p. 45.
37 Quoted in Burstyn, pp. 90–1.
38 Vicinus, p. 134.
39 Barbara Caine, *English Feminism 1780–1980* (OUP, Oxford, 1997), p. 114.
40 Dyhouse, p. 197.
41 Quoted in Blanche Athena Clough, *A Memoir of Anne Jemima Clough* (Edward Arnold London, 1897), pp. 197–8.
42 Clough, p. 232.
43 Margaret Cole, *Growing Up Into Revolution* (Longmans, Green, London, 1949), p. 36.
44 Dyhouse, pp. 7, 18, 23; Perry Williams, p. 189.

7 Imperialism

1 Jonathan Schneer, *London 1900: The Imperial Metropolis* (Yale UP, London, 1999), pp. 17–18; S. R. Gardiner, *A Student's History of England* (London, 1892), p. 954, quoted in Kathryn Castle, *Britannia's Children: Reading Colonialism Through Children's Books and Magazines* (Manchester UP, Manchester, 1996), p. 15.
2 John M. MacKenzie, 'Empire and Metropolitan Cultures', in Andrew Porter, ed., *The Oxford History of the British Empire*, vol. III: *The Nineteenth Century* (OUP, Oxford, 1999), pp. 270–93; John M. Mackenzie, *Propaganda and Empire: The Manipulation of British Public Opinion, 1880–1960* (Manchester UP, Manchester, 1984); Kelly Boyd, *Manliness and the Boys' Story Paper in Britain: A Cultural History, 1855–1940* (Palgrave, Basingstoke, 2003), pp. 100–1; David Cannadine, *Ornamentalism: How the British Saw Their Empire* (OUP, Oxford, 2001), pp. 102–3, 186.
3 Roxann Wheeler, *The Complexion of Race: Categories of Difference in Eighteenth-Century British Culture* (U Penn. P, Philadelphia, 2000), pp. 4, 5, 7, 289.
4 Catherine Hall, *Civilising Subjects: Colony and Metropole in the English Imagination, 1830–1867* (Chicago UP, Chicago, 2002), pp. 23, 74, 75.
5 Hall, p. 48.
6 Hall, p. 17.
7 Kate Teltscher, *India Inscribed: European and British Writing on India 1600–1800* (OUP, Delhi, 1995), p. 160; Mrinilini Sinha, *Colonial Masculinity: the 'Manly Englishman' and the 'Effeminate Bengali' in the Late Nineteenth Century* (Manchester UP, Manchester, 1995).
8 Julia Bush, *Edwardian Ladies and Imperial Power* (Leicester UP, London, 2000), p. 113.
9 Penelope Tuson, 'Mutiny Narratives and the Imperial Feminine: European

Women's Accounts of the Rebellion in India in 1857', *Women's Studies International Forum* 21.3 (1998), p. 298.

10 Quoted in Bush, p. 113.

11 Quoted in Bush, p. 2.

12 Quoted in Barbara Ramusack, 'Cultural Missionaries, Maternal Imperialists, Feminist Allies: British Women Activists in India, 1865–1945', in Nupur Chaudhuri and Margaret Strobel, eds., *Western Women and Imperialism: Complicity and Resistance* (Indiana UP, Bloomington, 1992), p. 133.

13 Quoted in Bush, p. 166.

14 Anna Davin, 'Imperialism and Motherhood', in Frederick Cooper and Ann Laura Stoler, eds., *Tensions of Empire: Colonial Cultures in a Bourgeois World* (U California P, Berkeley, 1997), p. 92.

15 Antoinette Burton, *At the Heart of the Empire: Indians and the Colonial Encounter in Late-Victorian Britain* (U California P, Berkeley, 1998), p. 32.

16 Angela Woollacott, 'The Colonial Flaneuse: Australian Women Negotiating Turn-of-the-Century London', *Signs* 25.3 (Spring 2000), pp. 2, 4.

17 Quoted in Bush, p. 113.

18 Hall, p. 72.

19 Frank Cundall, ed., *Lady Nugent's Journal: Jamaica One Hundred Years Ago* (A. & C. Black, London, 1907), p. 118.

20 Charlotte Sussman, *Consuming Anxieties: Consumer Protest, Gender, and British Slavery, 1713–1833* (Stanford UP, Stanford, 2000), pp. 164, 184.

21 Quoted in Adele Perry; ' "Oh I'm Just Sick of the Faces of Men": Gender Imbalance, Race, Sexuality, and Sociability in Nineteenth-Century British Columbia', *BC Studies* 105/106 (Spring/Summer 1995), p. 33.

22 Marilyn Lake, 'Australian Frontier Feminism and the Marauding White Man', in Clare Midgley, ed., *Gender and Imperialism* (Manchester UP, Manchester, 1998), pp. 125–7.

23 Wheeler, pp. 138–9.

24 Durba Ghosh, *Colonial Companions: Sexual Transgression, Racial Mixing and Gendered Order in Early Colonial India, 1760–1840* (forthcoming). I am grateful to the author for sharing her work with me before publication.

25 Douglas M. Peers, 'Soldiers, Surgeons and the Campaigns to Combat Sexually Transmitted Diseases in Colonial India, 1805–1860', *Medical History* 42 (1998), p. 139; Philippa Levine, 'Rereading the 1890s: Venereal Disease as "Constitutional Crisis" in Britain and British India', *Journal of Asian Studies* 55.3 (August 1996), pp. 587–8; Linda Bryder, 'Sex, Race, and Colonialism: An Historiographical Review', *International History Review* 20.4 (Dec. 1998), pp. 809, 815.

26 Douglas M. Peers, 'Privates off Parade: Regimenting Sexuality in the Nineteenth-Century Indian Empire', *International History Review*, 20.4 (1998), p. 853.

27 Quoted in Kathleen Wilson, *The Island Race: Englishness, Empire and Gender in the Eighteenth Century* (Routledge, London, 2003), p. 154.

28 Cundall, ed., p. 131.

29 Quoted in Nupur Chaudhuri, 'Memsahibs and Motherhood in Nineteenth-Century Colonial India', *Victorian Studies* 31.4 (1988), p. 531.

30 Peers, 'Privates off Parade', p. 849; Hall, p. 233.

31 Theon Wilkinson, *Two Monsoons* (Duckworth, London, 1976), p. 108.

32 Chaudhuri, 'Memsahibs and Motherhood', pp. 522, 526, 533.

33 Sinha, pp. 33–68.

34 Quoted in Sinha, p. 56.

35 Quoted in Vron Ware, *Beyond the Pale: White Women, Racism, and History* (Verso, London, 1992), p. 122.

36 Richard Hillier, 'A Vindication of the Address to the People of Great Britain, on the use of West India Produce: with some observations and facts relative to the situation of slaves: in a reply to a female apologist for slavery', (London, 1791), p. 7, quoted in Sussman, p. 112.

37 Elizabeth Kowaleski-Wallace, *Consuming Subjects: Women, Shopping, and Business in the Eighteenth Century* (Columbia UP, New York, 1997), p. 41.

38 Quoted in Nupur Chaudhuri, 'Shawls, Curry, and Rice in Victorian Britain', in Chaudhuri and Strobel, eds., pp. 233–5, 238–41.

39 Amelia Falkland, *Chow-Chow; Being Selections from a Journal kept in India, Egypt, And Syria* (Hurst and Blackett, London, 1857), vol. 1, pp. 9, 283.

40 Mrs. Colin MacKenzie, *Six Years in India* (R. Bentley, London, 1857), p. 173.

41 Emily Eden, *Up the Country: Letters written to her sister from the Upper Provinces of India* (1866; Oxford UP, London, 1930), p. 294.

42 Fanny Parkes, *Wanderings of a Pilgrim in Search of the Picturesque*, edited with notes and an introduction by Indira Ghose and Sara Mills (1850; Manchester University Press, Manchester, 2001), p. 259.

43 Quoted in Indira Ghose, *Women Travellers in Colonial India: The Power of the Female Gaze* (Oxford UP, Delhi, 1998), p. 63.

44 Susan L. Blake, 'A Woman's Trek: What Difference Does Gender Make?', in Chaudhuri and Strobel, eds., pp. 19–34; James Wolf, 'A Woman Passing Through: Helen Caddick and the Maturation of the Empire in British Central Africa', *Journal of Popular Culture* 30.3 (Winter 1996), pp. 35–56.

45 Hall, p. 96.

46 Jane Haggis, 'White Women and Colonialism: Towards a Non-Recuperative History', in Midgley, ed., pp. 51, 58.

47 Quoted in Nancy L. Paxton, 'Complicity and Resistance in the Writings of Flora Annie Steel and Annie Besant', in Chaudhuri and Strobel, eds., p. 163.

48 Susan Thorne, *Congregational Missions and the Making of an Imperial Culture in Nineteenth-Century England* (Stanford UP, Stanford, 1999), esp. pp. 5–10, 16–17, 69, 78, 99, 106; Susan Thorne, ' "The Conversion of Englishmen and

the Conversion of the World Inseparable": Missionary Imperialism and the Language of Class in Early Industrial Britain', in Cooper and Stoler, eds., pp. 238–62.

49 Janaki Nair, 'Uncovering the Zenana: Visions of Indian Womanhood in Englishwoman's Writing, 1813–1940', in Catherine Hall, ed., *Cultures of Empire: A Reader. Colonizers in Britain and the Empire in the Nineteenth and Twentieth Centuries* (Manchester UP, Manchester, 2000), pp. 224–5.

50 Clare Midgley, 'Female Emancipation in an Imperial Frame: English women and the campaign against *sati* (widow-burning) in India, 1813–1830', *Women's History Review* 9.1 (2000), pp. 95–121.

51 Quoted in Clare Midgley, *Women Against Slavery: the British Campaigns, 1780–1870* (Routledge, London, 1992), p. 101.

52 Midgley, *Women Against Slavery*; Clare Midgley, 'Anti-slavery and the Roots of "Imperial Feminism" ', in Midgley, ed., pp. 161–79.

53 Antoinette Burton, 'Fearful Bodies into Disciplined Subjects: Pleasure, Romance, and the Family Drama of Colonial Reform in Mary Carpenter's *Six Months in India*', *Signs* 20.3 (1995), pp. 545–74.

54 Ramusack, pp. 123–4.

55 Nancy Fix Anderson, 'Bridging Cross-Cultural Feminisms: Annie Besant and Women's Rights in England and India, 1874–1933', *Women's History Review* 3.4 (1994), pp. 563–80.

56 Antoinette Burton, *Burdens of History: British Feminists, Indian Women, and Imperial Culture, 1865–1915* (U North Carolina P, Chapel Hill, 1994), pp. 5–12.

57 Burton, *Burdens of History*, p. 114.

58 Rita S. Kranidis, *The Victorian Spinster and Colonial Emigration: Contested Subjects* (Macmillan, Basingstoke, 1999), p. 21.

59 From an 1865 letter, quoted in Marion Diamond, *Emigration and Empire: The Life of Maria S. Rye* (Garland Publishing, London, 1999), p. 137.

60 Marjory Harper, 'British Migration and the Peopling of Empire', in Porter, ed., p. 82; Cecillie Swaisland, *Servants and Gentlewomen to the Golden Land: The Emigration of Single Women from Britain to Southern Africa, 1820–1939* (U Natal P, Berg, 1993), p. 34.

61 Quoted in Raewyn Dalziel, 'Southern Islands: New Zealand and Polynesia', in Porter, ed., p. 582.

62 A. James Hammerton, *Emigrant Gentlewomen: Genteel Poverty and Female Emigration, 1830–1914* (Croom Helm, London, 1979), p. 92.

63 Bush, *Edwardian Ladies*, pp. 146–7.

64 Deborah Oxley, *Convict Maids: The Forced Migration of Women to Australia*, (CUP, Cambridge, 1996), pp. 17, 28–9.

65 Robin Haines, 'Indigent Misfits or Shrewd Operators? Government-assisted Emigrants from the United Kingdom to Australia, 1831–1860', *Population Studies* 48 (1994), pp. 225, 235–36, 246.

66   The first quote is from 1857; the second two are from 1862. All three are quoted in Jan Gothard, 'A Compromise With Conscience: the Reception of Female Immigrant Domestic Servants in Eastern Australia 1860–1890', *Labour History* [Australia] 62 (1992), p. 40.

67   Quoted in Oxley, p. 180.

68   Helen Vellacott, ed., *A Girl at Government House. An English Girl's Reminiscences: 'Below Stairs' in Colonial Australia* (Curry O'Neil, South Yarra, Victoria, 1982), p. 37.

69   Swaisland, pp. 5–6.

70   Quoted in Hammerton, pp. 136, 139.

71   Quoted in Marilyn Barber, 'In Search of a Better Life: A Scottish Domestic in Rural Ontario', *Polyphony* 8 (1986), pp. 13–16. Jean Burns was Scottish, but her experience was probably similar to that of a typical English emigrant.

8 Domestic Politics

1   Helen Rogers, *Women and the People: Authority, Authorship and the Radical Tradition in Nineteenth-Century England* (Ashgate, Aldershot, 2000), p. 1.

2   Barbara Caine, *English Feminism 1780–1980* (OUP, Oxford, 1997), p. 24.

3   Quoted in Introduction, Kathryn Gleadle and Sarah Richardson, eds., *Women in British Politics, 1760–1860: The Power of the Petticoat* (Macmillan, Basingstoke, 2000), p. 7.

4   Quoted in Maurice J. Quinlan, *Victorian Prelude: A History of English Manners 1700–1830* (Columbia UP, New York, 1941), p. 141.

5   Dorice Williams Elliott, ' "The Care of the Poor is Her Profession": Hannah More and Women's Philanthropic Work', *Nineteenth-Century Contexts* 19 (1995), p. 181.

6   Susan Pedersen, 'Hannah More Meets Simple Simon: Tracts, Chapbooks, and Popular Culture in Late Eighteenth-Century England', *Journal of British Studies* 25.1 (Jan. 1986), pp. 84–113.

7   Anne Stott, 'Patriotism and Providence: The Politics of Hannah More', in Gleadle and Richardson, eds., p. 40.

8   Sarah Richardson, 'The Role of Women in Electoral Politics in Yorkshire During the Eighteen-Thirties', *Northern History* 32 (1996), pp. 133–51.

9   Jon Lawrence, 'Contesting the Male Polity: The Suffragettes and the Politics of Disruption in Edwardian Britain', in Amanda Vickery, ed., *Women, Privilege, and Power: British Politics, 1750 to the Present* (Stanford UP, Stanford, 2001), p. 205.

10 Matthew Cragoe, ' "Jenny Rules the Roost": Women and Electoral Politics, 1832–1868', Gleadle and Richardson, eds., pp. 153–68.

11 Linda Colley, *Britons: Forging the Nation 1707–1837* (Yale UP, New Haven, 1992), pp. 257–63.

12 John Stevenson, *Popular Disturbances in England 1700–1832* (Longman,

London, 1992), p. 125; John Bohstedt, 'Gender, Household and Community Politics: Women in English Riots 1790–1810', *Past & Present* 120 (Aug. 1988), pp. 92, 122.

13 Iain McCalman, *Radical Underworld: Prophets, Revolutionaries and Pornographers in London, 1795–1840* (CUP, Cambridge, 1988), pp. 32, 124; Rogers, *Women and the People*, p. 52.

14 John Belchem, *Popular Radicalism in Nineteenth-Century Britain* (St Martin's Press, New York, 1996), pp. 46–7.

15 From the *Manchester Observer*, quoted in James A. Epstein, *Radical Expression: Political Language, Ritual, and Symbol in England, 1790–1850* (OUP, New York, 1994), p. 87.

16 Iowerth Prothero, *Radical Artisans in England and France, 1830–1870* (CUP, Cambridge, 1997), pp. 147–53.

17 Anna Clark, 'Queen Caroline and the Sexual Politics of Popular Culture in London, 1820', *Representations* 31 (Summer 1990), p. 47.

18 Thomas W. Laqueur, 'The Queen Caroline Affair: Politics as Art in the Reign of George IV', *Journal of Modern History* 54.3 (Sept. 1982), p. 417.

19 Prothero, p. 14. See also Laqueur, pp. 417–66, and Clark, pp. 47–68.

20 Laqueur, p. 442.

21 Quoted in Tamara L. Hunt, 'Morality and Monarchy in the Queen Caroline Affair', *Albion* 23.4 (Winter 1991), p. 716.

22 Barbara Taylor, *Eve and the New Jerusalem: Socialism and Feminism in the Nineteenth Century* (Pantheon, New York, 1983), p. 118.

23 Quoted in Taylor, p. 67.

24 Quoted in Taylor, p. 98.

25 Taylor, p. 247. See also Jutta Schwarzkopf, *Women in the Chartist Movement* (St Martin's Press, New York, 1991).

26 Rogers, *Women and the People*, p. 81.

27 Cragoe, p. 161.

28 Quoted in Schwarzkopf, p. 89.

29 Anna Clark, 'The Rhetoric of Chartist Domesticity: Gender, Language, and Class in the 1830s and 1840s', *Journal of British Studies* 31 (Jan. 1992), pp. 62–88; Michelle de Larrabeiti, 'Conspicuous Before the World: the Political Rhetoric of the Chartist Women', in Eileen Janes Yeo, ed., *Radical Femininity: Women's Self-Representation in the Public Sphere* (Manchester UP, Manchester, 1998), pp. 79–105.

30 Lynn Hollen Lees, *The Solidarities of Strangers: The English Poor Laws and the People, 1700–1948* (CUP, Cambridge, 1998), pp. 135–9.

31 Dorothy Thompson, *The Chartists: Popular Politics in the Industrial Revolution* (Pantheon, New York, 1984), p. 122; Anna Clark, *The Struggle for the Breeches: Gender and the Making of the British Working Class* (U California P, Berkeley, 1995), p. 191; Helen Rogers, ' "The Good Are Not Always Powerful, Nor the

Powerful Always Good": The Politics of Women's Needlework in Mid-Victorian London', *Victorian Studies* 40.4.

32 Quoted in Clark, p. 191.

33 Quoted in Schwarzkopf, p. 92.

34 Schwarzkopf, p. 199.

35 Kathryn Gleadle, *The Early Feminists: Radical Unitarians and the Emergence of the Women's Rights Movement, 1831–51* (St Martin's Press, New York, 1995), pp. 57, 59, 81, 92; Kathryn Gleadle, ' "Our Several Spheres": Middle-Class Women and the Feminisms of Early Victorian Radical Politics', Gleadle and Richardson eds., pp. 134–9.

36 Quoted in Sandra Stanley Holton, *Suffrage Days: Stories from the Women's Suffrage Movement* (Routledge, London, 1996), p. 49.

37 Margot Finn, *After Chartism: Class and Nation in English Radical Politics, 1848–1874* (CUP, Cambridge, 1993), pp. 160–1.

38 Simon Morgan, 'Domestic Economy and Political Agitation: Women and the Anti-Corn Law League', in Gleadle and Richardson, eds., pp. 115–33.

39 Martin Pugh, *The Tories and the People 1880–1935* (Basil Blackwell, Oxford, 1985), p. 68; G. E. Maguire, *Conservative Women: A History of Women and the Conservative Party, 1874–1997* (Macmillan, London, 1998), pp. 42–44.

40 Linda Walker, 'Party Political Women: A Comparative Study of Liberal Women and the Primrose League, 1890–1914', in Jane Rendall, ed., *Equal or Different: Women's Politics 1800–1914* (Basil Blackwell, Oxford, 1987), p. 174.

41 Karen Hunt, *Equivocal Feminists: The Social Democratic Federation and the Woman Question 1884–1911* (Cambridge UP, Cambridge, 1966), pp. 1, 8, 9, 251–4.

42 Karen Hunt, 'Negotiating the Boundaries of the Domestic: British Socialist Women and the Politics of Consumption', *Women's History Review* 9.2 (2000), pp. 398–402.

43 Maguire, pp. 42, 44.

44 Ellen Jordan, *The Women's Movement and Women's Employment in Nineteenth Century Britain* (Routledge, London, 1999).

45 Quoted in Philippa Levine, *Victorian Feminism 1850–1900* (Hutchinson Education, London, 1987), p. 134.

46 R. H. Graveson and F. R. Crane, *A Century of Family Law, 1857–1957* (Sweet & Maxwell, London, 1957), p. 8, quoted in Mary Lyndon Shanley, *Feminism, Marriage, and the Law in Victorian England* (Princeton UP, Princeton, 1989), p. 37.

47 Out of the 224 that were granted. See Lee Holcombe, *Wives and Property: Reform of the Married Women's Property Law in Nineteenth-Century England* (U Toronto P, Toronto, 1983), p. 96.

48 Shanley, pp. 23–9.

49 Caroline Norton, *English Laws for Women in the Nineteenth Century* (printed for Private Circulation, London, 1854), p. 175.

50 Shanley, p. 35.

51 Quoted in Gail L. Savage, ' "Intended Only for the Husband": Gender, Class, and the Provision for Divorce in England, 1858–1868', in Kristine Otteson Garrigan, ed., *Victorian Scandals: Representations of Gender and Class* (Ohio UP, Athens, 1992), pp. 24, 32.

52 Savage, p. 26.

53 Shanley, pp. 39, 40.

54 Shanley, p. 109.

55 Shanley, pp. 112–24.

56 Mary Hume-Rothery, *A Letter Addressed to the Right Hon. W. E. Gladstone, M.P. . . . Touching the Contagious Diseases Acts of 1866 and 1869* (Manchester, 1870), quoted in Susan Kingsley Kent, *Gender and Power in Britain, 1640–1990* (Routledge, London, 1999), p. 199.

57 Judith P. Walkowitz, *Prostitution and Victorian Society: Women, Class, and the State* (CUP, Cambridge, 1980), pp. 14–15, 29, 201, 204, 209.

58 Caine, p. 122.

59 Lucy Bland, *Banishing the Beast: English Feminism and Sexual Morality 1885–1914* (Penguin, 1995), pp. 95, 105–8, 113–14.

60 Caine, pp. 39, 125.

61 Eliza Lynn Linton, 'The Girl of the Period', *Saturday Review*, 14 March 1868.

62 Lucy Bland, 'Marriage Laid Bare: Middle-Class Women and Marital Sex 1880s–1914', in Jane Lewis, ed., *Labour and Love: Women's Experience of Home and Family, 1859–1940* (Basil Blackwell, Oxford, 1986), p. 133.

63 Quoted in Ann Heilmann, 'Mona Caird (1854–1922): Wild Woman, New Woman, and Early Radical Feminist Critic of Marriage and Motherhood', *Women's History Review* 5.1 (1996), p. 70.

64 Sally Ledger, *The New Woman: Fiction and Feminism at the Fin de Siècle* (Manchester UP, Manchester, 1997), pp. 6, 69–70; Bland, *Banishing the Beast*, p. 44; Lesley A. Hall, *Sex, Gender and Social Change in Britain Since 1880* (St Martin's Press, New York, 2000), pp. 49–50, 62.

65 Kali Israel, *Names and Stories: Emilia Dilke and Victorian Culture* (OUP, New York, 1999), pp. 190, 226.

66 Quoted in Gillian Scott, *Feminism and the Politics of Working Women: The Women's Cooperative Guild, 1880s to the Second World War* (UCL Press, London, 1998), p. 22.

67 Pamela M. Graves, *Labour Women: Women in British Working-Class Politics 1918–1939* (CUP, Cambridge, 1994), p. 1.

68 Quoted in Scott, p. 210.

9 Suffrage

1 Quoted in Barbara Caine, 'Feminism, Suffrage and the Nineteenth-Century English Women's Movement', *Women's Studies International Forum* 5.6 (1982), p. 547. See also Jane Rendall, 'Citizenship, Culture and Civilisation: The Languages of British Suffragists, 1866–1874', in Caroline Daley and Melanie Nolan, eds., *Suffrage and Beyond: International Feminist Perspectives* (NYUP, New York, 1994), p. 130.

2 June Hannam, ' "I Had Not Been to London": Women's Suffrage – A View From the Regions', in June Purvis and Sandra Stanley Holton, eds., *Votes for Women* (Routledge, London, 2000), pp. 229–30; Jill Liddington and Jill Norris, *One Hand Tied Behind Us: The Rise of the Women's Suffrage Movement* (1978; 2nd edn Oram Rivers Press, London, 2000); Vicinus, *Independent Women*, p. 248.

3 Mary Lyndon Shanley, 'Suffrage, Protective Labor Legislation, and Married Women's Property Laws in England', *Signs* 12.1 (1986), p. 67.

4 Quoted in June Purvis, 'The Prison Experiences of the Suffragettes in Edwardian Britain', *Women's History Review* 4.1 (1995), p. 115.

5 Gillian Scott, *Feminism and the Politics of Working Women: The Women's Cooperative Guild, 1880s to the Second World War* (UCL Press, London, 1998), p. 38.

6 Elizabeth Crawford, *The Women's Suffrage Movement: A Reference Guide 1866–1928* (UCL Press, London, 1999), pp. 474–9.

7 Crawford, pp. 149–51.

8 Quoted in Margot Finn, 'Women, Consumption and Coverture in England, c. 1760–1860', *Historical Journal* 39.3 (Sept. 1996), p. 705. See also David Rubinstein, 'Millicent Garrett Fawcett and the Meaning of Women's Emancipation, 1886–99', *Victorian Studies* 34.3 (1991), pp. 365–80.

9 Sandra Stanley Holton, 'The Suffragist and the "Average Woman" ', *Womens History Review* 1.1 (1992), pp. 9–24.

10 Quoted in Sophia A. van Wingerden, *The Women's Suffrage Movement in Britain, 1866–1928* (Macmillan, Basingstoke, 1999), p. 41.

11 Sandra Stanley Holton, *Feminism and Democracy: Women's Suffrage and Reform Politics in Britain 1900–1918* (CUP, Cambridge, 1986), p. 7.

12 Lisa Tickner, *The Spectacle of Women: Imagery of the Suffrage Campaign 1907–1914* (U Chicago P, Chicago, 1988), p. 48.

13 Elizabeth Wolstenholme-Elmy, 'Woman's Franchise: The Need of the Hour' (1907), quoted in Antoinette Burton, *Burdens of History: British Feminists, Indian Women, and Imperial Culture, 1865–1915* (U North Carolina P, Chapel Hill, 1994).

14 Quoted in Burton, p. 187.

15 Sandra Stanley Holton, ' "British Freewomen": National Identity, Constitutionalism and Languages of Race in Early Suffragist Histories', in Eileen Janes

Yeo, ed., *Radical Femininity* (Manchester UP, Manchester, 1998), pp. 149–71.

16 Deborah Epstein Nord, *The Apprenticeship of Beatrice Webb* (U Mass. P, Amherst, 1985), p. 149; Lisanne Radice, *Beatrice and Sidney Webb: Fabian Socialists* (St Martin's Press, New York, 1984), p. 177.

17 Julia Bush, 'British Women's Anti-Suffragism and the Forward Policy, 1908–1914', *Women's History Review* 11.3 (2002), pp. 432, 437.

18 Quoted in Wingerden, p. 115.

19 Bush, p. 436; James Thayne Covert, ed., *Memoir of a Victorian Woman: Reflections of Louise Creighton, 1850–1936* (Indiana UP, Bloomington, 1994), pp. 88–9, 145–6.

20 Quoted in Brian Harrison, *Separate Spheres: The Opposition to Women's Suffrage in Britain* (Holmes & Meier, New York, 1978), p. 75.

21 Quoted in Wingerden, p. 11.

22 Harrison, p. 52.

23 Quoted in Wingerden, p. 26.

24 Lesley A. Hall, 'Suffrage, Sex and Science', in Maroula Joannou and June Purvis, eds., *The Women's Suffrage Movement: New Feminist Perspectives* (Manchester UP, Manchester, 1998), pp. 191, 194, 198.

25 Quoted in Tickner, pp. 214–15.

26 Laura E. Nym Mayhall, 'Defining Militancy: Radical Protest, the Constitutional Idiom, and Women's Suffrage in Britain, 1908–1909', *Journal of British Studies* 39.3 (July 2000), p. 344.

27 Jon Lawrence, 'Contesting the Male Polity: The Suffragettes and the Politics of Disruption in Edwardian Britain', in Amanda Vickery, ed., *Women, Privilege, and Power: British Politics, 1750 to the Present* (Stanford UP, Stanford, 2001), pp. 202, 225.

28 Mayhall, p. 346.

29 Quoted in Crawford, pp. 503, 505.

30 Crawford, pp. 504–512.

31 Quoted in Crawford, p. 488.

32 Quoted in Marie Mulvey-Roberts, 'Militancy, Masochism or Martyrdom? The Public and Private Prisons of Constance Lytton', in Purvis and Holton, eds., p. 171.

33 Tickner, p. 209.

34 Sandra Stanley Holton, 'Women and the Vote', in June Purvis, ed., *Women's History: Britain 1850–1945, An Introduction* (2000; Routledge, London, 1995), p. 288.

35 Quoted in Crawford, p. 489.

36 Hilary Frances, ' "Pay the Piper, Call the Tune!": The Women's Tax Resistance League', in Joannou and Purvis, eds., pp. 66–7.

37 Mayhall, pp. 357–8; Hilary Frances,' "Dare To Be Free!" The Women's Freedom League and its Legacy', in Purvis and Holton, eds., p. 189.

38 Ian Christopher Fletcher, ' "A Star Chamber of the Twentieth Century":
   Suffragettes, Liberals, and the 1908 "Rush the Commons" Case', *Journal of
   British Studies* 35 (1996), pp. 504–30.

39 Barbara Caine, *English Feminism 1780–1980* (OUP, Oxford, 1997), pp. 161, 164.

40 Quoted in Wingerden, p. 101.

41 Tickner, pp. 82–4.

42 Quoted in Tickner, p. 94.

43 Quoted in Michelle Myall, ' "No Surrender!" The Militancy of Mary Leigh, a
   Working-Class Suffragette', in Joannou and Purvis, eds., p. 179.

44 Quoted in Sandra Stanley Holton, ' "In Sorrowful Wrath": Suffrage Militancy
   and the Romantic Feminism of Emmeline Pankhurst', in Harold L. Smith, ed.,
   British Feminism in the Twentieth Century (U Mass. P, Amherst, 1990), p. 16.

45 June Purvis, 'A "Pair of . . . Infernal Queens"? A Reassessment of the Dominant
   Representations of Emmeline and Christabel Pankhurst, First Wave Feminists
   in Edwardian Britain', *Women's History Review* 5.2 (1996), p. 261.

46 Quoted in June Purvis, ' "Deeds, Not Words": The Daily Lives of Militant
   Suffragettes in Edwardian Britain', *Women's Studies International Forum* 18.2
   (1995), p. 94.

SUGGESTIONS FOR FURTHER READING

Many valuable essays are not listed separately by their authors but can be found in the edited collections listed below. Each book or essay is listed only once, though some are relevant to more than one chapter.

Multi-chapter books

Olive Banks, *The Biographical Dictionary of British Feminists*, vol. I: *1800–1930* (New York UP, New York, 1985).

Kathryn Gleadle, *British Women in the Nineteenth Century* (Palgrave, Basingstoke, London, 2001).

Kathryn Gleadle and Sarah Richardson, *Women in British Politics, 1760–1860: The Power of the Petticoat* (Macmillan, London, 2000).

Catherine Hall, *White, Male and Middle Class: Explorations in Feminism and History* (Routledge, London, 1992).

Susan Kingsley Kent, *Gender and Power in Britain, 1640–1990* (Routledge, London, 1999).

June Purvis, ed., *Women's History: Britain 1850–1945, An Introduction* (2000; Routledge, London, 1995).

Pamela Sharpe, ed., *Women's Work: The English Experience 1650–1914* (Edward Arnold, London, 1998).

F. M. L. Thompson, ed., *The Cambridge Social History of Britain 1750–1950*, vol. 3: *Social Agencies and Institutions* (CUP, Cambridge, 1990).

Martha Vicinus, *Independent Women: Work and Community for Single Women 1850–1920* (U Chicago P, Chicago, 1985).

Amanda Vickery, ed., *Women, Privilege, and Power: British Politics 1750 to the Present* (Stanford UP, Stanford, 2001).

Introduction

Eric J. Evans, *The Forging of the Modern State: Early Industrial Britain 1783–1870* (2nd edn, Longman, New York, 1983, 1996).

Colin Matthew, ed., *The Nineteenth Century: The British Isles: 1815–1901* (OUP, Oxford, 2000).

Norman McCord, *British History 1815–1906* (OUP, Oxford, 1991).

Trevor May, *An Economic and Social History of Britain 1760–1970* (Longman, Harlow, 1987).

Simon Sretzer, *Fertility, Class and Gender in Britain, 1860–1940* (CUP, Cambridge, 1996).

Robert Woods, *The Demography of Victorian England and Wales* (CUP, Cambridge, 2000).

Chapter 1 Working-class women

Gregory Anderson, ed., *The White-Blouse Revolution: Female Office Workers since 1870* (Manchester UP, Manchester, 1988).

Andrew August, *Poor Women's Lives:, Gender, Work, and Poverty in Late-Victorian London* (Farleigh Dickinson UP, Madison, WI, 1999).

Peter Bailey, 'White Collars, Gray Lives? The Lower Middle Class Revisited', *Journal of British Studies* 38.3 (July, 1999), pp. 273–90.

Joanna Bourke, 'Housewifery in Working-Class England 1860–1914', *Past and Present* 143.2 (May, 1994), pp. 167–97.

Dina M. Copelman, *London's Women Teachers: Gender, Class and Feminism 1870–1930* (Routledge, London, 1996).

Anna Davin, *Growing Up Poor: Home, School, and Street in London, 1870–1914* (Oram Rivers Press, London, 1996).

Mary Freifeld, 'Technological change and the "Self-Acting" Mule: A Study of Skill and the Sexual Division of Labour', *Social History* 11.3 (1986), pp. 319–46.

Katrina Honeyman, *Women, Gender and Industrialisation in England, 1700–1870* (Macmillan, London, 2000).

Angela V. John, ed., *Unequal Opportunities: Women's Employment in England 1800–1918* (Basil Blackwell, Oxford, 1986).

Ellen Jordan, *The Women's Movement and Women's Employment in Nineteenth Century Britain* (Routledge, London, 1999).

Marjorie Levine-Clark, *Beyond the Reproductive Body: The Politics of Women's Health and Work in Early Victorian England* (Ohio State UP, Columbus, 2004).

Judith Lown, *Women and Industrialization: Gender at Work in Nineteenth-Century England* (U. Minnesota Press, Minneapolis, 1990).

Carol E. Morgan, *Women Workers and Gender Identities, 1835–1913: The Cotton and Metal Industries in England* (Routledge, London, 2001).

Ivy Pinchbeck, *Women Workers and the Industrial Revolution 1750–1850* (1930; Frank Cass & Co., London, 1930).

Jane Rendall, *Women in an Industrializing Society: England 1750–1850* (Basil Blackwell, Oxford, 1990).

Elizabeth Roberts, *A Woman's Place: An Oral History of Working-Class Women, 1890–1940* (Basil Blackwell, Oxford, 1984).

Sonya O. Rose, *Limited Livelihoods: Gender and Class in Nineteenth Century England* (Berkeley, U California P, 1992).

Ellen Ross, *Love and Toil: Motherhood in Outcast London 1870–1918* (OUP, Oxford, 1993).

Louise Tilly and Joan Scott, *Women, Work, and Family* (1978; rpt Routledge, New York, 1987).

Deborah Valenze, *The First Industrial Woman* (OUP, New York, 1995).

Nicola Verdon, *Rural Women Workers in Nineteenth-Century England: Gender, Work and Wages* (Boydell Press, Woodbridge, Suffolk, 2002).

2 Middle-class women

Thomas Neville Bonner, *To the Ends of the Earth: Women's Search for Education in Medicine* (Harvard UP, Cambridge, MA, 1992).

Ricki Burman, 'Jewish Women and the Household Economy in Manchester, *c.* 1890–1920', David Cesarini, ed., *The Making of Modern Anglo-Jewry* (Basil Blackwell, Oxford, 1990), pp. 55–75.

Antoinette Burton, ' "Contesting the Zenana": The Mission to Make "Lady Doctors for India", 1874–1885', *Journal of British Studies* 35 (July 1996), pp. 368–97.

Leonore Davidoff and Catherine Hall, *Family Fortunes: Men and Women of the English Middle Class, 1780–1850* (U Chicago P, Chicago, 1987).

Anne Digby and John Stewart, eds., *Gender, Health and Welfare* (Routledge, London, 1996).

Carol Dyhouse, 'Driving Ambitions: Women in Pursuit of a Medical Education, 1890–1939', *Women's History Review* 7.3 (1998), pp. 321–41.

Jane Lewis, *Women in England 1870–1950: Sexual Divisions and Social Change* (Wheatsheaf, Brighton, 1984).

Jane Martin, *Women and the Politics of Schooling in Victorian and Edwardian England* (Leicester UP, London, 1999).

Judith Moore, *A Zeal for Responsibility: The Struggle for Professional Nursing in Victorian England, 1868–1883* (U Georgia P, Athens, 1988).

F. K. Prochaska, *Women and Philanthropy in Nineteenth-Century England* (Clarendon Press, Oxford, 1980).

Anne Summers, 'The Costs and Benefits of Caring: Nursing Charities, *c.* 1830–1860', in Jonathan Barry and Colin Jones, eds., *Medicine and Charity Before the Welfare State* (Routledge, London, 1991), pp. 133–48.

Alex Tyrell, ' "Woman's Mission" and Pressure Group Politics in Britain (1825–60)', *Bulletin of the John Rylands University Library of Manchester*, 63.1 (1980), pp. 194–230.

Ronald G. Walton, *Women in Social Work* (Routledge, London, 1975).

Ruth Watts, *Gender, Power and the Unitarians in England 1760–1860* (Longman, London 1998).

3 Elite women

Hannah Barker and Elaine Chalus, eds., *Gender in Eighteenth-Century England: Roles, Representation and Responsibilities* (Longman, London, 1997).

Stephen C. Behrendt, *Royal Mourning and Regency Culture: Elegies and Memorials of Princess Charlotte* (Macmillan, London, 1997).

David Cannadine, 'The Context, Performance and Meaning of Ritual: The British Monarchy and the "Invention of Tradition", c. 1820–1977,' in Eric Hobsbawm and Terence Ranger, eds., *The Invention of Tradition* (CUP, Cambridge, 1983).

Elaine Chalus, 'Elite Women, Social Politics, and the Political World of Late Eighteenth-Century England', *Historical Journal* 43.3 (2000), pp. 669–97.

Linda Colley, *Britons: Forging the Nation 1707–1837* (Yale UP, New Haven, 1992).

Amanda Foreman, *Georgiana, Duchess of Devonshire* (Random House, New York, 2000).

Jessica Gerard, *Country House Life: Family and Servants 1815–1914* (Basil Blackwell, Oxford, 1994).

Margaret Homans, *Royal Representations: Queen Victoria and British Culture, 1837–1876* (U Chicago P, Chicago, 1998).

Margaret Homans and Adrienne Munich, eds., *Remaking Queen Victoria* (CUP, Cambridge, 1997).

P. J. Jupp, 'The Roles of Royal and Aristocratic Women in British Politics, c. 1782–1832', in Mary O'Dowd and Sabine Wichert, eds., *Chattel, Servant or Citizen: Women's Status in Church, State and Society*, Historical Studies XIX (Institute of Irish Studies, The Queen's University of Belfast, 1995), pp. 103–13.

William Kuhn, *Democratic Royalism: The Transformation of the British Monarchy, 1861–1914* (Macmillan, London, 1996).

Judith S. Lewis, *In the Family Way: Childbearing in the British Aristocracy, 1760–1860* (Rutgers UP, New Brunswick, NJ, 1986).

K. D. Reynolds, *Aristocratic Women and Political Society in Victorian Britain* (Clarendon Press, Oxford, 1998).

Dorothy Thompson, *Queen Victoria: The Woman, The Monarchy, The People* (Pantheon, New York, 1990).

4 Sexuality

Francoise Barret-Ducrocq, *Love in the Time of Victoria: Sexuality, Class and Gender in Nineteenth-Century London*, trans. by John Howe (Verso, London, 1989).

Paula Bartley, *Prostitution: Prevention and Reform in England, 1860–1914* (Routledge, London, 2000).

Lucy Bland, *Banishing the Beast: English Feminism and Sexual Morality 1885–1914* (Penguin, London, 1995).

Lucy Bland and Laura Doan, eds., *Sexology in Culture: Labelling Bodies and Desires* (U Chicago P, Chicago, 1998).

Anna Clark, 'Anne Lister's Construction of Lesbian Identity', *Journal of the History of Sexuality* 7.1 (1996), pp. 23–50.

Shani D'Cruze, *Crimes of Outrage: Sex, Violence and Victorian Working Women* (UCL Press, 1998).

Roger Davidson and Lesley A. Hall, eds., *Sex, Sin and Suffering: Venereal Disease and European Society since 1870* (Routledge, London, 2001).

Lesley A. Hall, *Sex, Gender and Social Change In Britain since 1880* (St Martin's Press, New York, 2000).

A. James Hammerton, *Cruelty and Companionship: Conflict in Nineteenth-Century Married Life* (Routledge, London, 1992).

Tim Hitchcock, *English Sexualities, 1700–1800* (St Martin's Press, New York, 1997).

Thomas W. Laqueur, *Making Sex: Body and Gender from the Greeks to Freud* (Harvard UP, Cambridge, MA, 1990).

Michael Mason, *The Making of Victorian Sexuality* (OUP, Oxford, 1994).

Angus McLaren, *A History of Contraception from Antiquity to the Present Day* (Basil Blackwell, Oxford, 1990).

Linda E. Merians, ed., *The Secret Malady: Venereal Disease in Eighteenth-Century Britain and France* (UP Kentucky, Lexington, 1996).

Douglas M. Peers, 'Soldiers, Surgeons and the Campaigns to Combat Sexually Transmitted Diseases in Colonial India, 1805–1860', *Medical History* 42 (1998), pp. 137–60.

Roy Porter and Lesley Hall, *The Facts of Life: The Creation of Sexual Knowledge in Britain, 1650–1950* (Yale UP, New Haven, 1995).

Barry Reay, 'Sexuality in Nineteenth-Century England: The Social Context of Illegitimacy in Rural Kent', *Rural History* 1.2 (1990), pp. 219–47.

Martha Vicinus, ed., *Lesbian Subjects: A Feminist Studies Reader* (Indiana UP, Bloomington, 1996), pp. 21–40.

Judith R. Walkowitz, *Prostitution and Victorian Society: Women, Class, and the State* (CUP, Cambridge, 1980).

Judith R. Walkowitz, *City of Dreadful Delight: Narratives of Sexual Danger in Late-Victorian London* (Virago, London, 1992).

5 Religion

Olive Anderson, 'Women Preachers in Mid-Victorian Britain: Some Reflections on Feminism, Popular Religion and Social Change', *Historical Journal* 12.3 (1969), pp. 467–84.

David Feldman, *Englishmen and Jews: Social Relations and Political Culture 1840–1914* (Yale UP, New Haven, 1994).

Sean Gill, *Women and the Church of England from the Eighteenth Century to the Present* (SPCK, London, 1994).

Kathryn Gleadle, *The Early Feminists: Radical Unitarians and the Emergence of the Women's Rights Movement, 1831–51* (Macmillan, London, 1995).

Frances Knight, *The Nineteenth-Century Church and English Society* (CUP, Cambridge, 1995).

Susan Mumm, *Stolen Daughters, Virgin Mothers: Anglican Sisterhoods in Victorian Britain* (Leicester UP, London, 1999).

James Obelkovich, Lyndal Roper, and Raphael Samuel, eds., *Disciplines of Faith: Studies in Religion, Politics and Patriarchy* (Routledge, London, 1987).

Susan O'Brien, 'Terra Incognita: the Nun in Nineteenth-Century England', *Past and Present* 121 (Nov. 1988), pp. 110–40.

Rosemary O'Day, 'Women in Victorian Religion', in David Englander and Rosemary O'Day, eds., *Retrieved Riches: Social Investigation in Britain 1840–1914* (Scolar Press, Aldershot, 1995), pp. 339–63.

Alex Owen, *The Darkened Room: Women, Power and Spiritual Late Victorian England* (U Pennsylvania P, Philadelphia, 1990).

Raphael Samuel, 'The Roman Catholic Church and the Irish Poor', in Roger Swift and Sheridan Gilley, eds., *The Irish in the Victorian City* (Croom Helm, London, 1985), pp. 267–300.

Raphael Samuel and Gareth Stedman Jones, eds., *Culture, Ideology and Politics: Essays for Eric Hobsbawm* (History Workshop Series, Routledge & Kegan Paul, London, 1982).

R. N. Swanson, ed., Gender and Christian Religion (Boydell Press, Woodbridge, Suffolk, 1998).

Susan L. Tananbaum, 'Philanthropy and Identity: Gender and Ethnicity in London', *Journal of Social History* 30.4 (1996), pp. 937–61.

Susan Thorne, *Congregational Missions and the Making of an Imperial Culture in Nineteenth-Century England* (Stanford UP, Stanford, 1999).

Deborah Valenze, *Prophetic Sons and Daughters: Female Preaching and Popular Religion in Industrial England* (Princeton UP, Princeton, 1985).

Pamela J. Walker, *Pulling the Devil's Kingdom Down: The Salvation Army in Victorian Britain* (U California P, Berkeley, 2001).

Barbara Walsh, *Roman Catholic Nuns in England and Wales, 1800–1937: A Social History* (Irish Academic Press, Dublin, 2002).

John Wolffe, ed., *Religion in Victorian Britain*, vol. V: *Culture and Empire* (Manchester UP, Manchester, 1997).

6 Education

Joan N. Burstyn, *Victorian Education and the Ideal of Womanhood* (1980; Rutgers UP, New Brunswick, NJ, 1984).

Carol Dyhouse, *Girls Growing Up in Late Victorian and Edwardian England* (Routledge & Kegan Paul, London, 1981).

Carol Dyhouse, *No Distinction of Sex? Women in British Universities, 1870–1939* (UCL Press, London, 1995).

Meg Gomersall, *Working-Class Girls in Nineteenth-Century England: Life, Work and Schooling* (Macmillan, Basingstoke, 1997).

Stephen Heathorn, *For Home, Country, and Race: Constructing Gender, Class, and Englishness in the Elementary School, 1880–1914* (U Toronto P, Toronto, 2000).

Felicity Hunt, ed., *Lessons for Life: The Schooling of Girls and Women, 1850–1950* (Basil Blackwell, Oxford, 1987).

June Purvis, *Hard Lessons: The Lives and Education of Working-Class Women in Nineteenth-Century England* (U Minnesota P, Minneapolis, 1989).

June Purvis, *A History of Women's Education in England* (Open UP, Milton Keynes, 1991).

7 Imperialism

Kenneth Ballhatchet, *Race, Sex and Class Under the Raj: Imperial Attitudes and Policies and their Critics, 1793–1905* (Weidenfeld & Nicolson, London, 1980).

Antoinette Burton, *Burdens of History: British Feminists, Indian Women, and Imperial Culture, 1865–1915* (U North Carolina P, Chapel Hill, 1994).

Antoinette Burton, *At the Heart of the Empire: Indians and the Colonial Encounter in Late-Victorian Britain* (U California P, Berkeley, 1998).

Julia Bush, *Edwardian Ladies and Imperial Power* (Leicester UP, London, 2000).

Nupur Chaudhuri, 'Memsahibs and Motherhood in Nineteenth-Century Colonial India', *Victorian Studies* 31.4 (1988), pp. 517–35.

Nupur Chaudhuri and Margaret Strobel, eds., *Western Women and Imperialism: Complicity and Resistance* (Indiana UP, Bloomington, 1992).

Frederick Cooper and Ann Laura Stoler, eds., *Tensions of Empire: Colonial Cultures in a Bourgeois World* (U California P, Berkeley, 1997).

Indira Ghose, *Women Travellers in Colonial India: The Power of the Female Gaze* (OUP, Delhi, 1998).

Durba Ghosh, *Colonial Companions: Sexual Transgression, Racial Mixing and Gendered Order in Early Colonial India, 1760–1840* (forthcoming).

Janice Gothard, 'A Compromise With Conscience: the Reception of Female Immigrant Domestic Servants in Eastern Australia 1860–1890', *Labour History* [Australia] 62 (1992), pp. 38–51.

Catherine Hall, *Cultures of Empire: A Reader. Colonizers in Britain and the Empire in the Nineteenth and Twentieth Centuries* (Manchester UP, Manchester, 2000).

Catherine Hall, *Civilising Subjects: Colony and Metropole in the English Imagination, 1830–1867* (U Chicago P, Chicago, 2002).

A. James Hammerton, *Emigrant Gentlewomen: Genteel Poverty and Female Emigration, 1830–1914* (Croom Helm, London, 1979).

C. J. Hawes, *Poor Relations: The Making of A Eurasian Community in British India 1773–1833* (Curzon Press, Richmond, Surrey, 1996).

Elizabeth Kowaleski-Wallace, *Consuming Subjects: Women, Shopping, and Business in the Eighteenth Century* (Columbia UP, New York, 1997).

Philippa Levine, 'Rereading the 1890s: Venereal Disease as "Constitutional Crisis" in Britain and British India', *Journal of Asian Studies* 55.3 (Aug. 1996), pp. 585–612.

Lata Mani, *Contentious Traditions* (U California P, Berkeley, 1998).

Clare Midgley, *Women Against Slavery: the British Campaigns, 1780–1870* (Routledge, London, 1992).

Clare Midgley, 'Female Emancipation in an Imperial Frame: English Women and the campaign against *sati* (widow-burning) in India, 1813–1830', *Women's History Review* 9.1 (2000), pp. 95–121.

Clare Midgley, ed., *Gender and Imperialism* (Manchester UP, Manchester, 1998).

Deborah Oxley, *Convict Maids: The Forced Migration of Women to Australia* (CUP, Cambridge, 1996).

Adele Perry, *On the Edge of Empire: Gender, Race, and the Making of British Columbia, 1849–1871* (U Toronto P, Toronto, 2001).

Indrani Sen, 'Between Power and "Purdah": The White Woman in British India, 1858–1900', *Indian Economic and Social History Review*, 34.3 (1997), pp. 355–76.

Mrinalini Sinha, *Colonial Masculinity: The 'Manly Englishman' and the 'Effeminate Bengali' in the Late Nineteenth Century* (Manchester UP, Manchester, 1995).

Charlotte Sussman, *Consuming Anxieties: Consumer Protest, Gender, and British Slavery, 1713–1833* (Stanford UP, Stanford, 2000).

Cecillie Swaisland, *Servants and Gentlewomen to the Golden Land: The Emigration of Single Women from Britain to Southern Africa, 1820–1939* (U Natal P, Berg, 1993).

Penelope Tuson, 'Mutiny Narratives and the Imperial Feminine: European Women's Accounts of the Rebellion in India in 1857', *Women's Studies International Forum* 21.3 (1998), pp. 291–303.

Roxann Wheeler, *The Complexion of Race: Categories of Difference in Eighteenth-Century British Culture* (U Pennsylvania P, Philadelphia, 2000).

Kathleen Wilson, *The Island Race: Englishness, Empire and Gender in the Eighteenth Century* (Routledge, London, 2003).

Anand A. Yang, 'Whose Sati? Widow Burning in Early 19th Century India', *Journal of Women's History* 1.2 (Fall 1989), pp. 8–33.

8 Politics

John Belchem, *Popular Radicalism in Nineteenth-Century Britain* (St Martin's Press, New York, 1996).

John Bohstedt, 'Gender, Household and Community Politics: Women in English Riots 1790–1810', *Past and Present* 120 (Aug. 1988), pp. 88–122.

Barbara Caine, *English Feminism 1780–1980* (OUP, Oxford, 1997).

Anna Clark, 'Queen Caroline and the Sexual Politics of Popular Culture in London, 1820', *Representations* 31 (Summer 1990), pp. 47–68.

Anna Clark, 'The Rhetoric of Chartist Domesticity: Gender, Language, and Class in the 1830s and 1840s', *Journal of British Studies* 31 (Jan. 1992), pp. 62–88.

Anna Clark, *The Struggle for the Breeches: Gender and the Making of the British Working Class* (U California P, Berkeley, 1995).

James A. Epstein, *Radical Expression: Political Language, Ritual, and Symbol in England, 1790–1850* (OUP, Oxford, 1994).

Margot Finn, *After Chartism: Class and Nation in English Radical Politics, 1848–1874* (CUP, Cambridge, 1993).

Margot Finn, 'Women, Consumption and Coverture in England, *c.* 1760–1860', *Historical Journal* 39.3 (Sept. 1996), pp. 703–22.

Patricia Hollis, *Ladies Elect: Women in English Local Government 1865–1914* (Clarendon Press, Oxford, 1987).

Thomas W. Laqueur, 'The Queen Caroline Affair: Politics as Art in the Reign of George IV', *Journal of Modern History* 54.3 (Sept. 1982), pp. 417–66.

Sally Ledger, *The New Woman: Fiction and Feminism at the Fin de Siècle* (Manchester UP, Manchester, 1997).

Lynn Hollen Lees, *The Solidarities of Strangers: The English Poor Laws and the People, 1700–1948* (CUP, Cambridge, 1998).

G. E. Maguire, *Conservative Women: A History of Women and the Conservative Party, 1874–1997* (Macmillan, London, 1998).

Iain McCalman, *Radical Underworld: Prophets, Revolutionaries and Pornographers in London, 1795–1840* (CUP, Cambridge, 1988).

Rohan McWilliam, *Popular Politics in Nineteenth-Century England* (Routledge, London, 1998).

Susan Pedersen, 'Hannah More Meets Simple Simon: Tracts, Chapbooks, and Popular Culture in Late Eighteenth-Century England', *Journal of British Studies* 25 (Jan. 1986), pp. 84–113.

Iowerth Prothero, *Radical Artisans in England and France, 1830–1870* (CUP, Cambridge, 1997).

Martin Pugh, *The Tories and the People 1880–1935* (Basil Blackwell, Oxford, 1985).

Jane Rendall, ed., *Equal or Different: Women's Politics 1800–1914* (Basil Blackwell, Oxford, 1987).

Sarah Richardson, 'The Role of Women in Electoral Politics in Yorkshire During the Eighteen-Thirties', *Northern History* 32 (1996), pp. 133–51.

David Rubinstein, *Before the Suffragettes: Women's Emancipation in the 1890s* (St Martin's Press, New York, 1986).

Jutta Schwarzkopf, *Women in the Chartist Movement* (St Martin's Press, New York, 1991).

Gillian Scott, *Feminism and the Politics of Working Women: The Women's Cooperative Guild, 1880s to the Second World War* (UCL Press, London, 1998).

Mary Lyndon Shanley, *Feminism, Marriage, and the Law in Victorian England* (Princeton UP, Princeton, 1989).

Anne Stott, *Hannah More: The First Victorian* (OUP, Oxford, 2003).

Barbara Taylor, *Eve and the New Jerusalem: Socialism and Feminism in the Nine-teenth Century* (Pantheon, New York, 1983).

Dorothy Thompson, 'Women and Nineteenth-Century Politics: A Lost Dimension', in Juliet Mitchell and Ann Oakley, eds., *The Rights and Wrongs of Women* (Penguin, New York, 1976), pp. 112–38.

Eileen Janes Yeo, ed., *Radical Femininity: Women's Self-Representation in the Public Sphere* (Manchester UP, Manchester, 1998).

9 Suffrage

Julia Bush, 'British Women's Anti-Suffragism and the Forward Policy, 1908–1914', Women's History Review 11.3 (2002), pp. 431–54.

Elizabeth Crawford, *The Women's Suffrage Movement: A Reference Guide 1866–1928* (UCL Press, London, 1999).

Caroline Daley and Melanie Nolan, eds., *Suffrage and Beyond: International Feminist Perspectives* (NYUP, New York, 1994).

Ian Christopher Fletcher, Laura E. Nym Mayhall, Philippa Levine, eds., *Women's Suffrage in the British Empire* (Routledge, London, 2000).

Brian Harrison, *Separate Spheres: The Opposition to Women's Suffrage in Britain* (Holmes & Meier, New York, 1978).

Sandra Stanley Holton, *Feminism and Democracy: Women's Suffrage and Reform Politics in Britain 1900–1918* (CUP, Cambridge, 1986).

Sandra Stanley Holton, *Suffrage Days: Stories from the Women's Suffrage Movement* (Routledge, London, 1996).

Maroula Joannou and June Purvis, eds., *The Women's Suffrage Movement: New Feminist Perspectives* (Manchester UP, Manchester, 1998).

Jill Liddington and Jill Norris, *One Hand Tied Behind Us: The Rise of the Women's Suffrage Movement* (1978; 2nd edn., Oram Rivers Press, London, 2000).

Laura E. Nym Mayhall, 'Defining Militancy: Radical Protest, the Constitutional Idiom, and Women's Suffrage in Britain, 1908–1909', *Journal of British Studies* 39.3 (July 2000), pp. 340–71.

June Purvis, 'The Prison Experiences of the Suffragettes in Edwardian Britain', Women's History Review 4.1 (1995), pp. 103–33.

June Purvis, *Emmeline Pankhurst: a Biography* (Routledge, London, 2002).

June Purvis and Sandra Stanley Holton, eds., *Votes for Women* (Routledge, London, 2000).

Harold L. Smith, ed., *British Feminism in the Twentieth Century* (U Massachusetts P, Amherst, 1990).

Lisa Tickner, *The Spectacle of Women: Imagery of the Suffrage Campaign 1907–1914* (U Chicago P, Chicago, 1988).

INDEX

Aberdeen, Ishbel, Countess of, 91
Aboriginal people, 208, 293
abortion/abortifacients, 130, 131–2
Abraham, May, 77
ACCL *see* Anti-Corn Law League
Acton, Eliza: *Modern Cookery*, 218
Acton, William: *The Functions and
    Disorders of the Reproductive Organs*, 117
Actresses' Franchise League, 288
adult education, 180–1
Africa, 57, 199, 207, 221, 222, 225
    immigrants from, 207
    troops from, 199–200
    see also North Africa; South Africa
Afro-Caribbean immigrants, 207
agricultural work, 16–17
Aide, Hamilton, 95
Aiken, Lucy, 91
Ajnala, 204
Akroyd Beveridge, Annette, 216, 228–9
Albert, Prince, 102, 104, 105–6
Albert Memorial Chapel, Windsor, 105
Alcott House, 256
Alexander, Mrs: *Hymns for Little Children*,
    144
Allbut, Henry Arthur, 130, 131
    The Wife's Handbook, 130, 131
Allen, J.M., 114
American colonies, 202, 204
Anderson, Elizabeth Garrett, 73, 79, 80, 182,
    188, 190, 191, 230, 264, 286
Anglicans/Anglican Church (Church of
        England), 50, 58, 145, 226
    and Conservative Party, 239, 245
    and education, 178, 182, 187, 190, 191
    and religion, 141, 142, 143–5, 147, 148, 156,
        158, 159, 160, 161
    and sexual and marital issues, 115, 116
Anglo-Catholics, 143, 159
Anne, Queen, 97

Annesley, James: *Memoirs of an Unfortunate
    Nobleman*, 211
Anti-Corn Law League (ACLL), 58, 257–8,
    283, 286
anti-slavery movement *see* slavery
Anti-Slavery Society, 226, 227
anti-suffrage movement, 294–6, 304
Anti-Sweating League, 78, 281
aristocratic women *see* elite women
Aristotle's Masterpiece, 116
Arkwright, Lucy, 89
Ashurst, Caroline *see* Stansfield, Caroline
    Ashurst
Ashurst, Eliza, 256
Ashurst, Emilie *see* Venturi, Emilie Ashurst
Ashurst, Matilda, 256
Ashurst, William, 256
Ashurst circle, 256
Ashworth, Mrs, 59
Asian immigrants, 207
Asquith, Herbert, 77, 240, 280, 281, 298, 310,
    313
Association for the Promotion of the
    Higher Education of Women in
    Cambridge, 189
atheism, 153
Austen, Jane, 52, 53
Austin, Mary, 136
Australia, 57, 59, 208, 211, 212, 236, 237, 293
    emigration to, 230, 231, 232–4, 235
    immigrants from, 208
    troops from, 199–200
ayah, 214, 216

Bagehot, Walter: *The English Constitution*,
    103
Baker Brown, Isaac, 117
Baldock, Minnie, 289
Balfour, Lady, 310
Bank of England, 38–9

Baptist Missionary Society (BMS), 156, 157, 222
Baptist Zenana Mission, 157
Baptists, 144, 148, 167
Barbados, 202
Barclay's Bank, 145
Barlow, Miss, 235
Barnier, Mary, 59
Bartrum, Katherine, 205
Bass, Matilda, 167
Bath, 123, 174, 185, 287
bazaars, 57–8
Beale, Dorothea, 186, 188, 265
Beale, Dr Lionel S., 67
Becker, Lydia, 257, 264, 272, 273, 274, 275, 290, 297, 299, 302, 304
Bedchamber crisis (1839), 104
Bedford College, London, 188
Beeton, Mrs: Book of Household Management, 18, 19, 48, 218
Bell, Blair, 118
Benares, 215
Bengal, 204
Bengal Army, 204
Bentley, Elizabeth, 25–6
Bergami, Bartolomeo, 248
Bernhardt, Sarah, 58
Besant, Annie, 130, 133, 170–1, 193, 229
The Law of Population, 130
Beveridge, Henry, 229
Bible Christians, 148, 164–5, 166
Biblewomen, 158, 160
Billington-Greig, Theresa, 306, 307
Birch, Louisa, 129
Bird, Isabella, 220
Birmingham, 11, 33, 71, 146, 149, 151
birth control see fertility, controlling
Bishop Otter College, Chichester, 71
Black, Clementina, 78, 277, 281
A Case for Trade Boards, 281
Married Women's Work, 78
Sweated Industry and the Minimum Wage, 281
Black Country, 33
Blackburn, Helen, 290
Blackburn Female Reform Society, 247
Blackfriars Settlement, 76
Blackheath, 185
Blackstone, William, 267
Blackwell, Elizabeth, 80
Blavatsky, Madame Helena, 170

BMS see Baptist Missionary Society
Board of Trade, 78, 281
boarding schools, 173, 174
Bodichon, Barbara Leigh Smith, 65, 188, 189, 191, 263, 265, 270, 272, 285
A Brief Summary in Plain Language of the Most Important Laws of England Concerning Women, 263, 270
Boer War, 184, 201, 204, 209, 221, 277, 304
Bombay, 204
Booth, Mrs Alfred, 287
Booth, Catherine, 168
Female Teaching, 168
Booth, Charles, 153
Life and Labour of the People in London, 78
Booth, William, 168
Bostock, Benedicta, 161
Boston, 57
Boucherett, Jessie, 263, 265, 266, 272
Boy's Own Magazine, 201
Boy's Own Paper, 201, 202
Braddon, Mary Elizabeth, 52, 53, 54
Bradlaugh, Alice, 193
Bradlaugh, Charles, 130, 153
Brahmo Samaj, 207
breast-feeding, 13, 87, 127
Bright, Mrs Allan, 287
Bright, Jacob, 264, 286, 297
Bright, John, 264
Bright, Ursula Mellors, 264, 273, 275, 286
Brighton, 174, 259
Brisbane, 233
Bristol, 61, 71, 146, 207, 244
British and Foreign School Society, 180
British Columbia, 211
British Empire, 199–237, 293, 296, 317, 318–19
British Ladies' Society 60–1
British Nursing Association, 68
British Orphan Asylum, 57
British Socialist Party (BSP), 261
British Society of Ladies for Promoting the Reformation of Female Prisoners, 60–1
British Women's Emigration Association (BWEA), 232
British Women's Temperance Association (BWTA), 150
Brocas, Bernard, 136
Brocas, Jane, 136
Brontë, Charlotte, 52, 53, 54
Brontë, Emily, 52, 53

Brooke, Emma, 52
  A Superfluous Woman, 279
Brooke, Henry: *Fool of Quality*, 211
Brooks, Johanna, 166
Brougham, Lord, 270
Brown, Nessie Egerton Stewart, 287
Browning, Elizabeth Barrett, 270
Browning, Robert, 280
Bruton, Mrs E.H., 92
Bryant & May, 281
Buchan, Luckie, 162
Buckingham, Marchioness of, 89
Buckingham Palace, 106
Bultitude, Elizabeth, 166
Burdett-Coutts, Angela, 56, 231
Burgess, Anne, 21
Burke, Edmund, 244
Burma, 200
Burns, Jean, 235–6
Burstall, Sara, 68, 69
businesses
  family, 45, 50
  owned by women, 51
Buss, Mary Frances, 185, 188, 265, 266
Butler, Lady Eleanor, 122
Butler, Fanny, 81
Butler, Josephine, 185, 191, 263, 271–2, 276,
  291, 308
  and campaign against Contagious
    Diseases Acts, 144, 185, 264, 274–5, 276,
    300
Buttledoor, Hannah, 232

Caddick, Helen: *A White Woman in Central
  Africa*, 221
Caine, Barbara, 241
Caird, Mona, 52, 277, 279–80
  The Daughters of Danaus, 279
Calcutta, 204, 216, 228–9
Cambridge University, 69, 70, 189, 191, 192,
  245 *see also individual colleges*
Canada, 208–9, 211, 213, 230, 235–6, 237
  immigrants from, 208
  troops from, 199–200
Cannadine, David, 83–4
Cantonment Act (1889), 276
Cape of Good Hope, 209
Caribbean, the, 199, 202–3, 210, 217, 225,
  236–7
Carlile, Jane, 247
Carlile, Mary-Ann, 247

Carlile, Richard, 247
Carlisle, Lady, 92
Caroline, Queen, 97, 99, 100–1, 248–50
Carpenter, Edward, 117
Carpenter, Mary, 61, 62, 71, 146–7, 206, 223,
  228, 229
  Six Months in India, 228
Carr, Ann, 166, 167
Cartwright, John, 247
Cat and Mouse Act (Prisoners' Temporary
  Discharge for Ill Health Act) (1913),
  314–15
Catholic Emancipation (1829), 150
Catholic Women's Suffrage Society, 288
Catholics, 50, 142, 144, 146, 150–1, 152, 158,
  159, 160, 161, 182
Cawnpore, 204–5
Cecil, Lady Gwendolen, 96
censuses
  as historical source, 10
  1851, 10, 153, 234, 266
  1871, 10
  1881, 10
  1891, 18
Central Committee of the National Society
  for Women's Suffrage *see* Great College
  Street Society
Central National Society for Women's
  Suffrage *see* Parliament Street Society
Central Poor Law Commission, 253
Ceylon, 156
Chalus, Elaine, 84
Chamberlain, Joseph, 206, 221
Chambers, Mary Ann, 157
Chant, Laura Ormiston, 276–7
charity *see* philanthropy
Charity Organization Society (COS), 76,
  78
charity schools, 178–9
Charles, Amelia, 74
Charlotte, Princess, 97, 98–100, 101, 107
Charlotte, Queen, 97–8
Chartism, 149, 252–6, 285
Chartist Abstinence Unions, 149
Chartist Temperance Tea Parties, 149
Cheltenham College for Boys, 175
Cheltenham Ladies' College, 185, 186
Cheshire, 24, 77
Chessar, Jane, 73
Chew, Ada Nield, 289
childbirth, 99–100, 102, 126–33

children, 13, 48–50, 86–8, 102, 132, 133, 201–2, 215
    custody of, 268–9, 273
    education of see governesses; schools
    illegitimate, 86, 120–1, 255
Children's Country Holiday Fund, 76
Children's Employment Commission Inquiring into the Factories (1833), 26
China, 200, 220
Chisholm, Caroline, 231
Chorlton v. Lings, 297
Church League for Women's Suffrage, 288
Church Missionary Gleaner, The, 222
Church of England see Anglicans/Anglican Church
Church of England Purity Society, 144
Church of England Temperance Society, 143, 149
Church of England Zenana Missionary Society, 157, 220
Church Missionary Society, 156, 157
Churchill, Clementine, 96
Churchill, Jenny, 96
Civil Registration Act (1837), 145
Clarendon, Earl of, 83
Clarendon Street Girls' Club, Manchester, 192
Clark, Alice, 286
Clark, Anna, 250
clerks, 34, 35, 36–9, 65–6
Clerks' Women's Social and Political Union, 288
Clough, Anne Jemima, 189, 191, 192–3
Cobbe, Frances Power, 245, 272, 301
Cole, Margaret, 193
Coleman, Charlotte, 271
Collet, Clara, 78, 277, 281
Colley, Linda, 100
Colonial and Indian Exhibition (1886), 201
Colonial Office, 200
Coltman, Elizabeth, 232
Common Cause, The, 291, 310
Conciliation Bill (1911), 313, 314
Conciliation Committee, 313
condoms, 128, 129, 131
Congregationalists, 144, 156
Conservatives/Tories, 94, 95, 96, 104, 239, 244, 245, 259
    and suffrage movement, 288, 298, 302, 313, 315
consumer goods, 216–18

Consumers' League, 78, 281
Contagious Diseases Acts, 138, 144, 185, 212, 264, 266, 273–6, 290, 296, 300–1
contraception see fertility, controlling
contraceptive sponges, 131, 133
convents/sisterhoods, 158–62
convicts, 232–3
Cook, Captain, 200, 208
Cook, Florence, 170
Co-operative Wholesale Society, 283
Corelli, Marie, 52
Cornwall, 166
Corrupt Practices Act (1883), 95, 259
Cottle, Em, 166
Coultart, Revd James, 157
Courtauld family, 146
courtship, 124–5
Coventry, 24, 32, 77
'coverture', 268, 270, 272, 299, 300
Craigen, Jessie, 282, 290
Craik, Dinah Mulock, 52, 53–4
Cranworth, Lord Chancellor, 271
Creighton, Louise, 295
Creighton, Mandell, 295
Crimean War, 36, 66
Crompton, Samuel, 27, 30, 32
Crompton's mule (spinning), 27, 32
cross-dressing, 121–2
Crystal Palace, 105
Cullwick, Hannah, 20–1
Curnow, Elizabeth, 21
Curzon, Lord, 296
Custody of Children Act (1839), 269
Cutler, Ann, 164

Daily Herald, 161
Daily Mail, 305
Daily Telegraph, 279–80
dame schools, 177–8
Dart, Elizabeth, 166
Darwin, Charles: Descent of Man, 117
Davey, Elizabeth, 21
Davidoff, Leonore, 45
Davies, Emily
    and education, 182, 185, 188, 189, 191, 244–5, 264, 265, 286, 291
    and feminism, 244–5, 263, 264, 265
    and politics, 244
    and suffrage, 289
Davison, Emily Wilding, 314
Dawes, William Pettit, 271

deaconesses, 159, 160
Deane, Lucy, 77
Derby, 77, 166
Derby Day (1913), 314
desire, sexual, 113–14
Despard, Charlotte, 298, 307
Devonshire, Duke of, 83, 92
Devonshire, Georgiana, Duchess of, 93, 121
Devonshire House, 95
diaphragm (contraceptive), 131
Dickens, Charles, 58, 67, 231
    Hard Times, 29
    Oliver Twist, 254
Dilke, Lady Emilia, 77, 277, 280–1
Disraeli, Benjamin, 239, 298
divorce, 86, 126, 138, 268, 270–1, 283
Divorce Act (1857), 270–1
doctors, 127–8, 129, 132, 137, 138
    female, 64, 79–81
domestic service, 18–22, 62–3
domestic violence, 126
domesticity, 87, 105, 147, 152, 209–16
    see also home
Douglas, Madame (pseudonym of Louisa
    Fenn), 130
Dufferin, Harriet, Countess of, 81
Dufferin Fund, 81

East, Mary, 123
East End of London, 135, 156, 158, 168, 169
East India Company, 203, 204, 207, 211, 212
eastern England, 16, 23
Eastwood, Annie, 190
Eden, Emily, 219, 220
    Up the Country, 219
Edgeworth, Maria, 52
Edinburgh University, 80
education, 42, 68, 91, 146, 172–95, 318
Education Acts
    1870, 37, 175, 177, 182, 297
    1880, 182
    1899, 182
    1902, 40, 182, 187
    1918, 182
Edward Albert, Prince of Wales, 102, 106
Edwards, George, 176
effeminacy, 203, 238
Election Fighting Fund (EFF), 314, 315
elections, 92–3, 95, 245–6
elementary schools, 70, 71–2, 182–4
    teachers, 34, 39–41, 71

Eliot, George (Marian Evans), 52, 53, 270,
    280
elite women, 83–107, 124, 173–4, 231–2, 245
    aristocratic, 83–97, 121, 127, 128, 172, 173–4,
        289
    royal, 83, 84, 97–107, 127 *see also*
        individual royal women
Elizabeth I, Queen, 97
Ellacombe, Jane, 160
Ellis, Havelock, 280
    Studies in the Psychology of Sex, 118
Elmy, Benjamin, 264, 301
Ely, Lady, 105
Emigrant and Colonial Gazette, The, 233
*Emigrant Gazette and Colonial Settler's
    Guide, The*, 233
emigration, 230–6, 266–7
Empire Day, 201
Englishwoman's Domestic Magazine, The,
    218
Englishwoman's Journal, The, 188, 263
Englishwomen's Review, 230
Enlightenment, 241, 291
Erle-Drax, W.S., 92
Essex, 17, 26, 32, 89
evangelicalism, 90–1, 96, 115, 142, 147–8
Evans, Janet, 247
Evans, Mary, 162
Evans, Thomas, 247
extramarital sex, 120–1

Factory Acts, 25
    1833, 177, 179
    1844, 179
Factory Department, 77, 78, 281
factory inspectors, 76–8
factory schools, 179
factory work, 23–9
Faithfull, Emily, 264
Falkland, Amelia: *Chow-Chow*, 219
family businesses, 45, 50
Family Colonialisation Loan Society, 231
family income
    aristocratic, 83
    middle-class, 43–4, 47, 50–4
fancy fairs,   57–8
Far East, 223
Farningham, Marianne, 149
Fawcett, Henry, 272, 285, 286, 291
Fawcett, Millicent Garrett, 79, 230
    and feminism, 263, 264, 266, 272, 278, 280

Fawcett, Millicent Garrett—*cont*
 political orientation, 245
 and suffrage, 286, 291, 294, 295, 299, 301,
  302, 304, 310, 316
Female Middle-Class Emigration Society
 (FMCES), 231, 266–7
Female Revivalists, 164–5, 166–7
Female Society for Birmingham, 226
Female Visitor to the Poor, The, 60
feminists, 3, 65, 80, 129, 138, 139–40, 170, 172,
  242, 318
 and domestic politics, 238, 240, 244–5,
  251, 262–83, 284
 and Empire, 229–30, 231, 234
 suffrage movement, 285–316
Fenn, Louisa (Madame Douglas), 130
Fern, Ann, 21
fertility, controlling, 49, 87, 127, 128–33,
  139–40
Fidoe, Amelia, 35
Fildes, Mary, 247
financial independence, 85
finishing schools, 174
First Concordium (Ham Common
 Concordium), 256
First World War, 81, 138, 199–200, 261, 277,
  315, 316
food riots, 246
force-feeding, 311–12, 314–15
Forster, William, 37, 182
'Forward Policy' (of anti-suffragists), 294
Foster family, 20–1
Fox, Charles James, 93
Fox, George, 145
Fox, Helen, 308–9
Fox, William, 256–7
Francis, Marianne, 91
Freewoman (journal), 139
French Revolution, 241, 294
Fry, Elizabeth, 49, 60–1
Fuseli, Henry, 241

Garrett, Elizabeth *see* Anderson, Elizabeth
 Garrett
Garrett, Millicent *see* Fawcett, Millicent
 Garrett
Gaskell, Elizabeth, 52, 53, 270
Gaskell, Peter, 24
Gaunt, Elizabeth Gorse, 166
Gawthorpe, Mary, 289, 291
Geals, Sarah, 123

Geddes, Patrick, 118
gender history, 3–4
General Medical Council, 131
General Post Office *see* Post Office
George III, King, 97, 98, 100, 184
George IV, King, 97, 98, 101, 248, 250
Gill, Helga, 289
Girl's Friendly Society (GFS), 143, 232, 233
Girl's Own Paper, 202
Girls' Public Day School Trust, 185
Girton College, Cambridge, 68, 70, 189, 191,
  193, 244, 264
Gladstone, William Ewart, 105, 107, 240,
  274, 298, 302
Glasgow, 151
Gloyne, Elizabeth, 271–2
Godwin, William, 52, 241
gonorrhoea, 135, 138 *see also* venereal disease
Gordon, Duchess of, 94
Gospel Temperance movement, 150
governesses, 51, 174–5
Governesses' Benevolent Institution (GBI),
  175, 187
Gower, Countess of, 87–8
Graham, Mrs Elizabeth, 246
Graham, Maria, 219
 Journal of a Residence in India, 219
grammar schools, 185–7
Grand, Sarah, 52
 The Beth Book, 279
 The Heavenly Twins, 279
Granville, Harriet, 99
Great College Street Society (Central
 Committee of the National Society for
 Women's Suffrage), 301, 302, 303
Great Western Railway, 37
Greg, W.R., 234–5
Grey, Maria, 185
grille protest (1908), 308–9
Grimstone, Mary Leman, 256–7
Grosvenor, Lord Robert, 90
Grosvenor House, 95
Guest, Lady Charlotte, 93–4, 180
Gurney, Catherine, 49–50
Gurney, Mary, 185

Hall, Catherine, 45
Hall, Lesley, 137
Hall, Mary: *A Woman's Trek from Cape to
 Cairo*, 221
Hallelujah Lasses, 168, 169

Ham Common Concordium (First Concordium), 256
Hamilton, Cicely, 139, 277, 280
  How the Vote Was Won (written with Christopher St John), 280
  Marriage as a Trade, 280
Hargreaves, James, 27, 32
Harrison, Jane, 70, 175
Hartshead Moor, 254
Havergal, Frances, 143
Havergal, Maria, 143
Hawkins, Jane, 119, 125
Hawkins v. Pring, 119, 125
Hay, Alexander, 120
Hays, Matilda, 256
Hazlitt, William, 248
Hervey, Lady, 94
Heyrick, Elizabeth, 145, 227
Hicks, Margaretta, 261
Hill, Matthew Davenport, 270
Hill, Octavia, 70, 74–5, 76
Holford, Mrs Gwynne, 92–3
Holland, Elizabeth, Lady, 87, 94, 245
Holloway Prison, 310
Holyoake, G.J., 51
Homans, Margaret, 101
home
  aristocratic, 85–92
  middle-class, 46–50
  working-class, 12–16
Home for Business Ladies, 38
Home Rule, 95, 245, 302, 313
Hong Kong, 212, 274
Hook, Mrs, 15
Hopkins, Jane Ellice, 144
hospital dispensers, 66
House of Commons, 104, 270, 285, 286, 296, 308–9
House of Lords, 83, 95, 248, 270
housing managers, 74–5
How, James (pseudonym of Mary East), 123
Howard sisters, 92
Howe, Hannah, 166
Huddersfield, 254
Hufton, Olwen, 11
Hughes, Molly, 185
Hull, 166, 175
Hume-Rothery, Mary, 274
Humphries, Caroline, 232
Hunt, Henry, 247

Hutchins, Mary Ann, 155
Hyde Park, 105, 310

Ilbert, Courtenay, 215–16
Ilbert Bill controversy (1883), 204, 215–16
illegitimate children, 86, 119–21, 255
Illustrated London News, 233
Imlay, Gilbert, 241
immigrants, 151, 152, 207–8
imperialism, 80, 199–237, 293–4
income *see* family income
Indecent Advertisements Act (1889), 131
Independent Labour Party (ILP), 305
Independent Methodists, 164–5 *see also* Methodists
India, 57, 170, 206, 244, 274, 276, 318
  goods from, 217–18
  history of British involvement in, 204–5
  Indian Rebellion (1857), 204–5
  Indian women, 80, 81, 220, 223–5, 228–9, 230, 293
  as 'jewel in the crown', 204
  missionaries in, 157, 222–3
  population, 199
  and reformers, 223–5, 228–30
  travel narratives about, 219–20
  troops from, 199–200
  Victoria as Empress of, 102, 200
  visitors to England from, 207–8
  white domesticity in, 211–13, 214–16, 236, 237
India Act (1784), 212
Indian Army, 133–4, 213
Indian National Congress, 204
indigenous populations, 208
Industrial Revolution, 9
industrialization, 9, 23, 42
infanticide, 129, 132
inspectors, 76–8
Institution of Nursing Sisters, 60
interracial relationships, 209–10, 211–12, 213
Ireland, 5, 24, 77
Irish College of Physicians, 80
Irish immigration, 146, 150
Irish Home Rule, 95, 245, 302, 313
Irish nationalists, 308, 313
Isle of Man, 293
Isle of Wight, 102

Jack the Ripper, 22, 135
Jackson, Annabel, 186

Jamaica, 202–3, 204, 210, 211, 212, 213–14, 318
    missionaries in, 155, 157, 222
    troops from, 199–200
Jersey, Sarah Sophia, Countess of, 87, 89, 94
Jersey, Margaret Elizabeth, Countess of, 96
Jesup, Mary, 48–9
Jewish Association for the Protection of
    Girls and Women, 152
Jewish Board of Guardians (JBG), 152
Jewish League for Woman Suffrage, 288
Jews, 143, 151–3
Jex-Blake, Sophia, 79, 80
Joan of Arc, 307
Jones, Agnes, 67
Jubilee celebrations, 106–7, 200

Kashmir shawls, 218
Kenney, Annie, 290, 301, 307, 308
Kensington, 73, 74
Kensington Society, 185, 263
Kent, 51, 120
Kent, Duke of, 99
Kenyon Baptist Church, 153
King's College, London, 187
Kingsley, Mary, 221
    Travels in West Africa, 221
Kirkland, Sarah, 166
Knight, Anne, 145, 228
Knightley, Lady, 289
Knowlton, Charles: Fruits of Philosophy, 130

Labour Party, 261, 282, 288, 313, 314, 315
Ladies' Companion for Visiting the Poor,
    The, 60
Ladies' Educational Associations, 189
Ladies' National Association (LNA), 144,
    274, 275, 276, 300–1, 308
'Ladies of Llangollen', the, 122
Ladies' Treasury, 218
Lady Margaret Hall, Oxford, 189, 193
Lady Margaret Hall Settlement, Lambeth,
    76
Lancashire
    church attendance in, 153
    factory schools in, 179
    socialism in, 261
    suffrage movement in, 287, 289, 306
    textile industry in, 24, 25, 26, 27, 28, 77,
        177, 287, 289
Lancet, The, 54, 117
Lander, Elizabeth, 271

Landon, Letitia Elizabeth: 'Princess
    Charlotte', 100
Langham Place circle, 65, 188, 263, 266, 285
Lansdowne House, 95
Laqueur, Thomas, 112, 250
laundry work, 77
Lawton, Marianna, 123
Layton, Mrs, 183
Leatham, E.A., 300
Lee, Ann, 162
Leeds, 25, 71, 130, 146, 151, 166, 291
    Workhouse, 62
Leeds Vigilance Association (LVA), 131
Leicester, 26
Leicestershire, 24
Leigh, Mary, 312
Leisure Hour, The (periodical), 222
Lennox, Emily, 6
Leopold, Prince, 102
Leopold of Saxe-Coburg (later King of
    Belgium), 99
lesbians, 121–3
Lewis, Sarah, 54
Liberals, 95, 239–40, 245, 260–1, 273, 274
    and suffrage, 288, 298, 302, 303, 304, 308,
        309, 312–13, 313–14, 315
    see also Whigs
Linton, Eliza Lynn, 278–9
Lister, Anne, 123, 245
Liverpool, 71, 151, 207, 287
    workhouse, 67
Liverpool, Lady, 94
Llewelyn Davies, Margaret, 277, 282, 283,
    289
Lloyd George, David, 309, 313
LNA see Ladies' National Associaton
local education authorities, 182–3
Local Government Act (1894), 303
local politics, 258–9, 297–8
London, 127, 221, 231, 249, 253, 256, 261
    aristocratic women in, 88, 89, 90, 93–4
    education in, 182, 183, 185
    feminism in, 262, 263–4
    growth of, 6
    immigrants in, 151, 207
    and imperialism, 200, 201
    Jubilee celebrations in, 106–7
    middle-class women in, 56, 57, 58, 60, 62,
        67, 72, 74, 76
    religion in, 149, 151, 153, 156, 158, 159, 160,
        162, 168

sexuality in, 114, 123, 134, 135, 137
suffrage movement in, 285, 286, 288, 299–300, 301, 305, 310–11
working-class women in, 10, 13, 18, 24, 33, 34, 36, 38, 39, 41
London Female Bible and Domestic Mission, 156
London Foundling Hospital, 111, 120
London Gazette, 104
London Lock Hospital, 137
London Missionary Society, 156
London National Society for Women's Suffrage, 188
London Obstetrical Society, 117, 190
London School Board (LSB), 72, 73, 183
London School of Medicine for Women (LSMW), 80, 230, 264
London Season, 83, 86, 88, 93–4, 124
London Suffrage Committee, 185
London University, 71, 80, 187–8 *see also individual colleges*
Londonderry, Frances Anne, Marchioness of, 86, 87, 94
Lovett, William, 54
Lowe, Louisa, 170
Lucas, Helen, 152
Lumsden, Louisa, 70
Lyttelton, Mrs Arthur: *Women and their Work*, 46
Lytton, Constance, 312

McCaw, Elizabeth, 136
M'Connel & Co., 179
MacDonald, Flora, 216
McIlquham, Harriet, 74
Mackenzie, Mrs Colin: *Six Years in India*, 219, 220
Madras, 204
'magdalene homes', 60, 134–5 *see also penitentiaries*
Maitland, Julia Thomas, 214
Malmesbury, Countess of, 96
Malthusian League, 130, 171
Manchester
anti-Corn Law League, 258
education in, 173, 179, 192
factory wages in, 25
feminism in, 262, 264, 272
population, 5–6
radicalism in, 247, 248
religion in, 146, 151
suffrage movement in, 272, 285, 286–7, 297, 300, 303, 304, 305, 308
workhouse, 73–4
Manchester and Salford Asylum for Female Penitents, 60
Manchester Female Reformers, 247
Manchester High School for Girls, 68
Manchester University, 71, 192
Manchester Women's Suffrage Society, 272
Mansfield, Lady, 94
Manual of Midwifery, A, 113
Maori Wars (1861–65), 204
Maoris, 208
Marjoribanks, Ishbel, 91
Markham, Violet, 294
Marlborough, Consuelo, Duchess of, 90
marriage, 46–7, 86, 125–6, 151
laws regarding married women, 267–73
Marriage Act (1836), 143
marriage bars, 39, 41
Married Women's Property Act
1870, 272–3
1882, 273, 299, 303
Married Women's Property Committee (MWPC)
first, 270
second, 272–3
Martineau, Harriet, 46, 228, 270
Martins, Sarah, 60
Maslin, Harriet, 165
Matthews Duncan, Dr, 190
Matters, Muriel, 308–9
Maudsley, Henry, 190
Maugham, Isabella, 233
Maurice, F.D., 62, 187
Maxwell, John, 54
Maxwell, Lily, 297
Mayhew, Henry, 31, 33–4, 176
Mazzini, Giuseppe, 257
Mechanics' institutes, 180–1
Medical Register, 79, 80, 131
medicine, 64, 79–81 *see also* doctors; nursing
mediums, 170
Melbourne, 235
Melbourne, Lord, 104, 219, 269
memsahibs, 214–16, 218
Men's League for Women's Suffrage, 310
Men's Social and Political Union, 310, 314
Merrington, Martha, 74
Messiahs, 162–3
Methodist Magazine, 164

Methodists, 141–2, 144, 145, 147–9, 155, 163–7, 168, 178
Metropolitan Association for Befriending Young Servants, 76
Metropolitan Athenaeum, 180
middle-class, 19, 43–82, 92
    and domestic politics, 240, 245, 250, 256–7, 258, 261, 262, 266, 280
    and education, 174–5, 185–7, 187–8
    and imperialism, 207, 214, 223, 231, 235
    and 'redundancy crisis', 234–5, 266
    and religion, 147, 154, 156, 158, 167–8
    and sexuality, 119, 124, 125, 127
    and suffrage movement, 288, 289–90, 306
Middle East, 222
Midlands, 16, 23, 24, 144, 246
militancy, 304–15
Mill, John Stuart, 285–6, 296, 297, 301
Millbank Prison, 61
millenarians, 163, 167
Milner, Alfred, 206
missionaries, 81, 155–8, 221–3, 237
Molesworth, Lady, 94
monarchy, 103, 105, 107
money, units of, 320–1
Monthly Repository, 256–7
Morant Bay Rebellion (1865), 204
More, Hannah, 45, 90, 91, 176, 225, 239, 240, 242–4
    Cheap Repository Tracts, 243
    Coelebs in Search of a Wife, 91, 243
    Hints Towards Forming the Character of a Young Princess, 243
    Strictures on the Modern System of Female Education, 243
Morocco, 156, 220
Morpeth, Lady Georgiana, 99
mortality rate, 6, 215
motherhood, 48–50, 206–7, 228, 229, 277
    see also children
Mothers' Union, 144
Mud March (1907), 310
Mulock, Dinah see Craik, Dinah Mulock
Munby, Arthur J., 33
music halls, 201, 276–7
Muter, Elizabeth McMullin: My Recollections of the Sepoy Revolt, 205
MWPC see Married Women's Property Committee
Mysore, 204

Napoleonic wars, 246
Nash, Rosalind, 282
Nashoba, 251
National and British schools, 180, 182
National Association for the Promotion of Social Science, 147, 272
National Chartist Association see Chartism
National Council for Combating Venereal Diseases, 138
National Gallery, 314
National League for Opposing Woman Suffrage, 295
National Review, 234
National Secular Society, 153, 170–1
National Society for Promoting the Education of the Poor in the Principles of the Established Church, 178, 179–80
National Society for Women's Suffrage (NSWS), 299, 301, 302
National Union of Women's Suffrage Societies (NUWSS), 286, 289, 303–4, 305–6, 309–10, 310–11, 312, 313–14, 315
National Vigilance Association (NVA), 276
Native Americans, 209
needlewomen, 25, 31, 33–4
Nevill, Lady Dorothy, 94
New France (Quebec), 208
New South Wales, 232
'new women', 139, 278–80
New York City, 170
New Zealand, 204, 208, 230, 231, 237, 293
    immigrants from, 208
    troops from, 199–200
Newcastle, 255
Newcastle, Duchess of, 96
Newcastle-under-Lyme, 26
Newgate Prison, 60, 61
Newnham College, Cambridge, 69, 189, 192–3
Nichols, Polly, 22
night schools, 146, 180
Nightingale, Florence, 36, 62, 66, 67
'Nightingale nurses', 67
Nineteenth Century, The, 294
non-conformists, 144–5, 145–50 see also individual religious groups
Norfolk, 16, 24, 176–7, 180
Norman, G.W., 252
North Africa, 200
North London Collegiate School for Girls, 68, 73, 185, 186

north of England, 23, 24, 144, 149, 264
North of England Council for Promoting
   the Higher Education of Women, 188,
   264
North of England Suffrage Society, 289
Northampton, 254, 261
Northern Star, 255
Northumberland, 17
Northumberland, Duke of, 83
Norton (née Sheridan), Caroline, 269–70
   *English Laws for Women in the Nineteenth
      Century*, 270
   *Observations on the Natural Claim of a
      Mother to the Custody of her Children*,
      269
Norton, George, 269
Norwich, 185
Nottingham, 166, 185
Nottingham Female Political Union, 253
Nottingham Journal, 254
Nottinghamshire, 24, 254
novels/novelists, 51–4, 279
NSWS *see* National Society for Women's
   Suffrage
Nugent, Maria, Lady, 210, 213–14
nursing, 34, 35, 36, 64, 66–8
NUWSS *see* National Union of Women's
   Suffrage Societies

Octavia Hill system (of housing), 75
office work *see* clerks
Oliphant, Mrs Margaret, 52
'one-body' model (of human anatomy),
   112–13
Ontario, 235–6
orgasm, 113
'Orientalism', 203, 219
Osborne House, 102
outwork, 29–34
Owen, Robert, 250
Owenism, 250–1, 265, 285
Oxbridge, 69, 80 *see also* Cambridge
   University; Oxford University
Oxford University, 70, 188, 189, 192 *see also
   individual colleges*
Oxfordshire, 17, 177

Paddington Board of Guardians, 74
Pain, James, 124
Paine, Thomas: *Rights of Man*, 246–7
Paley, Mary, 192–3

Pall Mall Gazette, The, 135, 161
Palmer, Phoebe, 168
Palmerston, Lord, 219
Palmerston, Lady Emily, 94
Pankhurst, Christabel, 264, 278, 292, 304,
   306, 307, 308, 309, 315
   The Great Scourge, 278
Pankhurst, Emmeline
   and suffrage, 264, 286, 292, 298, 303, 304,
      306, 307, 308, 309, 314, 315
   and workhouse, 73–4
Pankhurst, Richard, 264, 303
Pankhurst, Sylvia, 264, 304, 306
Paris, 80, 315
Parkes, Bessie Rayner, 65, 263
   Some Remarks on the Education of Girls,
      263
Parkes, Fanny: *Wanderings of a Pilgrim in
   Search of the Picturesque*, 219, 220
Parliament, 85, 86, 103, 245, 248, 249, 268,
   271, 272, 284, 295, 296, 298, 302, 303,
   318
   petitions to, 224, 227, 254, 262, 303
   see also House of Commons; House of
      Lords
Parliament Street Society (Central National
   Society for Women's Suffrage), 260, 302–3
Pater, Walter, 280
patriotism, 246
Pease, Elizabeth, 145, 228
Peck, Winifred, 186–7
Peel, Robert, 104
penetration, vaginal, 114–15
penicillin, 138
penitentiaries, 161 *see also* 'magdalene
   homes'
Persia, 156, 220
Peterloo Massacre (1819), 248
Phayne, Rosa, 235
Philadelphia, 57
philanthropy, 15–16, 45–6, 54–63, 81, 84, 85,
   89–91, 102, 192
Philippo, Hannah, 222
Phipps, Harriet, 105
Pioneer, The, 251
Pirie, Jane, 123
Pitt, William, 212
Place, Francis, 114–15, 124
politics
   and aristocratic women, 92–7
   domestic, 107, 238–84

politics—*cont*
  and imperialism, 199–237
  suffrage movement, 285–316
Ponsonby, Sarah, 122
Poor Law, 35, 54–5, 127, 137, 161
  Guardians, 73, 74, 253, 258–9, 265
  New Poor Law (1834), 18, 61–2, 76, 120,
    179, 253–5
  opposition to, 252–6
popular culture, imperialism in, 200–2
population growth, 5–6
Porter, Roy, 137
Post Office, 37, 38, 39
preachers, 163–8
pregnancy, 87, 126–7
premarital sex, 114–15, 119–20, 125
Presbyterians, 144
Preston, 19, 26
Price, Ann, 136
Priestman, Anna Maria, 290
Priestman, Mary, 290
Primitive Methodist Magazine, 149
Primitive Methodists, 148, 164–5, 166 *see also*
  Methodists
Primrose League, 95–6, 232, 259–60, 261,
  295, 302
Prince, Mary, 207, 226
Prisoners' Temporary Discharge for Ill
  Health Act (Cat and Mouse Act) (1913),
  314–15
prisons
  suffragettes in, 311–12
  visitors, 60–1
Proctor, Adelaide, 263–4, 265, 266
professions, 46–7, 63–82, 265
property, 85, 267–8, 270, 272–3, 299
prostitutes, 31, 33–4, 60, 114, 133–5, 136, 138,
  209, 212, 213, 273–7
Prudential Assurance Company, 37, 38, 66
Punch, 161
purdah, 224

quacks, 130, 137
Quakers
  and anti-slavery movement, 226, 227, 228
  and education, 175, 178
  and religion, 143, 144, 145, 146, 159, 165
  and suffrage, 286, 308
Queen, 218
Queen Caroline Affair (1820), 101, 248–50,
  283

Queen's College, London, 187–8, 190
Queensland, 236

race/racism, 202–3, 203–6, 207–9, 211–12,
  213, 215–16
radicalism, 240, 246–8, 256–7
Rae, Lucy, 66–7
Ragged School Union, 178
ragged schools, 71, 146, 178–9
Ramabai, Pandita, 208
Randborn, Harriet, 165
'Ranters' *see* Primitive Methodists
Raynard, Ellen, 156, 158
Recreative Evening Classes Association, 76
Reddish, Sarah, 289
'redundancy crisis', 234, 266
Reform Act
  1832, 57, 92, 252
  1867, 92, 95, 285, 296, 297
  1884, 92, 95, 301–2
reformers, 223–30
Reid, Elizabeth Jesser, 188
religion, 90–1, 115–16, 141–71
rent collectors, 74, 75
Representation of the People Act (1918),
  315–16
Republican, The, 247
reputation, sexual, 118–21
respectability, 14, 265
Richardson, Mary, 288, 290, 312, 314
Ridding, Laura, 205–6, 209
Robson, Emma, 149
Roedean (school), 186
Rokeby Venus, 314
Roman Catholics *see* Catholics
Roper, Esther, 290
Rose, Field Marshal Hugh, 200
Rose, Sir John, 136
Rosman, Alice Grant, 208
Rossetti, Christina, 144
Rothschild, Lionel, 151
Roussel, Pierre, 112
Roy, Rammohun, 207–8
Royal Commission on Divorce, 138, 283
Royal Commission on Labour, 78, 281
Royal Geographical Society, 73
Royal Holloway College, London, 188
royal household, 104–5
royal women *see* elite women
'Rush the Commons' protest (1908), 309
Ruskin, John, 74, 280

Russian immigrants, 151
Rutland, Duchess of, 94
Rye, Maria, 230–1, 263

Sadler, Michael, 25
St George's Chapel, Windsor, 98, 100
St Hilda's College, Oxford, 186
St John, Christopher: *How the Vote was Won* (written with Cicely Hamilton), 280
St Leonard's (school), 186
St Mary's Abbey, London, 161
St Matthew's Church, Brixton, 153
St Patrick's Church, Soho Square, 151
St Paul's Cathedral, 106
St Saviour's Church, Brixton Hill, 153
Sala, George, 234
salaries, 69, 77
Salford, 297
Salisbury, Lady, 94
Salvarsan (drug), 138
Salvation Army, 116, 155, 168–9, 231
Sand, George, 256
sati, 224–5, 237
Saturday Review, The, 279
Saurin, Susanna Mary, 162
Saurin v. Star, 161–2
School Boards, 72–3, 74, 182, 258–9, 298
school managers, 72
schools, 71–3, 91, 146, 173–4, 175, 176–7, 177–80, 194
Schools Enquiry Commission (1856), 185
Schreiner, Olive, 52, 277, 280
    Story of an African Farm, 279
    Women and Labour, 280
Scotland, 5, 23, 24, 150, 225
secondary-school teaching, 68–9
Sen, Keshub Chandra, 228
Senior, Jane Nassau, 76
separate-spheres, ideology of, 12, 44
servants, 47, 89, 120 *see also* domestic service
settlement house movement, 75–6
sexology, 117–18, 140
sexual advice, 116–17
sexual danger, 203–6
sexuality/sexual issues, 111–40, 274, 275, 278, 301, 317, 318
Shaftesbury, Lord, 178
Shafts (journal), 139, 278, 279
Shakers, 162
Sharples, Eliza, 247
Sheffield, 25, 132

Shelley, Mary, 52, 241
Sheridan, Father, 151
Sherwin, Joseph and Mrs, 11
Shibden Hall, Halifax, 245
Shield, The, 275, 276
Shiriff, Emily, 185
shop assistants, 35, 36
Showers, Mary Rosina, 170
Shrewsbury, Countess of, 96
Sidgwick, Henry, 189, 191
sisterhoods, 158–62
Sisters of the Poor, 159
slavery, 203, 210–11, 217
    campaign against, 145, 203, 210, 217, 225–8, 237
Smith, Barbara Leigh *see* Bodichon, Barbara Leigh Smith
Smith, Caroline, 123
Smith, Mary, 177–8
Smith, Rosamond, 233
Smith, William (pseudonym of Sarah Geals), 123
Social Democratic Federation (SDF), 261
social services, 70–8
socialism, 261, 280–3
socializing, 93–5
Society for the Mitigation and Gradual Abolition of Slavery throughout the British Dominions *see* Anti-Slavery Society
Society for Promoting the Return of Women as Poor Law Guardians, 74
Society for the Promotion of the Employment of Women (SPEW), 65, 188, 266
Society for the Suppression of Vice, 144
Society of Friends *see* Quakers
Somerset, 243
Somerville College, Oxford, 189, 193
Soulsby, Miss, 186
sources, historical, 2–3, 10
South Africa, 204, 205–6, 208, 209, 221, 230, 237
South Pacific, 222
South Place Chapel, London, 256
South Wales, 23
Southcott, Joanna, 162–3, 166
Southwark Settlement, 76
Spence, Thomas, 246–7
Spenceans, 246–7
Spencer, Countess, 90

Spencer, John, 26
spermicides, 131
SPEW *see* Society for the Promotion of the
    Employment of Women
spinning, 26–7, 32
spinning jenny, 23, 27, 32
spinsterhood, 140
Spiritualists, 169–70
Spitalfields, 24, 32, 240
Springett, Reverend, 153
Squire, Rose, 77
Srinagar, 81
Stafford, 35
Stafford, Marchioness of, 94
Staffordshire Potteries, 26, 77
Stanley, Lady Constance, 92
Stanley of Alderley, Lady, 185
Stansfield, Caroline Ashurst, 256, 257, 264
Stead, W.T., 135
Steel, Flora Annie, 223
Stibbs, Bartholomew: *Journal of a Voyage
    up the Gambia*, 202
Stockport, 11, 19, 23
Stokes, Agnes, 233–4
Stopford, Horatia, 105
Stride, Miss, 60
subscriptions, and raising money, 56–7
Suffolk, 176–7, 180
suffrage, 92, 95, 247, 248, 252, 253, 260, 265,
    272, 273, 280, 282, 285–316
sugar, 217
Sunday schools, 91, 153, 176, 178
Sutherland, Harriet Leveson-Gower,
    second Duchess of, 89
Sutherland, Millicent Leveson-Gower,
    fourth Duchess of, 289
Swanwick, Helena, 291, 293
Swindon, 165
Swiney, Frances, 171
    The Awakening of Women, 171
syphilis, 135–6, 138 *see also* venereal disease

Taft, Mary, 164
Tasmania, 208
Taylor, Barbara, 251
Taylor, Clementia, 272
Taylor, Helen, 285, 292, 298
Taylor, Peter, 272
teachers, 35, 39–41, 64, 65, 68–70, 71
temperance movement, 149–50
Terry, Ellen, 58

Tewkesbury, 74
textile industry, 23–9, 29–33
Theobald family, 170
theoretical approaches, 3–4
Theosophical Society, 170
theosophists, 169–70, 170–1
Thompson, Flora: *Lark Rise to Candleford*,
    17
Thompson, William, 285
    *Appeal to One-Half the Human Race,
    Women, against the Pretensions of the
    Other Half, Men*, 251
Thomson, J. Arthur, 118
Thorburn, John, 190
Thorne, Mary, 166
Tillard, Violet, 308–9
Times, The, 98, 161, 308, 311
Tod, Isabela, 272
Tomlinson, Elizabeth, 166
Tories *see* Conservatives/Tories
Townley, Jane, 162
trade unions, 28–9, 78, 281–2
Training School for Nurses, 67
travel narratives, 218–21
Trimmer, Sarah, 90
Trollope, Anthony: *Phineas Finn*, 94
trusts, 85, 268
TUC (Trades Unions Congress), 281, 282
Tuckwell, Gertrude, 71
Tuke, Margaret, 69
Tunbridge Wells, 73
Twining, Louisa, 50–1, 62, 64, 70, 73, 74, 76,
    265, 298
    Workhouses and Women's Work, 62
'two-bodies' model (of human anatomy),
    113

Underwood, Ann, 162
Unitarians
    and anti-slavery movement, 226, 228
    and education, 146, 175, 178, 179, 180, 188
    and politics, 256–7, 265, 286
    and religion, 144, 146
    and sexuality, 116
United States, 80, 150, 162, 170, 209, 248, 250
United Suffragists, 315
universities, 187–94
    and medical training, 79, 80, 81
    and qualifications of teachers, 68, 69
    teaching in, 69–70
    see also individual universities

University College, London, 193
University College Hospital, London, 136
Urania Cottage (rescue home), 231
urbanization, 5–6

Vanderbilt, Consuelo, 90
venereal disease, 133–9, 212–13, 273, 275, 278
Venturi, Emilie Ashurst, 256, 257, 272, 275
Vicinus, Martha, 122
Victoria, Queen, 1–2, 43, 56, 83, 95, 97, 99,
    101–7, 200, 201, 266
Victoria League, 232
Victoria Press, 264
violence
    domestic, 126
    suffragettes' use of, 311, 314
visitors, 58–63, 90
vote see suffrage

wages, 11, 18, 25, 38, 40
Wakefield, Edward, 231
Waldegrave, Lady, 94
Wales, 5, 23, 122, 256
Walker, Anne, 123
Walker, Mary Ann, 255
Walpole, Horace, 241
Ward, Ben, 124
Ward, Mrs Humphrey, 294, 297–8
    'An Appeal Against Female Suffrage', 294
Warren, Mrs Eliza: How I Managed My
    House on Two Hundred Pounds a Year, 47
Wasserman test (for syphilis), 138
Watson, Jane, 120
WCG (Women's Co-operative Guild), 277,
    282–3
weaving, 27–8
Webb, Beatrice, 78, 294
Webster, Augusta, 72
Wedgwood family, 146
Weininger, Otto: Sex and Character, 117
Wellington, Duke of, 104
Wesley, John, 148, 164
Wesleyan Methodist Missionary Society,
    156
Wesleyan Methodists, 145, 148, 159, 164–5,
    166, 167, 182 see also Methodists
West, Benjamin, 98
West Country, 24, 256
West Indies, 202–3, 210–11, 222
    immigrants from, 207
Westfield College, London, 188

Westminster, Lady, 90
Westminster Abbey, 106
Westminster Review, The, 279
Wheeler, Anna, 251, 268
Whigs, 94, 104 see also Liberals
White, Elizabeth, 165
white-collar work, 34–41
'white slavery' scandals, 135
Whittington Club, 180
Wigan, 25
Wightman, Mrs Julia, 149
    Haste to the Rescue, 149
Wilberforce, William, 144, 244
William IV, King, 101
William of Orange, 99
Windsor, 98, 100, 105
WLF see Women's Liberal Federation
Wollstonecraft, Mary, 52, 256, 291–2
    and anti-slavery movement, 225
    compared with Hannah More, 240,
        242–4
    and education, 172, 195
    and feminism, 240–1, 241–2, 265, 277–8
    and politics, 240–2, 244
    relationships, 241
    and suffrage, 285
    The Female Reader, 225, 240
    Maria, or the Wrongs of Women, 240–1
    A Vindication of the Rights of Women,
        241–2, 252, 278
Wolstenholme (Wolstenholme-Elmy),
    Elizabeth, 263, 264, 271–2, 275, 285, 293,
    301, 303, 307
Woman's Signal, 279
Women Writers' Suffrage League, 280, 288
Women's Co-operative Guild (WCG), 277,
    282–3
Women's Franchise League (WFL), 303
Women's Freedom League, 307, 308–9, 310,
    311, 312
women's history, 3, 4
Women's Industrial Council (WIC), 78, 281
Women's Labour League (WLL), 261, 282
Women's Liberal Associations (WLAs),
    260, 261, 302
Women's Liberal Federation (WLF), 96,
    260, 261, 302
Women's Liberal Unionist Association, 260
Women's Local Government Society, 258
Women's National Anti-Suffrage League,
    294–5

Women's National Liberal Association, 260

Women's Social and Political Union (WSPU), 286, 289, 304–8, 309–10, 311–12, 313, 314–15

Women's Suffrage Committees, 285, 286

Women's Suffrage Journal, 264, 297

'Women's Sunday' (1908), 311

Women's Tax Resistance League (WTRL), 308

Women's Trade Union League (WTUL), 29, 78, 281–2

Women's University Settlement, Southwark, 76

Wood, Mrs Henry, 52

Woods, Marianne, 123

work, paid, 9–12, 16–42, 44, 51, 265, 266–7, 317, 318 *see also* professions

workhouse, 18, 73–4, 253–4
  inspectors, 76
  schools, 179
  visiting, 61–3

Workhouse Visiting Society, 62–3, 73

working-class, 9–42, 62–3, 66, 78, 92
  and domestic politics, 240, 246–8, 249, 252–6, 257, 261, 273, 280–3

and education, 172, 175–81, 182–4

and imperialism, 206, 214, 231, 232–4

and religion, 147, 148, 149, 154, 156, 159, 160, 163, 165, 168, 169

and sexuality, 119–20, 124–5, 127, 128

and suffrage movement, 287, 288, 289, 290, 301–2, 306

Working Gentlewoman's Journal, The, 82

working men's colleges, 180–1

Wright, Fanny, 251

WSPU *see* Women's Social and Political Union

WTUL *see* Women's Trade Union League

Wyatt, James, 100

Wycombe Abbey (school), 186–7

Yarmouth prison, 60

Yonge, Charlotte, 52, 144

York, 19, 132, 185

Yorke, Louisa, 87

Yorkshire, 16, 24, 25, 123, 149, 254
  East Riding, 16, 17
  West Riding, 166

Young, Arthur, 91

zenanas, 80, 81, 157, 220–1, 223, 224